TIME
ANNUAL
1991
The Year in Review

Library of Congress catalog Card No.

Printed in the United States of America

First edition

10 9 8 7 6 5 4 3 2 1

TIME
ANNUAL

1991
The Year in Review

By the Editors of TIME

A
TIME
BOOK

TIME
1991
The Year in Review

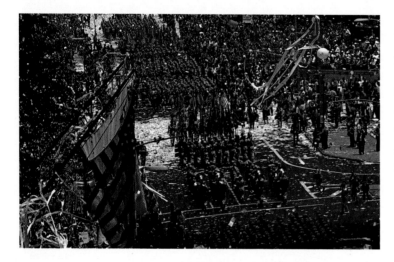

TIME

Editor-in-Chief: Jason McManus
Editorial Director: Richard B. Stolley
Corporate Editor: Gilbert Rogin

TIME INC. MAGAZINES
President: Reginald K. Brack Jr.
Executive Vice Presidents: Donald J. Barr, Donald M. Elliman Jr., S. Christopher Meigher III, Robert L. Miller
Senior Vice President: Richard W. Angle Jr.

Founders: Briton Hadden 1898-1929   Henry R. Luce 1898-1967
MANAGING EDITOR: Henry Muller
EXECUTIVE EDITORS: Richard Duncan, Edward L. Jamieson, Ronald Kriss
CHIEF OF CORRESPONDENTS: John F. Stacks
ASSISTANT MANAGING EDITORS: Walter Isaacson, James Kelly
EDITOR AT LARGE: Strobe Talbott
EDITORIAL OPERATIONS DIRECTOR: Oliver Knowlton
SENIOR EDITORS: Charles P. Alexander, Nancy R. Gibbs, Stephen Koepp, Christopher Porterfield, George Russell, Thomas A. Sancton, Barrett Seaman, Claudia Wallis, Jack E. White
ART DIRECTOR: Rudolph C. Hoglund
GRAPHICS DIRECTOR: Nigel Holmes
CHIEF OF RESEARCH: Betty Satterwhite Sutter
PICTURE EDITOR: Michele Stephenson
COPY CHIEF: Susan L. Blair   **PRODUCTION MANAGER:** Gail Music
SENIOR WRITERS: George J. Church, Richard Corliss, Martha Duffy, Otto Friedrich, Paul Gray, John Greenwald, William A. Henry III, Robert Hughes, Eugene Linden, Ed Magnuson, Lance Morrow, Bruce W. Nelan, Walter Shapiro
ASSOCIATE EDITORS: Richard Behar, Janice Castro, Philip Elmer-DeWitt, Richard Lacayo, Michael D. Lemonick, Thomas McCarroll, Richard N. Ostling, Priscilla Painton, Sue Raffety, Janice C. Simpson, Jill Smolowe, Anastasia Toufexis, Richard Zoglin
STAFF WRITERS: Guy Garcia, Christine Gorman
CONTRIBUTORS: Kurt Andersen, Carl Bernstein, Jesse Birnbaum, Jay Cocks, Barbara Ehrenreich, John Elson, Pico Iyer, Leon Jaroff, Stefan Kanfer, Michael Kinsley, Charles Krauthammer, Dennis Overbye, Richard Schickel, R.Z. Sheppard, John Skow, Richard Stengel, George M. Taber, Andrew Tobias
ASSISTANT EDITORS: Ursula Nadasdy de Gallo, Andrea Dorfman, Katherine Mihok, Brigid O'Hara-Forster, William Tynan, Sidney Urquhart, Jane Van Tassel (Department Heads); Bernard Baumohl, David Bjerklie, Nancy McD. Chase, Mary McC. Fernandez, Georgia Harbison, Anne Hopkins, Susan M. Reed, Elizabeth Rudulph
REPORTERS: Elizabeth L. Bland, Barbara Burke, Val Castronovo, Wendy Cole, Tom Curry, David Ellis, Kathryn Jackson Fallon, Sophfronia Scott Gregory, Janice M. Horowitz, Jeanette Isaac, Sinting Lai, Daniel S. Levy, Andrew Purvis, Michael Quinn, Andrea Sachs, Alain L. Sanders, David Seideman, David E. Thigpen, Susanne Washburn, Leslie Whitaker, Linda Williams, Linda Young
REPORTER-RESEARCHERS: Audrey Ball, Nancy Newman, Zona Sparks (Senior Staff)
COPY DESK: Judith Anne Paul, Shirley Barden Zimmerman (Deputies); Barbara Dudley Davis, Evelyn Hannon, Jill Ward (Copy Coordinators); Minda Bikman, Doug Bradley, Robert Braine, Bruce Christopher Carr, Barbara Collier, Julia Van Buren Dickey, Dora Fairchild, Judith Kales, Sharon Kapnick, Claire Knopf, Melinda J. McAdams, M.M. Merwin, Anna F. Monardo, Maria A. Paul, Jane Rigney, Elyse Segelken, Terry Stoller, Amelia Weiss (Copy Editors)
BUREAUS: Joelle Attinger, Paul A. Witteman (Deputy Chiefs of Correspondents); Suzanne Davis (Deputy, Administration) **Special Correspondent:** Michael Kramer **Correspondent at Large:** Bonnie Angelo **Washington Contributing Editor:** Hugh Sidey **Diplomatic Correspondent:** Christopher Ogden **National Political Correspondent:** Laurence I. Barrett
Senior Correspondents: David Aikman, Jonathan Beaty, Sandra Burton, Mary Cronin, Hays Gorey, Lee Griggs, Joseph J. Kane, J. Madeleine Nash, Edwin M. Reingold, Gavin Scott, Bruce van Voorst, James Wilde
Washington: Stanley W. Cloud, Margaret Carlson, Ann Blackman, Ricardo Chavira, Michael Duffy, Dan Goodgame, Ted Gup, S.C. Gwynne, Julie Johnson, J.F.O. McAllister, Jay Peterzell, Elaine Shannon, Dick Thompson, Nancy Traver **Boston:** Robert Ajemian, Sam Allis, Melissa Ludtke **Chicago:** Jon D. Hull, Elizabeth Taylor **Detroit:** William McWhirter **Atlanta:** Michael Riley, Don Winbush **Houston:** Richard Woodbury **Miami:** Cathy Booth **Los Angeles:** Jordan Bonfante, Jeanne McDowell, Sylvester Monroe, Martha Smilgis, James Willwerth, Sally B. Donnelly **San Francisco:** David S. Jackson
London: William Mader, Anne Constable **Paris:** Frederick Ungeheuer, Margot Hornblower **Brussels:** Adam Zagorin **Bonn:** James O. Jackson, Daniel Benjamin **Central Europe:** James L. Graff **Moscow:** John Kohan, James Carney, Ann M. Simmons **Jerusalem:** Lisa Beyer **Cairo:** Dean Fischer, William Dowell **Nairobi:** Marguerite Michaels **Johannesburg:** Scott MacLeod **New Delhi:** Edward W. Desmond **Beijing:** Jaime A. FlorCruz **Southeast Asia:** Richard Hornik **Hong Kong:** Jay Branegan **Tokyo:** Barry Hillenbrand, Kumiko Makihara **Latin America:** John Moody **Mexico City:** Laura López
Administration: Susan Lynd, David Richardson, Hope Almash, Melissa August, Breena Clarke, Donald N. Collins, Joan A. Connelly, Ann V. King, Lina Lofaro, Anne D. Moffett, Judith R. Stoler **News Desks:** Brian Doyle, Waits L. May III, Susanna M. Schrobsdorff, Pamela H. Thompson, Diana Tollerson, Ann Drury Wellford, Mary Wormley
ART: Arthur Hochstein (Deputy Art Director); Linda Louise Freeman (Covers); Steve Conley, Jennifer Napoli, Billy Powers, Irene Ramp, Ina Saltz, John F. White (Associate Art Directors); Joseph Aslaender, Nomi Silverman, Kenneth B. Smith (Assistant Art Directors); David Drapkin, Leah M. Purcell (Designers); John P. Dowd (Traffic)
Maps and Charts: Paul J. Pugliese (Chief); Leslie Dickstein, Steven D. Hart, Joe Lertola, Nino Telak, Deborah L. Wells **Administration:** Carrie A. Zimmerman
PHOTOGRAPHY: Richard L. Booth, MaryAnne Golon, Rose Keyser (Associate Editors); Kevin J. McVea (Operations); Renee Mancini (Syndication); Arnold H. Drapkin (Consulting Picture Editor); Dorothy Affa Ames, Sarah Buffum, Paula Hornak Kellner, Gary Roberts, Nancy Smith-Alam, Robert B. Stevens (Assistant Editors); Marie Tobias, Mary Worrell-Bousquette (Researchers) **Bureaus:** Martha Bardach, Sahm Doherty, Leny Heinen, Stanley Kayne, Barbara Nagelsmith, Anni Rubinger, Melanie Stephens, Simonetta Toraldo **Photographers:** Terry Ashe, P.F. Bentley, William Campbell, Greg Davis, Rudi Frey, Dirck Halstead, Kenneth Jarecke, Cynthia Johnson, Shelly Katz, David Hume Kennerly, Steve Liss, Christopher Morris, Robin Moyer, Carl Mydans, James Nachtwey, Matthew Naythons, Robert Nickelsberg, Chris Niedenthal, David Rubinger, Anthony Suau, Ted Thai, Diana Walker
MAKEUP: Charlotte J. Quiggle (Chief)
TECHNOLOGY: Ken Baierlein (Manager); Stephen F. Demeter (Systems Manager); Kevin Kelly, George Mendel, Peter K. Niceberg, Michael M. Sheehan, Lamarr Tsufura
IMAGING: Mark Stelzner (Manager); Gerard Abrahamsen, Charlotte Coco, Paul Dovell, John Dragonetti, Kin Wah Lam, Carl Leidig, Linda Parker, Robert Pfleger, Mark P. Polomski, Lois Rubenstein, Richard Shaffer, Jacqueline Shubitowski, David Spatz, Lorri Stenton, Paul White
PRODUCTION: Joseph J. Scafidi (Deputy); Trang Ba Chuong, Theresa Kelliher, L. Rufino-Armstrong (Supervisors); Robert L. Becker, Silvia Castañeda Contreras, Michael Dohne, Osmar Escalona, Garry Hearne, Nora Jupiter, Agustin Lamboy, Jeannine Laverty, Marcia L. Love, Janet L. Lugo, Peter J. McGullam, Sandra Maupin, Helen May, Michael Skinner
ADMINISTRATION: Rafael Soto, Alan J. Abrams, Catherine M. Barnes, Denise Brown, Tresa Chambers, Anne M. Considine, Tosca LaBoy, Marilyn V.S. McClenahan, Katharine K. McNevin, Elliot Ravetz, Teresa D. Sedlak, Deborah R. Slater, Marianne Sussman, Raymond Violini
EDITORIAL FINANCE: Eric A. Berk (Manager); Genevieve Christy (Deputy); Patricia Hermes, Esther Cederio, Morgan Krug, Katherine Young (Domestic); Camille Sanabria, Carl Harmon, Sheila Charney, Aston Wright (News Service); Linda D. Vartoogian, Wayne Chun, Edward Nana Osei-Bonsu (Pictures)
LETTERS: Amy Musher (Chief); Gloria J. Hammond (Deputy); Marian Powers (Administration)
EDITORIAL SERVICES: Christiana Walford (Director); Jennie Chien, Hanns Kohl, Benjamin Lightman, Beth Bencini Zarcone

TIME INTERNATIONAL
MANAGING EDITOR: Karsten Prager
Assistant Managing Editor: José M. Ferrer III
Senior Editors: Johanna McGeary, Christopher Redman, William E. Smith
Chief of Research: Jeanne-Marie North
Senior Writers: Frederick Painton, William Stewart, James Walsh
Associate Editors: Howard G. Chua-Eoan, William R. Doerner, Ariadna Victoria Rainert, Barbara Rudolph, Michael S. Serrill
Contributors: Robert Ball, Marguerite Johnson, Dominique Moisi, Michael Walsh
Assistant Editors: Oscar Chiang, Nelida Gonzalez Cutler, Lois Gilman, Tam Martinides Gray, Adrianne Jucius Navon
Reporters: Emily Mitchell, Lawrence Mondi, Jeffery C. Rubin, Megan Rutherford, Sribala Subramanian
Reporter-Researcher: Rosemary Byrnes (Senior Staff)
Art: James Elsis (Associate Director); Victoria Nightingale (Designer)
Photography: Julia Richer (Associate Editor); Eleanor Taylor, Karen Zakrison (Assistant Editors)
Makeup: Eugene F. Coyle (Chief); Alison E. Ruffley, Leonard Schulman
Administration: Helga Halaki, Barbara Milberg
PUBLISHER: Elizabeth P. Valk
Advertising Sales Director: Cleary S. Simpson
Associate Advertising Sales Manager: William J. Yonan
General Manager: Ellen F. Dealy
Consumer Marketing Director: David Gitow
Production Director: Brian F. O'Leary
Business Manager: A.P. Duffy
Communications Director: Jennifer Hillings Epstein
Marketing Director: Linda McCutcheon Conneally

TIME ANNUAL
1991
The Year in Review

Editor
Richard Duncan

Managing Editor
Kelly Knauer

Art Director
Christopher M. Register

Picture Editor
Katie Boal

Associate Editor
Alex Prud'homme

Essays
Paul Gray, John Greenwald, Michael D. Lemonick,
George Russell, Christopher Porterfield

Graphic Design
Nigel Holmes, Director; Steve Hart,
Joe Lertola, Nino Telak

Research
Ursula Nadasdy de Gallo, Director; Barbara Burke,
Susanne Washburn

Editorial Production
Michael Skinner

Photography Rights
Suzanne Richie

Project Director
David McGowan

Production Director
Joanne Pello

Consumer Marketing
Mary Warner, Kathy Lewis

The work of the following TIME writers and editors is represented in this volume:

Sam Allis, Jonathan Beaty, Lisa Beyer, Jesse Birnbaum, Cathy Booth, Margaret Carlson, Janice Castro, Howard G. Chua-Eoan, George J. Church, Jay Cocks, Richard Corliss, Michael Duffy, Richard Duncan, Philip Elmer-DeWitt, John Elson, Otto Friedrich, Nancy Gibbs, Dan Goodgame, Paul Gray, John Greenwald, S.C. Gwynne, William A. Henry III, Robert Hughes, Jon D. Hull, Pico Iyer, Leon Jaroff, Stefan Kanfer, Michael Kramer, Richard Lacayo, Michael D. Lemonick, Eugene Linden, Scott MacLeod, Thomas McCarroll, Lance Morrow, Bruce W. Nelan, Priscilla Painton, Alex Prud'homme, Joe Queenan, Barbara Rudolph, Richard Schickel, Walter Shapiro, Jill Smolowe, Strobe Talbott, Dick Thompson, Claudia Wallis, James Walsh, Michael Walsh, Jack E. White, Richard Woodbury, Richard Zoglin.

Additional thanks to: Sue Blair, John Calvano, Samuel Gold, Rudy Hoglund, Oliver Knowlton, Gail Music, Judy Paul, Mark Stelzner, Michele Stephenson

INTRODUCTION

This TIME Annual is a yearly version of the weekly magazine whose name it bears. It strives to tell the story of the world's year just as TIME magazine tells the story of the world's week: by identifying the most important news, issues and trends of the time, reporting them and charging them with meaning and perspective. As events slip from our news consciousness into history, it catches them, embodying some of both perspectives. It is not a "Best of TIME" collection; a few of the magazine's finer stories are not represented, because our goal is to elucidate the key events and issues of the year, and those pieces did not quite meet the history test.

From this news-as-history perspective, then, we have selected the most significant stories of 1991, and in most cases tightened them to eliminate the short-term details that, in all journalism, quickly fade into irrelevance. Occasionally we have combined stories on the same subject in order to eliminate duplication of background material. What we have *not* done is revise the analyses or judgments of the original stories. Our work, whether brilliant or flawed, is part of the record, and we will let the reader decide how well we did it.

Each section of the Annual is introduced by an essay, commissioned for this volume, by a senior writer or editor of TIME. These essays weigh events from an end-of-the-year perspective, pointing out coherences and patterns that are impossible to identify in a weekly rhythm. In addition, maps and charts created for the Annual provide new and illuminating views of the world's year. There is an index for ready access to the contents.

Here, then, is the year 1991. Ungainly, slippery, sometimes sullen and sometimes joyful, it came to us as news and we first grasped it in 52 parts. At the end of the year we looked back and found the parts made a whole—this volume. We hope that it informs and stirs your memories, as it did ours.

1991: The Year the World Tuned In

By PAUL GRAY

The passage of time is arbitrarily divided into minutes, hours, days, weeks. Nothing in nature strictly dictates these demarcations. Months are approximate and mismatched conveniences; why is June shorter than July and February shorter still?

But years are real. The ancients who scanned the heavens, seeking guidance or the solace of unearthly beauty, began to notice a pattern to the spectacle wheeling above them. Familiar clusters of stars appeared, vanished and reappeared, over and over again; the sun rose from a slightly different angle each morning, moving toward the center of the sky and then slowly sinking back, threatening to bury itself in the earth. When it halted and began ascending once more, as it always did, people celebrated and rejoiced.

Cultures and religions still disagree about when years begin and about what numbers or names should be attached to them. But most of civilization commemorates, in one form or another, the annual journey of the earth around the sun. Anniversaries—literally the turning of years—provide both the comfort of return, of a round-trip completed, and the unsettled sense of change. This play of sunlight is familiar, we have stood in it before; but we are, all of us, slightly different now.

Such alterations are the stuff of personal stories, the progress of lives. Larger shifts become the raw material of history, and when these are especially significant or influential, the years in which they happened become famous: among others, 1066, 1492, 1776, 1914, 1941. Such fame, however, is almost always retrospective. On a day-to-day basis, most people simply had no idea they were living through historic upheavals. In part this ignorance of events stemmed from slow or spotty methods of communication; before the 19th century, news could travel no faster than a rider on horseback. Few of those who were alive in 1492 knew anything of what Christopher Columbus had on his mind or what, late in the year, he actually accomplished.

But neither, in a sense, did Columbus. Decades would pass before the import of what had occurred—a meeting of the Old and New worlds—began to be realized. In fact, the aftershocks of that collision are still being felt as its 500th anniversary approaches.

So it is safe to say that 1991—the year this book chronicles—may assume a different shape and importance with the hindsight provided by a few decades or centuries. But the problem of interpreting the recent past, of gauging the lasting influence of daily events, has changed dramatically in the past few years. The difficulty now is not a paucity of available news, as it was in 1492 or even, in present terms, in 1941, but a deluge of data, a flood of facts. The world is wired. Computers chat with one another. Satellites in stationary orbits receive and beam out images and sound over vast swatches of the earth. While Wall Street sleeps, traders in Tokyo are busy setting the next day's financial agenda.

This electronic machinery has been in place for some time, to be sure. But 1991 is likely to be remembered, among other things, as the year when Marshall McLuhan's oft-proclaimed global village—a world audience huddled around cool, flickering fires—became truly operational.

Three events of the past year stand out as bench marks of this change: the gulf war, the failed coup in the Soviet Union and the Senate hearings on Anita Hill's charge of sexual harassment against Judge Clarence Thomas. Each of these will receive extended attention in the pages that follow; all were important in different ways and for different reasons, and the August plot in Moscow—which led directly to the subsequent dissolution of the U.S.S.R.—guarantees 1991's place on any future list of memorable years.

But Operation Desert Storm, the Soviet coup and the Thomas hearings not only met the traditional tests of news value—they were intense, dramatic and consequential in ways not yet entirely understood; each was also principally perceived by untold millions of people through the medium of television. Each was in some way photogenic, not intentionally made for the cameras, to be sure, but nonetheless particularly attractive to them. No other year has ever had three such significant news events being played out, while they happened, on home screens. Inevitably, the coverage of these stories became part of the stories themselves.

Author Michael Arlen once called Vietnam "the Living Room War," and TV certainly appears to have had an impact on the resolution of that long conflict. Many believe public support for the war faded as scenes of violence and carnage kept cropping up each night on the network news shows. It is easy to forget now that those scenes were always 24 hours old; film and videotape had to be carried in from the field and flown out of Vietnam and across the Pacific to the U.S., where the footage was edited for broadcast.

All this had changed by mid-January 1991, when the U.S. and its allies launched intensive bombing raids against Saddam Hussein's military structures in Iraq and his invading forces in Kuwait. There were no tape delays this time; cameras were in place, and sophisticated electronic gear, including satellites, was ready for whatever might happen. With no warning, the rockets' red (and green and magenta) glare eerily lit up the night sky over Baghdad, and millions of viewers suddenly found themselves facing more drama than they had anticipated over their suppers. Down there in the darkened streets of the Iraqi capital, people were presumably being killed. It was death, live on TV.

When Saddam retaliated by launching Scud missiles toward civilian areas in noncombatant Israel and against U.S. positions inside Saudi Arabia, the televised tension twisted several notches higher. TV reporters stood on hotel rooftops scanning the night sky for Scuds, flinching at unfamiliar noises, the edge in their voices clear whenever it seemed that something might be on the way. Some previously unsung names—Arthur Kent of NBC, Charles Jaco of the Cable News Network—rapidly became familiar household presences, surrogate civilians for everyone who stayed home from the war.

It was such riveting viewing that thousands of people began reporting an odd complaint; they found themselves unable to turn off their televisions or walk away from their sets. They did not want to miss the next reported Scud attack or the next doughty defense by the newly installed Patriot missiles. Only when the invasion phase of Desert Storm started did this TV mania begin to abate; normal military security and censorship asserted control, correspondents' access to combat units was restricted, and live pictures of actual fighting became practically and technically impossible. It is one of the ironies of the whole phenomenon that conventional warfare, when it finally arrived, produced conventional TV coverage.

One Monday in August, a thunderbolt: a group of Kremlin hardliners had staged a coup against the government of Mikhail Gorbachev, who was being detained at his resort retreat in the Crimea. This news—even though it involved one of the world's most recognizable figures—did not initially seem tailor-made for television. Coups, putsches, palace revolts are, by definition, carried out in secret. The only photo op likely to emerge from such endeavors is the one the world actually got some hours after the uprising was announced: the new leaders justifying their cause, declaring their legitimacy and announcing that everything was calm and under control.

But something was wrong with the picture this time. In boxy suits, seated uneasily behind a long table under the glare of lights and the scrutiny of cameras, these self-proclaimed new Soviet leaders were nervous, halting and altogether unsure of themselves. Worse still, some of the questions being asked by assembled reporters were downright rude. Would Lenin or Stalin or even Leonid Brezhnev have stood for such treatment?

What quickly became clear was that the continuing presence and operation of television cameras in Moscow—a legacy of Gorbachev's *glasnost*—sent a direct signal that this coup would fail. Two years earlier, in Tiananmen Square, the geriatric Chinese leadership, forced to choose between world censure and a popular democratic uprising, decided to crack down violently on demonstrating students in full view of cameras. No such brutal resolve was visible among the instigators of the Soviet coup or among the troops who would have to crush fellow citizens.

Russian President Boris Yeltsin, whom none of the putative new rulers had thought to arrest or detain, climbed on top of a vehicle to demonstrate his defiance; the cameras loved him and transformed what could have been a quixotic—and, in the bad old days, fatal—gesture into an international image of bravery and freedom. Scarcely two days into the coup, with the Russian Parliament Building prepared for a siege by Soviet police and army, live television coverage continued: another city, another nighttime filled with tension and odd lighting effects. Some minor skirmishes occurred. But as the scene dragged on, the conviction grew that as long as these pictures kept coming, as long as the transmissions that none of the new authorities had had the wit to squelch continued, nothing was going to happen. Bad news would not be seen but only registered as static or a screen suddenly gone black.

In October a very different sort of confrontation played itself out on television, and again the effect was mesmeric; a fine fall weekend in most parts of the U.S. was spent indoors, glued to the tube. Law professor Anita Hill's charge that Judge Clarence Thomas, nominated by President Bush to serve on the Supreme Court and awaiting a Senate vote on confirmation, had subjected her to sexual harassment on the job 10 years earlier proved explosive in ways few anticipated. Certainly not members of the Senate Judiciary Committee, who had learned of Hill's allegations and sent staff members to interview her; given her presumed reluctance to testify publicly, the committee decided it had done all it could do.

The leaking of Hill's charges to the press brought a fire storm of criticism and outrage down on the Senate. Judiciary Committee members, all of them male, might protest that they were scrupulously trying to balance the rights of the nominee against those of his accuser; the impression of power-wielding men siding with one of their own against the complaints of a woman proved overwhelming and repellent. Obviously the only place to settle this matter was . . . on television.

A tired old riddle goes: If a tree falls in the forest and no one is present to hear it, does it make any noise? Had the Hill-Thomas imbroglio happened 40 years ago, the only way to have heard it would have been over radio (doubtful, given programming practices at the time) or through written news accounts. These would no doubt have been informative, but they would not have generated much noise. The televised hearings were so deafening that they generally overrode a disarming truth: the proceedings were bound, barring an implausible, Perry Masonish breakdown on the stand by one of the witnesses, to end inconclusively. It was going to be Hill's word against Thomas' word. She said, he said.

Even if the plot was doomed to fizzle out into uncertainty, the drama proved irresistible. The cameras locked in on the faces of Hill and Thomas and waited for one of them to blink, to manifest some visible twitch of inner duplicity. Neither did. Their voices—hers patiently, reluctantly recounting past indignities, his laced with fury at the indignities to which he was now being subjected—were eloquent. Two highly educated African Americans found themselves in a struggle that went beyond race into the darker mysteries of gender and sex. The proceedings quickly took on a private, nightmarish aura, governed by the experience of each individual viewer. Women could look at Hill and recall all the slights and offensive gestures and comments they had received from males; men could observe Thomas, called on the carpet, embarrassed in front of the world, and think either, "There, but for the grace of God . . . " or wonder, "Have I been as innocent of this sort of behavior as I thought?" It was almost an anticlimax when Thomas was narrowly confirmed to the Supreme Court; the televised hearings had inaugurated a new front in the battle of the sexes.

As good as television was at conveying the feel and texture of these three stories, the worldwide reach and immediacy of this medium—proved as never before in 1991—raises some troubling questions, a legacy for the years to come. One is the possibility that what plays well on TV will be defined as important, and what does not will be ignored or dismissed. Television is wonderful with shocks but bad with repercussions. On the tube, the gulf war basically ended with a bravura press conference by General Norman Schwarzkopf and some upbeat footage of returning troops and welcome-home parades. A flurry of attention was later given to the Kurds, again being persecuted by Saddam Hussein and driven into the mountains to starve. And then, nearly nothing. But Saddam still terrorizes in Iraq, the Kurds still plot and suffer, and the old Kuwaiti oligarchy, most of

whom spent the unpleasant months of Iraqi occupation in comfortable exile, is back in power and looking for scapegoats. All this is both disheartening and fascinating, but little of it is picturesque.

When Boris Yeltsin stopped waving his arms and got down to the business of brokering the breakup of the Soviet Union, he all but disappeared from the television screen. The coup was high drama, while the collapse of an empire proved a long, complicated story spread over thousands of miles and hundreds of millions of individual hopes and fears. There will be no neat conclusion to this process—nothing suitable for film at 11—but its effects will rumble throughout the foreseeable future. Anita Hill is back teaching law in Oklahoma; the issue she dramatized and came to symbolize is still a vexing and serious problem in many workplaces. The individual solutions to come will not be hammered out under klieg lights.

And what of stories that develop slowly and largely out of public view? These would include the search for peace between Israel and its neighbors in the Middle East and the difficult progress toward representative government in South Africa. Many vital matters hardly lend themselves to pictures at all: trade and budget deficits, AIDS research, the decline of American public schools, the crumbling infrastructure of U.S. roads and bridges, the projected shape of the new European Community, the uncertainties of international financial markets and practices, the continued failures of most Third World economies.

And television, by its very nature, makes it hard for viewers to establish a context for what they see. Whatever is on the screen at the moment appears just as important as whatever was on the screen a minute ago. Across the world, rock videos follow clips of starving villagers; Madonna elbows out Mandela.

Amid so much indiscriminate information, what truly matters? When so much of what bombards the eyes and ears each day seems instantly forgettable, which impressions will prove memorable?

One purpose of this book is to suggest answers to questions like these. To be sure, some things are not yet known about 1991. Trends so broad and sweeping as to defy closeup analysis may have begun or changed direction or achieved critical mass during the past 12 months, and future historians may wonder why we failed to notice them, just as we now marvel at the innocence and lack of foresight with which Europe stumbled toward a cataclysmic war in 1914. The year just past perhaps also included private, as yet unreported accomplishments that future historians may perceive as fundamental to any understanding of our times: scientific, medical or artistic breakthroughs whose full fruitions are yet to occur. All of that remains to be seen. Even now, though, some of the vivid surfaces of 1991 look unforgettable.

A Changing World

CANADA

SEPT: Prime Minister Mulroney proposes revisions to the constitution that grant Quebec legal recognition as a "distinct society," establish an elected senate, and allow self-rule within 10 years for Indians and Eskimos

DEC: Government creates new territory for Eskimos, to be known as Nunavut

U.S.

1991: America's year was marked by victory in the gulf, economic doldrums, arguments over national identity, and the legal/sexual circuses of the Thomas hearings and the Smith rape trial. See Timeline: U.S.A. on the following pages for chronology

JULY: Total eclipse of the sun visible along a 9,300-mile path from the Pacific through Mexico and eight Latin American countries

Mexico

Guatemala

El Salvador

Haiti

Venezuela

Colombia

LATIN AMERICA

JULY: Colombia, Mexico and Venezuela announce agreement to create free-trade zone by Jan. 1992

Colombia
JUNE: Pablo Escobar, the leader of the Medellín cocaine cartel, surrenders after the assembly bans the extradition of citizens wanted abroad
JULY: The cartel says it is ending its terrorist campaign

El Salvador
SEPT: In New York, under U.N. auspices, President Cristiani and the Farabundo Marti Liberation Front (F.M.L.N.) agree to reintegrate F.M.L.N. guerrillas into civilian society. Court in San Salvador finds a colonel guilty of the murder of six Jesuit priests in 1989

Guatemala
JAN: Jorge Serrano Elías wins presidential election. First civilian transfer of power

Haiti
FEB: Jean-Bertrand Aristide, the first democratically elected president, is sworn in
SEPT: Military coup ousts Aristide. At least 26 are killed, 200 injured
OCT: As a result of the coup, OAS declares a trade embargo against Haiti

TIME Graphics by Nigel Holmes

WESTERN EUROPE

European Community
DEC: All nations except United Kingdom agree to adopt common currency and loose political union

NATO
MAY: Announces a reorganization of forces in Europe, to begin in 1994 and be completed in 1999. U.S. forces will be reduced by 50%

France
MAY: Prime Minister Rocard resigns. Edith Cresson, a Socialist, becomes first woman to hold that office

Germany
JUNE: Parliament agrees to move the seat of government from Bonn, capital since 1949, to Berlin

Italy
FEB: Italian Communist party renames itself the Democratic Party of the Left

Norway
JAN: King Olav V, oldest monarch in Europe, dies; his son Harald succeeds to the throne

Sweden
SEPT: In national elections, the five nonsocialist parties win 53% of the vote, the worst electoral defeat for the Social Democrats in 60 years

United Kingdom
FEB: Irish Republican Army (I.R.A.) fires at the Prime Minister's office while the cabinet is meeting. Two bombs explode at London railroad stations, killing one, injuring 40

EASTERN EUROPE

Warsaw Pact
MARCH: Ceases to exist

Albania
APRIL: In first free parliamentary elections the Communists win a majority of the seats
JUNE: Prime Minister Fatos Nano's government resigns. Parliament approves the first non-Communist cabinet since 1945

Czechoslovakia
JUNE: Protocol to end Soviet occupation is signed

Romania
SEPT: Coal miners strike. Prime Minister Roman resigns
OCT: Theodor Stolojan is named Prime Minister. Says he will continue economic reform policies

ANTARCTICA

OCT: 24 countries, including the U.S. and U.S.S.R., sign a protocol in Madrid banning oil and mineral exploration for 50 years

SOVIET UNION

JAN: 14 people are killed when Soviet troops storm Lithuania's radio-TV center in Vilnius ·
AUG 21: A coup against President Gorbachev fails; he returns to Moscow.
24: He resigns as Communist Party chief and urges that the party be disbanded.
27: He appeals to the republics to preserve military and economic union
SEPT: The Soviet Union recognizes the independence of the Baltic states
OCT: Eight other republics agree to economic union
NOV 6: After refusing to join the economic union, Ukraine and Moldavia agree. 16: Boris Yeltsin, President of Russia, takes control of the money supply and of trade in oil, gold, diamonds and foreign currency
25: Gorbachev suffers setback when seven republics refuse to endorse union treaty
DEC 1: Ukraine votes for independence.
8: Russia, Ukraine and Belorussia form a commonwealth. 13: Other republics join

MIDDLE EAST: The Gulf War and after

JAN 12: U.S. Congress authorizes use of force in the Persian Gulf crisis.
16: Desert Storm begins. 23: Iraq leaks millions of gallons of oil into the gulf. 29: Battle of Khafji; first major ground engagement
FEB 23: Ground war begins. 22–26: Iraq sets 732 Kuwaiti oil wells ablaze. 26: Iraq abandons Kuwait City. 27: Cease-fire after 100 hours of ground war
MARCH 6: Bush victory speech to Congress
APRIL: U.S., British and French begin to airlift supplies to Kurdish refugees
MAY: Coalition troops extend protection zone for Kurdish refugees
JULY 15: Last coalition forces withdraw from northern Iraq. 19: Kurds and Iraqis agree to end fighting. 30: U.N. inspectors find more than four times the number of shells and raw materials for chemical arms than Iraq had declared in April
SEPT: Iraq detains U.N. inspectors and the 25,000 pages of records documenting Iraq's secret nuclear program

Israel

APRIL: U.S. requests that Israel stop building new settlements, to no avail

Iran

MAY: President Rafsanjani says he wants to increase economic and political cooperation with the West

Jordan

JUNE: King Hussein signs charter to restore multiparty democracy

Hostages

AUG: U.N. Secretary-General Perez de Cuellar begins intensive efforts to free hostages. John McCarthy (U.K.) and Edward Tracy (U.S.) are freed
SEPT: Israel releases 51 Arab prisoners Jack Mann (U.K.) is freed
OCT: Israel frees 15 Lebanese prisoners. Jesse Turner (U.S.) is released
NOV: Terry Waite (U.K.) and Thomas Sutherland (U.S.) are released
DEC: Americans Joseph Cicippio, Alann Steen and Terry Anderson are freed. The release of two Germans is promised

Peace process

OCT: First round of talks in Madrid
DEC: Talks resume in Washington D.C.
U.N. repeals resolution equating zionism with racism

ASIA

Afghanistan
SEPT: President Najibullah calls for multiparty local elections. National elections are scheduled for 1992

Bangladesh
MARCH: Parliamentary elections; Khaleda Zia becomes Prime Minister
APRIL: 92,000 are killed during cyclone. Disease and starvation may increase the total to 200,000, causing $1 billion damage

Burma (Myanmar)
OCT: Aung San Suu Kyi, leader of the opposition National League for Democracy, who is under house arrest, is awarded Nobel Peace Prize

Cambodia
OCT: The government, the Khmer Rouge and two noncommunist guerrilla factions sign a peace treaty to end the 21-year civil war

China
MAY: Jiang Qing, widow of Chairman Mao, commits suicide

Hong Kong
OCT: Vietnam and Britain agree to the repatriation of Vietnamese refugees

India
MAY: Rajiv Gandhi is killed while campaigning to be Prime Minister

North Korea
SEPT: Becomes full U.N. member
DEC: Signs nonaggression treaty with South Korea, formally ending Korean War

Philippines
MAR: President Aquino says Imelda Marcos may return; will face $10 billion theft charges
JUNE: Mt Pinatubo erupts. 20,000 U.S. personnel evacuated. Clark Air Base is closed in November

Taiwan
APRIL: President Lee ends martial law decreed by nationalist government in 1948

Thailand
FEB: Military rebels seize Prime Minister
MAR: Civilian government is installed

AFRICA

Angola
MAY: Last Cuban soldiers leave, ending Cuba's role in the 16-year civil war. Free elections promised for 1992

Benin
MARCH: Nicephore Soglo becomes the first popularly elected president

Ethiopia
MAY: Guerrillas take Assab, the government-controlled port on the Red Sea. President Mengistu resigns

Liberia
JUNE: Rival factions agree to cease-fire in the civil war that has partitioned the country into two zones

Mali
MARCH: Military coup ousts President Moussa Traoré

APRIL: Soumana Sacko, a U.N. development officer, named interim Prime Minister

Somalia
JAN: Rebel forces take Mogadishu, and President Barre flees

Togo
AUG: After 24 years of military rule, President Eyadéma surrenders authority. Elections will be held in 1992
DEC: French troops intervene in coup attempt by Eyadéma troops

Zaire
SEPT: After riots, President Mobutu asks Etienne Tshisekedi to form a government but in October replaces him with Bernadin Mungul-Diaka

Zambia
NOV: President Kaunda, after 27-year rule, is defeated at ballot box

SOUTH AFRICA

FEB: President De Klerk announces that he will ask parliament to repeal apartheid laws
MAY: Winnie Mandela is found guilty of kidnapping, sentenced to six years, freed on bail pending an appeal
JULY: Olympic committee lifts its 21-year ban on participation in the games
SEPT: De Klerk proposes a new constitution that would establish universal suffrage and new two-chamber parliament

Norway
Sweden
U.K.
Germany
France
Czechoslovakia
Romania
Italy
Albania
N. Korea
S. Korea
Japan
China
Afghanistan
Taiwan
Bangladesh
Burma
Hong Kong
Thailand
India
Cambodia
Philippines
Mali
Ethiopia
Liberia
Togo
Benin
Somalia
Zaire
Angola
Zambia
South Africa

Timeline: U.S.A.

Nation   **Science Society**   **Arts Sport**   **Business**

JAN

A federal judge rules that pictures of nude women displayed in the work-place qualify as sexual harassment

61%

President Bush's popularity rating according to telephone polls taken for TIME/CNN throughout the year

Deadline expires; allies begin war by bombing Baghdad at night

Medical and Dental Association recommend that doctors and dentists infected with HIV virus notify patients of their condition

U.S. Postal Service raises price of a first-class stamp to 29 cents

Lincoln Center begins an ambitious program of performances to mark Mozart's bicentennial year

Sears eliminates 21,000 jobs

Eastern stops flying

Pan Am files for bankruptcy protection

The stock market Dow Jones Industrials, weekly closings

2501.5 Lowest point during the war

FEB

80%

Bush sends $1.45 trillion budget to Congress

Senate Ethics Committee clears four out of five senators; in November, Alan Cranston (D.-Calif.) is reprimanded

Allies invade Kuwait, liberate Kuwait City in "100-hour war"

Senate unanimously confirms Lynn Martin as Secretary of Labor

California Department of Water Resources suspends agricultural deliveries of water as drought enters fifth year

Neil Simon's *Lost in Yonkers*, the 1991 Pulitzer Prize play, debuts on Broadway

The Silence of the Lambs is released and becomes a surprisingly big hit

Treasury Department offers Congress a plan to reform the banking system

MAR

86%

Congress passes bill to provide $30 billion additional funds for savings and loan bailout

Bush travels to meet with Mulroney in Canada, Mitterrand on Martinique and Major on Bermuda

Los Angeles police are videotaped brutally beating a suspect

NASA announces plans for a simplified space station to cost $30 billion and be ready for occupancy by a four-member crew by September 1999

Walter Annenberg donates his unparalleled collection of artworks to New York's Metropolitan Museum of Art

2858.9 Donald and Ivana Trump reach agreement on a divorce settlement

APR

Nicaraguan President Violeta Barrios de Chamorro addresses a joint session of Congress

73%

The travels of White House Chief of Staff John Sununu come under close scrutiny

Carter aide Gary Sick charges a secret deal between Iran and the Reagan/Bush campaign team in 1980 delayed the release of hostages

NASA launches Gamma Ray Observatory from space shuttle Atlantis

William Smith accused of rape in West Palm Beach

FDA begins strict enforcement of labeling regulations

Miss Saigon opens on Broadway with a record-breaking advance ticket sale

Kitty Kelley's biography of Nancy Reagan causes a fuss and becomes an instant best seller

State regulators seize control of Executive Life of California, the largest failure of a U.S. insurer

Air Force selects Lockheed's prototype for the new F-22 fighter plane to replace the F-15 Eagle as the primary Air Force fighter

MAY

Bush suffers heart fibrillation while jogging at Camp David

House passes Brady bill, mandating seven-day wait for handgun purchases

The Supreme Court "gags" clinics receiving federal funds from discussing abortion.

Queen Elizabeth II addresses a joint session of Congress

Hispanics and blacks clash in the worst rioting in Washington, D.C., since 1968

Smith formally charged

Thelma & Louise, the summer's most talked-about film, is released

Nolan Ryan pitches his seventh no-hitter; Rickey Henderson becomes the all-time base-stealing champ

Losing a five-year fight for control, Carl Icahn sells his stake in USX

Detroit's Big Three report first-quarter losses of $2.4 billion, the largest ever

JUNE

House passes a civil rights bill

Associate Justice Thurgood Marshall resigns from the Supreme Court

Supreme Court rules that states may ban nude erotic dancing

Forbidden to use government planes to travel on private trips, Sununu takes an official limousine to a stamp auction in New York

Bush meets Boris Yeltsin, President of the Russian republic

Elizabeth Carl, a woman living in an openly lesbian relationship, is ordained an episcopal priest

President Zachary Taylor's body is exhumed to test for signs of poisoning. None are found

Spike Lee's *Jungle Fever* spearheads a new wave of successful black films

Jay Leno is named to succeed Johnny Carson as host of NBC's the *Tonight Show*

2906.8 Melvyn Paisley pleads guilty after a four-year investigation into the selling of Pentagon information to military contractors

Bush names Clarence Thomas to Marshall's seat on the Surpreme Court

Commerce Secretary Robert Mosbacher says he will not adjust the 1990 census figures

69%

Bush visits Kiev

68%

Federal charges against Oliver North are dropped

Democratic presidential race heats up as Brown, Wilder, Harkin and Kerrey announce candidacies

Bush travels to Madrid for Middle East peace conference

Congress blushes as a check-bouncing scandal surfaces

60%

Bush travels to the NATO meeting in Rome, visits the Pope and stops off in the Netherlands

Congress extends unemployment benefits and passes civil rights bill, banking bill and highway bill

Senate approves Robert Gates as new director of CIA

Sununu resigns as Chief of Stuff; Samuel Skinner takes over

Former head of California's Lincoln Savings & Loan Charles Keating is found guilty of securities fraud. He faces 10 years in prison and a $250,000 fine

Republican Patrick Buchanan announces his candidacy for President

Bush travels to Canada, France, London for the economic summit, Greece and Turkey; then Moscow for START treaty signing

CIA official Alan Fiers admits lying on aid to *contras*

Dick Thornburgh resigns as Attorney General to run for Senator from Pennsylvania

Dan Quayle criticizes lawyers at the American Bar Association convention

Bush announces cuts in the U.S. nuclear arsenal; Gorbachev follows suit shortly

Senate holds hearings for Clarence Thomas nomination; Anita Hill charges sexual harassment. Final vote is 52 to 48 to confirm Thomas

46%

Edwin Edwards defeats David Duke in the Governor's race in Louisiana

---

Total solar eclipse visible in Hawaii and across Latin America

Pro-life Operation Rescue sit-in heats up at abortion clinics in Wichita

Jeffrey Dahmer arrested in Milwaukee for murder

NASA launches earth probe satellite, beginning Mission to Planet Earth

Manuel Noriega goes on trial in a U.S. district court in Miami

23 killed in a Texas café by George Hennard

Fire ravages Oakland, Calif., destroying hundreds of homes

Magic Johnson says he is HIV-positive

The Michigan Board of Medicine suspends Jack Kevorkian for aiding patients' suicides

New York City high schools begin giving condoms to students

Salman Rushdie speaks at a symposium on free speech in New York City

William Smith acquitted of rape charges by a West Palm Beach jury

---

Terminator 2, Hollywood's most expensive film ever, is the year's biggest hit

Long-hitting golf newcomer John Daly wins the P.G.A. title

Aging veteran Jimmy Connors thrills tennis fans at the U.S. Open with his come-from-behind victories

Mike Tyson is charged with sexual assault and characterized as a "serial buttocks fondler"

The Minnesota Twins outlast the Atlanta Braves to win a classic World Series

Scarlett, the sequel to *Gone with the Wind*, is the fastest-selling novel in years

Harold Brodkey's long-promised novel *The Runaway Soul* is published to generally negative reviews

Disney's *Beauty and the Beast* opens and is hailed as an instant classic in the full-legth animated format

Michael Jackson's new album *Dangerous* immediately soars to the top of the charts

Bugsy, Hook, The Addams Family, Cape Fear and *JFK* are the major holiday attractions at the nation's movie theaters

---

IBM and Apple announce a pact to join forces and share technology

Bank of England seizes control of the assets of B.C.C.I.

Chemical Bank and Manufacturers Hanover say they will merge

BankAmerica acquires Security Pacific in the largest such deal ever

Salomon Brothers admits violations in bidding practices

Clark Clifford resigns as chairman of First American Bankshares

Abu Dhabi government detains former executives of B.C.C.I. in its investigation of the bank's fraudulent activities; the government and its ruler own 77.4% of B.C.C.I.

U.S. District Court accepts Exxon's plea agreement and a $1.25 billion settlement in 1989 *Exxon Valdez* oil spill

American Express writes off $155 million in bad loans on its Optima card

Robert Maxwell is found dead just eight months after saving the New York *Daily News*

IBM unveils the most radical shake-up in its history, planning to cut 20,000 jobs in 1992

Pan Am stops flying

2914.36
(12/13)

GM announces massive cuts and 21 plant shutdowns

TIME Chart by Nino Telak

15

America on the Move

The United States is a nation of people forever running toward bright new futures -- or away from bleak presents and past failures. The 1991 release of figures from the 1990 Census portrayed a nation that has been growing more rapidly and in more complex patterns than ever before, as this TIME chart reveals.

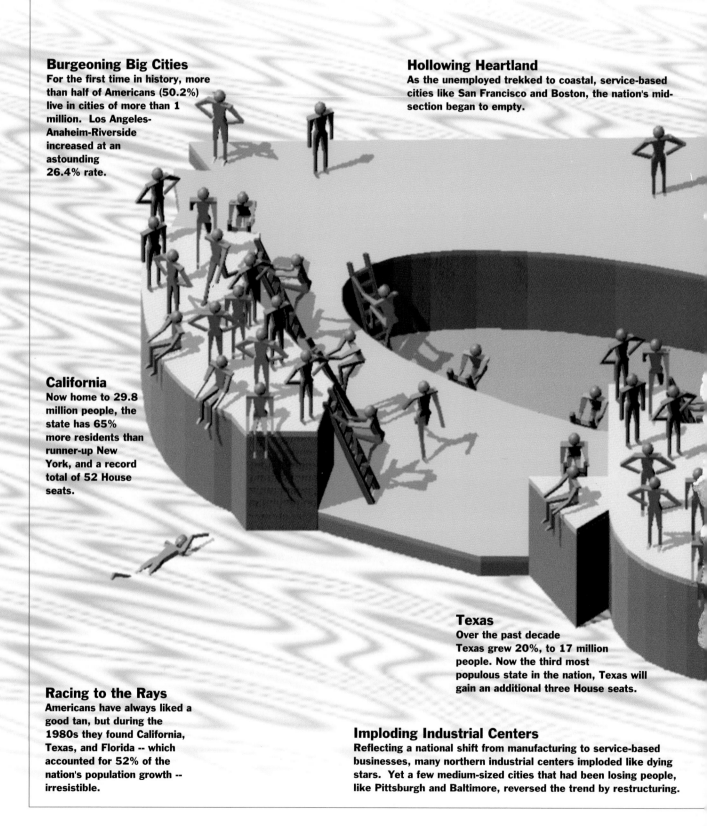

Burgeoning Big Cities
For the first time in history, more than half of Americans (50.2%) live in cities of more than 1 million. Los Angeles-Anaheim-Riverside increased at an astounding 26.4% rate.

Hollowing Heartland
As the unemployed trekked to coastal, service-based cities like San Francisco and Boston, the nation's mid-section began to empty.

California
Now home to 29.8 million people, the state has 65% more residents than runner-up New York, and a record total of 52 House seats.

Texas
Over the past decade Texas grew 20%, to 17 million people. Now the third most populous state in the nation, Texas will gain an additional three House seats.

Racing to the Rays
Americans have always liked a good tan, but during the 1980s they found California, Texas, and Florida -- which accounted for 52% of the nation's population growth -- irresistible.

Imploding Industrial Centers
Reflecting a national shift from manufacturing to service-based businesses, many northern industrial centers imploded like dying stars. Yet a few medium-sized cities that had been losing people, like Pittsburgh and Baltimore, reversed the trend by restructuring.

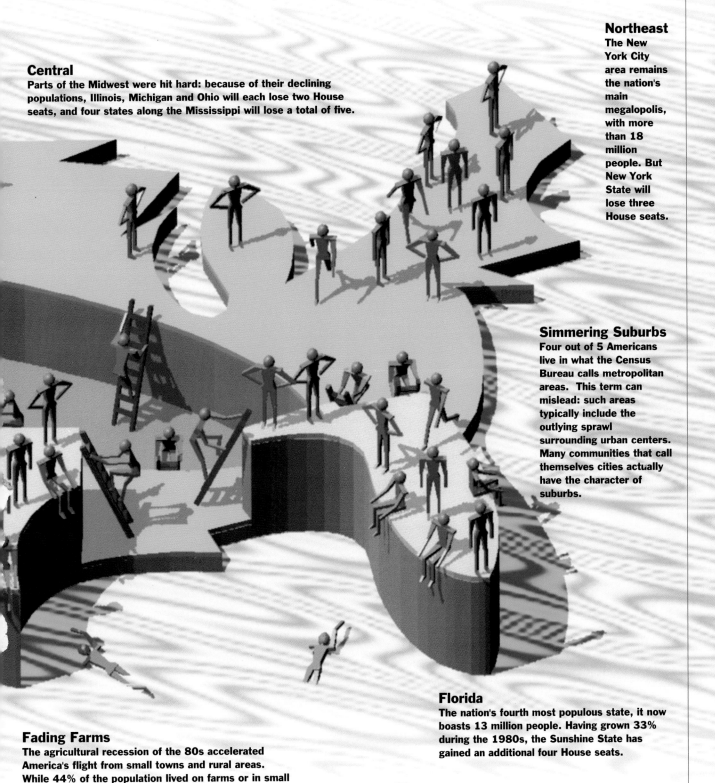

Staying Put
Surprisingly, some of the frostbelt towns that contributed to the migrant stream of the 1970s, like Toledo, Ohio, Fort Wayne, Ind., and Elmira, N.Y. stabilized in the 1980s, as the middle- and working-class residents of these cities aren't moving.

Booming Minorities
The ethnic makeup of the nation changed more radically than at any time in the past. The 1980 Census found that 1 of every 5 Americans belonged to a minority group. By 1990, 1 of every 4 Americans claimed Hispanic, Asian, African or Native American roots.

Central
Parts of the Midwest were hit hard: because of their declining populations, Illinois, Michigan and Ohio will each lose two House seats, and four states along the Mississippi will lose a total of five.

Northeast
The New York City area remains the nation's main megalopolis, with more than 18 million people. But New York State will lose three House seats.

Simmering Suburbs
Four out of 5 Americans live in what the Census Bureau calls metropolitan areas. This term can mislead: such areas typically include the outlying sprawl surrounding urban centers. Many communities that call themselves cities actually have the character of suburbs.

Florida
The nation's fourth most populous state, it now boasts 13 million people. Having grown 33% during the 1980s, the Sunshine State has gained an additional four House seats.

Fading Farms
The agricultural recession of the 80s accelerated America's flight from small towns and rural areas. While 44% of the population lived on farms or in small towns in 1950, that segment has dwindled to 23%.

Illustration for TIME by Joe Lertola

For the Record

TOP 10 MOVIES

1 Home Alone
2 Terminator 2
3 Dances With Wolves
4 Robin Hood
5 The Silence of the Lambs
6 City Slickers
7 Sleeping With the Enemy
8 Kindergarten Cop
9 Naked Gun 2 1/2
10 Teenage Mutant Ninja Turtles II

SPORTS

Football: SUPERBOWL The N.Y. Giants beat the Buffalo Bills 20-19

Tennis:
AUSTRALIAN OPEN
Women's champion, Monica Seles
Men's champion, Boris Becker
FRENCH OPEN
Women's champion, Monica Seles
Men's champion, Jim Courier
WIMBLEDON
Women's champion, Steffi Graf
Men's champion, Michael Stich
U.S. OPEN
Women's champion, Monica Seles
Men's champion, Stefan Edberg

Golf:
THE MASTERS Ian Woosnam
U.S. OPEN Payne Stewart
LPGA CHAMPIONSHIP Meg Mallon
BRITISH OPEN Ian Baker-Finch
PGA CHAMPIONSHIP John Daly

Hockey:
STANLEY CUP CHAMPIONSHIP
Pittsburgh Penguins over Minnesota
North Stars in 6 games

Boxing: Evander Holyfield retains his HEAVYWEIGHT TITLE over George Foreman

Motor Sports:
DAYTONA 500 Ernie Irvan
INDIANAPOLIS 500 Rick Mears
LeMANS Volker Weidler, Johnny Herbert, and Bertrand Gachot team
FORMULA ONE WORLD CHAMPIONSHIP
Ayrton Senna

Basketball: NBA CHAMPIONSHIP Chicago
Bulls defeat Detroit Pistons in a 4-game sweep
NCAA FINALS Duke outlasts Kansas 72-65 to win championship

Track & Field:
WORLD TRACK AND FIELD CHAMPIONSHIPS
Carl Lewis wins 100 meter dash in world record time of 9.86 seconds
Mike Powell leaps a record 29' 4 1/2" long jump

Figure Skating:
WORLD FIGURE SKATING CHAMPIONSHIPS
Ladies: Kristi Yamaguchi
Men: Kurt Browning
Pairs: Natalia Mishkuteniok & Artur Dmitriev
Ice Dancing: Isabelle & Paul Duchesnay

Baseball: WORLD SERIES Minnesota Twins defeat Atlanta Braves in 10th inning of the 7th game

Horse Racing:
KENTUCKY DERBY Strike the Gold
PREAKNESS Hansel
BELMONT STAKES Hansel

TOP 10 RENTAL VIDEOS

1	Dances with Wolves	6	The Hunt for Red October
2	Ghost	7	Days of Thunder
3	Die Hard 2	8	Sleeping with the Enemy
4	Kindergarten Cop	9	Three Men and a Little Lady
5	Dick Tracy	10	GoodFellas

12:35

Sources
Videos: Commtron's 1991 Annual Report
Books: Waldenbooks (through 12/14/91)
Movies: Boxoffice Magazine (through 12/17/91)
TV Shows: Nielsen Media Research (through 12/8/91)
TIME Chart by Joe Lertola and Steve Hart

ACADEMY AWARDS

Best Picture:
Dances with Wolves

Best Director:
Kevin Costner
Dances with Wolves

Best Actor:
Jeremy Irons
Reversal of Fortune

Best Supporting Actor:
Joe Pesci
GoodFellas

Best Actress:
Kathy Bates *Misery*

Best Supporting Actress:
Whoopi Goldberg
Ghost

Lifetime Achievement:
Sophia Loren and
Myrna Loy

TOP 10 TITLES

1	Scarlett	Alexandra Ripley
2	Sum of All Fears	Tom Clancy
3	Needful Things	Stephen King
4	Heartbeat	Danielle Steel
5	Nancy Reagan	Kitty Kelley
6	Star Wars #1	Timothy Zahn
7	No Greater Love	Danielle Steel
8	The Firm	John Grisham
9	Me	Katharine Hepburn
10	Doomsday Conspiracy	Sidney Sheldon

TOP 10 TV SHOWS

FALL 1991 TV RATINGS

1	**ROSEANNE**	ABC
2	**60 MINUTES**	CBS
3	**MURPHY BROWN**	CBS
4	**CHEERS**	NBC
5	**DESIGNING WOMEN**	CBS
6	**FULL HOUSE**	ABC
7	**COACH**	ABC
8	**HOME IMPROVEMENT**	ABC
9	**MAJOR DAD**	CBS
10	**MURDER, SHE WROTE**	CBS

TONY AWARDS

Best Play:
Lost in Yonkers

Best Musical:
The Will Rogers Follies

Best Actress, Play:
Mercedes Ruehl
Lost in Yonkers

Best Actor, Play:
Nigel Hawthorne
Shadowlands

Best Actress, Musical:
Lea Salonga
Miss Saigon

Best Actor, Musical:
Jonathan Pryce
Miss Saigon

NOBEL PRIZES

Literature: South African novelist Nadine Gordimer
Physiology or Medicine: German physiologists Erwin Neher and Bert Sakmann for their work in uncovering basic cell functions
Peace: Burmese opposition leader Aung San Suu Kyi for her nonviolent struggle for democracy and human rights

Economics: Ronald H. Coase, professor emeritus of the University of Chicago Law School. For *The Theory of the Firm* and *The Problem of Social Cost*
Physics: Pierre-Gilles de Gennes of the College de France in Paris. For his study of liquid crystals
Chemistry: Richard R. Ernst of Zurich, Switzerland. For refining nuclear magnetic resonance imaging

Weeks of Bombing, Hours of Victory

By PAUL GRAY

The new year of 1991 began with the near certainty of war. Much of the debate that raged during the waning months of 1990 had exhausted itself. Iraq's blitzkrieg invasion of Kuwait in August was an act of brutal simplicity, but the questions it posed for the U.S. and other world powers proved devilishly complex. What should be done about Saddam Hussein and this act of naked aggression against a small and powerless neighbor?

President George Bush had responded to the invasion quickly, vowing that "this will not stand." Saying that was easier than actually getting Saddam out, and the motives for doing so came under intense and often critical scrutiny. The noble view was that the U.S. and the world at large had an obligation to restore the independence of Kuwait. Critics wondered whether this obligation was not really based less on notions of liberty than on an interest in Kuwait's substantial oil reserves. Obviously, there was truth in both positions.

And then there was the raw threat of Saddam himself. Few outside his country took seriously his argument that Iraq had simply reclaimed part of its rightful territory. The overriding concern was that a ruthless strongman with a demonstrated contempt for human rights and international law stood poised to bestride the Middle East. In the near future—analysts disagreed over how near—Saddam would achieve nuclear capabilities. It would be easier to stop him now, the argument ran, than it would be later.

But how? In the most impressive stretch of his presidency to date, George Bush skillfully maneuvered along a number of difficult paths: pressing for negotiations, working behind the scenes at the United Nations for an international embargo against Iraq and building an impressive, if unlikely, alliance of nations willing to contribute to a military action against Saddam.

By January, hopes that some course other than combat could resolve the situation were guttering out. The sanctions imposed by the embargo, some argued, were working and would eventually bring Saddam to his knees. Not so, countered others; Saddam cared nothing about the deprivations the embargo imposed on his people and would use this economic pressure as an excuse for further aggressions. Negotiations stood at an impasse; the U.S. demanded as a precondition Iraqi withdrawal from Kuwait, and Saddam refused to budge. It was somewhere around here that the Saddam-as-madman theory began to take hold in earnest. Either he was suicidal or he actually believed that his army, the fourth largest in the world, could withstand the military might being assembled in Saudi Arabia.

And if Saddam believed that, maybe he knew something the rest of the world did not. Misgivings blossomed into fears. What if cadres of terrorists struck Europe and the U.S.? What if Israel were drawn into the conflict, enraging the Arab masses and splintering the delicate alliance of forces opposed to Saddam? What if the sophisticated modern weaponry proved inoperable in the swirling desert sands? How long would U.S. public opinion support a lengthy land war? Tensions mounted during a prolonged air bombardment, while Saddam retaliated with Scud missile attacks.

The ground invasion phase of Operation Desert Storm lasted roughly 100 hours. Iraq was driven out of Kuwait.

This smashing victory will be studied and analyzed for decades to come. It was one of those rare instances in military history when strategy translated perfectly into practice. For the allies who assembled against Saddam, just about everything went right.

Considering the worries and uneasiness that preceded the fighting, the euphoria among the victors—and the folks back home—was understandable. Among other things, the gulf war pushed further into the background the long soul-searching over the U.S. actions in Vietnam. Citizens once more had reason to be proud of American military might.

But even as the flags were waved, nagging doubts appeared. It became clear that Saddam's forces had been vastly overrated. His underfed, ill-equipped troops, softened up by weeks of pre-combat bombing, were often more eager to surrender than fight. And in spite of the military rout and humiliation administered to his forces and him, Saddam was still in charge in Iraq.

Getting rid of Saddam had never been an announced aim of Desert Storm. On the other hand, it was no secret that the U.S. would not mind the dictator's death or overthrow. But within hours of the cease-fire, voices were raised claiming Bush had relented too soon, giving Saddam and his remaining forces an escape hatch. Many in Washington believed or hoped Saddam's generals, outraged at the catastrophe he had wrought, would topple him. But the Iraqi leader is not the typical military strongman, at the mercy of his subordinates; he is a ferociously efficient wielder of political power, surrounded on all sides by loyal relatives and others whose lives depend on his survival. Iraq showed signs of coming apart in the weeks after the war, but Saddam, as he had done so often before, managed to crush all the uprisings.

And in the afterglow of victory came the sobering realization of what it had cost. Allied casualties were miraculously light, but the human loss in Iraq and Kuwait was enormous. The full extent of Iraqi deaths, military and civilian, will not be known for certain as long as Saddam rules, and may never be known at all; but they were fearsome. The destruction in Iraq has brought persistent malnourishment and disease. Many of the victims are children. And charges persist that Saddam still has the wherewithal to develop nuclear weapons. Sadly, the end of the war is not the end of this story.

Storm

in the Gulf

The enterprise is still surrounded by a daze of astonishment: that it should have been so quick, so "easy," so devastating in effect. Like some martial equivalent of the Reagan years, the victory in the gulf made Americans feel better about themselves. It was splendid and necessary, but also unreal—an action-adventure that, like most movies, was divided into three chapters, with decisive turning points: first, the Iraqi invasion and the buildup of coalition forces; then the onset of the air war; and finally the ground war and its denouement. The victory came with such merciless ease that on the winners' side, the deeper levels of experience (nobility, sacrifice, endurance and so on) were not engaged. By the end of the year, the glorious moment seemed a long time ago.

The prospects going into the war were horrifying. The Pentagon ordered 16,099 body bags to be shipped to the Persian Gulf to bring home dead Americans. (In the end, 15,773 of the bags were not necessary.) We were confronting the fourth largest army in the world, commanded by a thug whom we thought cunning at the time and even invested with satanic powers. Saddam was armed with chemical weapons and was working on the nuclear kind. All those dark possibilities gave the coalition, in effect, a license to kill. The killing was very well done. I hope it does not give us too much pleasure. **—From an essay by Lance Morrow**

A cruise missile hurtles skyward from the *Wisconsin*

Deadline For War

Holding its breath, the world awaited the Jan. 15 deadline

THE VOTE TO FIGHT

Never had Congress faced a challenge quite like it. In the Persian Gulf, 430,000 U.S. troops were prepared to launch into battle against the Iraqi invaders of neighboring Kuwait. An American President had dispatched those troops to the Middle East, and the United Nations had authorized the use of force against the Iraqis unless they withdrew by Jan. 15. Yet Congress, the only branch of government with the constitutional power to declare war, had still not spoken, and the President was threatening to move with or without the lawmakers' approval. In the second week of January, Congress took up the question of war and peace with a rare urgency. Perhaps the most effective argument in favor of war was made not in Washington, however—but in Geneva.

LAST GASPS ON THE NEGOTIATION TRAIL

When U.S. Secretary of State James Baker and Iraqi Foreign Minister Tariq Aziz met in Geneva on Jan. 9, a brown manila envelope lay unopened on the table, mute testimony to the breach between their positions. The package contained a letter from President Bush to Saddam Hussein conveying in stark terms Washington's determination to see Iraq leave Kuwait. Baker had given Aziz a photocopy of the letter at the outset of the meeting. As Baker looked on, the Iraqi read the message slowly, his hands trembling. Finally, he said he could not bring such a letter to his leader; its tone was not appropriate for communication between heads of state.

The rest of the meeting was no more productive, although the atmosphere was calm and professional. Though Baker, the diplomat, was clearly depressed by the outcome of the discussion, his boss, the Commander in Chief, was unfazed. As Bush aides explained it, the Baker-Aziz conference confirmed the President's expectations without realizing his worst fears.

A RELUCTANT GO-AHEAD

With most Republicans already behind him, the President moved quickly after the Geneva breakdown to gain support from Democrats, while the Democratic leadership was continuing the fight to give sanctions more time. The antiwar factions in both houses fell in behind nearly identical resolutions drafted by House majority leader Richard Gephardt and Georgia Senator Sam Nunn,

When Saddam's tanks rolled into Kuwait in August 1990, Bush's allied coalition issued a deadline for withdrawal

chairman of the Senate Armed Services Committee. Nunn, with his hard-line reputation on most other military issues, was particularly important for attracting wavering Democrats.

When the Senate opened debate, majority leader George Mitchell laid out the antiwar, pro-sanctions position, warning that "the grave decision for war is being made prematurely." In the House, Gephardt stressed that the opponents of war were not friends of Iraq. "The only debate here in the Congress is over whether we slowly strangle Saddam with sanctions or immediately pursue a military solution. The choice is really over tactics."

While Congress debated, the White House continued to canvass for votes. One morning, more than 100 members of the House mushed through a snowstorm to a White House breakfast at which the President pleaded for their backing. In contrast to the President's aggressive lobbying, the Democratic leadership took a more hands-off approach toward rank-and-file Congressmen.

Once the speeches were made and the votes counted, a majority of the lawmakers lined up behind the President, and the battle that everyone had hoped to avoid seemed closer than ever. The House, by a vote of 250 to 183, and the Senate, 52 to 47, adopted resolutions that, in language approved by the White House, authorized the President to use military force against Iraq after Jan. 15.

Both houses also defeated alternative resolutions, sponsored by the Democratic leadership, calling for a delay in military action until sanctions had been given more time to work. At a press conference afterward, George Bush called the outcome in Congress "a clear signal that Iraq cannot scorn the Jan. 15 deadline." The votes represented not only a tactical victory for Bush, but a stunning turnaround of congressional sentiment. When the newly elected 102nd Congress assembled in Washington on Jan. 3, few lawmakers believed a majority could be found in either chamber favoring a quick resort to force. For months Bush had avoided seeking congressional approval of his gulf policies, fearing that a narrow victory—or worse, a defeat—would further embolden Saddam Hussein. But the failure of the Geneva talks—and particularly the impression of Iraqi intransigence—swept congressional fence-sitters into the President's camp.

With the Jan. 15 deadline approaching, the Iraqi strongman would not blink

ANXIETY BEFORE THE STORM

For the American people, the interval between Saddam's invasion in August 1990 and the January deadline took on a peculiar unreality—a psychological suspension between peace and war. Much of the nation's opinion was clustered in the cautious middle ground; Americans were not yet sounding especially jingoistic or bellicose. Few questioned that Saddam Hussein was a villain who had raped Kuwait and had to be removed. Saddam made it easy by being a sort of caricature of an enemy, a heavy out of professional wrestling. The only question: should he be forcibly removed now, or slowly squeezed by sanctions? After the Geneva talks broke up, Americans seemed resigned that war would come. They thought it was necessary, but they did not much welcome it.

"I think it's stupid. I don't like why we're there," said Brian Scanlan, 34, a Boston carpenter. "But I feel it's inevitable." In Phoenix an engineer named Darin McDaniel expressed the same somewhat unhappy sense of a nation performing an international service in which it did not entirely believe: "I would have decided not to fight before Bush got us up to this point. He's already closed the door. The only thing to do now is finish it off. I'm for getting it over in a hurry."

As the deadline approached, TIME's Michael Kramer caught the national mood: "These are the longest days. End games fascinate. If clarity has been assured, only tragedy remains. Time moves in slow motion. An entire world waits with shallow breath, and the news never ends."

Canceled letter: meeting James Baker in Geneva, Iraqi Foreign Minister Tariq Aziz refused to deliver Bush's message to Saddam

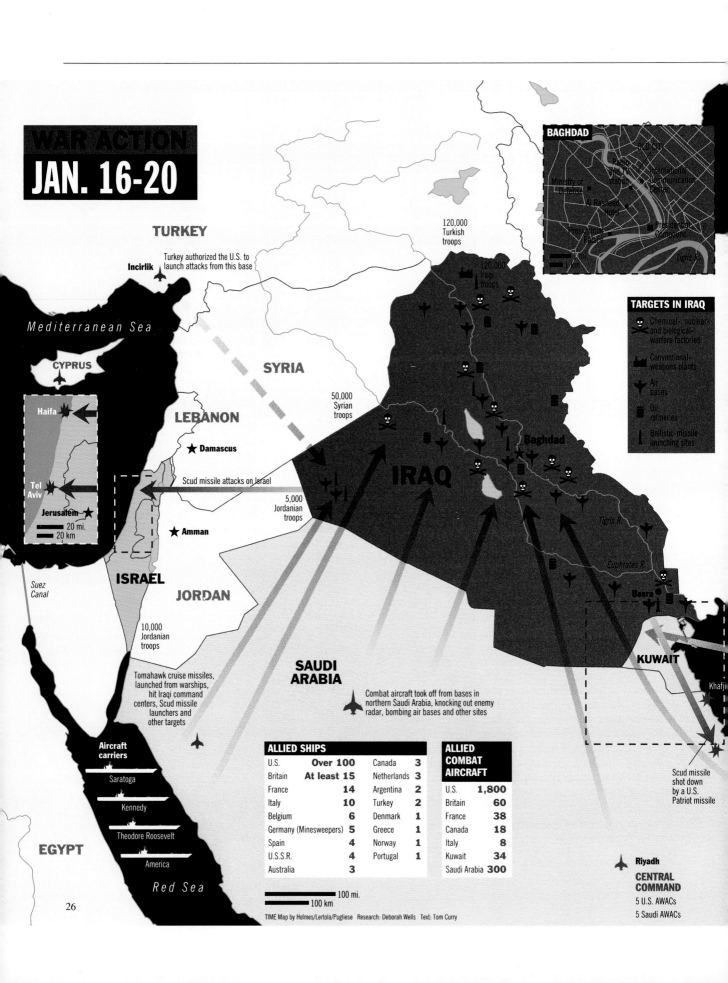

WAR ACTION
JAN. 16-20

BAGHDAD

OLD CITY
Radio and TV station
International Communication Center
Ministry of defense
Al Rasheed Hotel
Presidential Palace
Presidential Compound
Tigris R.
1 mi.
1 km

TURKEY

Turkey authorized the U.S. to launch attacks from this base
Incirlik

120,000 Turkish troops

120,000 Iraqi troops

Mediterranean Sea

CYPRUS

SYRIA

50,000 Syrian troops

TARGETS IN IRAQ

Chemical-, nuclear- and biological-warfare factories

Conventional-weapons plants

Air bases

Oil refineries

Ballistic-missile launching sites

LEBANON

★ **Damascus**

Haifa

Scud missile attacks on Israel

5,000 Jordanian troops

Baghdad

IRAQ

Tel Aviv

Jerusalem ★

20 mi.
20 km

★ **Amman**

Tigris R.

Suez Canal

ISRAEL

JORDAN

Euphrates R.

10,000 Jordanian troops

Basra

SAUDI ARABIA

KUWAIT

Tomahawk cruise missiles, launched from warships, hit Iraqi command centers, Scud missile launchers and other targets

Combat aircraft took off from bases in northern Saudi Arabia, knocking out enemy radar, bombing air bases and other sites

Khafji

Scud missile shot down by a U.S. Patriot missile

Aircraft carriers

Saratoga

Kennedy

Theodore Roosevelt

America

ALLIED SHIPS			
U.S.	**Over 100**	Canada	3
Britain	**At least 15**	Netherlands	3
France	14	Argentina	2
Italy	10	Turkey	2
Belgium	6	Denmark	1
Germany (Minesweepers)	5	Greece	1
Spain	4	Norway	1
U.S.S.R.	4	Portugal	1
Australia	3		

ALLIED COMBAT AIRCRAFT	
U.S.	**1,800**
Britain	60
France	38
Canada	18
Italy	8
Kuwait	34
Saudi Arabia	300

EGYPT

Red Sea

Riyadh

CENTRAL COMMAND

5 U.S. AWACs

5 Saudi AWACs

100 mi.
100 km

TIME Map by Holmes/Lertola/Pugliese   Research: Deborah Wells   Text: Tom Curry

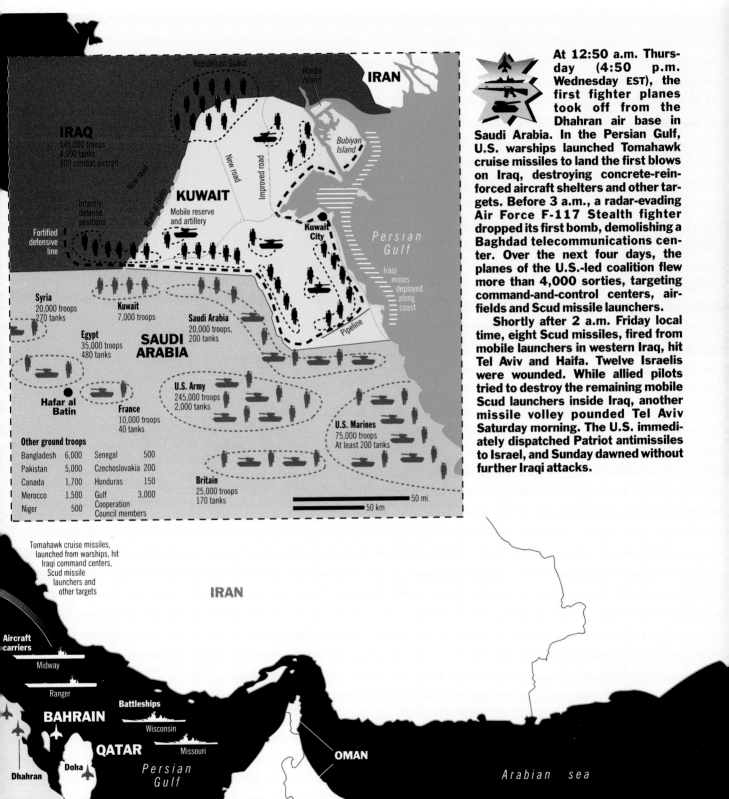

At 12:50 a.m. Thursday (4:50 p.m. Wednesday EST), the first fighter planes took off from the Dhahran air base in Saudi Arabia. In the Persian Gulf, U.S. warships launched Tomahawk cruise missiles to land the first blows on Iraq, destroying concrete-reinforced aircraft shelters and other targets. Before 3 a.m., a radar-evading Air Force F-117 Stealth fighter dropped its first bomb, demolishing a Baghdad telecommunications center. Over the next four days, the planes of the U.S.-led coalition flew more than 4,000 sorties, targeting command-and-control centers, airfields and Scud missile launchers.

Shortly after 2 a.m. Friday local time, eight Scud missiles, fired from mobile launchers in western Iraq, hit Tel Aviv and Haifa. Twelve Israelis were wounded. While allied pilots tried to destroy the remaining mobile Scud launchers inside Iraq, another missile volley pounded Tel Aviv Saturday morning. The U.S. immediately dispatched Patriot antimissiles to Israel, and Sunday dawned without further Iraqi attacks.

IRAN

IRAQ
545,000 troops
4,000 tanks
500 combat aircraft

Republican Guard

Warba Island

Bubiyan Island

KUWAIT
Mobile reserve and artillery

New road
Improved road
New road
Wadi al Batin

Kuwait City

Persian Gulf

Iraqi mines deployed along coast

Infantry defense positions

Fortified defensive line

Pipeline

Syria
20,000 troops
270 tanks

Kuwait
7,000 troops

Egypt
35,000 troops
480 tanks

SAUDI ARABIA

Saudi Arabia
20,000 troops,
200 tanks

Hafar al Batin

France
10,000 troops
40 tanks

U.S. Army
245,000 troops
2,000 tanks

U.S. Marines
75,000 troops
At least 200 tanks

Britain
25,000 troops
170 tanks

Other ground troops			
Bangladesh	6,000	Senegal	500
Pakistan	5,000	Czechoslovakia	200
Canada	1,700	Honduras	150
Morocco	1,500	Gulf Cooperation Council members	3,000
Niger	500		

50 mi.
50 km

Tomahawk cruise missiles, launched from warships, hit Iraqi command centers, Scud missile launchers and other targets

IRAN

Aircraft carriers
Midway
Ranger

Battleships
Wisconsin
Missouri

BAHRAIN

QATAR
Doha

Dhahran

Persian Gulf

OMAN

Arabian sea

Abu Dhabi

U.A.E.

The Battle Begins

The allies bomb Baghdad, and Saddam retaliates with Scud attacks on Israel and environmental terrorism in the gulf

War is an exercise in the unpredictable and often uncontrollable, following a course that cannot be foreseen hour to hour and leading to consequences that neither side had ever intended. Battle scenarios are crisp and clear cut, actual battles are anything but, and invariably bring surprises. No matter that the war starts on live television. Or that the deadline for combat is set six weeks in advance and is publicized more intensively than any other in history. Or that the attack proceeds in precisely the fashion that had all but officially been proclaimed in advance, with massive air attacks. The unexpected still occurs.

One surprise was surprise itself. After all the months that the war drums had been beating, the opening air and missile onslaught achieved almost complete tactical surprise. American weapons that had never been fired in anger worked as well as if the war were some elaborate training movie. Initial Iraqi resistance was so weak that Air Force Captain Genther Drummond,

who took part in the opening assault, remarked, "It was as if we had no adversary." The few unexpected developments were favorable: only scattered anti-American demonstrations broke out in the Arab world rather than the huge pro-Iraqi riots that some had feared.

BOMBS IN THE DARK

Previous generations of pilots had spoken of a "bomber's moon." But that was before technology revolutionized air warfare. Today the ideal condition for an air raid is a pitch-black night. Infrared devices and laser-guided bombs enable pilots to see and hit their targets through inky darkness; moonlight would serve only to make their planes more visible to antiaircraft gunners. Jan. 15 was the first of three moonless nights in Iraq and Kuwait. No good; the U.S. considered the deadline for using force to be midnight American Eastern standard time, and that was 8 a.m. Jan. 16 over Baghdad, after

The war begins as the allies bomb Baghdad in the early morning of Jan. 17, local time

sunup. The following night was the earliest time when both political and astronomical conditions would be ripe for war.

Just before 1 a.m. in the Middle East, pool reporters at U.S. air bases in Saudi Arabia heard and felt the ground-shaking thunder of wave after wave of jets taking off. The planes headed north toward Kuwait and Iraq. At about the same time, more jets were winging off six U.S. carriers in the Persian Gulf and Red Sea. Eventually about 2,000 planes of the U.S. and six allied nations—Britain, France, Italy, Canada, Saudi Arabia and the Kuwaiti government-in-exile—hit targets throughout Iraq and Kuwait.

The outside world got the first news from Western television correspondents at Al Rasheed Hotel in downtown Baghdad. Three reporters from CNN, the 24-hour news channel—anchorman Bernard Shaw, veteran combat correspondent Peter Arnett and reporter John Holliman—provided an exceptional, and perhaps unprecedented, live account of the start of war from inside an enemy capital.

Their reports were a low-tech throwback to Edward R. Murrow's famous radio broadcasts from London during the blitz. As viewers watched a still screen, disembodied voices described what was happening in graphic, excited, sometimes overwrought language. Arnett: "We're crouching behind a window in here . . . The antiaircraft is erupting again." Shaw: "This feels like we're in the center of hell." The dramatic scene was punctuated by interludes of awkward comedy, as the reporters scurried around the room on hands and knees and exchanged nervous banter.

With a spellbound world tuned in, the CNN trio told of hearing air-raid sirens and seeing tracer bullets and antiaircraft bursts lighting up the black skies. For a while, though, no bomb explosions could be heard; George Bush, listening to and watching TV in the White House, started to get a bit edgy. Finally, a noise that was indisputably a bomb blast could be heard over an open telephone line to correspondents at just about 7 p.m. EST—3 a.m. Thursday in Baghdad. "Just the way it was scheduled," noted Bush, who dispatched spokesman Marlin Fitzwater to tell reporters, "The liberation of Kuwait has begun."

Two hours later the President went on TV to deliver a speech that had been in preparation for weeks. His manner was somber and determined. The U.S. goal, he said, "is not the conquest of Iraq; it is the liberation of Kuwait."

FEEBLE RESPONSE

By that time, the destruction was well under way. Pilots returning from the first attack described an awesome pattern of flashing multicolored lights—some antiaircraft bursts, some bombs—brightening the dark ground and skies. One after another likened it to a Fourth of July fireworks display or a Christmas tree. A British television correspondent standing on a sixth-floor balcony of Al Rasheed Hotel reported a weird sight: a U.S. cruise missile whizzing past at eye level and slamming into the Iraqi Defense Ministry nearby.

The pinpoint accuracy of the attacks was spectacular. At a Friday briefing in Saudi Arabia, Air Force Lieut. General Charles Horner showed videotapes of two laser-guided bombs sailing through the open doors of a bunker in which an Iraqi Scud missile was stored, and a third plopping down the rooftop air shaft of a tall building in Baghdad and then blowing off the top floors. Bombs and missiles also hit other targets around and even in the heart of Baghdad—Saddam Hussein's presidential palace, for one—while apparently doing little damage to civilian lives or property.

A modern assault starts out with an attack on the enemy's air-defense capabilities. Ground-hugging cruise missiles, flying too low for radar to detect easily, hit targets initially judged too dangerous for manned aircraft to handle. In the assault on Baghdad, some of the first blows came from Tomahawk cruise missiles fired by ships far out in the Persian Gulf. As the first explosions rocked the city, Iraqi antiaircraft fire was directed into the sky at planes that were not there—yet. Stealth fighters also sneaked past radar to join the initial attack. Then high-flying aircraft, some launching missiles from far off, jammed or confused enemy radar and took out some antiaircraft guns, interceptor planes and airfields. Finally, when a path was cleared, bombers and fighter-bombers attacked at lower altitudes for great precision.

After the first raids, U.S. and allied planes pounded targets throughout Kuwait and Iraq around the clock, not so much in waves as in a steady stream, concentrating on missile sites, command and control units, troop complexes and artillery sites. Casualties among the allied airmen were phenomenally light: Iraqi antiaircraft fire was in some cases heavy, but inaccurate, and few planes rose to challenge the attackers.

POPGUN RETALIATION

From the very first, Saddam had loudly proclaimed that an important strategy for winning a war was to strike Israel, probably with missiles releasing clouds of poison gas. The idea was to goad Jerusalem into striking back, thus enabling the Iraqi dictator to claim that the war now pitted the Arab nation against Israel, its American ally and Arab stooges. His hope was that Egypt and Syria, rather than appear to be fighting in defense of Israel, would pull out of the anti-

CRUISE MISSILES

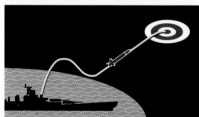

PURPOSE:
Long-range attack
USES:
Launched from ships and submarines
DISTINCTION:
Can fly under radar; 1,500-mile range
COST:
$1 million

30

Under a moonless sky over the Persian Gulf, 100 of these missiles initially blasted off from U.S. warships on a 700-mile flight to Iraq. Their TERCOM radar system compared landmarks with prerecorded maps to guide them to their targets. They struck nuclear, chemical and biological facilities.

STEALTH FIGHTER

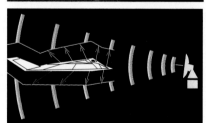

PURPOSE:
Long-range precision bombing
USES:
To penetrate air defenses undetected
DISTINCTION:
Extremely low radar profile
COST:
$106 million

Taking off from bases in Saudi Arabia, 27 of these single-seat twin-engine planes were the first aircraft to hit such targets as command-and-control centers and fixed Scud missiles. The plane's radar-evading Stealth technology, based on shape and materials, proved highly successful in the gulf.

ELECTRONIC JAMMING

PURPOSE:
Confuse or disable enemy radar
USES:
Carried by the Navy's EA-6B Prowler, the Air Force's F-4G Wild Weasel, EF-111A Raven and EC-130H Compass Call
DISTINCTION:
U.S. has the most advanced systems now deployed
COST:
For a Prowler, $32 million

The latest electronic-countermeasure systems have been placed on new planes as well as some of the oldest in the U.S. inventory. In the gulf war, ECM aircraft were among the first over Iraq and Kuwait, jamming air-defense radars and crimping their ability to detect intruding planes.

Iraq coalition or switch sides, and even Saudi Arabia would come under heavy pressure to end the battle.

The U.S. took the threat seriously enough to beg Israel in advance not to launch a pre-emptive attack. Washington promised in return to make the Scud missiles in western Iraq, the ones aimed at Israel, a primary target of the first alliance bombing raids. They were hit, and hit hard, at the start of the war. As the first 24 hours ticked by without an assault, hope grew that Saddam had been prevented from trying his cynical gambit.

No such luck. Early Friday morning, air-raid sirens went off through much of Israel. The government radio ordered all citizens to don the gas masks that had been distributed earlier and move into the sealed rooms that every household had been urged to prepare. Then blasts began rocking the Israeli cities of Tel Aviv and Haifa. Early reports said at least one missile warhead had released nerve gas and that a hospital in Tel Aviv was receiving gassed victims.

Not so. By Israeli count eight Scuds hit Tel Aviv, Haifa and the Ramallah area on Friday, but none of them released gas. They in-

jured about a dozen people, killing no one. Four elderly Israelis and a three-year-old girl, however, either suffocated inside gas masks that had been improperly adjusted or died of heart attacks. Despite the deaths, that amounted to a kind of popgun attack in contrast to the kind of assault the U.S. had feared Saddam would mount.

Washington and London immediately began a strenuous effort to persuade Israel not to retaliate and the Arab allies not to abandon the coalition if it did. The U.S. stepped up its aerial search for Scud missiles that could be fired from hard-to-locate mobile launchers. One Scud had been launched earlier against Saudi Arabia, but was blown up in midair by a Patriot antimissile missile. That was another technological triumph, the first known time that an attack missile had been destroyed by a defensive missile in combat.

On Saturday morning three more missiles fell on Tel Aviv. This time 10 people were injured, but again no one was killed. President Bush and British Prime Minister John Major separately telephoned

PATRIOT SYSTEM

RAYTHEON

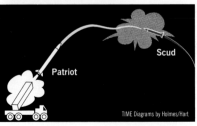

Scud

Patriot

TIME Diagrams by Holmes/Hart

PURPOSE:
Intercept aircraft and missiles
USES:
Protection of ground facilities
DISTINCTION:
Has remote launchers and high accuracy missiles
COST:
$123 million

This system won high marks when a U.S. Army Patriot destroyed an Iraqi Scud missile in Saudi Arabia. A Patriot battery has eight launchers with four missiles each. Israel received two batteries in late December, but they were not yet operational. The U.S dispatched more, including crews, at week's end. ʼ

SMART BOMBS

DEPARTMENT OF DEFENSE VIA ABC NEWS

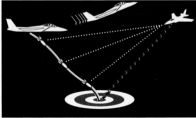

PURPOSE:
Precision bombing
USES:
Carried by most new fighter-bombers as well as B-52s
DISTINCTION:
Permits pilots to release bombs at safe distance from air defenses
COST:
Varies widely by type

The success of last week's air strikes was largely owing to the use of "smart bombs." Deployed in many forms, they are guided either by lasers, infrared or TV cameras. In one such system, a crewman can follow images relayed from the bomb and keep it on course toward its target by moving a joystick.

NIGHT-VISION DEVICES

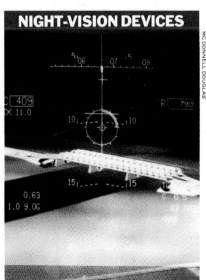

MC DONNELL DOUGLAS

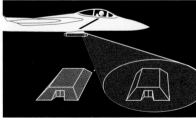

PURPOSE:
Light amplification
USES:
For aircraft, tanks and infantry
DISTINCTION:
Can amplify starlight 25,000 times
COST:
$200,000 for the fighter-bomber version

Night-vision goggles worn by fighter-bomber pilots, including those flying the F-15E Eagle that was used extensively in the gulf strikes, make objects visible at up to seven miles, even on dark nights. The device permits pilots to attack at low altitudes without using radar, which an enemy can detect.

Israeli Prime Minister Yitzhak Shamir, Bush at 3 a.m. Washington time, to plead again for restraint. After the Israeli Cabinet met in a concrete bunker on Saturday, the government once more assured Washington that for the moment it would not retaliate. The U.S. installed in Israel two batteries of the Patriot antimissiles, manned by American servicemen, the first time the U.S. had participated directly in Israel's defense.

THE HUNT FOR SCUDS

In the days that followed, Iraq launched salvos of Scud missiles at Israel and Saudi Arabia. Patriot antimissiles blew up most of them in the air, but six got through to hit Tel Aviv and Haifa, and at least one struck Riyadh. Four Israelis and one Saudi died during the raids; at least 130 Israelis and 30 Saudis were injured, and more than 1,000 Israelis were made homeless. During the first 10 days of the war, Iraq fired only about 50 Scuds, saving hundreds more for later use.

The raids made Saddam a hero to many Arabs, whose glee at seeing Israelis suffer was horrifying. But the attacks backfired in their political purpose. Though Jerusalem insisted that it would eventually retaliate, officials assured the U.S. that it would do so sooner rather than later only if future attacks released poison gas or killed large numbers of Israelis.

Searching for mobile Scud launchers did divert allied warplanes from bombing targets of greater military importance. That and heavy clouds over Iraq and Kuwait early in the war's second week briefly slowed the tempo of the air assault. Many allied planes carried infrared devices and guidance systems that enabled them to hit targets they could not see. But assessment of bomb damage can only be done visually, which is impossible through clouds. That in turn made it difficult to decide which planes should be sent to hit targets a second time and which could pound new ones.

As skies cleared late in the week, the bombing resumed with greater intensity than ever. On Thursday allied planes mounted a record 3,000 sorties (one plane on one flight); in the first 10 days, sorties totaled 20,000, of which more than half were combat missions.

The big change was a switch in targets. In the first days of the war, bombers concentrated on blasting Iraqi nuclear facilities, chemical- and biological-weapons plants (including one factory in Baghdad that the Iraqis said manufactured baby formula but that the White House insisted was devoted to preparations for germ warfare), command-and-control centers and, in particular, the Iraqi air force.

Saddam's planes were simply not a factor in the battle. Many were unable to take off because runways they might have used had been bombed full of craters. When the Iraqi planes did fly, their performance in dogfighting was miserable. When two Iraqi jets tried to stage an attack with Exocet missiles on British ships in the Persian Gulf, a Saudi pilot shot down both.

The allies used their superiority to shift into a new phase of the air war. They continued to revisit old targets, such as runways that

Soldiers inspect the smoking remains of an Iraqi Scud in Riyadh, Saudi Arabia

can often be repaired within 48 hours and must be bombed repeatedly to keep them out of action. But they concentrated increasingly on targets such as transport lines, fuel dumps and tank and artillery parks. Again and again they hit the southern city of Basra, which according to legend is near the site of the Garden of Eden and once was home port to Sinbad the Sailor. Under Saddam, it had become the main supply gateway and communications center for the Iraqi troops in Kuwait.

A WAR AGAINST THE EARTH

Unequipped to fight the allies in the air, Saddam turned to environmental terrorism. In a first taste of nightmares to come, a number of oil wells and storage tanks were set afire at Al-Wafra field in southern Kuwait and at the Shuaiba industrial complex just north of Mina al-Ahmadi. U.S. and Saudi officials claimed the fires were perhaps set to provide a massive shield of smoke that would confuse the guidance systems of allied missiles and planes and block the view of military satellites.

Then came word of a full-scale disaster. Early in the war's second week, the slightly nauseating odor of oil was noticeable along coastal areas of Saudi Arabia near the border with Kuwait. Within days, observers could see the source of the smell: a 10-mile band of crude, so thick in places that the water heaved like mud. Iraq had opened the spigots of Kuwait's main supertanker-loading pier, the Sea Island terminal, 10 miles offshore from the country's major petroleum refinery and loading complex at Mina al-Ahmadi. Through pipes leading from giant storage tanks, millions of gallons of crude had been poured straight into the water. At the same time, at least three tankers docked there were deliberately being emptied into the gulf.

Though the Pentagon first estimated that the spill was the largest in history, later reports indicated that it was 0.5 million to 3 million bbl. smaller than the 1979-80 Gulf of Mexico spill at the offshore drilling rig known as Ixtoc I. Saddam may have engineered the spill to foil any allied plans for an amphibious invasion, but he was also probably trying to shut down desalination plants that provide much of the fresh water for Saudi Arabia's eastern province. Another target may have been Saudi power stations and oil refineries, which rely on seawater for cooling.

The danger was vastly greater, though, for the billions of creatures that inhabit the Persian Gulf. The gulf waters, shores and islands are dotted with coral reefs, mangrove swamps and beds of sea grass and algae, brimming with birds, sea turtles, fish and marine mammals. The oil spill delivered a devastating blow to the ecology of the gulf, as hundreds of oil-soaked marine birds washed up on the shores of northern Saudi Arabia in the first days after the spill. One consolation for environmentalists: this was the first war in which the ecological consequences of battle had been the focus of world attention even as the fighting took place. In his quixotic madness, the Iraqi strongman seemed intent on waging what he called "the mother of battles" against the mother of us all—the earth itself.

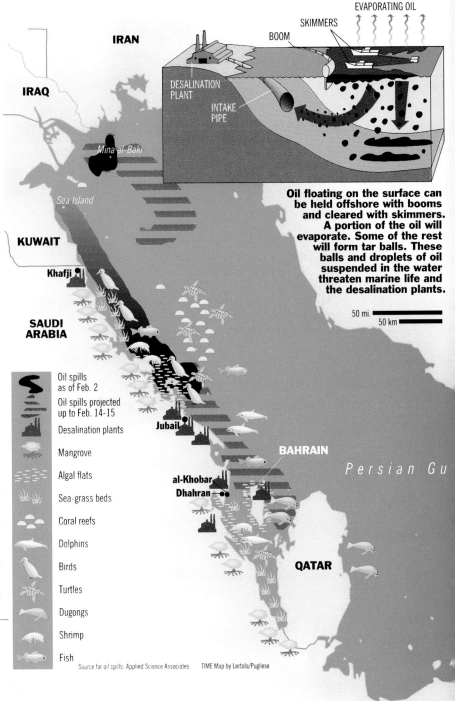

Oil floating on the surface can be held offshore with booms and cleared with skimmers. A portion of the oil will evaporate. Some of the rest will form tar balls. These balls and droplets of oil suspended in the water threaten marine life and the desalination plants.

50 mi.
50 km

Oil spills as of Feb. 2
Oil spills projected up to Feb. 14-15
Desalination plants
Mangrove
Algal flats
Sea-grass beds
Coral reefs
Dolphins
Birds
Turtles
Dugongs
Shrimp
Fish

Source for oil spills: Applied Science Associates   TIME Map by Lertola/Pugliese

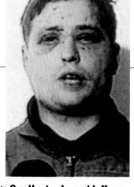

IRAQ'S HORROR PICTURE SHOW

Saddam also resorted to another form of terror. In the war's second week, he paraded allied captives before television cameras. The images were only too familiar. The men stared straight ahead, their eyes glazed and puffy, their bodies rigid, unmoving. Their faces, lined with fa-

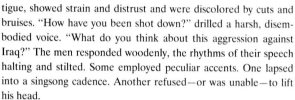
Saddam paraded American POWs Guy Hunter Jr. and Jeffrey Zaun before his TV cameras

tigue, showed strain and distrust and were discolored by cuts and bruises. "How have you been shot down?" drilled a harsh, disembodied voice. "What do you think about this aggression against Iraq?" The men responded woodenly, the rhythms of their speech halting and stilted. Some employed peculiar accents. One lapsed into a singsong cadence. Another refused—or was unable—to lift his head.

What did Saddam hope to achieve by this bizarre and revolting picture show? Did he believe that the grisly footage would turn Western public opinion against the war? Deter pilots from their missions? Raise doubts about the fortitude and courage of the allied fighting forces? If so, he had miscalculated. The clumsy propaganda seemed only to harden civilian and military resolve that Saddam must be stopped. Western viewers did not need expert commentary to conclude that the statements made by 13 captured pilots—eight Americans, two Britons, two Italians and one Kuwaiti—had been brutally coerced, in bald violation of the Geneva Conventions' provisions on the treatment of prisoners of war.

COMBAT IN THE SAND

Saddam's next move surprised everyone: he mounted an offensive. His army had been carefully positioned behind barbed wire, minefields and trenches, and had been fairly effectively hiding from air attack. His plan had always been to wait for an allied ground assault against his well-fortified troops, and then to inflict such heavy casualties on the attacking forces that President Bush would seek some sort of compromise peace.

As envisioned by allied military leaders, the standard scenario called for the long-awaited—and dreaded—ground war to begin in mid to late February with an all-out U.S. and allied aerial, artillery and missile barrage on the Iraqi army's fortifications in Kuwait, followed by a massive tank and infantry assault. But in the last days of January, Saddam's troops abandoned their defensive positions and mounted an attack on the Saudi Arabian ghost town of Khafji. More a skirmish than a true battle, the attack was launched on a penny-ante scale, with about 1,500 men and 80-odd tanks and other armored vehicles.

Iraqi troops, tanks and armored vehicles crossed the Saudi border at several points between Khafji and Umm Hujul, 50 miles to the west. On Wednesday night, Jan. 30, they occupied Khafji, six miles south of the border; it had been abandoned on Jan. 17 by residents fleeing out of the range of Iraqi artillery. Saudis and troops from the Persian Gulf sheikdom of Qatar, supported by Marine air attacks

and artillery fire, retook the town on Thursday, but only after house-to-house fighting that raged from 2:30 a.m. to 2 p.m. Sniper fire could still be heard on Friday. Marine planes and artillery repulsed the attacks at Umm Hujul.

Statistically, the Iraqis took a beating. By Friday afternoon the Saudis and Qataris had captured 500 Iraqis in and around Khafji. Allied officials said 30 Iraqis were killed and an additional 37 were wounded. Saudi casualties were not much lighter: 18 dead, 29 wounded and four missing.

Eleven Marines were killed in the fighting around Umm Hujul, and an AC-130 gunship with a crew of 14 was shot down over Kuwait. A male and a female soldier on a transport mission near Khafji were also missing. The woman, Army Specialist Melissa Rathbun-Nealy, became the first female American soldier ever to become a POW (though some nurses were captured in previous wars).

One tragic episode from the battle for Khafji: Iraqi tanks perched on the north side of a sand ridge near the Saudi-Kuwait border were firing at a company of U.S. Marines on the south side. The Marines were returning fire with TOW antitank missiles. Overhead, a U.S. Air Force A-10 Thunderbolt swooped toward one of the Iraqi tanks and released a heat-seeking Maverick missile.

But instead of flying straight for the target, the missile was diverted by the hot exhaust of a Marine light armored vehicle that stood between the U.S. plane and the Iraqi tank. The Maverick smacked into the left rear side of a LAV, blowing up the vehicle and killing all seven Marines inside. The tragic exchange was the war's first case of U.S. casualties from "friendly fire"—a combat euphemism for troops' getting shot, shelled or bombed by their own side.

In the battle, American 1-10 attack planes and Cobra and Apache helicopters and infantry weapons appeared to be quite as deadly as advertised against Iraqi armor. Allied commander General Norman Schwarzkopf would initially confirm only 24 Iraqi tanks definitely destroyed, but other counts for the border battles as a whole ran as high as 80 vehicles. The streets of Khafji were littered with the burning hulks of Soviet-made armored personnel carriers, knocked out by American TOW missiles fired by Saudi and Qatari infantrymen. U.S. Marines lost three LAVs in the fighting around Umm Hujul.

The battle also had other unpleasant surprises for the U.S. and its allies. Despite widespread reports of low morale among Iraqi frontline troops, those in Khafji fought tenaciously, prolonging the battle for hours after the Saudis announced they had retaken the town. One column of tanks had approached the Saudi border with their guns pointing backward, which allied forces took as a sign that the troops manning them wanted to defect; instead the Iraqis swiveled their turrets around rapidly and opened fire.

Allied commanders admitted to two other disappointments.

Scud-missile launchers in Iraq were taking a longer time to find and destroy than expected. General Schwarzkopf reported that 35 Scuds were lobbed against Israel or Saudi Arabia in the first seven days of the war, only 18 in the second seven days. In the first half of the war's third week only four launchings were recorded: three warheads fell on or near the Israeli-occupied West Bank, causing no reported casualties, and another aimed at Riyadh was destroyed by a Patriot missile. But 1,500 sorties were directed against Scuds, the most against any single type of target, and that delayed and lessened the assault against such other vital targets as supply lines and Saddam's well-entrenched élite fighting force, the Republican Guard. Also, Iraq proved more adept than expected at repairing runways, roads, radar and certain comunications lines, forcing allied planes to hit some of those installations again and again.

However, the happy surprises in the air war outweighed the disturbing ones. The most heartening development was that allied losses were so low. White House officials had braced themselves for the destruction of 100 or more American planes in the first few days: the actual figure lost in combat through the first 17 days was 15, plus seven allied craft. The principal reason: the allies had so seriously crippled the Iraqi air-defense system that Baghdad gave up all attempts to exercise central control: every antiaircraft and missile battery was on its own trying to track and intercept allied raiders. The Iraqi air force virtually disappeared: scores of its planes were destroyed on the ground or in the air; hundreds more were hiding in shelters and rarely taking off; another 150 or so of the best planes—in a surprising gambit—were flown to air bases in Iran.

Although early U.S. reports played down Iraqi casualties, later estimates indicated from 30,000 to 100,000 died

CALCULUS OF DEATH

As the war entered its fourth week, there seemed to be a lull in the conflict. Though air raids averaged one sortie a minute, the week brought no new oil spills, Iraqi raids into Saudi Arabia or any other surprise developments. The pace of Scud-missile attacks on Israel and Saudi Arabia dwindled further; Israel went five whole days without being the target of even one. Additional Iraqi planes fled to safety in Iran, though for the first time, American jets shot down six before they could cross the border. And there were more allied bombing and strafing runs than ever.

The big change was a perceptible shift in the type of bombing, toward the sort that would pave the way for a ground offensive. American and allied planes still carried out the kind of "deep penetration" strikes on factories, communications facilities, bridges and other fixed targets that began Jan. 16; Baghdad was hit 22 nights in a row. But the majority of strikes now consisted of what military men call battlefield interdiction—direct attacks on Iraqi tanks, artillery, troops and supply lines.

In the White House, President Bush faced a fateful decision: whether and when to start a ground offensive—a campaign that Baghdad radio said Iraq was "waiting impatiently" to fight. He dispatched Secretary of Defense Dick Cheney and Joint Chiefs of Staff Chairman Colin Powell to the gulf to talk with General Schwarzkopf and other allied commanders. En route to Saudi Arabia, Cheney identified as "the No. 1 priority" expelling Iraq from Kuwait "at the lowest possible cost in terms of loss of U.S. life." A considerable body of American political and military opinion favored holding off a ground attack not for weeks but for months, believing that prolonged bombing held the best hope of saving allied soldiers' lives.

Others argued for a relatively quick start to the ground war. Among their arguments: the air campaign would reach a point of diminishing returns; maintaining the fighting edge of allied troops would become more difficult the longer they sat in the sand; the strength-sapping gulf summer was approaching. The most important arguments for speed, however, were political. The more protracted the war, the greater the chance for a compromise settlement that would leave Saddam a menace for the future—and the more Saddam might seem a hero to the masses of Arabs who had long felt humiliated by the West.

Life on the Line

Rock the Casbah: G.I.'s brought jazz, Scrabble, volleyball and barbecues to the Saudi Arabian desert

To the U.S. ground soldiers of Operation Desert Storm, the shortest road home from Saudi Arabia cuts through Kuwait. But the prospect of traveling along it fills the grunts with dread.

In the evening, when the meals are over and the winds pick up and the temperatures drop below freezing, there are words of comfort. Some come from tentmates, some from letters, some from the radio muttering at cotside 24 hours a day. There are favorite songs, including one that is making the rounds of U.S. tents and bunkers in northern Saudi Arabia. It is a verse for a soldier, the 91st Psalm.

Under his wings you will find refuge.
His faithfulness is a shield and buckler.

Life at the front is a song of dark fear, deep pride, lost mail, long waits and improvisation. The white heat of the summer is hard to remember in February, when it becomes cold enough at night to leave ice rattling inside canteens. At the very front lines, the motto is "Travel light, freeze at night." Soldiers sleep in parka linings, with socks on their hands if their mittens are missing. They wish they could requisition extra toes.

It is a nuisance to lug around gas masks and protective gear, but no one complains. For the troops on the ground, the greatest fear is of chemical attack, a strike by an enemy they cannot see. That is why the troops love the chickens.

Near the gas-monitoring machines and scattered around the bases are live chickens. The machines' sirens will sound if there are chemical agents in the air, but the birds are the backup. Coal miners used canaries to warn against poisonous gases; the desert uses chickens. One

airbase named its newspaper after its chicken—*Buford Talks*—on the grounds that as long as the bird is squawking, they are safe. When peace comes, the soldiers daydream, they will hold a barbecue.

You will not fear the terror of the night,
nor the arrow that flies by day,
nor the pestilence that stalks in darkness,
nor the destruction that wastes at noonday.

The closer to the front, the more raw the nerves. "When we moved farther north, it helped morale because we broke the routine. The troops joke around a lot more," says a soldier. "We get T rations, which are hot and a lot better than MRES." MRES, or Meals, Ready to Eat, are the soldiers' most accessible enemy. Everyone hates them. Egyptian soldiers refused them. Only ravenous Iraqi prisoners of war wolf them down. When the milk runs out, there is pineapple drink to pour on the cornflakes.

The U.S. soldiers are older (average age: 27, compared with 21 in Vietnam) and better trained than the troops of past American wars. More than 95% of last year's recruits graduated from high school, in contrast to 54% a decade ago, and they are fitter. "I hate the new Army," says a sergeant looking for a cigarette. "Nobody smokes."

The American women, universally known as "females," who make up about one-tenth of the armed forces, are writing the rules as they go along. The Saudi government, rejecting the idea of female soldiers coming to their defense, designates them as males with female features. Some women are in traditional support roles as cooks, clerks and nurses. But they are also armorers, strategic planners and intelligence officers, serving close to the fire zone.

The men seem to take the women's presence in stride. "Once you work with them enough, they realize that you're a soldier like they are," says Lieut. Lynnel Bifora, 23, of Mohawk, N.Y., of the XVIII Airborne Corps. "I won't let them carry gear for me. I like to tell them that a bullet has no gender. Combat has no gender. You can kill the chivalry bit." She admits that it would be nice to put on a dress again, and clings to what femininity she can. "You can be tough and strong and still be a female," she says. The most precious distraction, the source of the most pleasure and some pain, is the mail, typically weighing in at 400 tons. A letter from home is reread until the pages crumble. "I had just opened the letter from my wife when we had a Scud alert," says Sergeant Darrell Thompson, 37, of the XVIII Airborne. "I dropped my mail to run off to the bunker, but I put the photo of my little girl in my pocket, like a good-luck charm."

A thousand may fall at your side, ten
thousand at your right hand; but
it will not come near you.

THE ENDGAME

On Feb. 15, Saddam dropped a diplomatic bombshell: he offered to pull out from Kuwait—if the Israelis withdrew from the West Bank and Gaza and the allied troops withdrew from the Persian Gulf, including naval forces that had been on patrol for decades. Plus forgiveness for all Iraqi debts. Plus reparations for the destruction caused by allied bombing. Plus . . .

But it *was* a bombshell. Not because the offer had the remotest chance of being accepted. But because Iraq for once was pointedly not boasting about making American and other allied soldiers drown in their own blood, not spurning all talk of a cease-fire with contempt, not claiming that Kuwait was and always would be Iraq's 19th province. The tone of Baghdad's propaganda had changed from swaggering bluster to pleas for sympathy for Iraq as the victim of a savage bombing campaign.

That line had some effect. In continuing air assaults on Baghdad, the 2,000-lb. bombs dropped from a Stealth fighter-bomber hit an air-raid shelter and, Baghdad said, killed several hundred civilians. U.S. officials insisted that there had been no mistake and the bunker was, in fact, a military communications center. The Iraqis treated the tragedy as manna from propaganda heaven. For millions of people around the world, pictures of the broken bodies dug out of the rubble drove home the horror of a war that had seemed, at least on the TV screens, to be rather tame.

However, the U.S. and its European allies suffered little if any public backlash against the war, and strong as Arab anger was, it was not quite sufficient to shake the governments (Saudi Arabia, Egypt and Syria) that had made major troop commitments to the coalition.

The imperfect success of the propaganda campaign left Iraq with one big hope for a face-saving way out of the war: Soviet diplomacy. Under pressure from hard-liners and a military that had equipped and trained the Iraqis—and seeking to prove the Soviet Union was still a superpower—Soviet President Mikhail Gorbachev began a period of diplomatic maneuvering. Following Baghdad's withdrawal proposal—which President Bush promptly denounced as a "cruel hoax"—Gorbachev proclaimed himself encouraged enough to invite Iraqi Foreign Minister Tariq Aziz to Moscow for new talks. There he handed Aziz a Soviet proposal: Iraq would withdraw, supposedly unconditionally, from Kuwait. In return, Moscow would undertake to preserve Saddam from any punitive actions, guarantee Iraq's territorial integrity, try to get economic sanctions against Iraq lifted and work for an overall Middle East peace conference.

The proposal was met with apprehension from the U.S. and other allies, who felt it might not only save Saddam and his regime from defeat but put him in a position to claim a political victory. When the Iraqis agreed to the proposal, on Thursday, Feb. 21, Bush convened his top aides in the White House for a council of war.

At 10:20 p.m. Bush returned from an evening at Ford's Theater to see *Black Eagles,* a play about black airmen in World War II. His war cabinet was waiting. It was a warm evening for February; the fireplace was dark. Joint Chiefs of Staff Chairman Powell was clad in a green turtleneck and sport jacket. Vice President Dan Quayle and Defense Secretary Cheney wore tuxedos, having come from a dinner for visiting Queen Margrethe II of Denmark. Cheney had removed his eyeglasses and was absentmindedly chewing one end of the frames. Like everyone else, he was studying a pair of freshly copied documents in his lap.

One was a list of "criteria" by which the allies would judge whether an Iraqi withdrawal was unconditional and worthy of an allied cease-fire. The second was a single-page argument about why the Gorbachev-Aziz agreement was "unacceptable."

Bush scanned the drafts, nodded and said, "I like both of these. Let's put them together. It's not enough to just say we don't accept the Soviet plan. I went through this with Gorbachev on the phone, and he knows it's unacceptable and he knows the specific reasons why, and we ought to lay them out to the whole world."

"Well, let's set a date and set a time," suggested Powell.

"I think that's a good idea," Bush replied immediately.

Powell explained that a deadline would be "helpful to the military because then my guys in the field know what to expect." National Security Adviser Brent Scowcroft agreed. "The diplomatic question was the toughest," said a participant. "We had 28 partners, and the highest concern was making sure we could get everyone on board."

Someone suggested that noon Saturday be the deadline; noon in Washington was sundown in Kuwait, where allied forces held the advantage in night-fighting ability. Bush said, "O.K., we're agreed then. It's noon Saturday."

On Friday morning the President appeared before the cameras in the Rose Garden of the White House, giving Saddam an ultimatum: withdraw from Kuwait without condition or further delay by the Saturday-noon deadline—or face the consequences.

The next 24 hours were filled with diplomatic flopping around that looked increasingly like playacting—or simple stalling. Vague hints emerged from a U.N. Security Council meeting as the deadline passed that maybe the Iraqis would respond positively. The hints came from the Soviet representative; the Iraqi delegate claimed not to know what he was talking about. The deadline passed.

On Saturday night Bush helicoptered from Camp David to the White House. Appearing before the cameras at 10 o'clock, the President looked somber, and his sentences were plain, devoid of any rhetorical flourish. Harking back to Friday's ultimatum, he remarked that he had given Saddam "one last chance . . . to do what he should have done more than six months ago: withdraw from Kuwait without condition or further delay." Saddam, he said, had responded only with "a redoubling" of efforts "to destroy completely Kuwait and its people—a reference to the "scorched earth" torching of oil wells and systematic executions of Kuwaitis. The war that began Jan. 16 with the start of history's most intense bombing campaign had "entered a final phase" that the President hoped could be concluded "swiftly and decisively." He asked all Americans to stop whatever they were doing for a moment to say a prayer. On the battlefront, the land war had already been under way for hours. But the final phase of the conflict had now been solemnized by the President.

Schwarzkopf's flanking maneuver succeeds and the ground war becomes a rout—but Saddam puts the torch to the oilfields of Kuwait as his troops retreat

Even before the ground campaign began, the war had been won to a greater extent than allied commanders would let themselves hope. It was known that five weeks of bombing had destroyed much of the Iraqis' armor and artillery. But not until coalition soldiers could see the corpses piled in Iraqi trenches and hear surrendering soldiers' tales of starvation and terror did it become obvious how bloodily effective the air campaign had been. One of the key questions about the bombing was how much it had disrupted Iraqi command and communications. The damage turned out to be almost total. Iraqi troops could not communicate even with adjoining companies and battalions; they fought, when they did fight, in isolated actions rather than as part of a coordinated force. One unit of the Republican Guard was caught and devastated on the war's last day while its members were taking a cigarette break; comrades in surrounding units had been unable to warn them that onrushing American forces were almost on top of them.

Bereft of satellites or even aerial reconnaissance, Saddam Hussein's commanders could not see what was going on behind allied lines. Thus General Norman Schwarzkopf was able to hoodwink Baghdad into concentrating its forces in the wrong places until the very end. Six of Iraq's 42 divisions were massed along the Kuwaiti coast, guarding against a seaborne invasion. U.S. Marines repeatedly practiced amphibious landings, as conspicuously as possible, and as zero hour approached, an armada of 31 ships swung into position to put them ashore near Kuwait City. The battleships *Missouri* and *Wisconsin* took turns, an hour at a time, firing their 16-in. guns at Iraqi shore defenses. It was all a feint; the war ended with 17,000 Marines still aboard their ships.

Most of Iraq's frontline troops hunkered down behind minefields and barbed wire along the 138-mile Saudi-Kuwait border, awaiting what Baghdad obviously expected to be the main allied thrust. Coalition troops did in fact initially concentrate in front of them. But in the last 16 days before the attack, more than 150,000 American, British and French troops moved to the west, as far as 300 miles inland from the gulf, setting up bases across the border from an area of southern Iraq that was mostly empty desert. Part of that allied force was to drive straight to the Euphrates River, cutting off retreat routes for the Iraqi forces in Kuwait; another part was to turn east and hit Republican Guard divisions along the Kuwait-Iraq border, taking them by surprise on their right flank.

The battle plan did call as well, however, for narrowly focused thrusts through the main Iraqi defensive works. Concerned that his troops would get caught in breaches and slaughtered by massed Iraqi artillery firing poison-gas shells, Schwarzkopf ordered a shift in the bombing campaign during the last week to concentrate heavily on knocking out the frontline big guns. The planes succeeded spectacularly, destroying so much Iraqi artillery that its fire was never either as heavy or as accurate as had been feared. Also in the last week, special-operations commandos expanded their activities deep in Iraqi territory. Many additional units landed by helicopter, checking out the lay of the land and fixing Iraqi troop, tank and artillery positions so they could guide both air strikes and, later, advancing ground units.

Schwarzkopf had initially got Washington's agreement to Feb. 21 as the day to begin the ground assault. But some subordinates thought they needed two more days to get ready. So he and George

The long-awaited ground campaign began in a hellish environment of bombardment and burning oil wells

Bush fixed 8 p.m. Saturday, Feb. 23—noon in Washington—as zero hour, and Bush and his war council made that the expiration time of the final ultimatum to Saddam. As the deadline approached, tanks equipped with bulldozer blades cut wide openings through the sand berms Saddam's soldiers had erected as a defensive wall along the border, and tanks and troops began pushing through on probing attacks; some were across hours before the deadline.

During the night, B-52s pounded Iraqi positions and helicopter gunships swept the defense lines, firing rockets at tanks and artillery pieces and machine-gunning soldiers in the trenches. Allied artillery opened an intense bombardment from howitzers and multiple-launch rocket systems that released thousands of shrapnel-like bomblets over the trenches. Everything was ready for the ground troops to begin moving in the last hours of darkness, taking advantage of the allies' superior night-vision equipment.

SUNDAY: THROUGH THE BREACH

Between 4 a.m. and 6 a.m., allied forces jumped off at selected points all along the 300-mile line. Though Hollywood has long pictured the desert as a place of eternal burning sunshine and total aridity, the attack began in a lashing rain that turned the sand into muddy goo. The first troops through were wearing bulky chemical-protective garb, in keeping with the allied conviction that Saddam would use poison gas right from the beginning. In fact, the Iraqis never fired their chemical weapons.

Saudi and other Arab troops hit the strongest Iraqi fortifications near the coast. To their left were the U.S. 1st and 2nd Marine divisions, which had moved inland. The Marines attacked at points known to allied commanders as the "elbow" of Kuwait, where the border with Saudi Arabia turns sharply to the north, and the "armpit," where it abruptly sweeps west again. They were led in person by Lieut. General Walter Boomer, the top Marine in the gulf area, according to operational plans he had forwarded only 16 days earlier to the Pentagon, where they caused raised eyebrows because of their audacity. But they worked.

The allied troops in Saudi Arabia had built sand berms and replicas of the other Iraqi entrenchments and practiced breaching them until they could virtually do it blindfolded. Among the tactics: remotely piloted vehicles, or pilotless drone planes, guided soldiers to the most thinly held spots in the Iraqi lines. Line charges, or 100-yd.-long strings of tubing laced with explosives, blasted paths through minefields. Tanks and armored personnel carriers drove through those paths in long, narrow files, observing strict radio silence. Their drivers communicated by hand signals—even in the dark, when night-vision devices worked perfectly.

Much had been written about the inferno the Iraqis would create by filling trenches with burning oil. But in the Marines' sector, U.S. planes had burned off the oil prematurely by dropping napalm. The Saudis did encounter trenches filled with blazing petroleum and in some cases with water, but crossed them by the simple expedient of having bulldozers and tanks fitted with earth-moving blades collapse dirt into the trenches until they were filled. It took only hours for the allied troops to burst through the supposedly impregnable Iraqi defenses and begin a war of maneuvers, sweeping right past some of the heaviest concentrations of troops and armor, and calling in withering air strikes and tank and artillery fire on those that fought. Throughout the 100-hour campaign, the allied soldiers avoided hand-to-hand fighting wherever possible, preferring to stand off and blast away at their foes at more than arm's length.

At the far western reach of the allied line, the French 6th Light Armored Division jumped off before dawn Sunday, attacking across the Iraqi border with the U.S. 82nd Airborne Division toward a fort and airfield named As Salman, 105 miles inside Iraq. On the way, American artillery and French Gazelle helicopter gunships firing HOT antitank missiles subdued a force of Iraqi tanks and infantry, many of whom surrendered.

To the right of the French, the U.S. 101st Airborne Division mounted a deep-penetration helicopter assault into southeastern Iraq. Chinook helicopters, some skimming only 50 feet above the sand, others slinging Humvees, modern versions of the old jeeps, below their fuselages, ferried 4,000 men with their vehicles and equipment into the desert. The force established a huge refueling and resupply base, then jumped off again from there deeper into Iraq. Other units—the British 1st Armored Division, seven U.S. Army divisions, and Egyptian, Saudi and Syrian units—attacked at various times throughout the day at points along the Saudi-Iraq border into the western tip of Kuwait. All moved fast and attained their most ambitious objectives. The 1st Marine Division, for example, by Sunday night had reached al-Jaber airport, half the 40-mile distance from the Saudi border to Kuwait City.

MONDAY: SPEEDING UP

Nearly all units continued moving at rapid rates: the Saudis and U.S. Marines in Kuwait toward the north; American Army units toward the Euphrates; British, other American, Egyptian and Syrian forces to the east. The French, having taken As Salman in 36 hours, stopped at midday on Schwarzkopf's orders to set up a defensive position guarding the units to their right against any Iraqi attack from the west.

Mass surrenders began almost with the first breaches of the Iraqi lines Sunday and by Tuesday had reached 30,000; the allied command stopped counting then. By war's end the number had easily

Moving quickly, allied forces rounded up Iraqi soldiers, many of whom surrendered eagerly

passed 100,000. They came out of collapsed bunkers, waving hand-kerchiefs, underwear, anything that was white. Everyone on the allied side had a favorite surrender story.

Two striking ones: about 40 Iraqis tried to surrender to an RPV, turning round and round, waving their arms as the pilotless drone circled above. An Iraqi tank and another armored vehicle bore down on a U.S. Humvee driven by a lone soldier and stuck helplessly in mud. The Iraqi vehicles pulled the Humvee out of the mire; then their crews surrendered to its driver.

Schwarzkopf was careful to state that the mass surrenders did not necessarily mean the Iraqis were poor fighters. Most, he noted, had no belief in what they were doing and did not regard holding on to Kuwait as a cause worth dying for. They were starved, thirsty, often sick—medical care was atrocious to nonexistent—and some had been terrorized by their own commanders, who employed roving execution squads to shoot or hang troopers who had attempted to desert or defect. That barbaric method of keeping discipline backfired: soldiers gave themselves up as soon as the guns pointing at them were American, British or Arab.

Baghdad radio on Monday broadcast an order, supposedly from Saddam, for his forces to withdraw from Kuwait; many complied with alacrity. Those who paused to fight were often cut to pieces. On Monday afternoon, for example, the 1st Marine Division encountered Iraqi units in the Burgan oil field near Kuwait International Airport and flushed them out with "time on target" fire, the opposite of a rolling barrage: all guns in the entire division opened up at the same time to lay down a devastating curtain of explosives on the same limited target area. That forced the Iraqis out of the oil field. Emerging into the open, they were hit with more fire from artillery, Cobra attack helicopters and Marine tanks. Some 50 to 60 Iraqi tanks were reported destroyed in this brief engagement. Marine losses: zero.

Oddly, though, this day of burgeoning victory brought the one U.S. tragedy of the war. An Iraqi Scud missile heading for Saudi Arabia broke up in flight: the warhead plunged onto an American barracks near the huge base at Dhahran. The blast killed 28 soldiers, causing in an eye blink almost a third of all American battle deaths in the entire war. An additional 90 soldiers were injured, many seriously.

TUESDAY: BUGGING OUT

Residents of Kuwait City awoke to the sound of tank engines revving up. The Iraqis were pulling out, sparing the city, its inhabitants and the allied forces closing in the agonies of house-to-house fighting. By afternoon Kuwaiti resistance fighters said they were in control of the city, though sniper fire continued for a while and Saudi and Kuwaiti troops did not stage their victory parade into the city until the following day.

Outside the city, said a U.S. briefing officer, "the whole country is full of people escaping and evading." Though some allied commanders described the Iraqi pullback as an orderly fighting retreat, at times it looked like a pell-mell bugout. Roads leading north to-ward the Iraqi city of Basra, military headquarters for the Kuwait theater, were so jammed with vehicles and troops that a pilot from the carrier U.S.S. *Ranger* in the gulf said it looked like "the road to Daytona Beach at spring break." Allied bombing of roads and bridges had created bottlenecks from which mammoth traffic jams backed up, making for still more inviting targets. So many allied planes converged on the main road from Kuwait City to Basra that combat air controllers feared they might collide, and diverted some of the attackers to secondary roads.

Pilots flying off the *Ranger* were so eager to refuel and get back into the air to kill more tanks that they had their planes loaded with whatever bombs or missiles happened to be available on the flight deck, rather than waiting for the ship's elevators to bring up ordnance specifically chosen for their mission. Pilot after pilot described attacks in which, after the first tank in a column was hit, the crews would abandon the others and set out on foot for home. Correspondents touring the road at week's end found mile after mile of blasted, twisted, burned, shattered tanks, trucks and other vehicles, many still incongruously carrying loot from Kuwait City: children's toys, carpets, television sets. Those Iraqi soldiers who reached the Euphrates threw up pontoon bridges to replace sturdier spans that had been destroyed by bombing; when more bombs wrecked the pontoon bridges too, some desperate troops crossed by walking along earthen dams.

WEDNESDAY: CLOSING THE RING

Some allied units had reached the Euphrates as early as Monday; by Wednesday morning they were established in enough force to prevent further crossings. British units cut the main Kuwait City-Basra highway early in the day; American Marines had reached it farther to the south the previous afternoon. The gate had slammed shut on Saddam's forces in Kuwait. Their escape routes were broken. Encirclement was complete.

The day was dominated by the two big tank battles of the war. U.S. Marines ran into a major Iraqi armored force at Kuwait International Airport. The sky was so dark because of the heavy smoke from oil wells set afire by the Iraqis that Marine Major General Michael Myatt had to read a map by flashlight. The Marines nonetheless resumed the battle by what light there was, and late in the day reported having destroyed all 100 Iraqi tanks they had engaged.

In a far bigger clash along the Kuwait-Iraq border, American and British troops pushing eastward after their flanking maneuver through the desert finally broke the Republican Guard. Schwarzkopf had defined these troops as the "center of gravity" of the Iraqi forces. Said a senior Army staff officer: "The whole campaign was designed on one theme: to destroy the Republican Guard."

British troops encountered some Guard units as early as Monday night, destroying a third of their armor at the first blow with long-range artillery fire and aerial attack. Fighting between American troops and Guard units also began Monday and steadily intensified; by nightfall Monday a briefer reported one of the Guard's seven divisions in the area rendered "basically ineffective." The big

Victory! U.S. soldiers celebrate the liberation of Kuwait City on Feb. 27, 1991

battle raged all day Wednesday. Some allied officers reported that the Guard fought about as well as could have been expected of troops battling without air cover, with minimal, if any, communications and under relentless allied bombing. But one American officer asserted that "basically, we are chasing them across the plains, shooting as we go."

The Guard fared no better than other Iraqi units. Not only was allied air power unchallenged and decisive; U.S. M1A1 tanks proved superior in maneuverability and firepower to Iraq's best, the Soviet-built T-72s. One correspondent witnessed a duel between an M1A1 and a T-72. When they sighted each other, the American tank backed up, outside the T-72's range. The Iraqi tank fired a round that fell short. The M1A1 fired its longer-range cannon, scoring a direct hit that put the Iraqi tank out of action, then promptly swiveled and went looking for another victim.

On Wednesday evening Schwarzkopf, in a masterly briefing on the war about to end, began by saying that Iraq had lost more than 3,000 of the 4,700 tanks it had deployed in the Kuwait theater at the start of the war—then added, "As a matter of fact, you can add 700 to that as a result of the battle that's going on right now with the Republican Guard." Saddam's forces lost similarly high proportions of their other armored vehicles, artillery and trucks. The result, said Schwarzkopf, was that Iraq was left with only an infantry army, no longer capable of offensive operations and therefore not a threat to other countries in the region. That fulfilled one of the two principal allied war aims; the other, clearing Iraq out of Kuwait, was just about accomplished as well. The war was as good as over.

THURSDAY: VICTORY

In a few more hours, the shooting officially ended. At 5 a.m. (9 p.m. Wednesday in Washington) Bush went on the air to announce that he was ordering a suspension of all offensive action, to take effect three hours later. Since it was a unilateral action rather than an agreement negotiated with the Iraqis, it was not officially a cease-fire, but it had the same result. Shooting in fact stopped at 8 a.m., and only sporadic incidents broke the silence as the weekend began. Some Iraqi units appeared not to get the word at first; allied troops set up loudspeakers blaring over and over again the message in Arabic that Iraqis would no longer be attacked if they held their fire. A warning to those that did not: on Saturday, a column of 140 Iraqi tanks and other armored vehicles ran into a U.S. force and began shooting. The Americans counterattacked with tank and helicopter fire, destroying 60 Iraqi vehicles and capturing the other 80.

Postmortems had already begun. Baghdad Radio claimed that Iraq had won but could give no rationale except some mumblings about spirit. In Moscow generals hastened to proclaim that the destruction of Iraq's mostly Soviet-built equipment said more about the deficiencies of the Iraqi military than about the quality of the weapons. Some of them hinted, however, that Soviet cuts in military spending, if carried much further, might begin to weaken the nation's defenses against the demonstrated proficiency of Western high-tech weaponry.

On the allied side, Schwarzkopf seemed right in terming the coalition's ability to achieve nearly total success with so few losses "almost miraculous." Not only were the pessimists and skeptics wrong, including all those who had said the aerial bombing was going badly, but the optimists were far off the mark too. American casualties were less than 5% of the *lowest* prewar Pentagon estimates. U.S. forces had prepared about 10,000 beds, aboard ships and in three field hospitals, to receive the wounded; only a tiny fraction were filled.

Such overwhelming success, in fact, may be unrepeatable. The U.S. and its partners are unlikely to face soon, or ever, another combination of a cause so clear that it unites a mighty coalition; ideal terrain for high-tech warfare; a dispirited and war-weary enemy army; an almost total lack of opposition in the air; and an adversary, Saddam, who made nearly every blunder in the book.

At the war's end, Saddam remained in power, shorn of the military might that had made him a menace, but not of all capacity for troublemaking. Kuwait, liberated, was a smoldering wreck needing perhaps years of reconstruction. Among Americans, the war finally laid to rest the ghosts of Vietnam. Whatever challenges to international security lurk in the future, chances are they won't be so morally stark and politically compelling. The U.S. emerged with new power and credibility—but also with an urgent need to define a vision of a new world order.

Having banished the ghosts of Vietnam, U.S. soldiers found a sympathetic welcome on their return to the States

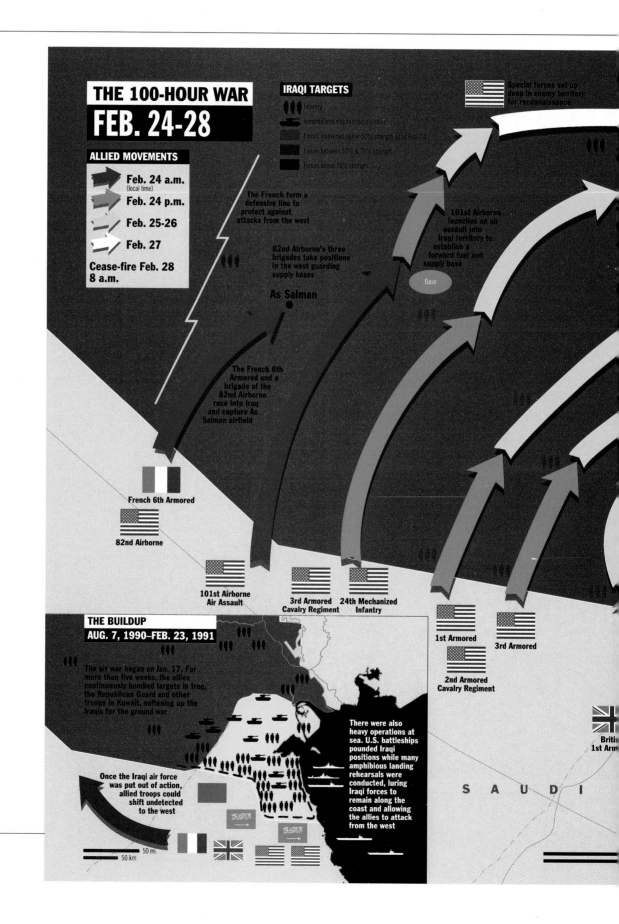

THE 100-HOUR WAR
FEB. 24-28

ALLIED MOVEMENTS

Feb. 24 a.m.
(local time)

Feb. 24 p.m.

Feb. 25-26

Feb. 27

Cease-fire Feb. 28
8 a.m.

IRAQI TARGETS

Infantry

Armored and mechanized divisions

Forces weakened below 50% strength as of Feb. 24

Forces between 50% & 75% strength

Forces above 75% strength

Special forces set up deep in enemy territory for reconnaissance

The French form a defensive line to protect against attacks from the west

82nd Airborne's three brigades take positions in the west guarding supply bases

101st Airborne launches an air assault into Iraqi territory to establish a forward fuel and supply base

Base

As Salman

The French 6th Armored and a brigade of the 82nd Airborne race into Iraq and capture As Salman airfield

French 6th Armored

82nd Airborne

101st Airborne
Air Assault

3rd Armored
Cavalry Regiment

24th Mechanized
Infantry

1st Armored

3rd Armored

2nd Armored
Cavalry Regiment

British
1st Arm

THE BUILDUP
AUG. 7, 1990–FEB. 23, 1991

The air war began on Jan. 17. For more than five weeks, the allies continuously bombed targets in Iraq, the Republican Guard and other troops in Kuwait, softening up the Iraqis for the ground war

There were also heavy operations at sea. U.S. battleships pounded Iraqi positions while many amphibious landing rehearsals were conducted, luring Iraqi forces to remain along the coast and allowing the allies to attack from the west

Once the Iraqi air force was put out of action, allied troops could shift undetected to the west

S A U D I

50 mi.

50 km

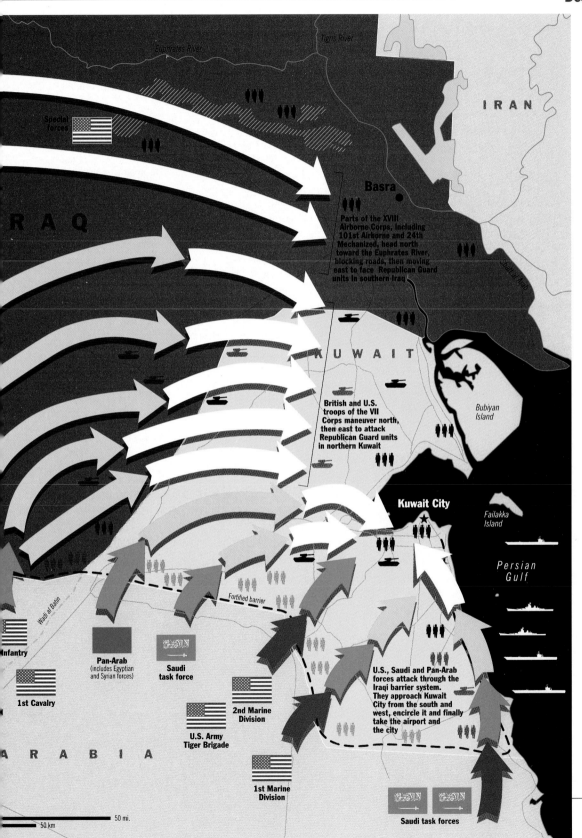

Special forces

I R A N

Euphrates River

Tigris River

I R A Q

Basra

Parts of the XVIII Airborne Corps, including 101st Airborne and 24th Mechanized, head north toward the Euphrates River, blocking roads, then moving east to face Republican Guard units in southern Iraq

Shatt al Arab

K U W A I T

Bubiyan Island

British and U.S. troops of the VII Corps maneuver north, then east to attack Republican Guard units in northern Kuwait

Kuwait City

Failakka Island

Persian Gulf

Fortified barrier

Infantry

Wadi al Batin

1st Cavalry

Pan-Arab (includes Egyptian and Syrian forces)

Saudi task force

2nd Marine Division

U.S., Saudi and Pan-Arab forces attack through the Iraqi barrier system. They approach Kuwait City from the south and west, encircle it and finally take the airport and the city

A R A B I A

U.S. Army Tiger Brigade

1st Marine Division

Saudi task forces

50 mi.

50 km

War's Bitter Wake

As the allies withdrew, rebellion rocked Saddam's Iraq, and the oil fields of Kuwait threatened an environmental holocaust

With the rout of Saddam Hussein's army and the rapid cease-fire, the war came to an abrupt conclusion. But three dramas were left to be played out: the revolt of the Shi'ites in southern Iraq; the rebellion, defeat and flight of the Kurds in northern Iraq; and the struggle to rebuild devastated Kuwait.

As Saddam reeled in defeat, he faced a revolt from Shi'ites in the south of Iraq, who sought to replace his secular Baathist regime with Islamic rule. Saddam gathered the remnants of his defeated army into a loyal force that rapidly overwhelmed the weak and ill-equipped Shi'ite insurgents. He dispatched two Republican Guard divisions to ensure the efficiency of the regular Iraqi troops who had failed so miserably against the allied coalition. This time it was the Shi'ite rebels who were doomed to failure. They lacked a joint command-and-communications system and were largely dependent on weapons and ammunition abandoned by Iraqi soldiers as they fled the allies. The holy sites of Karbala and Najaf, so meticulously avoided by coalition bombing raids, were ravaged. Thousands of civilians, in some cases targeted with napalm and phosphorus, streamed toward the southern sector of the country occupied by U.S. troops. Ordered not to intervene, American soldiers could offer little more than food, water and medical assistance. With the U.S. refusing to get involved, the rebels were finally crushed by Saddam's forces.

In the north things were different, and for almost a month the Kurds lived a dream. An uprising that began on March 4 in the town of Rania spread like a sandstorm to engulf all Iraqi Kurdistan. The *peshmerga* (those who face death), as the rebel fighters were called, did not need to capture towns, as local Iraqi Kurdish militiamen spontaneously joined the rebellion.

But their defeat was equally decisive. With the south subdued, Saddam was able to move 100,000 more troops north, rapidly outnumbering the Kurdish fighters. Within a week his forces had relieved the siege of Mosul; Kirkuk, Erbil and other Kurdish-occupied cities were reconquered.

The Kurds fought back bravely, but there was a stylized, almost medieval ferocity to their resistance. The *peshmerga* were dressed in turbans and baggy khaki trousers. Along with their AK-47s, SAMs and submachine guns, they carried a traditional dagger stuck into their sashes. Possessed of an incredible sense of honor, the *peshmerga* buried all the Iraqi soldiers they killed with full military honors. Attacked by gunships, the *peshmerga* wrapped their arms around one another and sang and danced. Washington had hinted it

might attack helicopters flying against the rebels and retaliate if Saddam attacked them. But—in a highly controversial decision—the Bush White House announced, "We do not intend to involve ourselves in the internal conflicts in Iraq."

So the defeated Kurds headed north and east toward Turkey and Iran. At first, it was impossible to estimate the number bottled up at those borders. Columns of people and vehicles, sometimes 50 miles long, snaked into the hills. Tehran claimed that more than 1 million Kurds and Shi'ites were seeking sanctuary; hundreds of thousands more fled toward Turkey, where, though the borders were declared closed, more than 400,000 of them crossed to refuge.

A stopgap solution was needed: U.N.-sanctioned safe havens inside Iraq, where the refugees would be protected from attack by Saddam's forces. Backed by Britain and France, the U.S. warned Saddam not to use either fixed-wing aircraft or helicopters north of the 36th parallel—where the Kurdish refugees were concentrated—with the implicit threat that if he did they would be shot down.

In Operation Haven, U.S., British and French troops built giant tent cities, each housing up to 100,000 Kurds. As Saddam watched, helpless to intervene, the refugee Kurds returned from the barren mountains where they had fled. By year's end, they had reached an uneasy peace with the regime.

Saddam's legacy continued to afflict Kuwait as well. In a typical act of revenge, his forces dynamited the oil fields as they withdrew. Of the country's 1,000 oil wells, 732 were wrecked or set on fire. Day

turned to night under the resulting thick, sooty clouds. Although early estimates had predicted the well fires could burn for years, 10,000 workers from all parts of the world, including the U.S., extinguished all the fires by year's end. However, other challenges remain for Kuwait: no one can yet predict how long it will take for the oil spilled into the gulf to be absorbed, and the desert remains littered with land mines that must be disarmed or exploded.

George Bush

During the gulf war, when George Bush gave his State of the Union address to the joint session of Congress and triggered a great ovation to U.S. desert forces, there was a moment when the cameras in the House chamber caught the face of Senator Ted Kennedy, as enraptured as everyone else by the applause that would not cease. But in the din came a tiny echo from the 1988 Democratic Convention, when Kennedy fevered his audience with his litany of Bush's ditherings, following each charge with the taunt, "Where was George?"

In the gulf war George was there, the Commander in Chief who organized and launched one of this century's most awesome military exercises. Most Americans marched with Bush, and from the beginning of the crisis there was no doubt just where he was.

The aura of war followed Bush in the weeks after the conflict began, visibly enhancing his stature. More than 3,500 people jammed the Washington Hilton for the national prayer breakfast he attended in January. And a few days later, when Bush visited three military bases in the South that had units in the gulf battle, there was an emotional intensity that topped anything Bush had ever encountered in this country.

How could the man Kennedy taunted be so resolute? And let's not forget those who derided him as a wimp, a lapdog, every divorced woman's first husband, a terminal preppie. His painful politeness and unwavering loyalty to Ronald Reagan through mountainous deficits and Iran-*contra* bumbling raised the question of his backbone. He waffled on issues like abortion and taxes, and even his supporters wondered in dark moments about his inner stuff.

History shows that the demands of war often reveal special qualities in Presidents not easily detected in the babble of a political campaign. For 5½ months Bush went down a straight road to battle. There were no black moods for him as there had been for John F. Kennedy in the Cuban missile crisis when he believed there was a likelihood of a nuclear exchange. Nor did Bush wander through the darkened White House as Lyndon Johnson used to do, as confused by his own experts as by his enemies in Vietnam. Richard Nixon sometimes sought solitude and brooded for hours over decisions on using American power. Bush sought out friends and Chinese food.

It may be that Bush went through all the known tortures on the way to his decision. But they must have been entirely internal. There is as yet no enemy or friend who claims to have been witness when Bush was either uncertain or unclear. Some wimp.

Saddam Hussein

Confronted by a formidable coalition of arms, he fires missiles at civilians in a noncombatant state. Taking a terrible pounding from the air, he sends some of his best planes and pilots to the airfields of a neutral country. He releases millions of gallons of oil into the Persian Gulf, threatening his own people with ecological disaster.

Seen simplistically and from afar, Saddam Hussein comes across as a figure seldom found outside the pages of comic books or pulp fiction: the villain who will stop at nothing, an Arab Dr. No, alive and menacing in the Middle East.

But the reason so many in the West find him baffling is an unwillingness or an inability to understand the conditions of the world that spawned him.

He grew up in a culture soaked in conspiracy. Living impoverished in a mud hut, he witnessed a world up for grabs. Power was being abandoned or ceded by the colonialist overlords. In the fresh air of change, Iraq experienced bloody and repeated coups and countercoups in the three decades after independence in 1932. The upheavals ceased in 1968, when the Baath Party won power and installed a regime so ruthless that effective opposition was simply crushed.

One of the principal architects of the Baath success was Saddam. Placed in charge of domestic security, he forged Iraq's ubiquitous and terrifying intelligence network. He murdered his enemies and, when appropriate, his friends. He did not finally get to be President of Iraq by being a nice guy. If he now thinks people all around him are trying to kill him, that may be because, for much of his adult life, people all around him have been trying to kill him.

The frequent allusions in the West to Saddam's "paranoia" thus make his behavior seem more complicated than it really is. He does not have to fantasize enemies; he has inherited and made enough to last several lifetimes.

Has he exploited Middle East tensions and hatreds for his own purposes and hunger for power? Certainly. Are those tensions real, no matter what use he has made of them? Unfortunately, yes.

Saddam's most enduring legacy may be his refusal to halt the wheel of rage that has been grinding in his part of the world for centuries. Even his enemies concede him a certain charisma and brilliance. Could he, after suffering and clawing his way to power, have used his influence to bring peace to the region? He did not try, and, in any case, the world could not wait for an answer.

Stormin' Norman

He lacks the heroic mien—steel forged in Camelot—of central casting's great military strategists: Wellington, MacArthur, Cordesman. His stare, which can be ferocious, is undercut by a fretful brow; the small, almost gentle features are stranded in his moon face. You look for John Wayne, and you find Jonathan Winters crossed with Willard Scott.

The man who commanded the vast military might of Operation Desert Storm prepared all his professional life for his role. This passionately engaged leader of considerable talents is possessed of a startling, prophetic mind.

As long ago as 1983, H. Norman Schwarzkopf foresaw the possibility that the U.S. might one day find itself at war in the Middle East if an unfriendly nation succeeded in taking over a neighbor. In 1989, as boss of the U.S. Central Command (which covers some North African countries and areas farther east), Schwarzkopf set out on his own to design a contingency plan. Five days before Saddam Hussein launched his invasion, Schwarzkopf and his staff happened to be running an exercise predicated on the possibility that Iraq might overrun Kuwait.

The son of a West Pointer, Schwarzkopf was first posted over-

seas, at 12, to Tehran with his father. During his years at West Point, he impressed friends with his single-minded ambition: he desperately wanted to lead his country's forces into battle. Later Schwarzkopf served two tours in Vietnam, first as a paratrooper advising Vietnamese airborne troops, then as commander of an infantry battalion. Twice he was wounded in action; three times he won a Silver Star. On one occasion, he tiptoed into a minefield to rescue a wounded soldier.

In the war room as in the field, noncoms and enlisted soldiers were as devoted to Schwarzkopf as his officers. None seemed overly intimidated by his gruffness, his size (6 ft. 3 in., 240 lbs.) or even his flare-ups. He was, after all, the Bear, whom some described as only part grizzly and the rest Teddy.

His famous post-victory briefing found the Bear gruff and compassionate. Speaking in flinty, illuminating sentences, he made sense of the battle plan in its grandeur and awful human cost. For 57 minutes, without toupee or TelePrompTer, he displayed all the seductiveness of the performer's art, prowling like a stand-up comic, tamping his rage into questions intimidating and rhetorical, letting his emotions now and then stumble over his eloquence. In Operation Desert Storm, Schwarzkopf gave the nation a warrior to be proud of.

Colin Powell

In the war in the gulf, the Chairman of the Joint Chiefs of Staff emerged as a model of Americans as they like to imagine themselves—a man of action who is deeply reflective as well, direct, lucid and unflappable. Born in Harlem and raised in the South Bronx by Jamaican immigrants, he was a veteran of almost two decades of capitol political experience before the Persian Gulf war. After completing two tours in Vietnam, Powell came to the attention of official Washington in 1972, when a White House fellowship placed him in the Office of Management and Budget. He rarely ventured outside the Beltway again, meanwhile filling some of the most powerful jobs in America, including National Security Adviser to Ronald Reagan. "I don't know anybody in this town who's served so long in such sensitive jobs who's been as free of criticism as Colin," says former Secretary of Defense Caspar Weinberger, his onetime boss.

No sooner had the war ended when polls showed that a large majority of Americans preferred Colin Powell to Dan Quayle as a running mate for George Bush in 1992. Powell's response was double edged: "I have no interest in politics at the moment," he declared.

Peter Arnett

With his balding pate, excited voice and habitual twitching of the mouth, he was hardly the image of a smooth network honcho. His colleagues pointed out that his TV work still had a heady taste of print, the ineradicable remnant of more than 20 years as a wire-service correspondent in Vietnam and around the world. Tapped by CNN to cover the fledgling network's war beat in 1981, he jumped at the chance. The job took him to Nicaragua, El Salvador, Moscow, Angola and Beirut. Along the way, he battled constantly with TV producers who wanted pictures to do more of the talking and him less. In short, CNN's Peter Arnett was just the right man for the job he held at the beginning of the war: the last American reporter in Baghdad.

Arnett, 56, is a correspondent's correspondent who believes it is better to get out some of the news—even when censored and sometimes manipulated by Iraq—than none at all. The decision to stay put at Baghdad's al-Rasheed Hotel after his colleagues had departed was his alone, and he made it with a typical lack of fuss. "I've been in much more dangerous situations in my career with much less attention than I'm getting now," he said from Baghdad. "It's just another story."

49

Down in the Dumps and Irritable

By PAUL GRAY

This should have been a very good year in the U.S. The gulf war, which had caused so many national jitters as 1990 drew to a close, ended with miraculous speed and a rousing lift to patriotic feelings. After the failed Soviet coup in August, what had seemed unthinkable only a few years earlier became inescapably obvious. The cold war had ended, and the entity that Ronald Reagan had called "the evil empire" was falling apart. Not only was the U.S.S.R. no longer a superpower; it was not the U.S.S.R. any more. Democratic ideals caught fire among peoples formerly oppressed by ideology and force; in unexpected places, the U.S. was being flattered by imitation. So why were so many Americans so down in the dumps and irritable with one another?

The bitterness surrounding the Clarence Thomas–Anita Hill hearings in October seemed symptomatic of a national bad mood. Although Professor Hill's testimony was free of rancor and recriminations, her charge that Judge Thomas had subjected her to sexual harassment when she worked on his staff ten years earlier touched raw nerves everywhere. Women, it became clear, were mad as hell— at men—and not going to take insensitive male behavior any more. When an obviously furious Thomas called the televised Senate Judiciary Committee proceedings "a high-tech lynching," another painful image of injustice—this time racial rather than sexual—thrust itself into the public domain.

Even before Hill's accusation, Judge Thomas had become a lightning rod for discontent and anger. President Bush's nomination of a black conservative with little experience on the bench to fill the Supreme Court vacancy left by retiring Justice Thurgood Marshall angered a broad coalition of advocacy groups. Many worried about Thomas' position on abortion and about what his presence on the court would mean when, as seems inevitable, an opportunity to reconsider the landmark *Roe v. Wade* decision arrives. Any thoughts that passions might be cooling over the question of legal abortions vanished in mid-July in Wichita, Kans. Operation Rescue, an out-of-state pro-life organization, came to town to stage large, noisy demonstrations against abortion clinics; confronted with this open invitation to protest, pro-choice groups responded with equal vehemence.

Although he declined the Senate Judiciary Committee's invitations to discuss his views on *Roe v. Wade*, Thomas' opinions on another subject were well known, and they drew wide criticism. The judge had spoken out on several occasions against racial quotas and affirmative-action programs. This position sparked outrage among civil rights organizations, especially since, as it was frequently pointed out, Thomas' rise from rural poverty in Pinpoint, Ga., to the élite halls of the Yale Law School had been helped by precisely the type of programs he now opposed.

Affirmative action has always been controversial in some quarters, but 1991 may have marked the time when opinion began to turn heavily against it. Many blamed such policies for a troubling increase in racial and bias incidents on college campuses across the country; white students resented what they saw as favoritism for nonwhites in admission standards and financial aid, while minority students complained that their qualifications were automatically deemed inferior by majority fellow-students. In a more philosophical vein, some argued that affirmative action largely benefited minority members of the middle classes while doing virtually nothing to help those in the inner-city underclass.

Colleges were not the only places where race relations soured. The videotaped beating of an unarmed black motorist by members of the Los Angeles police department was played and replayed on television, arousing protests and new doubts about equal treatment under the law where minorities are concerned. In Brooklyn's Crown Heights section, a car driven by a Jew accidentally struck and killed a black child; in the melee that ensued, a group of blacks surrounded and stabbed a Jewish passerby to death. Several tense days of hurled bottles and epithets followed. In Louisiana a candidate with former ties to the Ku Klux Klan ran on the Republican slate for Governor; David Duke lost, but he gathered nearly 40% of the vote.

Americans also spent a lot of time last year shouting at their elected representatives. It suddenly became uncomfortable in 1991 to be an incumbent. Widespread revelations about congressional perks—including no-fault check-bouncing privileges on Capitol Hill—thoroughly outraged taxpaying constituents back home. Many state officials, facing budget deficits and shrinking revenues, were forced to choose between cutting services or raising taxes—neither act a recipe for re-election. The recession, which showed signs of ending or abating in late summer, hung on through the fall, spreading more gloom: more job layoffs, persistent unemployment and a pinched Christmas retail season.

Other, isolated events only deepened the sense of national malaise. A record-breaking mass murder in Texas; the grisly discovery of body parts in a Minneapolis apartment. Magic Johnson's dramatic announcement that he had tested positive for the HIV virus and was retiring from professional basketball shocked a nation; it also reminded everyone of the devastation caused by AIDS.

Not all the domestic news was bad in 1991, of course, but bright spots proved to be the exception. One of them was the undiminished eagerness of immigrants to stream to these shores, looking for the same opportunities that millions of their predecessors sought and found. Perhaps they know something that Americans last year showed signs of forgetting.

She Said, He Said

As the nation looked on, two credible witnesses presented irreconcilable views of what happened nearly a decade ago

I t was hard to imagine two more unlikely or reluctant witnesses. On one side of the divide was Anita Hill, 35, a specialist in the dry area of commercial law, a reserved woman who by all accounts is given more to listening than to talking. On the other was Clarence Thomas, 43, a courtly man who has enjoyed a reputation for treating women with respect. Yet there she was, this prim law professor from the University of Oklahoma, seated before the Senate Judiciary Committee, calmly detailing graphic charges of sexual harassment against the man who seemed virtually certain to be confirmed as the next Justice to the Supreme Court.

He said, "I have not said or done the things Anita Hill has alleged."

She said, "I am not given to fantasy. This is not something I would have come forward with if I was not absolutely sure of what I was saying."

For witnesses to this spectacle, whether there in the Senate Caucus Room or at home in their living rooms, deciding who was telling the truth was all but impossible. Viewers had to weigh the testimony of two admirable people—both of whom had escaped a background of rural poverty to scale great heights, both of whom are known to be grounded in strong religious and spiritual values, both of whom have reputations for great personal integrity—and pronounce one of them a liar. In the final analysis, it came down to this: the specificity of Hill's charges against the intensity of Thomas' denials.

Before the days of exhaustive testimony would end, Hill would coolly and impassively detail the nature of Thomas' alleged harassment while she worked for him in government positions from 1981 to 1983. Words like "penis" and "breasts" and "pubic hair" would enter the public record repeatedly in so somber a fashion that no one in the hearing room would blanch. It was clear that the differences in the Hill and Thomas versions on what transpired a decade ago were not a simple matter of differing sensibilities—oversquea-mishness on her part vs. bad taste on his. If Hill's description of Thomas' words and actions was truthful, then the Supreme Court nominee was guilty of sexual harassment in the past and perjury in

Anita Hill, the accuser: "What happened and telling the world about it are the two most difficult . . . experiences of my life."

the present. If Hill's account was a flight of fantasy, then she was delusional and a candidate for medical attention.

Republican Senator Orrin Hatch aimed squarely at the accuser, implying that Hill was working in tandem with "slick lawyers" bent on destroying Thomas' chances to join the court. When committee chairman Joseph Biden asked if he believed that Hill had fabricated a tale of sexual harassment, Thomas replied, "This story was developed specifically to destroy me." In the course of the hearing, which Thomas angrily characterized as "a high-tech lynching for uppity blacks," other witnesses came forward. Some tried to buttress Hill's charges, either by affirming that she had complained of sexual harassment at the time of the alleged incidents or by putting forward their own allegations of misconduct by Thomas. Others sought to cast doubt on Hill's testimony, either by dredging up recollections that conflicted with hers or by offering stories that aimed to weaken Hill's credibility.

But nothing could match the devastating effect of both Hill's and Thomas' testimony. Cool and unflappable, Hill painted a vivid and sobering portrait of what it means to be victimized by sexual harassment—from the fears and humiliations she experienced to the repercussions it had on her work, health and career choices. Given the detail and consistency of her testimony, it was almost inconceivable that Hill was fabricating the portrait of a sexual-harassment victim.

No less poignant, or believable, however, were Thomas' adamant denials. In his opening remarks—which he wrote himself, by a friend's account, after telling the White House to "butt out"—he said he felt "shocked, surprised, hurt and enormously saddened" on learning of Hill's charges. While Hill would maintain that he had asked her out five to 10 times during the period in question, he denied that he had ever asked her for even a single date. Rather, he said, Hill was someone he had helped at every turn, someone he considered a friend. That accusations of harassment should come from her seemed to him particularly hurtful. "I lost the belief," he said, "that if I did my best, all would work out."

Then Thomas enlarged his field of pain. He spoke of the long ordeal—105 days by week's end—that he had endured since his nomination to the Supreme Court, of reporters picking through his garbage cans and poring over his divorce papers. "This is not American; this is Kafkaesque," he declared. "It has got to stop. No job is worth what I've been through—no job. No horror in my life has been so debilitating. Confirm me if you want. Don't confirm me if you are so led." Said he: "I will not provide the rope for my own lynching. These are the most intimate parts of my privacy, and they will remain just that, private."

The tone of his opening statement was so bitter, in fact, that many listeners thought he was leading up to a withdrawal of his candidacy. But he stopped short of that, insisting he would "rather die than withdraw."

After Hill concluded her testimony, Thomas said, "I deny each and every single allegation against me." He called the hearing a travesty, a circus, a national disgrace. During his two days of testimony, Thomas returned repeatedly to a central theme of his rebuttal: that

Clarence Thomas, the embattled nominee: "I deny each and every single allegation against me . . . I will not provide the rope for my own lynching."

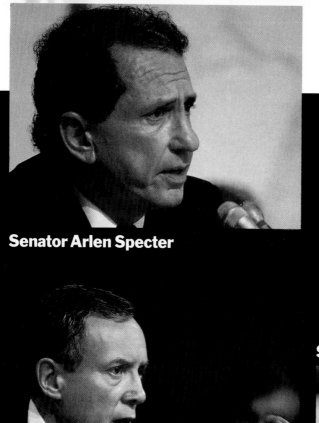

Senator Arlen Specter

Senator Joseph Biden

Senator Alan Simpson

Senator Orrin Hatch

he was the victim of a racially motivated attack. "I cannot shake off these accusations because they play to the worst stereotypes we have about black men in this country," he declared.

At only one point did he offer a hint of anything that might smack of a personal relationship with Hill. "I would drive her home and sometimes stop in and have a Coke or a beer or something and continue arguing about politics for maybe 45 minutes to an hour," he said. "But I never thought anything of it." Later, Thomas elaborated on this aspect of their relationship by stating that there were a "number of instances" when he visited Hill's home while working with her at the Education Department.

Thomas' two sessions of angry rebuttal were compelling. But even so riveting an appearance could not mitigate the impact of Hill's own eight hours of virtually uninterrupted testimony. In her opening statement, she spoke about the general nature of her office exchanges with Thomas while working under his supervision, initially at the Department of Education's office for civil rights in 1981 and '82, then at the Equal Employment Opportunity Commission from 1982 to '83. "He spoke about acts that he had seen in pornographic films involving such matters as women having sex with ani-

mals, and films showing group sex or rape scenes," she alleged.

One of the "oddest episodes," she said, involved an exchange in Thomas' office when he reached for a can of Coke and asked, "Who has put pubic hair on my Coke?" (Later, Hatch accused Hill of stealing the story from a work of fiction. Holding aloft a copy of the book *The Exorcist*, Hatch quoted, "There seems to be an alien pubic hair in my gin.") On other occasions, Hill maintained, "he referred to the size of his own penis as being larger than normal" and spoke of the pleasure he had "given to women with oral sex."

Under questioning, she also recalled an exchange in Thomas' office where Thomas alluded to the large penis of an actor in a pornographic film by referring to the character's name.

"Do you recall what it was?" pressed Senator Biden.

"Yes, I do." Hill, permitting herself a rare display of emotion, wrinkled her nose in disgust. "The name that was referred to was Long Dong Silver." Hatch, who emerged as one of the panel's most aggressive interrogators, later dug up a 1988 decision by a federal appeals court, citing an obscene photograph of a character by that name. Hatch suggested it was this court case that had brought the name to Hill's attention—not Clarence Thomas.

Hill was also quite specific about her last encounter with Thomas, in 1983, while still an employee at the EEOC. Up until then, she said, she had declined all social invitations from Thomas, explaining to the Senators that she had repeatedly told him she did not feel it was appropriate to date her supervisor. But this was her last day at the EEOC before proceeding to a teaching post at Oklahoma's Oral Roberts University. So, she said, after he "assured me that the dinner was a professional courtesy only," they went to a restaurant after work. "He made a comment I vividly remember," she said. "He said that if I ever told anyone of his behavior, that it would ruin his career."

The most moving aspect of Hill's testimony was the portrait she painted of the vulnerability, humiliation and frustration she experienced while working under such conditions. "It wasn't as though it happened every day," Hill explained. "But I went to work during certain periods knowing that it might happen." She spoke of her fear of being squeezed out of good assignments, losing her job, maybe even not being able to find any job at all within the Reagan Administration if she continued to resist Thomas' alleged overtures. At one point, she said, the stress she experienced from the tension of her relationship with Thomas caused her to be hospitalized for five days with acute stomach pains.

Although the panel of male Senators seemed to have an especially hard time with this part of Hill's testimony, her tale struck a resonant chord with countless women across America. Judith Resnick, a law professor at the University of Southern California Law Center, characterized Hill's testimony: "You're seeing a paradigm of a sexual-harassment case."

The point most rigorously pursued by the Senate panel, particularly Pennsylvania's Senator Arlen Specter, the chief Republican interrogator on the committee, was why Hill decided in 1982 to follow Thomas from the Education Department to the EEOC. At that point, Hill said, she thought "the sexual overtures which had so troubled me had ended." Besides, she noted, there was talk that President Reagan was thinking of phasing out the Education Department, and she feared she might wind up jobless.

Once she got to the EEOC, Hill said, the overtures from Thomas resumed. If that was true, Senators wondered, then why in the years since she turned to teaching had she remained in touch with Thomas? Hill said she saw little harm in maintaining cordial relations with Thomas now that she no longer worked with him and no longer felt threatened by him.

Specter made much of the fact that while at Oral Roberts University, Hill remained friendly enough with Thomas to volunteer to drive him to the airport on one occasion. She suggested that the university's founding dean, Charles Kothe, had asked her to do so. (Kothe was not only her boss at that time but a good friend of Thomas' as well.) And what of the 11 phone calls she made to Thomas over a six-year period? Those, she explained, were work-related calls, and each "was made in a professional context."

Each time committee members tried to probe her possible motivations for denouncing Thomas publicly, they came up dry. "There is no motivation to show I'd make up something like this," she said. It became clear that it was members of various Senate staffs who had approached Hill, not the other way around. She maintained her silence publicly until her FBI statement fell into reporters' hands on Oct. 5. At that point, she said, "I could not keep silent."

Democratic Senator Patrick Leahy confronted the issue of motive and asked if she stood to gain in any way from coming forward. "I have not gained anything except knowing that I came forward and did what I felt that I had an obligation to do," she said. "That was to tell the truth."

The only moment when Hill seemed at all evasive came during an exchange with Specter over an Oct. 9 account in *USA Today*. In it, Keith Henderson, an old friend of hers who is also a former Senate Judiciary staff member, is quoted as saying Hill was advised by Senate staff members that her FBI affidavit would be the instrument that "quietly and behind the scenes" would force Thomas to withdraw, without her name ever becoming public. Specter pressed her to recall discussing such a scenario with anyone. First she demurred that she did not recall that specific comment. Pressed again, she allowed, "There might have been some conversation about what could possibly occur." Later, Specter attacked Hill's change in testimony as "flat-out perjury."

Senators returned to the point, plainly unwilling to accept that Hill had not at least entertained this scenario when she made her statement to the FBI agents. They, like many viewers, could not fathom how Hill would have failed to anticipate that her charges might not remain anonymous and that at some point she might have to face Thomas. When asked by Biden if she considered herself part of an "organized effort" to keep Thomas from the bench, she said, "I had not even imagined that this would occur."

There was one attempt at producing a smoking gun: Specter's presentation of an affidavit by John Doggett, a Yale classmate of Thomas' and a Washington acquaintance of Hill's. In it Doggett alleged that at a going-away party shortly before she left the EEOC, Hill steered him to a quiet corner and chastised him with the words "I am very disappointed in you. You really shouldn't lead on women and then let them down." Doggett called her charge "completely unfounded" and added that he came away "feeling that she was somewhat unstable, and that, in my case, she had fantasized about my being interested in her romantically." Hill responded that she barely knew Doggett and stated flatly, "I did not at any time have any fantasy about romance with him."

When the hearing concluded, everyone who had witnessed Hill's and Thomas' dramatic testimony knew for certain only what they had known at the start: one was telling the truth, and the other was lying. There was no way to imagine a happy ending to this very sad confrontation. For both Hill and Thomas, it was the hardest ordeal of their lives. But one of them was shouldering the burden unfairly, and it may never be known which one. While both had been sullied and injured by the proceedings, only one had been dragged through the mud on the strength of a very convincing lie.

A Question of Character

**Clarence Thomas and Anita Hill were both known
for truthfulness and integrity—
until the hearings**

*Anita Hill's accusations against Clarence Thomas raised the
question of sexual harassment to national prominence, only to reduce it
again to its toughest and most intractable kernel: her word against his.
Neither Hill nor Thomas was able to bring decisive evidence before the
committee. Thus the evidence of character counted all the more
heavily. But even that appeared to weigh equally on both sides. Based
on their backgrounds, Hill and Thomas seemed to be the two least likely
people in the world to be involved in an exchange of accusations about
sexual misconduct or false charges. Both have devoted their lives to
hard work and public service. He is said to be sensitive to women. She
has a reputation for integrity. One of them is lying.*

A Reputation for Integrity

Some people have always found it hard to reconcile the fact
that Clarence Thomas is both black and a conservative. It is
harder still to match the image of Thomas offered by Anita
Hill—of a boss who pressured and humiliated her—with the picture
offered by friends and co-workers, who portray him as a model of
courteous and respectful relations with women. The bedeviling paradox that emerged during the hearings was this: How could Thomas
have been one man to the world and another to Hill?

Even as her charges were electrifying the country, Thomas' defenders were rushing to his side. Former colleagues insist that if
anything, Thomas had a special sensitivity toward women's concerns. Janet Brown, who met Thomas when both were on the staff of
Missouri Senator John Danforth, recalled that when she was subjected to sexual harassment some years ago, Thomas was the most
sympathetic of her friends. "Outside my immediate family, there
was no one who exhibited more compassion, more outrage, more
sensitivity, more caring than Clarence Thomas."

Friends from his undergraduate days at Holy Cross College in
Worcester, Mass., maintain that Thomas tried to set an example
among the black students on the dormitory corridor where he lived.
"He was always respectful of women and critical of those who were
not," says classmate Leonard Cooper. Those who know him shake
their head at the idea that Thomas has any preoccupation with porn
films. Moreover, says an old friend, his methods of flirtation before
he remarried were hardly those of a Lothario. "Clarence's idea of a
date was to call up a woman and ask if he could come over and have
a beer and talk," says the friend.

It is just one of the ironies of his situation that while heading the
Equal Employment Opportunity Commission, Thomas strongly

**Could Thomas have been one man to the world and another to Hill?
It was hard to watch his testimony and not view him as a victim**

urged the Justice Department to back the commission's sexual-harassment guidelines in arguments before the U.S. Supreme Court. But
while he firmly denies it, Thomas has been accused of dragging his feet
on the 1983 case of an EEOC attorney who was accused of making un-
welcome sexual advances to several women in his office. After an internal investigation found the charges to have substance, Thomas urged
that the attorney be fired, but the dismissal never took place.

Thomas' defenders insist that he could act decisively in dealing
with cases of sexual harassment. Dolores Rozzi cites one case of a
male field supervisor under her jurisdiction at EEOC who she felt had
been unfairly charged with harassment. "I tried to convince Thomas
that I didn't feel this gentleman was guilty," she says. "He down-
graded the person two grades, a severe punishment." If Thomas is
the man his friends say he is, that penalty might have been pure justice. If he is the man Anita Hill says he is, it was pure hypocrisy.

A Real Straight Arrow

If Clarence Thomas had been a woman, he might have been Anita Hill. The childhood without much money, the hard work that led to college and Yale Law School, the career achievements in the private sector and public service that followed—much of Thomas' up-by-the-bootstraps life story has its equivalent in hers. And just as his reputation for integrity makes the charges against him hard to believe, her reputation makes them hard to dismiss. "She is scrupulous, conscientious and ethical beyond reproach," says Teree Foster, associate dean of the University of Oklahoma's law school.

Among most of the people whose paths Hill has crossed, she has left behind the impression of quiet but unquestionable achievement and a sober but not solemn disposition. She dates, though not a lot. She enjoys a laugh, though she doesn't tell the jokes. The youngest of 13 children in a devout Baptist family, she grew up near Morris, Okla., a small town (pop. 1,200) where her father raised cattle and farmed.

Though reserved, Hill was popular among classmates at Morris High School before graduating as valedictorian. "She was so smart it wasn't even funny," recalls Bill Bearden Sr., the former basketball coach. "She was very polite, well groomed and never missed a day of school." At Oklahoma State University she majored in psychology, and graduated with honors in 1977.

Hill's friends insist that she has never been hypersensitive. Says one: "I would not hesitate to invite her to an R-rated movie."

After earning a law degree from Yale in 1980, also with honors, Hill spent a year in private practice in Washington before being hired as special counsel to Thomas at the Department of Education's office for civil rights. She had reservations about living in Washington, which seemed too loose and unbuckled a place. "She was a real straight arrow," says Michael Middleton, who worked with both Hill and Thomas at the Department of Education and later at the EEOC. "Very proper and straitlaced. She was certainly no bimbo."

In 1982 Hill followed Thomas to the EEOC as his special assistant, but surprised colleagues a year later by leaving to take a job as law professor at Oral Roberts University. Five years ago, she moved to the University of Oklahoma, where she specializes in commercial law. Hill works on the faculty senate and the dean's committee and advises minority students, often inviting them to dinner at her modest one-story brick house.

Hill, who is single, allows few diversions from her work. But her friends insist she has never been prudish or hypersensitive. Bill Hassler is a Washington attorney who was a friend of Hill's at law school, where he would confide to her the details of his romantic ups and downs. She would listen, he recalls, without embarrassment. "I wouldn't hesitate to invite her to an R-rated movie," he says.

Hill gives no signs of having a political ax to grind. "She's a scholar in commercial law," says professor Harry Tepker, a colleague at Oklahoma. "That's not exactly the sort of field that firebrands go into." Those who know her describe her as both a conservative and a feminist but not an ideologue in either area. "I suspect she's a card-carrying Republican," says Joel Paul, a friend who recalls arguments in which Hill would loudly support Judge Robert Bork's unsuccessful nomination to the Supreme Court. "She is cut from the same political cloth as Thomas."

The Ultimate Men's Club

As pampered denizens of a virtually all-male bastion, many Senators were slow to grasp the seriousness of the sexual-harassment issue

There may be no better place in America for a referendum on male domination than the U.S. Senate. All white, mostly over 50, cosseted by fawning aides, uninhibited by women, the Senate may be the most visible concentration of full-frontal prefeminist thinking left.

If it weren't for that, the Judiciary Committee might have found a way to evaluate Professor Anita Hill's charges against Judge Clarence Thomas confidentially. But it was easier to consign her to the category of she-devils, like Fanne Foxe, Elizabeth Ray and Donna Rice, who rise from a public official's past to bring down a man simply for being, well, a man. In this postgraduate Skull and Bones, most of whose members hardly need to worry where their next million is coming from, it is hard to empathize with someone worried enough about her career that she would overlook offensive conduct until it became literally a federal matter.

Senators don't interact with women as colleagues—they have only two—and most of the other women they come in contact with are subservient. According to a 1991 study by the Congressional Management Foundation, women hold 31% of the top four positions on Senate staffs. Among those, women account for 24% of the very top post of administrative assistant. They earn 78¢ to every dollar their male counterparts pull in. Still, the preponderance of females is found in the catchall legislative jobs, where, as a staff member says, "taking good notes and neatness count."

In the absence of production quotas or a bottom line, the only measure of performance in the Senate is how much one pleases the boss. Getting coffee is not a courtesy but part of the job description; being sent to the boss's house to pick up a tux and a change of underwear is all in a day's work. In a Senate dining room, a young aide delivering papers to her boss was asked to remove her jacket so that a constituent could get a better look. She did. To someone operating in that atmosphere, perhaps, as Senator Arlen Specter said at the hearing, talk of "women's large breasts" hardly seems such a big deal.

While the Senate is full of selfless older women, happy to substitute the life of the office for a life, it also has a huge contingent of postfeminist younger women, who think being asked to walk the dog is the price one pays for invaluable experience. Says an aide to a Democratic Senator : "You know what the code is, and if you want to be involved, you know what you have to tolerate."

Fear of hypocrisy may have kept Democrats on the Judiciary Committee from taking charges of a personal nature seriously. Certainly Senator Edward Kennedy—recently shamed for taking his son and nephew barhopping on a night that ended in an accusation of rape—is not the ideal person to sit in judgment of someone else's sexual manners. Other members have had personal embarrassments as well: Senator Dennis DeConcini is one of the Keating Five; Senator Joseph Biden had to drop out of the 1988 presidential race because of plagiarism; Senator Patrick Leahy had to resign from the Intelligence Committee after admitting he had leaked a confidential document.

When a contingent of seven House members marched to the Democratic Caucus Room to ask for a meeting about sexual harassment, they were told they couldn't come in. Said California Congresswoman and Senate candidate Barbara Boxer: "What could be more symbolic than that closed door?" Some Senators "got it" better after some sensitivity training at home. Senators Daniel Patrick Moynihan and Jim Exon said they didn't realize how serious the issue was until they talked to their wives. Said Boxer: "If there were more women in the Senate, they wouldn't need to rely on spouses to tell them what's important to 51% of the American population."

But something happened during the hearings that may, for better or worse, permanently destroy all that comity. What debates over the budget, arms control, abortion or the gulf war did not destroy was finished off by televised hearings that stripped bare the sensibilities of two witnesses and the Senators who questioned them. The club may never be the same again.

Fraternity brothers: Biden, Kennedy and Metzenbaum confer

Woman Power

Outraged over the Thomas confirmation, women vow political revenge. But they face rank-and-file divisions.

A few Americans have picked over the detritus of the Clarence Thomas–Anita Hill bonfire and found something they can use. The owners of Spytech, a firm that supplies pocketbook-size recorders, came up with a new ad campaign: "Sexually harassed? Prove it. Stop it. Sue." Jesse Jackson, the sloganeer of American politics, is now talking about "economic harassment."

But mostly what was discovered in the wreckage of the Supreme Court confirmation hearings was the charred skeletons of some American myths. When the 52-to-48 vote was over, confirming Clarence Thomas as a Supreme Court Justice by the lowest margin of this century, some Americans had to give up a few illusions about fair play and about the complicated dynamics of racial and sexual solidarity. They learned that a woman who comes forward in good faith to make an accusation can become the accused, that skin color matters more to blacks than ideology, and that gender matters less to women than the causes women espouse in the name of feminism.

This last lesson is perhaps most startling. When Hill walked into the Senate Caucus Room, women across America saw her as the bearer of an old secret about the ugly politics of accommodation between men and women on the job. But by the end of the hearings, a majority of women had decided she did not speak for them. On the eve of the vote, polls showed that 55% of men found Thomas more believable and that 49% of women agreed.

Faced with this female skepticism, some feminists argue that Hill lost the ideological battle in part because she lost the tactical one. For one thing, she missed prime time. "Anita Hill spoke to 5 million Americans during the day; Thomas spoke to 30 million that night," says University of Southern California law professor Susan Estrich. More important, perhaps, Hill's putative Democratic allies on the Senate Judiciary Committee sat back while the Republicans attacked, ultimately painting the Yale-educated law professor as a delusionary careerist with a split personality. "Hill was savaged for three days by Republicans who played to win," says a Democratic strategist. "No one cross-examined Thomas in the same tone."

In the end, however, Hill lost her own female constituency because of an unspoken factor that has kept the women's movement from becoming a consistent force in American politics: class. When J.C. Alvarez came forward as a witness for the judge and described Hill as aloof and ambitious, she played a real-life version of Tess, the secretary pitted against a Wall Street shrew in the movie *Working Girl*. "Both working-class women and highly educated women put up with sexual harassment every day," says Anne Reingold, media director for the Democratic Party. "But the perception among working-class women is that a Yale law degree just gives you the right to make a federal case out of it."

Instead of dwelling on October's setback, women lashed out at the Senate's 98 male members and threatened to target those who put Thomas on the high court. They staged demonstrations; they donated money to women' groups. Said Eleanor Smeal, president of the Fund for the Feminist Majority: "The Senate did more in one week to underscore the critical need for more women in the Senate than feminists have been able to do in 25 years."

There was predictable talk about forming a third political party dedicated to women's causes. The Democratic Senatorial Campaign Committee—headed by Virginia Senator Charles Robb, who cast his vote for Thomas—took a double hit. Its annual fund raiser in Washington was picketed by feminists, and the liberal direct-mail firm of Craver, Matthews, Smith announced it was dropping the group as a client. Some of the Democrats' most loyal contributors said they would not raise a dime for the 11 Democratic Senators who gave Thomas his slim victory.

But even as they threatened retaliation, women's groups were forced to confront the fragmentation of their movement. Since its peak two decades ago, the women's movement has spawned subgroups whose diverse interests range from pushing day care to combating pornography. Women's groups christened 1990 the Political Year of the Woman, but only one of seven women who ran for the Senate last year, Nancy Kassebaum of Kansas, was elected; she voted to confirm Thomas. In some ways, feminist politics have expanded too much to keep women under one tent.

Perk City

Wonder why Congress is so arrogant about bounced checks? Perhaps because its members are used to the freebie life.

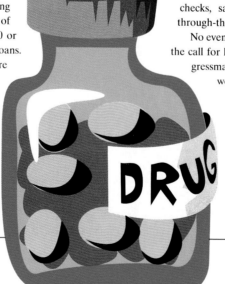

Members of Congress expect to be called Honorable, but their claim to that honorific looks pretty flimsy. First came the check-bouncing scam, when investigators found that lawmakers wrote more than 8,000 rubber checks at their private bank last year, free of charge. Then came word of members' stiffing the House restaurant, where prices are already dirt cheap. Suddenly, talk-show comedians, newspaper editorialists and the mailman were all wondering, How can members of Congress balance a budget and spend tax dollars wisely when they can't even balance their own checkbooks?

What could be a better invitation to civil disobedience than watching lawmakers who earn $125,100 travel around the world for free and have their parking tickets fixed, refusing to pay for the few perks that are not granted outright? Hoping it would all go away, House Speaker Tom Foley at first declared that check-bouncing privileges would be canceled and members would be required to pay the same penalties as everyone else for overdrawing their accounts. But the storm only gathered strength. Republican Pat Roberts of Kansas and Democrat Mary Rose Oakar of Ohio revealed that roughly 300 legislators owed the main House restaurant and catering service more than $300,000.

With a flutter of contrition, House members voted 390 to 8 to shut down their private bank, which by this time had been dubbed B.C.C.I., the Bank of Corrupt Congressional Incumbents. Dozens of lawmakers admitted writing bad checks.

The furor began when the General Accounting Office revealed that in one year alone, members of Congress bounced 8,331 checks—581 for $1,000 or more—giving themselves, in effect, interest-free loans. Millionaire lawmakers, said investigators, were among the worst offenders, but the habit was shared by Foley, majority leader Richard Gephardt and minority whip Newt Gingrich. In some cases, debts of $10,000 and more were rolled over for months, with no penalties and no interest charged. Those who were innocent of any creative financial activity rushed to clear their names in a spectacle of finger pointing. Other members would not, as they say, dignify the charges with a response. Ways and Means Committee chairman Dan Rostenkowski was particularly forthright. "None of your damn business," he told reporters. Majority leader Gephardt was at pains to explain that lawmakers had been irresponsible only with each other's money. "The public should be aware that no taxpayer funds were used to cover insufficiencies," he said.

Members of Congress seemed in some cases to be genuinely surprised at the public's rage. Which only served to confirm the impression of a body of lawmakers out of touch with the lives of their constituents.

Many Congressmen consider public service a personal sacrifice. If they were lawyers in private practice, they could make many times the salary they earn as legislators. They are often required to maintain two homes, attend costly fund raisers, live in an expensive city and work long hours. A cheap car wash may not seem much in return.

But this culture of privilege, so stubbornly protected, is not well suited to these hard times. When uninsured workers live in fear that one illness could wipe out their life savings, it is enraging to hear of the House pharmacy dispensing free prescription drugs. When young families cannot get a mortgage on a house, the idea of free loans to lawmakers is bound to rankle.

Those members of Congress who ventured back to their districts got an earful. Democrat Pat Schroeder, who insists that she has not bounced any checks, says the furor "captures the brick-through-the-window political mood."

No event could have better breathed life into the call for limiting the number of terms a Congressman can serve. But for what it was worth, legislators could take some comfort in the fact that few people could claim to be perfectly clean. The culture of special privilege, it turns out, is so pervasive that those using the House bank included not only members and their staffs but also journalists who cover Capitol Hill. Maybe it's time to move the nation's capital to Omaha.

Toward a Safer World

Bush cuts the U.S. arsenal and invites Gorbachev to do the same. But Moscow should read the fine print.

I t was a solid Bush-plus performance. In his televised address to the nation from the Oval Office on Sept. 27, the President was proposing nothing less than a new set of guidelines for nuclear peace in the post–cold war world. He was, for once, ahead of the curve, demonstrating real leadership in his capacity as Commander in Chief of the doomsday arsenal.

Yet this was no nuclear abolitionist, no Jimmy Carter daring to dream about the "elimination of all nuclear weapons from this earth." Nor was it Ronald Reagan, putting his faith in a pure defense that would render nuclear weapons "impotent and obsolete." Instead, it was classic George Bush, a traditionalist and pragmatist, striving for boldness without undermining a quality he values even more: prudence. Bush did his best to make his initiative seem visionary, even magnanimous. For a sweetener, he announced several unilateral steps, such as removing all nuclear-tipped cruise missiles from U.S. surface ships and attack submarines. But these are for the most part minor gestures that will leave intact the main concepts and structures of American defense. The implications of Bush's proposals are far more onerous for the U.S.S.R. In his own statesmanlike way, he was all but dictating to the Kremlin how it should restructure its nuclear forces.

Bush's essential purpose is to accelerate the retirement of some of the Soviet Union's most advanced military programs while protecting key elements of the U.S.'s "strategic modernization": the Trident II submarine missile and a scaled-back version of the Star Wars antimissile defense.

Arms-control proposals, like the arms themselves, have targets. Bush's plan is aimed squarely at two categories of nuclear weaponry: 1) intercontinental ballistic missiles (ICBMs) with multiple warheads, known as independently targetable re-entry vehicles (MIRVs); and 2) short-range missiles and other so-called tactical weapons. Not coincidentally, those are the Soviet systems that most worry the U.S. Because the U.S.S.R. is a land power with a preference for heavy artillery, it has more of these monsters than the U.S.

Traditionally it was U.S. policy to redress this imbalance in two ways: through negotiations, like the Strategic Arms Reduction Talks (START), and by developing America's own 10-warhead MX missile. This time Bush said in effect, Let's agree to eliminate MIRVed ICBMs altogether. While the U.S. has some 350 MIRVed ICBMs, the Soviets would have to give up 763 such weapons.

In targeting tactical nukes, Bush was addressing what has been a growing concern about the disintegration of the Soviet Union. For months, the U.S. government has been studying the danger that dissident groups might seize weapons and use them for intimidation. Furthermore, Bush's proposal was intended to help him get a grip on a more general political problem: the difficulty in keeping up with seismic changes in the geopolitical landscape.

Bush opened his speech with the image of the world facing a "fresh page of history before yesterday's ink has even dried." He might have been speaking about the ink on two documents in particular. In November 1990 the leaders of 22 nations met in Paris to sign a treaty on Conventional Forces in Europe that had been under negotiation for nearly 17 years. In July, Bush and Gorbachev signed another pact capping a decade of START talks.

Gorbachev had trouble getting his marshals to accept concessions in the negotiations. But that was before the coup. Now many obstreperous senior officers have been summarily retired. Still, there are plenty of people in Moscow who are desperate to cling to Soviet strategic nuclear strength as the last symbol of their country's superpower status. For that reason alone they will resist further cuts.

Yet the U.S.S.R. itself is crumbling. The leaders of Russia, Kazakhstan, Belorussia and Ukraine—the independent Soviet republics that have long-range nuclear weapons—have promised to carry out all the cuts required of them under the Gorbachev–Bush agreements. Indeed, Ukraine and Belorussia said they hope to become completely nonnuclear states, and asked for U.S. aid in dismantling the warheads.

From the American point of view, the fewer Soviet nukes the better. Bush calculated that Soviet leaders will have an easier time persuading the military to swallow more cuts if they're part of a bilateral deal.

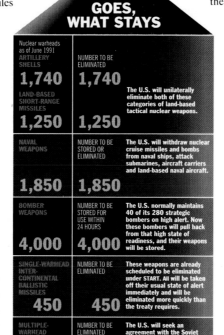

WHAT GOES, WHAT STAYS

Nuclear warheads as of June 1991	NUMBER TO BE ELIMINATED	
ARTILLERY SHELLS 1,740	1,740	The U.S. will unilaterally eliminate both of these categories of land-based tactical nuclear weapons.
LAND-BASED SHORT-RANGE MISSILES 1,250	1,250	
NAVAL WEAPONS 1,850	NUMBER TO BE STORED OR ELIMINATED 1,850	The U.S. will withdraw nuclear cruise missiles and bombs from naval ships, attack submarines, aircraft carriers and land-based naval aircraft.
BOMBER WEAPONS 4,000	NUMBER TO BE STORED FOR USE WITHIN 24 HOURS 4,000	The U.S. normally maintains 40 of its 280 strategic bombers on high alert. Now these bombers will pull back from that high state of readiness, and their weapons will be stored.
SINGLE-WARHEAD INTERCONTINENTAL BALLISTIC MISSILES 450	NUMBER TO BE ELIMINATED 450	These weapons are already scheduled to be eliminated under START. All will be taken off their usual state of alert immediately and will be eliminated more quickly than the treaty requires.
MULTIPLE-WARHEAD INTERCONTINENTAL BALLISTIC MISSILES 2,000	NUMBER TO BE ELIMINATED ?	The U.S. will seek an agreement with the Soviet Union to modify or eliminate all ICBMs with multiple warheads. Development of the mobile MX Peacekeeper and the mobile option for the Midgetman missile will be abandoned.
SUBMARINE-LAUNCHED BALLISTIC MISSILE WARHEADS 5,400	NO CHANGE	This category is untouched. Bush will seek full funding for the Strategic Defense Initiative and the B-2 bomber.

TIME Graphic by Joe Lertola

Source: Arms Control Association

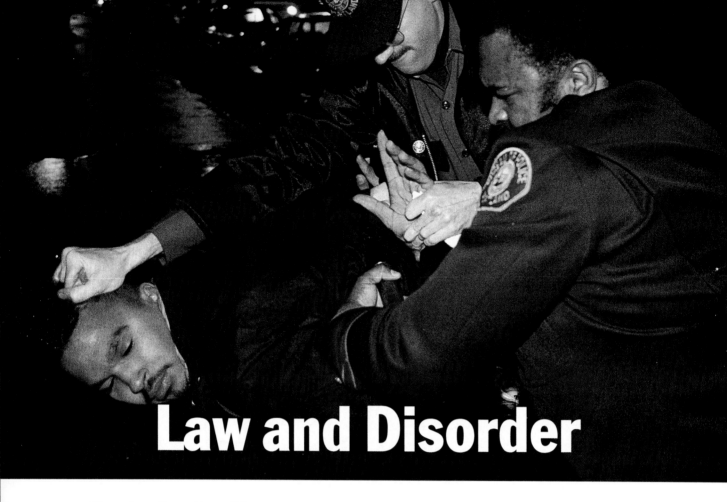

Law and Disorder

Four Los Angeles officers are arrested for a vicious beating, and the country plunges into a debate on the rise of complaints against cops

The incident was over in a matter of minutes.

It began with wailing police cars chasing a motorist through the night, cornering his car in a Los Angeles suburb and surrounding the driver as he stepped into the street. A sergeant fired a 50,000-volt Taser stun gun at the unarmed black man, then three officers took turns kicking him and smashing him in the head, neck, kidneys and legs with their truncheons. A hovering helicopter bathed the scene in a floodlight as 11 other policemen looked on. When the beating was over, Rodney King, 25, an unemployed construction worker, had suffered 11 fractures in his skull, a crushed cheekbone, a broken ankle, internal injuries, a burn on his chest and some brain damage.

The matter might have ended there had not a bystander captured the March 3 incident with his video camera. Within hours, the horrific scene was being replayed on national television. Within days, outraged protesters were demanding the resignation of Los Angeles police chief Daryl Gates. Four officers were arrested for assault and 11 others were investigated by the FBI, the L.A.P.D.'s internal affairs division and the Los Angeles County district attorney's office. Said D.A. Ira Reiner: "It is a terrible moment, and time for serious reflection, when officers who have sworn to uphold the law are indicted for the most serious felonies." George Bush bluntly summarized the prevailing shock: "What I saw made me sick."

The scandal reverberated far beyond Los Angeles, stirring a na-

tionwide debate over excessive police violence. Was the beating an aberration, as Los Angeles police chief Daryl Gates insists? Or did it affirm yet again that many cops resort to violence when no threat to their safety can justify it? Is racism so pervasive that the fight against crime all too often becomes a war on blacks? Has the criminal-justice system become so ineffectual that officers feel the need to play judge and jury on the spot? Has police work become so dangerous that even well-meaning officers can snap under the pressure?

Those questions became more urgent as evidence grew that the officers involved in King's beating might have expected their behavior to be winked at. In tapes of radio calls and computer records of police communications on the night of the attack, some of the officers involved could be heard swapping racist jokes and boasting about the beating. Their lighthearted exchanges sound nothing like the words of men who fear they have done something out of the ordinary. Two nurses at Pacifica Hospital, where King was taken after the beating, testified that the officers who assaulted King showed up later at the hospital room to taunt him. One allegedly told the victim, "We played a little hardball tonight, and you lost."

Los Angeles is far from the only place where police play hardball, dispensing curbside justice regularly, especially in ghetto neighborhoods. Those who live outside such areas can usually ignore that reality. Fed up with violent street crime, they are often content to send in the police force while they look the other way.

Skull-drumming tactics have an enduring place in police history, and commonly accompany charges of racism. Many of the ghetto riots of the 1960s were prompted by police incidents. More recently, Miami has suffered five street uprisings in 10 years, all ignited by episodes of perceived police brutality.

Spotty record keeping makes it hard to measure the frequency of police misconduct. Departments often refuse to disclose the number of complaints they receive. Citizens often bring their accusations to civil rights or police-watchdog groups, which complicates attempts to compile a comprehensive count.

In the end, many cases doubtless go unreported, especially in cities where complaints have to be filled out at the station house that is the home base of the very officers against whom the charge is being brought. "The general feeling out on the streets is that you can't get justice when a cop mistreats you," says Norman Siegel, executive director of the New York Civil Liberties Union.

But while the experts cannot agree on whether abuses are up or down, few dispute that they are common. Even in the best of times, police work is dangerous and stressful, and an officer can face several life-or-death decisions during a single eight-hour watch. The pressures have mounted in recent years as crack has poured into the inner cities, giving rise to gangs armed with automatic weapons— and the hair-trigger temperament to use them.

In New York City, which has highly restrictive guidelines for when police may use their guns, the number of people shot by local cops soared in the past three years from 68 to 108. At the same time, police have been fired on by suspects in greater numbers every year since 1980. Though the number of officers killed nationally has fallen from 104 in 1980 to 66 in 1989, that is partly the result of wider use of bulletproof vests. As inner cities have degenerated into free-fire zones, many officers have become more aggressive, if only in self-defense. Danger "is something you get used to," says Officer Dennis Rhodes, a 20-year veteran of the L.A.P.D., "but every time you check in for a shift, you don't really know if you're going to go home that night."

Indeed, police have been saddled with a task for which they are singularly ill equipped. Most authorities believe that urban street crime arises from a combination of poverty, poor education and a

Under fire: police chief Daryl Gates

Rodney King was viciously beaten

lack of opportunity in inner-city neighborhoods, problems that the police can do nothing about. Officers, who tend to be recruited from places far from the neighborhoods they will patrol, often have little in common with the citizens they must serve and protect. "The bulk of police forces are white males of the middle class," says Ron DeLord, head of the Combined Law Enforcement Associations of Texas. "Yet we send them into large urban centers that are black and Hispanic and poor, with no understanding of the cultural differences."

Experts on police psychology insist that most officers are attracted to police work by the opportunity to protect and serve. But a certain number of rotten apples, predisposed to brutality, make it through psychological testing that can be woefully inadequate.

A few cities have revamped their training and supervision to make abuses less likely. Since 1988, all 2,400 police officers on the Metro-Dade county force have undergone violence-reduction training to school themselves in ways to defuse potentially violent situations and to avoid overreaction to typical confrontations.

Critics of the police say that legal-damage suits are a more useful deterrent to police brutality and that they would work even better if jury awards were paid out of individual officers' pockets instead of by city treasuries. While courts have decided that public employees are not individually liable for most of their actions on the job, taxpayer concern about the rising cost of lawsuits has revived the popularity of civilian review boards. Such panels are at work in 26 of the nation's 50 largest cities, up from 13 seven years ago.

In the end, discipline must come from rank-and-file police with courage enough to break the so-called Blue Code, which prohibits one officer from ratting on another. A few signs exist that some officers are abandoning the tradition of blind loyalty to one another. In Houston more than half of all complaints now come from other officers. During the King beating, two California highway-patrol officers reportedly took down the names of those involved from their breast-pocket name tags.

Episodes of police brutality are likely never to vanish entirely. But they could be significantly curtailed if more officers concluded that so long as their fellow police take the law into their own hands, there is no law at all.

Exoneration for a Kennedy

The prosecution had strong evidence against William Smith but could not use it in court

William Kennedy Smith: months of unease, acquittal in an hour

Palm Beach will never be the same. Last March the Kennedy clan arrived at the family compound for what Senator Ted Kennedy called a "traditional Easter weekend." The weekend included a Good Friday night outing for the Senator, his son Patrick and nephew William Kennedy Smith at Au Bar, the club of the moment. Ted Kennedy and his son had some drinks and returned to the estate. Smith stayed until closing time, about 3 a.m., and left with a woman who drove him to the Kennedy compound.

The next thing anyone knows for sure is that the woman, a 29-year-old single mother, went to the police and said she had been raped at the estate. She was taken to a nearby hospital and treated for injuries. The other thing known for sure is that the complaint turned Palm Beach into a media circus. In the greatest assemblage of journalists since Operation Desert Storm, reporters from as far away as Norway descended on the enclave, foraging for details.

After a delay, the cops named William Smith as a suspect. The son of Jean Kennedy and the late Stephen Smith, William was a medical student at Georgetown University, and is described as one of the least arrogant of the young Kennedys. But after the story surfaced, Smith declared his innocence and virtually disappeared.

In December a trial was held in West Palm Beach. After 10 days of wrenching testimony, it took the six-member jury only 77 minutes to find William Kennedy Smith not guilty of rape. The swift decision raised questions about the prosecution's case, which pitted the accuser's tale of being pinned to the ground and violated against Smith's equally vehement denials. Many prosecutors would have dropped the case as unwinnable. Why then did State Attorney David Bludworth and Moira Lasch, his chief felony attorney, decide to press ahead?

Smith's lawyer, Roy Black, asserts that Bludworth's motive was to avoid seeming soft on the Kennedy family. But there was more to it than that. During their investigation, the prosecutors became convinced that the woman was telling the truth about Smith. The police, rape counselors and the doctors who examined the woman believed her. Their problem was proving that in court. Furthermore, seven years ago, Bludworth was accused of kowtowing to the family by not thoroughly investigating the drug-overdose death of Robert Kennedy's son David in Palm Beach. Bludworth, who faces re-election next year, risked renewed accusations of a cover-up had he declined to move against another Kennedy.

His and Lasch's suspicions were further aroused when the Kennedys gave police investigators what seemed to be a runaround. William Barry, a former FBI agent, incorrectly told detectives that Senator Kennedy had left, when in fact he was at the Palm Beach estate. For two weeks the family rebuffed police attempts to survey the grounds where the alleged assault took place. That was sufficient time for wind and sea to obliterate any evidence that might have corroborated the woman's story. A Palm Beach County grand jury declined to indict Barry for obstruction of justice.

Any doubts the prosecutors might have harbored about Smith's guilt seem to have been swept away when three women came forward to claim that they too had been sexually attacked by Smith. But Florida prohibits testimony about a rape defendant's sexual history unless it shows a striking and detailed similarity to the crime with which he is charged. Moreover, none of the women had filed charges against Smith. One of Lasch's most controversial moves was to release the three women's stories. Bludworth says Florida law, which requires that public records be made available on request, left Lasch with no choice but to make the stories public—as well as details of the accuser's sexual past, which included three abortions and sexual abuse by her father.

Defense attorney Black mounted a devastating counterattack, arguing that the three cases did not represent a "signature style," and that the only real question in the Palm Beach case was whether the woman consented or not. When Judge Mary Lupo ruled that the women could not testify because Lasch had failed to establish enough parallels between their stories and the one from Smith's accuser, the prosecution's case, for all practical purposes, was over.

Its cause was not helped by Lasch's plodding courtroom style. She was despondent after Smith's boy-next-door performance on the witness stand. He calmly described accepting the woman's offer of a ride home from Au Bar, and then walking with her along the beach. After exchanging kisses, he testified, the couple had two sexual encounters—though the romantic mood was broken when he mistakenly called her "Cathie." Unable to shake Smith's story, Lasch resorted to expressions of incredulity that two people who had met in a notorious pickup joint could be having sex only a few hours later.

After his exoneration, Smith celebrated with his family. For a short while, his accuser remained in hiding, in a vain attempt to maintain her anonymity. But TV technicians on some channels began to dissolve the blurry blob that had hidden her face while the trial proceeded. On Dec. 19, she agreed to be interviewed on national television and identified herself as Patricia Bowman, the stepdaughter of Michael Gerald O'Neil, former chairman of GenCorp., a multimillion-dollar conglomerate that owns General Tire. From now on she will be recognizable as the woman who accused William Kennedy Smith of rape—and was not believed.

Little Flat of Horrors

Recalling The Silence of the Lambs, a Milwaukee man is seized in a den of mutilated body parts

Psycho: Jeffrey L. Dahmer turned his apartment into a slaughterhouse

For months residents sensed that all was not right at the Oxford Apartments on Milwaukee's crime-infested west side. A power saw buzzed at odd hours. The putrid odor of rotting meat flooded the corridors.

When police entered Apartment 213, they were shocked to find a freezer covered with Polaroid photographs of mutilated men. Various body parts were strewn around the apartment.

Unlike Hannibal ("the Cannibal") Lecter, the brilliant mass-murdering psychiatrist in *The Silence of the Lambs,* the creature who turned Apartment 213 into a private slaughterhouse is an unassuming 31-year-old ne'er-do-well named Jeffrey L. Dahmer. The pale, sandy-haired Dahmer eventually confessed to 17 murders over the past 13 years.

Many of the victims were black males, and some were homosexuals. One trait Dahmer seems to share with the fictional Lecter is an apparent penchant for cannibalism: he told police he had saved a human heart "to eat later."

The investigation suggested that Dahmer fit classic patterns of a serial killer. Says Robert Ressler, a former FBI agent: "Dahmer falls into the subcategory of the sadistic, sexually oriented serial killer who is inevitably a white male loner." This type of killer, says Ressler, generally comes from a broken home, has had poor parenting and/or was abused early in his life, usually doesn't marry, is often an alcoholic or drug addict and can be suicidal.

Jeffrey Dahmer spent 10 months in prison for fondling a 13-year-old Laotian boy in 1988. On his release, Dahmer was put on probation. Although he showed up at the probation office every month, his caseworker never visited Dahmer in his home, as is usually required. A state department of corrections spokesman said the requirement had been waived because the agent was overworked. Another serious lapse occurred in May, when police officers were called by two black women who found a naked, bloodied Asian boy on the street. The cops laughed off the incident as a gay love spat and delivered the 14-year-old to Dahmer's apartment. As soon as they left, Dahmer reportedly strangled the boy and dismembered his body.

Dahmer's murderous rampage might have continued indefinitely had one of his victims not escaped and told police Dahmer was trying to kill him. Dahmer, who was arrested without a struggle, expressed remorse.

Said the parents of one of Dahmer's victims: "We have spent a great deal of time trying to understand the motivation for such a heinous crime and concluded that some acts are so evil they simply cannot be explained."

Ten Minutes in Hell

In the worst mass murder in U.S. history, a gunman turns a Texas café into a killing field, leaving 23 dead

As the usual lunchtime crowd jammed Luby's Cafeteria in Killeen, Texas, on Oct. 16 a blue Ford Ranger pickup tore across the parking lot and barreled straight through the restaurant's plate-glass window. A few startled customers ran to help the driver. To their horror, a muscular young man sprang from behind the wheel with a semiautomatic pistol and began firing. "This is what Bell County did to me . . . This is payback day!" he shouted as he pumped bullets in every direction.

Pausing only long enough to pack fresh clips into his two semiautomatic pistols—a Glock 17 and a Ruger P-89— the killer continued to shoot people point-blank in the head or chest for a full 10 minutes. When four police officers arrived on the scene, they returned his fire and wounded him. The gunman then stumbled into a rear alcove, where he shot himself in the head. By the time he slumped to the floor, the death toll stood at 23. It was the worst mass murder in U.S. history, surpassing the 1984 massacre at a McDonald's restaurant in San Ysidro, Calif., that left 21 dead.

The killer was quickly identified as George Hennard, 35, an unemployed seaman with a reputation as an oddball. An intemperate recluse, Hennard was thrown out of the merchant marine in 1989 for possessing a small amount of marijuana. Because 14 of his 22 victims were female, there was speculation that he had been driven by misogyny. As Hennard stomped through the restaurant, he shouted, "Take that, bitch!" several times.

Investigators found that Hennard had had no trouble obtaining his weapons. He purchased both in Nevada and registered them with the Las Vegas police last winter.

George Hennard: an unemployed seaman who hated women

The Army had brought psychological counselors to the Fort Hood region to deal with the heavy casualties that were expected during Desert Storm. As it turned out, the community lost twice as many people in the October rampage as it did in the entire gulf war.

A City Sundered

Operation Rescue supporters show their colors at a rally

Pro-choice forces in Wichita fight to uphold the law

The protests finally subsided in Wichita, but the healing will take time.

Before Operation Rescue came to town in mid-July, Linda Barber and her brother Rick Middleton hardly ever talked about abortion. Now they hardly ever talk. Rick, 39, enlisted with the pro-life forces and was twice arrested for trying to shut down one of the city's three abortion clinics. Linda, 35, volunteered to escort the terrified female patients past the demonstrators. "I had no clue she was pro-choice," says Rick. "The relationship in our family is definitely strained." Linda is less polite. "I feel he's in bed with a bunch of criminals," she says. "I can't imagine spending this Christmas together."

Just about every bar, restaurant and dining-room table in Wichita played reluctant host to an impassioned debate on abortion this summer. "It's going to take some time to regain a center of gravity," says Mayor Bob Knight. "The passions and feelings are so deep, and the city of Wichita has been criticized by everybody."

City officials were relieved when the number of protesters dropped dramatically in the last week of August, after rallies that drew at least 25,000 pro-lifers and 6,000 pro-choicers from across the country. 2,600 arrests and countless screaming matches left tempers high. At a proudly counterculture bar called Kirby's, blatant pro-lifers were likely to be booted from the premises. Elsewhere, pro-choicers faced similar hazards. "I've been elbowed, stepped on, spit on and called Satan's mistress," says Marina Clemente, 26, who unwittingly entered a pro-life sandwich shop and found herself "verbally abused" by 20 patrons once she revealed her views.

Before July 15, most residents were preoccupied with rising property taxes, gang violence and renewed efforts to ban nude dancing. But all the factors that make Wichita a nice place to raise a family—its manageable size and heartland values—also proved irresistible to out-

of-state Operation Rescue activists. Though largely pro-choice, Wichita contains all the ingredients for staging a militant morality play on abortion. Says Steve Smith, assistant managing editor of the Wichita *Eagle:* "We're on the fringes of the Bible Belt; we have a strong evangelical presence, a pro-life Governor and an arguably pro-life mayor." More important, Wichita is home to the Women's Health Care Services clinic, where George Tiller is one of a handful of U.S. physicians known to perform late-term abortions.

Tiller, who wears a bulletproof vest to work and checks his car for bombs every morning, has emerged as a hero to the pro-choice movement, refusing to be intimidated by protesters and death threats. To pro-lifers, he is a modern-day Mengele. Says Paula Winter, a "sidewalk counselor" who tries to dissuade patients from entering the clinic: "He kills 10 to 20 babies a week in his 'abortuary' and then puts them into his incinerator and burns them."

Along the thoroughfare that adjoins Tiller's clinic, a dozen pro-lifers and half as many pro-choicers petition passersby with wrenching pictures and alarming slogans. Commuters honk to register their vote—or throw cans, bottles and even bags of urine. The abortion debate has a way of inducing indignation even among the timid. "I came out of the closet a week ago," says pro-choicer Paul Wilson, 75. "The silent majority is sick and tired of this invasion by outsiders."

While everybody claimed victory, Operation Rescue's tactics appear to have backfired. In a poll published Aug. 11 by the Wichita *Eagle,* nearly 80% of respondents opposed the group's methods. The same number said the protests had no impact on their views on abortion, while 15% said they now felt more inclined to support abortion rights, and less than 8% felt more supportive of abortion restrictions.

Wichita will have an easier time recouping its national reputation than repairing its internal divisions. "I think there are some people so inflamed that they won't cool down for a lifetime," says the Rev. Jack Middleton of Wichita Bible Church. Middleton's own healing process begins at home, as he tries to get his children Linda and Rick back on speaking terms in time for Christmas.

"It Can Happen to Anybody."

Basketball's beloved star retires and vows to become a spokesman in the battle against AIDS.

For years he has been a walking—no, a running, jumping, slithering—suspension of disbelief. Not just on the basketball court, where he has all but remade the game and brought in a whole new dictionary to cover the moves that bear his monogram—the "no-look pass," the "triple double," the "coast to coast" drive. And not just in America, but from Bali to the Bahamas, where many kids wear his picture on their chest. Hundreds in Paris were calling out for "Ma-JEEK" when he went to play in France in October, and everyone was preparing for the unprecedented prospect of seeing him, the consummate professional, bring an amateur's enthusiasm to the 1992 Olympics.

Even outside the world of sports, Mr. Showtime's enormous smile and unquenchable grace have become almost ubiquitous—on music video shows, on billboards, at fund-raising dinners. For more than a decade, Earvin "Magic" Johnson Jr. has commanded the world of entertainment on the court and off with an irreplaceable blend of poise and surprise.

On Nov. 7, however, Magic delivered what was clearly his most serious shock. At a press conference on the ground he has made his own, the Great Western Forum, home to the Los Angeles Lakers, Johnson, 6-ft. 9-in. tall and 32 years old, at the top of his career, announced that he had been infected by the human immune-deficiency virus (HIV) that causes AIDS and would "have to retire from the Lakers today." Although he has as yet no symptoms of AIDS, the man who had defied gravity, and belief, for so long would suddenly, overnight, vanish from the court. "I'm going to miss playing," said Johnson, dry-eyed and dignified as ever, "but my life is going to go on. I'm going to go on a happy man."

The disclosure left millions in a state of disbelief. It was not just a celebrity who was endangered by a life-threatening disease, but of all things an athlete whose strength and endurance had made him the most admired player in the world. "A situation like this just doesn't make sense," said Kevin McHale, Johnson's longtime rival from the Boston Celtics. "When you look at a big, healthy guy like Magic Johnson, you think this illness wouldn't attack someone like him. But it did." Many others were sobered at the thought that if even the most enchanted and mobile of bodies was vulnerable, it could, as Johnson pointed out, "happen to anybody."

Yet Johnson's characteristic refusal to be cowed, even by AIDS, suggested that the star might, as so often before, alchemize disaster with his irresistible hopefulness. He was, after all, not unusual in contracting the virus, but he seemed to recognize that he was in an unusual position to campaign for protection against it. Vowing to educate people about AIDS, Johnson said he would use his plight to tell others that "safe sex is the way to go." Just by his public acknowledgment, he began the process: calls to AIDS hot lines and testing centers more than doubled in most places the next day.

The virus has already claimed the young, the famous: symbols of Hollywood like Rock Hudson, symbols of youth such as 18-year-old Ryan White, even symbols of athletic prowess like the All-Pro former Washington Redskin Jerry Smith. Yet Magic is perhaps the first celebrity to come out instantly to admit his condition, and unprompted. And he is certainly the most famous: even people with no interest in basketball recognize his name and smile. In addition, because he contracted the disease through heterosexual contact, he drove home the fact that anyone is vulnerable.

Johnson is also ideally placed to speak on AIDS to the groups most in need of counsel: poor minority communities and the young. Though blacks represent only 12% of the nation's population, they account for 25% of the AIDS patients: more than half the women with AIDS in the U.S. are African American. Yet even many of the best-intended AIDS-prevention programs have failed to speak the language of the groups that are most at risk. "Clearly this is tragic," said Norm Nickens, chairman of the National Minority AIDS Council. "But we couldn't ask for a better spokesman."

Johnson's swift and brave admission also casts light on many of the darker issues shadowing the world of sports. Many sports stars use their heroism to advantage and then almost boast of their immunity from consequence. Wilt Chamberlain devotes an entire chapter in his recent autobiography to elaborating on his claim that he has slept with 20,000 different women. Football's Jim Brown, formally charged with violence against women, was equally unapologetic in his memoir about totting up his sexual scores. Johnson's fellow Angeleno Steve Garvey had hardly ended his All-American career before it was revealed that he was seriously involved with at least two women other than his wife. No one would begin to suggest that Johnson should bear the blame for the ways many athletes abuse their status, but his tragedy does raise many searching questions about the immortality we expect of our sporting heroes.

At the announcement of his retirement, however, the big man's characteristic calm helped temper, a little, the sadness of the occasion. While there is no reason to deify the player or accord him any more sympathy than that lent to the roughly 1 million others in the U.S. and millions elsewhere in the world who have been infected, there is ample reason to feel grateful for his courage and his sanity and to hope that somehow, with his dauntless smile, he might even give us something more to cheer about at the saddest moment of his life.

When Magic Johnson announced that he had the AIDS virus, he put the risk of heterosexual transmission squarely in center court

Cracked Cover

In early July the seemingly moribund Iran-*contra* scandal roared back to life with a series of stunning developments. Alan Fiers, head of the CIA's Central America task force from 1984 to 1986, pleaded guilty to two counts of lying to Congress about when top intelligence officials learned of the illegal diversion of funds—from secret arms sales to Iran—to the Nicaraguan rebels. Fiers said he became aware of the diversion of funds in the summer of 1986, but that Clair George, then the CIA's deputy director for operations, ordered him to deny any knowledge of the transfers when he testified before the House intelligence committee that October. Fiers' admissions left investigators wondering: Just what did Ronald Reagan and George Bush know? And when did they know it?

Furthermore, investigators disclosed that U.S. intelligence agencies, including the CIA, kept secret accounts with the Bank of Credit & Commerce International—the shady financial empire accused of laundering billions of illicit dollars around the world.

October Surprise?

It is hard to solve a mystery if all the people who actually know the truth are either accomplished liars, adamantly mute, or already dead. Such a conundrum faces those lawmakers curious about the purported "October Surprise" hostage deal—an alleged 1980 agreement between the Reagan campaign and Iranian officials to delay the release of American hostages until after the U.S. elections. Last April, Gary Sick, a former Carter White House official, focused attention on the possibility of such a deal after a lengthy investigation. Then Ari Ben-Menashe, a former Israeli intelligence officer and veteran spinner of stunning yarns, charged that Robert Gates (now director of the CIA) was present at three 1980 meetings between William Casey, then Reagan's campaign manager, and Iranian officials in Madrid. Allegedly, they discussed delaying the release of the 52 hostages in Iran in return for shipments of arms. Ben-Menashe also claims that Gates attended a meeting in Paris, which included then vice-presidential candidate George Bush. President Bush calls the charges "bald-faced lies," and neither ABC's *Nightline* nor the *Financial Times* of London was able to confirm Ben-Menashe's claims. But others, like veteran investigative reporter Seymour Hersh—who has written a book about Israel's secret nuclear program—have found some of Ben-Menashe's testimony credible. If Casey in fact cut a deal with Iran to delay the release of the hostages, the act would verge on treason. If no such bargain was ever struck, the reputations of innocent men have been smeared.

North Walks

It was probably inevitable. In September all charges against Oliver North, the former White House aide who carried out Iran-*contra*, were dismissed by a federal judge. As the news sped through Washington, some of the air went out of the hearings on Robert Gates' appointment to head the Central Intelligence Agency. The North dismissal, dimming any prospect of further immunity deals for key Iran-*contra* players, all but ensured that the Senate would never fully learn what Gates knew about the scandal.

Four years ago, Senate select committees on Iran-*contra* granted North limited immunity from prosecution in return for hearing his side of the story. That gave North a large opening: though he was subsequently found guilty of obstructing Congress and mutilating government documents, his attorneys convinced an appeals-court judge that the case should be reviewed to ensure that none of the witnesses in his trial had been influenced by the televised hearings. In early September, North's old boss, former National Security Adviser Robert McFarlane, said he had indeed been swayed by the retired Marine's emotional testimony.

Independent counsel Lawrence Walsh faced a choice: he could either prosecute North again or let the matter drop. Walsh chose to write North off and concentrate on prosecuting Clair George, the CIA's former chief of covert operations, who was indicted for lying or obstruction during a series of investigations into the Iran-*contra* affair. Pronouncing himself "totally exonerated," North declared, "I've had my last hearing."

Many experts predicted this outcome when lawmakers granted North immunity. Today some who supported that decision question its wisdom. "The lesson is that the Congress, when they grant immunity now, must be very cautious," said Democrat Lee Hamilton, "because doing so probably defeats any criminal prosecution."

Shootout over Gun Control

Like rival gunfighters, the National Rifle Association and Handgun Control Inc. stalked each other for months. With 2.7 million members and an annual budget of $86 million, the giant N.R.A. seemed to tower over the bantamweight gun-control group, which has only 1 million members and a $6.5 million budget. But after the smoke cleared on Capitol Hill last May, advocates of gun control had triumphed in a 239-to-186 House vote for the so-called Brady bill. Named after James S. Brady, the former White House press secretary who was crippled in the attempted assassination of President Reagan in 1981, the bill calls for a seven-day waiting period for the purchase of handguns. The proposal is designed to give police time to check a purchaser's criminal and mental-health records (although it does not require such checks); furthermore, say advocates, the wait will provide a "cooling-off" period for hot-headed customers.

But in October, the same week that George Hennard killed 23 people with semiautomatic pistols at Luby's Cafeteria in Killeen, Texas, the N.R.A. triumphed when the House voted 247 to 177 to defeat a measure banning 13 different assault weapons.

The Gag Rule

When politicians latched on to the abortion issue as the sort of emotional question that extracts votes and campaign funds from true believers, they unleashed a venomous public argument. That debate heated up again last May when the Supreme Court voted 5 to 4 to uphold a federal regulation conceived in 1988 that bans discussion of abortion in federally funded health clinics.

Critics call the regulation the "gag rule," and, indeed, the court's ruling in *Rust v. Sullivan* made little medical or intellectual sense. It does not forbid women to seek abortion counseling and referrals. But it narrows—and in some cases may even eliminate—access to such services for many poor and low-income women who cannot afford private medical advice, thereby placing informed choice beyond their reach. "For these women," Justice Harry Blackmun warned in a harsh dissenting opinion, "the government will have obliterated the freedom to choose as surely as if it had banned abortions outright." In early November, House and Senate both approved legislation to overturn *Rust v. Sullivan* and restore Government aid to thousands of clinics under Title X of the Public Health Service Act. But on Nov. 19, President Bush vetoed Congress's initiative in order to assuage his conservative constituency.

The Keating One

In November, after 22 months, the Senate Select Committee on Ethics finally punished the last of the Keating Five. The committee found that only California Democrat Alan Cranston, 77, had engaged in "fund raising and official activities [that] were substantially linked." Cranston was reprimanded for accepting $850,000 in contributions from financier Charles Keating while interceding on his behalf with bank regulators who were trying to seize Keating's failing savings and loan.

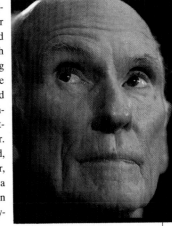

The committee found that Cranston's conduct had been "improper and repugnant," but those were mild words to describe the dealings with Keating. In one instance, a Keating aide gave Cranston $250,000 at the same meeting during which he agreed to plead Keating's case. Cranston insisted that what he had done for Keating was not unusual for a Senator. How many lawmakers, he demanded, "could rise and declare you've never, ever helped—or agreed to help—a contributor?" To which Republican Warren Rudman snapped, "Everybody doesn't do it."

A Heartbeat Away

It seemed like a routine Saturday for George Bush. The President was relaxing at Camp David after flying home from Ann Arbor, where he had given a commencement address at the University of Michigan. In the middle of the afternoon he donned his running togs and began to pound the trails of the retreat. At 4:20 the President was suddenly stricken with fatigue and shortness of breath. Secret Service agents walked him to the Camp David infirmary, and from there he was rushed by helicopter to Bethesda Naval Hospital.

Tests indicated that Bush had suffered from an irregular heartbeat, or atrial fibrillation, a condition that was caused by Graves' disease, a thyroid ailment, but is not a serious health threat. There were no signs of heart damage. By early evening the President was dining on steak and salad. Vice President Dan Quayle had been immediately informed, but no moves were made to activate the lines of presidential succession. Public concern about Bush was probably intensified by the fact that his designated successor is not highly regarded as a potential President. Bush's attack provided a momentary scare—and a stark reminder that even the most vigorous of Presidents is only a heartbeat away from eternity.

Sununu's Slide

For weeks, as his standing in the polls dropped and fears grew that the economy might stagger back into recession, George Bush had been under pressure from both friend and foe to do something to get his presidency back on track. In early December, Bush finally did something. He replaced contentious White House chief of staff John Sununu with a man who is temperamentally his exact opposite: Transportation Secretary Samuel Skinner, a likeable moderate who is one of the Administration's smoothest troubleshooters.

Sununu's tenure as Bush's right-hand man was anything but smooth. His troubles began in earnest last spring, when it was reported that Sununu had made frequent flights on Air Force executive jets—including trips to ski resorts and his New Hampshire home—that have cost the taxpayers more than $500,000 during the past two years. And what Sununu did once he got off the planes raised serious ethical questions. Since he joined the Bush Administration, Sununu and his family have taken at least four trips that were financed in large part by corporate interests. Yet federal law forbids officials to accept valuable gifts, including travel and recreation, except from certain charitable and educational organizations.

In the Bush Administration, the cardinal rule is not merely to avoid conflicts of interest but to avoid even the appearance of doing wrong. There were signs that Bush, while careful to support his lieutenant in public, was smoldering in private. Then, in June, Sununu ordered the driver of his government limousine to take him to New York City, where he spent the day buying rare stamps at Christie's. Dismissing the driver, Sununu returned to Washington on a private jet owned by Beneficial Corp. Once again, Bush was embarrassed.

Sununu had been insensitive to conflicts of interest since he was Governor of New Hampshire from 1983 to 1988. He took trips on state planes for purposes that aides considered personal. He used personal computers that were "lent" to him by firms doing business with the state. He accepted tuition wavers and subsidies from Tufts University for his children long after he had stopped teaching there. Says a Sununu ally from New Hampshire: "John was a taker even when he was Governor. He is one who has always seen fit to exercise power rather than discretion."

While Sununu was valuable to Bush as a link to the G.O.P.'s right wing, his real value was as the President's enforcer, the "abominable no man" who acted as a lightning rod for the Commander in Chief. But at year's end, Sununu's ethical lapses began to catch up to him, and Beltway insiders questioned his leadership. At one point, Sununu seemed to criticize the President for a remark about high interest rates on credit cards; at another point, he accosted a Washington *Post* reporter, shouting, "Everything you write is lies!"

By mid-November, after several of Bush's political strategists warned that they would find it difficult to work with Sununu on the 1992 campaign, Bush concluded that his chief of staff had become a serious liability. Yet the President, who values loyalty above all else, could not bring himself to personally give the bad news to his old friend. Instead, he delegated the assignment to his oldest son, George W. Bush, who met with Sununu on Nov. 27.

But Sununu deluded himself into thinking that he could save his job by rallying conservatives behind him. Instead of resigning, he began phoning conservatives on Capitol Hill and elsewhere, imploring them to let the President know they supported him.

Some lawmakers responded positively to Sununu's appeal. But the chief of staff's many enemies in Washington saw an opportunity to take revenge. Republican leader Robert Dole, who has seethed since Sununu helped Bush win the 1988 New Hampshire primary by suggesting that Dole was a closet advocate of higher taxes, coldly spurned him. Then Dole twisted the knife by describing Sununu's phone call to a television interviewer. Some White House officials and G.O.P. strategists were miffed that Sununu was trying to end-run the President. Bush himself was reported to be "chapped" by what seemed to be an attempt to blackmail him into retaining Sununu.

On Dec. 3, Sununu gave in. He delivered a handwritten resignation, stating that as a private citizen he would continue supporting Bush "in pit bull mode or pussey [sic] cat mode (your choice, as always)." He will remain at the White House as a counselor to the President until March 1, presumably to help steer the Bush campaign through the New Hampshire primary.

Sununu's downfall pleased many White House staff members who had long chafed under his imperious management. A senior official answered a reporter's call by singing, "Ding, dong, the witch is dead." Said a somewhat disgusted David Carney, a White House political aide who has worked for Sununu for 11 years: "Are people gleeful today that John Sununu is leaving? Absolutely . . . Is he surprised? Not at all. He played hardball, and he got hardball. He knows how politics works, and he wasn't in this to win any popularity contests."

A Lawyer Who Changed America

Thurgood Marshall did his best to outlast the Republican Presidents he frequently calls "those bastards." But his 83rd birthday was approaching, his health was so poor that he said he was "coming apart," and there was not much hope that a liberal Democrat would recapture the White House and name his successor. On June 27, Marshall, the first African American to serve as a Justice of the Supreme Court, gave up the seat he had held since 1967. Four months later, Clarence Thomas was sworn in as Marshall's replacement—but only after an acrimonious confirmation process in which Thomas was charged with sexual harassment by Anita Hill, a former colleague.

Despite his physical frailty and growing philosophical isolation from his fellow Justices, Marshall's was no meek or defeated departure. His last words from the bench were a stinging rebuke to the court's conservative majority. In a 6-to-3 decision, the Justices ruled that prosecutors in death-penalty cases could introduce evidence about the character of the victim and the suffering caused by the crime—thereby reversing a precedent that was only four years old. This brought thunder from Marshall. "Power, not reason, is the new currency of this court's decision making," Marshall wrote. In the cases overturned, "neither the law nor the facts . . . underwent any change in the last four years. Only the personnel of this court did."

The implications of discarding established legal principles to

pursue a political agenda, Marshall charged, were staggering. High on his list of "endangered precedents" are cases involving the right to abortion, affirmative action, limitations on the death penalty, and separation of church and state. The new approach, he added, "will squander the authority and legitimacy of this court as a protector of the powerless."

More than any other Justice of his era, Marshall brought an experience of the real world, of growing up poor, of fighting for principle. His views on the death penalty, for instance, were shaped by the lessons he learned defending people charged with murder. He is the only one to have put his own life at risk by trying volatile cases in the segregated South. Indeed, he was the victorious attorney in *Brown v. Board of Education*, the 1954 landmark decision that prohibited racial segregation in public schools. As a Justice, Marshall sometimes helped change American law. As a civil rights lawyer he changed America. "He is truly a living legend," says Harvard law professor Laurence Tribe. "It is hard to think of another lawyer in the 20th century who has played a more important role."

Toughie, Smoothy, Striver, Spy

Robert Gates was an eagle scout and an A student, a wholesome Kansas kid who met his wife-to-be on a hayride. He yearned to become a doctor or a teacher, and volunteered to tutor needy students. His college honored him as the graduate "who has made the greatest contribution to his fellow man." So how did a nice guy like Gates get into the spy business?

Nominated in May by President Bush to serve as director of Central Intelligence, Gates began his CIA career "on a lark" in 1965. He accepted a recruiter's invitation to an interview just for "a free trip to Washington." Once he got there, however, things got serious. The agency asked Gates to join, not as a "spy" but as a deskbound analyst, and he accepted. He scrambled rapidly up the career ladder, drawing praise for cogent analysis and crisp writing. Fast-forward a quarter-century and Gates, now 48, is the youngest—and most experienced—CIA director since the agency was founded in 1947.

Before he was confirmed on Nov. 5, Gates had to win the Senate confirmation that eluded him in 1987. Then the agency's deputy director, he was criticized for not acting on indications that the Iran-*contra* scandal was afoot. No wrongdoing by Gates was proved, but he withdrew his name from nomination to spare President Reagan further embarrassment.

This time, a number of his former colleagues suggested that Gates helped enforce a kind of political correctness on the way information was assessed and presented at the CIA. They said they believed Gates leaned on analysts to stretch evidence in support of sus-

picions—that the Soviets were behind the 1981 assassination attempt on the Pope, that the Kremlin had a master plan to deny the U.S. access to critical natural resources in Africa and elsewhere. Oozing contrition, Gates put up a spirited defense. He apologized for not pressing his CIA boss, the late William Casey, harder about Iran-*contra*. Gates also admitted the agency had placed too much emphasis on cloak and daggery, and even vowed to resign if illegal activity occurred on his watch.

The CIA of Robert Gates will attempt to outgrow its cold war roots. Policymakers demand intelligence on new topics, from industrial counterespionage to the AIDS epidemic's devastation of the élite in several African countries. Budget cutters hungrily eye the estimated $30 billion in often redundant spending by the CIA and other elements of the intelligence community. To address these challenges, Gates offers close ties with the White House and Pentagon, broad CIA experience and a black belt in bureaucratic politics.

Overwhelming Changes, Uncertain Outcomes

By PAUL GRAY

If all the world's a stage, its scenery shifted dramatically in 1991. Iraq, which menaced the Middle East when the year began, was driven out of Kuwait, its armies humiliated and its infrastructure pounded. The general sigh of relief at this outcome was checked by Saddam Hussein's continued hold on power in his battered country, but at least his capacity to wreak havoc in his neighborhood had been thwarted. Order, it seemed, had been restored.

But while matters sorted themselves out around the Persian Gulf, another story with vast implications was slowly, inexorably unfolding. Mikhail Gorbachev's long attempt to reform the Soviet Union while simultaneously maintaining its unity began to fail visibly. The two goals had always seemed inherently at war with each other. In arguing for less centralization of production and more individual initiative at the local level of factories and farms, Gorbachev had implicitly undermined communist economics and the authority of the Communist Party itself. The system was collapsing of its own weight. Long lines of shoppers waiting to browse over emptying shelves provided daily testimony that things were falling apart. The question was, Could the center hold?

No clear answer seemed in sight as the year began. In late January, while the world's attention hovered over Iraq, the three Baltic states of Estonia, Latvia and Lithuania declared their independence from the Soviet Union. This action posed a direct and potentially fatal threat to Gorbachev's vision of an improved but still united U.S.S.R. If the Baltics were allowed to go their own way, others of the 15 Soviet republics would surely wish to follow. Under pressure from Kremlin hard-liners, Gorbachev sent in the troops. Skirmishes and some bloodshed followed. But the brute, implacable power that had crushed anti-Soviet uprisings in Hungary in 1956 and Czechoslovakia in 1968 seemed largely missing in the Baltics. What in the old days would have been a rout resolved itself into a stalemate.

The breaking point for this impasse began during several astonishing days in August. The coup against Gorbachev was not entirely unexpected; a number of observers, both in the U.S.S.R. and in the West, had predicted that old-line Communists would not tolerate Soviet deterioration indefinitely. Still, news that Gorbachev had been toppled and was being detained in the Crimea came as a shock. What happened next proved even more surprising: the rapid collapse of the coup, thanks in part to the ineptitude of the plotters and the spirited public resistance rallied by Russian President Boris Yeltsin. Behind these factors rested a larger lesson, clear amid the civilian barricades and defiant crowds of Muscovites. It was no longer possible to clamp the Soviet Union together through force.

One of the surpassing ironies of those few, hectic days in August was that Gorbachev's restoration to power resulted in the dissipation of that very power. The coup and its failure stood as final repudiations of the old Soviet way of doing things. Having been rescued by the reformers, Gorbachev was no longer in a position to enforce obedience or unity. The Communist Party was banned because of its support of the attempted coup. The Baltic states were allowed to go free. With dizzying speed, other Soviet republics announced their independence, in varying degrees, from the central government in Moscow. In December 11 republics, led by Russia, Ukraine and Belorussia, ratified a commonwealth among themselves and named Minsk its capital. In less time than anyone could have foreseen, Mikhail Gorbachev had become a man without a country.

It is impossible to predict all the effects that will follow from the disappearance of the Soviet Union. The presence of nuclear arms and the question of who will control them remain worrisome. There is a threat of further disintegration within the old U.S.S.R. into warring ethnic or religious groups. The evidence of Eastern Europe is not comforting on this point. In the most glaring case, Yugoslavia collapsed into a bloody civil war between Serbs and Croats.

But the waning of Soviet influence even before the collapse manifestly affected other areas of the globe during the past year. The allied effort against Saddam Hussein would have been much harder to mount and sustain if the U.S.S.R. still had the will or inclination to oppose it. The tentative talks between Israel and its neighbors surely were prompted in part by Arab recognition that Moscow is no longer a reliable ally. The same realization may have hastened the release of all but two of the Western hostages by terrorist groups in the Middle East.

Against this backdrop of overwhelming and uncertain change, some of the events of 1991 still seemed familiar, and occasionally dismaying. On the positive side, the South African government and members of the once outlawed African National Congress made substantial, startling progress in the dismantling of apartheid and the building of a representative government. European nations proceeded along the path that is to unite them economically in 1992. More bad but not especially surprising news came out of Haiti, where a military coup toppled the first democratically elected President in the nation's history. And in India, while campaigning to become Prime Minister, Rajiv Gandhi met the violent fate of his mother Indira, dead of assassination.

Any year that included the collapse of a superpower would be considered eminently memorable. The historic importance of 1991 is already beyond debate. Something important ended. What will take its place remains to be seen.

The Russian Revolution

No Soviet Union? That huge blob of blood red that dominated maps of the Eurasian landmass for 70 years now broken up into a crazy quilt of squirming lines enclosing a kaleidoscope of colors? The concept is even harder to grasp than the idea of a noncommunist Soviet Union. Well, almost anything may yet emerge out of the chaos that has followed the second Russian Revolution. But on two central facts everyone is agreed: the old unitary state in which the Kremlin tightly controlled life is dead; the Other Superpower that overshadowed the 20th century is no more. "The former union has ceased to exist, and there is no return to it," says Anatoli Sobchak, the reformist mayor of St. Petersburg—a city once called Leningrad.

ANATOMY OF A COUP

It may have been the most widely advertised coup in history. Rumors and warnings had begun as early as the summer of 1990. According to British intelligence, elements of the Soviet army and KGB actually rehearsed a coup (under the guise of a countercoup) in February 1991. June brought what was soon called the "constitutional-coup attempt." Prime Minister Valentin Pavlov asked the Supreme Soviet for the authority to issue decrees without Mikhail Gorbachev's knowledge but was rebuffed. In late July hard-liners published an announcement appealing for "those who recognize the terrible plight into which our country has fallen" to support dramatic action to end disorder. They might as well have put up billboards shouting COUP!

In hindsight, even the timing seems screamingly obvious. Gorbachev had designated Tuesday, Aug. 20, for the ceremonial signing of a new union treaty with the presidents of the Russian and Kazakh republics; other republics were expected to sign later. The treaty would transfer so many powers—over taxes, natural resources, even the state security apparatus—to the republics as to make restoring ironfisted Kremlin control of the whole country impossible. Moreover, a new national Cabinet would have been named by the republics. Some of the eventual coup leaders, including KGB chairman Vladimir Kryuchkov, Defense Minister Dmitri Yazov and Interior Minister Boris Pugo, would almost certainly have lost their jobs. The plotters could not afford to let that treaty go into effect.

Yet Gorbachev by his own testimony was totally unprepared. To some scholars and Soviet officials that appears so

Boris Yeltsin, fist upraised, rallies his forces in the center of Moscow

odd as to suggest that the President himself had staged a Potemkin coup to win sympathy. But that seems farfetched. More probably, the very volume and intensity of coup talk had dulled his political antennae. Alexander Yakovlev, a close adviser, claimed after it was all over that he had even given Gorbachev the names of some likely—and, as it turned out, actual—plotters. The President, according to Yakovlev, had scoffed that they "lack the courage to stage a coup."

A little before 5 p.m. on Sunday, Aug. 18, the head of the President's security guards entered Gorbachev's office at his Crimean vacation retreat at Foros and announced that "a group of people" were demanding to see him. Who were they, asked Gorbachev, and why had they been let into the house? They were accompanied by Yuri Plekhanov, the chief of the state security-guard organization, said Gorbachev's man; that was all he knew. Gorbachev picked up a phone to call Moscow. "It didn't work. I lifted the second [phone], the third, the fourth, the fifth. Nothing." All his communications had been cut.

Instantly realizing what might be up, Gorbachev went to another room, called in his wife, daughter and son-in-law and warned them that his visitors might "attempt to arrest me or take me away somewhere." Returning to his office, he found that the delegation had already bulled its way in. There were four besides Plekhanov. Gorbachev initially named only one: Valeri Boldin, his own chief of staff. It was as if John Sununu had joined a coup against George Bush. The others were finally identified as Oleg Baklanov, deputy chairman of the National Defense Council; a Communist Party hack named Oleg Shenin; and General Valentin Varennikov. In the name of the so-called State Committee for the State of Emergency, the visitors demanded that Gorbachev sign a decree proclaiming an emergency

and turning over all his powers to Vice President Gennadi Yanayev. Gorbachev's reply: "Go to hell."

By then, a special detachment of KGB troops had surrounded his vacation house. Just in case Gorbachev somehow got out and tried to return to Moscow, KGB units drove tractors across the runway of the nearby airport to prevent Gorbachev's TU-134 presidential jet from taking off.

Roughly 12 hours passed before the outside world knew anything. But at 6 a.m. Monday, Aug. 19, TASS, the Soviet news agency, reported falsely that Gorbachev was ill and had yielded his powers temporarily to Yanayev. An hour later, TASS announced the formation of the eight-member State Committee for the State of Emergency, ostensibly headed by Yanayev. Actually, this gray apparatchik was only a figurehead; the real power probably was held by Kryuchkov, Pugo and Yazov, plus possibly lesser-known figures. Some of Russian republic president Boris Yeltsin's aides later fingered Baklanov as the chief plotter. The committee announced that it would rule by decree for six months. All newspapers except for nine pro-coup sheets were ordered to stop publishing, political parties were suspended and protest demonstrations banned. Muscovites had to maneuver around troops and tanks that were moving to seize key installations.

Yet it was obvious even that early that the coup was ill planned and curiously halfhearted. The plotters neglected to immediately arrest popular potential enemies before they could begin organizing a resistance. In particular, the failure to make sure that Yeltsin was taken into custody was fatal. Inexplicably, the putschists did not even pull the plug on the communications of anyone except Gorbachev. Bush was amazed at how easily he could get through by telephone to Yeltsin, and Yeltsin seems to have had no difficulty coordinating action with other coup opponents.

Most successful coup organizers also begin by moving reliable troops into key positions. Yet the Soviet plotters used only troops and equipment that happened to be on hand and gave the soldiers only the vaguest idea of what they were supposed to be doing.

Far from being prepared to crush opposition, the troops were obviously under orders to avoid confrontation and above all not to shoot. Citizens shouted at the troops and scrawled swastikas on tanks parked outside the Russian Parliament Building with impunity. When the coup leaders decreed a curfew from 11 p.m. to 5 a.m., the soldiers made no attempt to enforce it.

Why were the coup plotters so inept? Simple incompetence might be one answer; several were party hacks who had never displayed much imagination . They may have thought that the economic collapse that had made Gorbachev wildly unpopular, coupled with a Russian tradition of submissiveness to authority, would win the populace to their side without bloodshed. They may even have been corrupted, so to speak, by the new atmosphere of democracy— at least to the extent of feeling a need to give their coup a cloak of constitutionalism, which in turn prevented them from acting with the ruthlessness a successful coup generally requires. Alternatively, some American officials think plotters were not so much inept as unable to round up enough support.

But many powerful Soviet figures who wound up opposing the coup were initially noncommittal or played highly ambiguous roles. Alexander Dzasokhov, a secretary of the Central Committee of the Soviet Communist Party, tried to paint the party as a resolute opponent of the conspirators. "From the very beginning of the coup," he said, the committee secretariat "demanded that they see Gorbachev." In fact, though, Nursultan Nazarbayev, president of Kazakhstan, says the Central Committee on Monday secretly urged local party organizations to support the junta.

Soviet Foreign Minister Alexander Bessmertnykh came down with a vaguely defined illness, one of several seeming cases of "coup flu." (Symptoms: cold feet and a weakening of the backbone.) Bessmertnykh climbed out of his sickbed to denounce the plot only after it was falling apart—too late to keep from getting fired. General Mikhail Moiseyev, Chief of the Soviet General Staff, was perhaps conveniently on vacation in the Crimea when the coup began. But some of his subordinates claimed he

wrote out the orders for the troops to occupy key points in Moscow—as well as the orders for them to go back to their barracks when the coup was failing.

Even Yeltsin reportedly had a moment of irresolution. On Monday morning he hurried to the Russian republic headquarters— nicknamed the White House because of its marble façade—and was joined by other coup opponents. One of them, former Soviet Interior Minister Vadim Bakhatin, says they urged Yeltsin to proclaim himself in command of all army and KGB units on Russian republic soil. Bakhatin recounts that Yeltsin was reluctant. He feared that such an order would split the army and perhaps start a bloody civil war. Bakhatin and others, however, convinced Yeltsin that if no one exercising constitutional authority was willing to countermand orders from the junta, the army might eventually invade the White House and arrest them all, and the coup would succeed.

From then on, Yeltsin never wavered. At 12:30 p.m. Monday he clambered atop an armored truck outside the White House to announce the decree assuming command. He denounced the coup as illegal and unconstitutional and called for a general strike to thwart it. In retrospect, that was the first and perhaps the biggest turning point. Yeltsin had made it obvious that the coup would face determined resistance; his appearance helped inspire protest demonstrations throughout the country. At the time, however, its significance was not entirely apparent. No more than about 200 Muscovites had gathered outside the Russian republic building to see and hear his fiery performance. But as word spread, the crowd grew and grew until it eventually numbered in the tens of thousands.

At 5 p.m. Monday the conspirators finally called a press conference. Their performance was a disaster. Far from coming across as a take-charge group, they appeared nervous and half apologetic. They gave a preposterous excuse for assuming authority (Gorbachev was too tired and ill to retain command); stressed that the coup was a constitutional devolution of authority to Yanayev, although it clearly was not; and proclaimed a highly dubious devotion to continued reform. Junta member Vasili Starodubtsev sniffled continually, and Yanayev seemed twitchy. As Gorbachev later commented, "They said I was sick, but they were the ones whose hands were shaking."

Gorbachev apparently was listening if not watching. His security guards stayed with him at the Foros dacha and scrounged up some old radio receivers

Looking drawn but relieved, Gorbachev arrived back in Moscow at the end of his ordeal in August

so they could monitor foreign radio coverage of the coup. Though he said he had been subjected to "psychological pressure," this apparently consisted of isolation rather than any actual interference with his activities. The President spent part of his time drafting an angry condemnation of the coup and made four videotapes of himself to prove he was not sick. Fearing that the worst might happen to him, he also recorded his last will and testament. Gorbachev's wife Raisa was apparently quite shaken by the experience and was later reported to be receiving medical treatment.

In the outside world, the tide was beginning to turn. By Tuesday morning the Western powers unanimously, though separately, proclaimed a clear line: no normal relations with the Soviet Union until legitimate authority was restored, and a quick and indefinite cutoff of most of the economic aid that the U.S.S.R. desperately needed.

Tuesday afternoon brought one telltale indication that the junta was losing what grip it had established. After obediently reporting all the pronouncements of the so-called Emergency Committee and little else, TASS suddenly began interspersing them with reports of the burgeoning resistance. For example, it let Soviet citizens know that Aleksei II, Patriarch of the Russian Orthodox Church and a signer of a December 1990 appeal for a law-and-order crackdown, had come out against the coup.

Tension nonetheless built toward a climax Tuesday night. It was obvious that the junta could no longer prevail unless it began using deadly force, starting with an armed assault on Yeltsin's White House. All afternoon and evening, loudspeakers blared warnings that tanks were rolling toward the building and 60 planes filled with paratroopers were preparing for an airborne assault. Thousands of people worked through the night building barricades to deter an attack, supplemented by human chains of unarmed protesters. Just before midnight, short bursts of gunfire did echo from nearby streets. It was not, however, the start of an assault but a scuffle between tanks and protesters around a barricade. Three demonstrators were left dead—the only Moscow casualties of the coup.

Otherwise, nothing happened. All day Tuesday and Wednesday morning, Yeltsin's aides were on the phone to KGB chief Kryuchkov and Defense Minister Yazov, asking them point-blank if the junta planned to storm the White House. "Yazov did not deny it," they reported. Finally Kryuchkov promised, "You can sleep soundly." There would be no shoot-out.

Why not? Reports differed in detail but agreed in essence: the armed forces would not carry out any order to attack.

Wednesday morning there was a seemingly ominous flurry of military activity. Soviet troops in Lithuania and Estonia took control of several radio and TV stations; in Moscow paratroopers shut down an independent radio station that had resumed broadcasting the day before. But those actions quickly turned out to be the plotters' last gasp. The failure to storm the White House on Tuesday made clear that the junta would not or could not resort to the serious bloodshed that by then would be necessary to crush resistance. By Wednesday the plotters evidently concluded that the jig was up, and the coup fell apart with astonishing speed.

THE BALTICS
Aug. 19
Massive military movements in the area begin, including naval blockades. Soviet troops seize communication centers and other key buildings in the republics' capitals.
Aug. 20–21
Estonia and Latvia declare immediate independence. Clashes occur outside the Latvian and Lithuanian parliaments; one man is killed in Lithuania. After the coup's collapse, the Soviet troops begin their withdrawal and finally abandon all institutions they had seized, some of them occupied since January.
Aug. 22–23
In Lithuania and Latvia, the parliaments outlaw the Communist Party. In Estonia and Lithuania, statues of Lenin are torn down.

LENINGRAD
Aug. 19
Anatoli Sobchak, mayor of Leningrad, immediately proclaims the coup committee unconstitutional, and calls on the population to rush to the defense of the city council. Thousands protest the coup outside the Winter Palace. Sobchak's decisive actions and protest stop the army from entering the city.
Aug. 21
5,000 people spend the night outside the city council building to protect it from possible attack.

BELORUSSIA
Aug. 20
The central committee of the Communist Party supports the coup, but members of the republic's supreme soviet oppose it.

MOLDAVIA
Aug. 20
Mass anticoup demonstrations take place in Kishinev. Prime Minister Valeriu Muravski bans the nine newspapers sanctioned by the coup.
Aug. 23
Republic adopts resolution outlawing Communist Party activities.

UKRAINE
Aug. 19
Republican radio and TV are shut down.
Aug. 20
8,000 rally to protest the coup. The parliament declares the actions of the coup's leaders to be null and void.

THE CRIMEA
Aug. 18
Gorbachev is placed under house arrest at his summer home in Foros.
Aug. 21
Four conspirators fly to see him as the coup crumbles and are promptly arrested. Gorbachev leaves for Moscow.

GEORGIA
Aug. 19
When the coup starts, President Zviad Gamsakhurdia asks his people to remain calm.
Aug. 23
Gamsakhurdia calls for a ban of the Communist Party and nationalization of party property.

ESTONIA
Baltic Sea
LATVIA
LITHUANIA
Tallinn
Riga
Leningrad
Vilnius
POLAND
Minsk
BELORUSSIA
Moscow
MOLDAVIA
Kiev
ROMANIA
UKRAINE
Kishinev
Odessa
Black Sea
Yalta
Foros
Black Sea
Caspian Sea
GEORGIA
Tbilisi
Yerevan
Baku
ARMENIA
AZERBAIJAN

0   500   1,000 miles
0   500   1,000 km

Army tanks and troops
Those that defected to Yeltsin
Barricades erected by Yeltsin supporters

On Tuesday, Yeltsin addresses a crowd of 150,000 in front of **Russian Parliament.**

New U.S. Embassy (under construction)

On Friday, Gorbachev and Yeltsin purge top officials and appoint proven reformers. The move reflects a possible power-sharing arrangement between the two leaders.

Riot police are ordered to wait near the **Bolshoi Theater**

KGB headquarters

Statue of Dzerzhinsky (founder of the secret police) is pulled down on Thursday.

U.S. Embassy

Moscow River

Kalinina Prospect

Manezh Square

Red Square

Communist Party headquarters

Kalininsky Bridge

Three Yeltsin supporters are killed here on Tuesday

On Wednesday, junta members try to flee to Vnukovo Airport, 19 miles (30 km) away.

The coup is run from the general staff headquarters in the **Ministry of Defense.**

Kremlin and surrounding area are sealed off by dozens of armored vehicles and hundreds of riot troops.

The putschists station truckloads of riot police behind **St. Basil's Cathedral.**

Moscow River

MOSCOW
1 mile
1 km

THE ARMY

On Aug. 19, two élite armored divisions, the Tamanskaya and the Kantemirovskaya, and one airborne division, the Tulskaya, are moved into Moscow. Of those, the Tulskaya division and a tank detachment of the Tamanskaya division side with Yeltsin.

When the putschists realize that troops are defecting, they decide to send in the élite KGB airborne Vitebskaya division. The units of that division, however, halt some 12 miles (19 km) from the Russian Parliament and never enter the city.

Three special KGB battalions and two special-purpose battalions of the military intelligence service are deployed in the capital as well.

More than 300 men from the police schools in Bryansk, Orel and Vladimir side with the Russian government, rushing to Moscow to defend the parliament building.

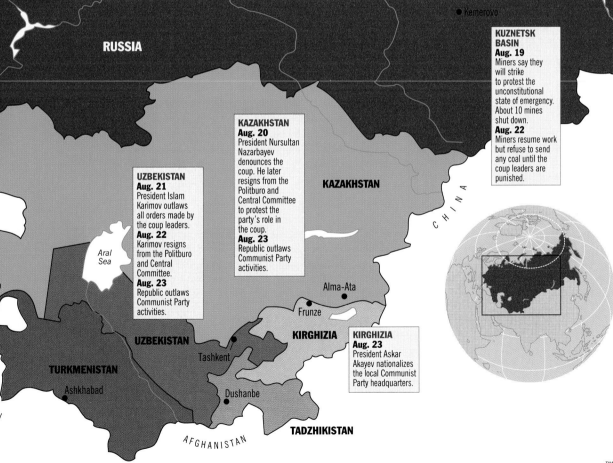

● Kemerovo

RUSSIA

KUZNETSK BASIN
Aug. 19
Miners say they will strike to protest the unconstitutional state of emergency. About 10 mines shut down.
Aug. 22
Miners resume work but refuse to send any coal until the coup leaders are punished.

KAZAKHSTAN
Aug. 20
President Nursultan Nazarbayev denounces the coup. He later resigns from the Politburo and Central Committee to protest the party's role in the coup.
Aug. 23
Republic outlaws Communist Party activities.

KAZAKHSTAN

CHINA

UZBEKISTAN
Aug. 21
President Islam Karimov outlaws all orders made by the coup leaders.
Aug. 22
Karimov resigns from the Politburo and Central Committee.
Aug. 23
Republic outlaws Communist Party activities.

Aral Sea

Alma-Ata

Frunze

UZBEKISTAN

KIRGHIZIA

KIRGHIZIA
Aug. 23
President Askar Akayev nationalizes the local Communist Party headquarters.

Tashkent

TURKMENISTAN

Ashkhabad

Dushanbe

TADZHIKISTAN

AFGHANISTAN

TIME Map by Nigel Holmes
Research by Deborah L. Wells
and Leslie Dickstein

A new balance of power: Yeltsin—not Gorbachev—is now the senior partner

At 2:15 p.m., Yeltsin announced to the Russian parliament that some of the conspirators were running to Vnukovo Airport to get out of town. A delegation headed by Yeltsin's vice president, Alexander Rutskoi, chased after them. One hour earlier, TASS announced that the Defense Ministry had ordered all troops to clear out of Moscow. Bystanders cheered as soldiers, some waving prerevolutionary Russian flags, rode atop armored vehicles on their way back to bases.

After two days of isolation, Gorbachev was suddenly again besieged by visitors from Moscow, this time competing for his favor. Some of the conspirators tried to flee the capital. Pugo, for example, was originally rumored to be aboard a plane headed for Central Asia, but in fact was soon admitted to a Moscow hospital with gunshot wounds, apparently self-inflicted, from which he died. Kryuchkov and Yazov, however, did get to Vnukovo Airport ahead of their pursuers, and hopped a plane for Gorbachev's resort. They were accompanied by Anatoli Lukyanov, chairman of the Soviet parliament. Though he is an old friend of Gorbachev's, Lukyanov played at best an ambiguous role in the coup; he has been accused by some of Yeltsin's aides of being the mastermind behind the whole plot. Hard on their heels, Rutskoi and his avengers also took off for the Crimea.

Possibly Kryuchkov and Yazov hoped to negotiate with Gorbachev an end to the coup that would preserve some of their power. Or maybe they simply intended to beg forgiveness. Rutskoi and his friends, however, feared they might want to kill the Soviet President. When Kryuchkov and Yazov arrived at his dacha, Gorbachev demanded that they be arrested (Lukyanov was not arrested but was suspended from his job pending an investigation). Rutskoi and his gun-toting party, who got to the dacha shortly after, were delighted to do that job.

All this took so long that Gorbachev did not get back to Moscow until 2:15 a.m. Thursday. Stepping off the plane, he looked haggard but flashed a relieved smile, rather like the released hostage that he was. In theory, at least, he was back in full command. In fact, he faced gigantic tasks of rounding up the plotters, alleviating the economic and social chaos that had provided the excuse for the coup, and working out a modus vivendi with Yeltsin. As for the surviving plotters, all of whom had been arrested by week's end, they were facing not only treason trials but also the knowledge that their mismanaged coup had intensified the move toward democracy and decentralization they had tried to stop. The three days that shook the world were over.

INTO THE VOID

Something new was born, improvised on a grand scale. But its final shape has yet to be chiseled. In the wake of the popular upheaval that defeated the putsch, the Treaty of Union—designed to limit Moscow's control, and worked out by the Kremlin and nine of the Soviet Union's 15 republics in June—quickly became a dead letter, judged totally inadequate to slake the republics' thirst for independence.

After the collapse of the coup, the three Baltic republics—Latvia, Lithuania and Estonia—achieved independence and were formally recognized by Gorbachev. But the headlong trend toward dissolution did not stop there. In early December, 90% of Ukrainians approved a referendum calling for complete independence from the Soviet Union, seeming to scuttle Gorbachev's hopes of forming some sort of viable new union.

Nor was there any guarantee that the remaining republics could hold together. Carried to its extreme, in fact, the movement toward

Like the fallen statue of Dzerzhinsky, the KGB's fate hangs in the balance

disintegration could splinter the former U.S.S.R. into upwards of 40, mostly mini, countries—the 15 full republics plus some of the 20 autonomous republics, eight autonomous regions and 10 smaller autonomous areas. Most are homelands of distinct ethnic groups that cherish ambitions to become autonomous in fact as well as name.

To be sure, nobody expects the dissolution to go that far. Certainly, one reason for the republics' eventual decision to form a commonwealth was the concern over a self-destructive splintering of authority. Gorbachev refused to resign until assured that some sort of union would be preserved, and St. Petersburg's Sobchak called a complete dissolution of the union "suicidal."

In retrospect, the Soviet government dissolved at breakneck speed. In the wake of the coup attempt, the Communist Party virtually disappeared overnight, its leadership disbanded, its offices padlocked, its funds frozen. The Supreme Soviet suspended party activities throughout the U.S.S.R., formalizing what had already been accomplished by decree in the republics. The Soviet parliament also dismissed the entire Cabinet of Ministers after Gorbachev bluntly declared, "I cannot trust this Cabinet, and that is that."

That left a "transitional government" to be run by a variety of makeshift executive bodies. The most important of these was a four-member commission headed by Ivan Silayev, prime minister of the Russian republic, charged with drawing up an economic-reform plan for the former Soviet Union. As the commonwealth took shape, however, the transitional effort soon withered away.

An air of confusion marks much of the democratic upheaval. The Institute of Geography of the Soviet Academy of Sciences counts 75 border disputes, the great majority entangled with ethnic conflicts. In fact, much of the secessionist spirit reflects real ethnic hostility; indulging it could be a recipe not just for chaos but for bloodshed. Another threat is the specter of economic collapse, possibly leading to outright famine. Soviet production and distribution of food, fuel and virtually everything else are already in a deep slump because the old system of central planning and commands has long since broken down and nothing coherent has taken its place. A splitting up of political authority among heaven knows how many republics could make the situation much worse.

Indeed, as the year came to an end, the Soviet Union simply ceased to exist. On Sunday, Dec. 8, three newly independent states—Ukraine, Belorussia and Russia, which together constituted 75% of the U.S.S.R.—declared the end of the Soviet Union and the formation of a commonwealth of independent states; eight other republics eventually joined them. The new commonwealth will be governed from Minsk rather than Moscow. Gorbachev, his power base eroding since the August coup, resigned in late December. In the West, some Sovietologists looked forward to the formation of a new, stable union. But others were concerned by the prospect of another civil war and the possibility that dissidents would try to gain control of Soviet nuclear weapons.

Outside powers have only marginal ability to influence what happens inside the former Soviet Union. Soviet citizens must decide their fate themselves, while the world holds its breath. The failed coup and the turmoil that has followed are fundamentally enormously hopeful events. If the immediate results are chaotic—well, revolutions by their nature cannot be tidy. The trouble is that the most democratic revolutions can so easily degenerate into lasting chaos, out of which a new dictatorship can be born. Remember the February 1917 revolution that overthrew the Czar, the chaos that followed, and the November 1917 Bolshevik coup, which established the tyranny that has only now been broken—maybe.

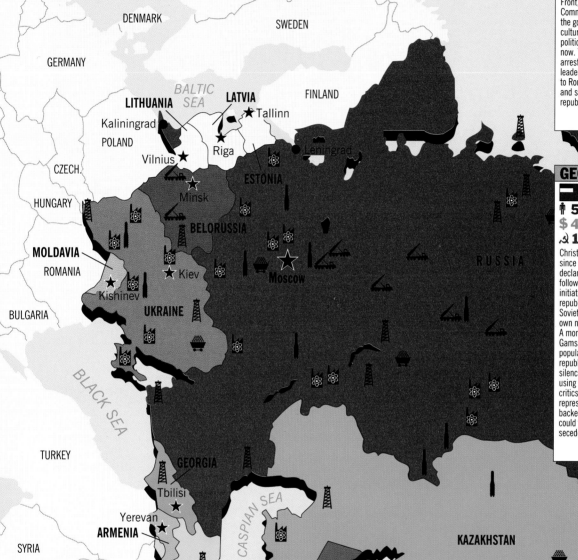

Silo-based ICBMs **Mobile-based ICBMs**

Oil **Coal** **Nuclear power**

REPUBLIC

Flag   Ethnic breakdown

👤 Population, 1990

$ Per capita GNP, 1989

☭ Established as a separate republic of the Soviet Union

MOLDAVIA

👤 **4.4m**

$ **3,830**

☭ **1940**

64% Moldavians
14% Ukrainians
13% Russians
4% Gagauzi
2% Bulgarians

The parliament voted for independence last week, but the republic's rich vineyards and tobacco fields seem inadequate for self-sufficiency. Prior to 1940 Moldavia was part of Romania, and two-thirds of its population is ethnic Romanians. The nationalist Moldavian Popular Front, which progressively ousted the Communists from power and took over the government in 1990, favors close cultural links with Romania, but a political merger seems unlikely for now. The front used the failed coup to arrest troublesome ethnic minority leaders who rejected the 1989 change to Romanian as the official language and set up their own "sovereign" republics last year.

GEORGIA

👤 **5.5m**

$ **4,410**

☭ **1936**

70% Georgians
8% Armenians
6% Russians
6% Azerbaijanis

Christian Georgia, boldly nationalistic since Khrushchev's days, formally declared independence in April, following a series of parliamentary initiatives that exempted the republic's youth from service in the Soviet army and created Georgia's own national guard, 12,000 strong. A month later, noncommunist Zviad Gamsakhurdia became the first popularly elected President of a Soviet republic. But he is accused of silencing the independent press and using harsh methods to intimidate his critics. Ossetians, who complain of repression by Georgian nationalists, backed the failed Moscow coup, and could fight for their own right to secede.

NORWAY

DENMARK

SWEDEN

GERMANY

FINLAND

BALTIC SEA

LITHUANIA   LATVIA

Kaliningrad   ★ Tallinn

POLAND

Vilnius ★   Riga

ESTONIA

CZECH.

Minsk

HUNGARY

BELORUSSIA

Leningrad

MOLDAVIA

RUSSIA

ROMANIA   ★ Kiev

BULGARIA

Kishinev ★   Moscow

UKRAINE

BLACK SEA

TURKEY

GEORGIA

Tbilisi ★   *CASPIAN SEA*

Yerevan ★

SYRIA   ARMENIA

KAZAKHSTAN

★ Baku   *ARAL SEA*

AZERBAIJAN

LAKE BALKHASH

IRAQ

UZBEKISTAN

Ashkhabad   Alma-Ata ★

IRAN   ★

Tashkent ★   Frunze

TURKMENISTAN   Dushanbe ★   KIRGHIZIA

AFGHANISTAN   CHINA

TADZHIKISTAN

Sources: PlanEcon; *Soviet Military Power*; *Journal of Soviet Nationalities*; Flag Research Center
Time Graphic by Pugliese/Lertola

UKRAINE

51.8m
$4,700
1922

73% Ukrainians
22% Russians
1% Belorussians
1% Jews

Because of Ukraine's abundant industry and agricultural production, Moscow viewed its declaration of independence last week with alarm. Kiev was equally fearful when Russia reserved the right to challenge the borders of secessionist neighbors, which Ukrainians took as a threat to reclaim the former Russian territories of the coal-rich Don basin and the Crimea. The republics have now promised to respect each other's borders and have formed a temporary military and economic alliance, which they urged other states of "the former U.S.S.R." to emulate.

BELORUSSIA

10.3m
$5,960
1922

78% Belorussians
13% Russians
4% Poles
3% Ukrainians

The parliament's declaration of independence came as a surprise from the most conservative of the western republics, but since communists still control the legislature, the move was seen as a way of holding on to power. The same session forced government leader Nikolai Dementei to resign because of his complicity in the coup, but General Eduard Shirkovski, head of the local KGB, and General Prosecutor Georgi Tarnavski, both of whom had supported it, kept their posts. Though there has been little nationalist pressure for secession, there have been strong protests against food-price increases and calls for an end to one-party rule. There is also lingering resentment over the central government's handling of Chernobyl.

ARCTIC OCEAN

BERING SEA

0 — 500 MILES
0 — 800 KILOMETERS

ARMENIA

3.3m
$4,710
1936

93% Armenians
3% Azerbaijanis
2% Kurds
2% Russians

The parliament announced a year ago that it would seek independence under the April 1990 Soviet law on secession, the first republic to invoke it, and a referendum on independence is scheduled later this month. Christian Armenia has been embroiled in a blood feud with its mainly Muslim neighbor Azerbaijan since 1988. In that year the Armenian enclave of Nagorno-Karabakh voted to secede from Azerbaijan, and thousands of Azerbaijanis subsequently fled from Armenia, leaving it one of the few republics with virtually no ethnic minorities. Hostility toward the Muslim republic remains strong. Many citizens fear that independence could also leave them vulnerable to their ancient enemy, Turkey, without protection from Moscow.

AZERBAIJAN

7.1m
$3,750
1936

83% Azerbaijanis
6% Russians
6% Armenians

Late last week Azerbaijan joined the independence club, a considerable turnaround for the conservative republic and for communist leader Ayaz Mutalibov, who long resisted secessionist pressures from the Popular Front. The move could also further the nationalists' long-term goal of uniting with their ethnic kin in Iran. Most Armenians have fled in the wake of pogroms, and minority Russians also fear Azerbaijani nationalism. Two days after the Moscow coup began, Mutalibov issued a statement supporting the Emergency Committee. When the coup collapsed, the statement was suppressed, but a copy was found by the Popular Front and published. To fend off calls for his resignation, Mutalibov ordered closure of communist headquarters in Baku.

KAZAKHSTAN

16.7m
$3,720
1936

40% Kazakhs
38% Russians
6% Germans
5% Ukrainians

Politically, Kazakhstan has been slow to change. It declared sovereignty in October 1990 only after 13 other republics had done so. President Nursultan Nazarbayev, who resigned from the Politburo and Central Committee to protest the coup, wants a new union treaty establishing a commonwealth. To calm Kazakhs angry at renewed Russian territorial claims, the two republics signed a pledge to respect common borders and work at preventing the "uncontrolled disintegration" of the Soviet Union. But ethnic tensions could flare up.

RUSSIA

148m
$5,810
1922

82% Russians
4% Tatars
3% Ukrainians
1% Chuvashes

No republic has profited so richly from the failed coup. What remains of the Soviet central government is rapidly being taken over by the largest republic, but President Boris Yeltsin's strengthening of Russian authority has antagonized leaders of other republics as well as Soviet President Gorbachev. He authorized Russia to take control of union ministries like the Kremlin that are situated on its territory. But he has had to rescind imperialist orders commandeering the Soviet Union's central banks. Although Yeltsin still sees a role for a streamlined central government, he champions a union treaty and has been wooing other republics to join in.

TURKMENISTAN

3.6m
$3,370
1925

72% Turkmen
10% Russians
9% Uzbeks
3% Kazakhs
1% Ukrainians

Usually the Soviet Union's calmest republic, little has been heard from its capital since the coup. Except for a declaration of sovereignty in August 1990, democratization has achieved minimal progress. But the republic has quietly made known its discontents. Before the coup, President Saparmurad Niyazov called the new union treaty ambiguous and said he did not think it would be signed for some time. He also said Kremlin leaders should not have the right to levy taxes in his republic and reap exclusive profit from its rich natural-gas reserves and cotton harvest. Now, Niyazov may be willing to work out a new kind of alliance with Russia.

UZBEKISTAN

20.3m
$2,750
1925

71% Uzbeks
8% Russians
5% Tadzhiks
4% Kazakhs

Trying to cling to power, President Islam Karimov resigned from the Communist Party Central Committee and Politburo two weeks ago and instructed parliament to draft legislation on independence. But conditions are not favorable: high population growth has led to privation and unemployment, which have fueled ethnic and social unrest, and pollution is diminishing cotton production. Leaders of the five Central Asian republics—the U.S.S.R.'s poorest—signed an economic cooperation pact this month, and nationalists are increasingly demanding that if the five break free from Moscow, they should unite into a single state. But many in the other four fear domination by the more numerous Uzbeks.

TADZHIKISTAN

5.3m
$2,340
1929

62% Tadzhiks
24% Uzbeks
8% Russians
1% Tatars
1% Kirghiz
1% Ukrainians

The smallest of the Central Asian republics declared sovereignty in August 1990, and two noncommunist political parties, one Islamic, have been established. In April leaders tried to carry out Moscow's price reforms, but citizens resisted. Unemployment has been rising in the impoverished republic. Riots in February 1990, triggered by rumors that Armenian refugees would receive preferential housing, resulted in the mass emigration of non-Tadzhiks—mostly Uzbeks and Russians who fear that they will be victims of nationalist violence—shrinking the pool of professionals and skilled workers. The push to revive Tadzhik culture is growing stronger, and interest in Islam is rising, including the improvement of business and cultural ties with Iran.

KIRGHIZIA

4.4m
$3,030
1936

52% Kirghiz
22% Russians
13% Uzbeks
3% Ukrainians
2% Germans

The Central Committee of the Communist Party fired its entire staff after the coup attempt and scheduled a congress for November. The liberalization drive begun last October by President Askar Akayev has launched a market-oriented reform program. But progress is slowed by ethnic rivalry. A 1990 land dispute sparked fighting between Uzbek and Kirghiz communities in Osh, leaving some 200 dead. The area remains mired in poverty, rising unemployment and land shortages, and sporadic violence continues among Tadzhik, Uzbek, Kirghiz and Russian residents.

Perils of Nationhood

The Baltics have reclaimed their independence, but won't be able to break from Moscow's grip entirely

The general growled his warning over the telephone. As élite Soviet paratroopers were ordered into the Baltic republics in early January, Fyodor Kuzmin, the regional commander, rang up the presidents of secessionist Lithuania, Latvia and Estonia with a stony message. If your people obstruct the mission to round up draft dodgers, he said, the troops will shoot. On Jan. 11, in an atmosphere of mounting confrontation, General Kuzmin kept his word.

Moving to seize Lithuania's self-defense headquarters and main printing plant in Vilnius, armed assault forces opened fire at the plant. Though most soldiers apparently fired blanks and only one colonel used live ammunition, eight people were reported wounded, one young man shot in the face. Angry young civilians at the publishing center surrounded a tank. "Why are you here?" they screamed. "What are you doing?" Lithuanian President Vytautas Landsbergis, charging that troops were "spilling blood," placed an urgent call to Mikhail Gorbachev. The Soviet President could

not come to the phone, Landsbergis was told; he was having lunch.

Fretful foreign governments wondered whether Gorbachev would countenance bloodshed to suppress the independence movements. A chilling indication came when thousands of Lithuanians, singing freedom songs, tried to prevent Soviet troops and tanks from taking control of a television tower outside Vilnius. Shots were fired, and 15 unarmed demonstrators were killed. At least two of the dead had been crushed beneath the treads of Soviet tanks.

A week later, a squad of thuggish Soviet special forces troops, known as black berets, attacked the Interior Ministry in neighboring Riga, Latvia. In a 30-minute exchange of gunfire, they killed two Latvian militiamen, a well-known filmmaker and a bystander.

"Gorbachev is using the world's attention on the gulf to get away with this," said Geoffrey Hosking, a Soviet-affairs expert at London University. Indeed, the confrontations in the Baltics began to recall events in Hungary in 1956, when the Soviet army moved against a restive population under cover of another Middle East flare-up, the Suez crisis.

All three Baltic states took the position that they were illegally absorbed into the U.S.S.R. in 1940 and were not part of the union. The republics were under no illusions that they could defeat the Kremlin, but they refused to sign Gorbachev's proposed union treaty or consider anything short of full independence. A lopsided stalemate set in. But the Soviet President soon found himself in an untenable situation: old-line communists attacked him for not bringing the rebels to heel, while reformers condemned him for using force to halt nonviolent political activity. The bloodletting touched off a 100,000-strong protest march in Moscow and a stream of warnings from abroad.

What broke the impasse was the desperate attempt by communist hard-liners to seize control of the Soviet Union in August. When the coup failed, Gorbachev was restored to the Soviet presidency and renounced any attempt to keep the Baltic republics in the Soviet Union.

Once Lithuania, Latvia and Estonia reclaimed their freedom, foreign ministers and diplomats from around the world seemed almost breathless in their rush to establish diplomatic relations. The first new ambassador on the scene was Denmark's Otto Borch, who arrived Aug. 27 and said, "No assignment I have received has brought me greater pleasure than this one."

The same day, the 12-nation European Community announced its recognition of the Baltics. At an emotional ceremony in Bonn, the foreign ministers of the three republics personally accepted Germany's recognition. The 1939 nonaggression treaty between Nazi Germany and the Soviet Union set the stage for Stalin's annexation of the Baltic states the following year. "It is only today," said Estonian Foreign Minister Lennart Meri, "that the last consequences of the Second World War have been done away with."

Meanwhile, the French and Swedish foreign ministers flew to the Baltics to prepare for the opening of their new embassies. By early September more than 30 countries—including the U.S.—had recognized the states as independent. Later in the month, all three states became members of the United Nations.

Crushing dissent: tanks roll against protesters at the television center in Vilnius, but Moscow says they brought it on themselves

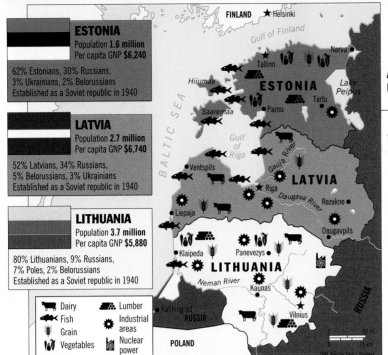

TIME Map by Paul J. Pugliese

ESTONIA
Population 1.6 million
Per capita GNP $6,240

62% Estonians, 30% Russians,
3% Ukrainians, 2% Belorussians
Established as a Soviet republic in 1940

LATVIA
Population 2.7 million
Per capita GNP $6,740

52% Latvians, 34% Russians,
5% Belorussians, 3% Ukrainians
Established as a Soviet republic in 1940

LITHUANIA
Population 3.7 million
Per capita GNP $5,880

80% Lithuanians, 9% Russians,
7% Poles, 2% Belorussians
Established as a Soviet republic in 1940

Dairy
Fish
Grain
Vegetables
Lumber
Industrial areas
Nuclear power

After 51 years, Estonia, Latvia and Lithuania have reclaimed their freedom from the U.S.S.R.

— World

bassies open in Vilnius, Riga and Tallinn, the Baltics will remain dependent on trade with the other 12 Soviet republics.

About 60% of the Baltics' gross national product comes from trade, almost all of it in raw materials imported from the other Soviet republics and processed goods re-exported to them. Hopes for large-scale foreign investment remain only hopes, in spite of the generous tax exemptions that have been offered over the past year. Baltic officials say Western businessmen have stayed away because of political instability, and it is likely to be a while before many foreigners feel confident enough about the region's future to invest.

Perhaps the biggest problem for the Baltics is the oil supply. They import 97% of their fuel and pay for it in rubles at low, centrally subsidized prices. While overall trade between the Baltics and the other republics will probably hold level for some time, oil-rich republics like Russia will want to charge market prices, up to 10 times the present rate, for their fuel. That could cost Lithuania $700 million a year in hard currency it does not have. In July Lithuania charted a new course by signing an economic-cooperation treaty with the Russian republic, and it now hopes to barter food for oil. Latvia is less fortunate, since it doesn't even produce enough grain to feed itself. In Estonia both industrial and agricultural production are declining.

To make the burden worse, local officials and what remains of the central government will have to settle who owns which portions of the major Moscow-controlled industries that are based in the Baltics. They include electronics factories, locomotive plants and telecommunications and semiconductor producers. Not only will the Baltic governments have to compensate Moscow for those enterprises, they will have to manage them with a work force that consists overwhelmingly of ethnic Russians who were recruited specifically to move to the Baltics for those jobs.

A treaty between Lithuania and Russia ratified in August guarantees the civil rights of their citizens in both republics. Even so, many of the 1.7 million Russians in the Baltics are so fearful of retribution that Yeltsin apparently decided he had to fly to Latvia for two days to reassure them.

The Baltic governments would welcome some reassurance. On the day the European Community recognized the Baltics, its commission published a report estimating that the three new nations would need financial aid totaling $3 billion to carry them through their painful transition to a market economy. The E.C. invited the Baltic foreign ministers to meet to sign a special agreement on association with the Community. The Balts will attend with high hopes that special-association status may bring aid and investment with it. But, wisely, they are hedging their bets. Though all three Baltic countries plan eventually to issue their own currency, they will continue to use the ruble for the immediate future.

While officials in Moscow did not dispute the fact that the Baltics were out of the Soviet Union—and Russia's Boris Yeltsin recognized them—Gorbachev insisted that the final terms of their departure be negotiated. Baltic leaders shared that view to some extent, if only to ensure a process that frees their republics from the grip of the more than 100,000 Soviet military, KGB and Interior Ministry troops still based there.

Those negotiations have born fruit. Lithuanians will no longer be drafted for the Soviet army, and those in uniform now will be released. Lithuanians and Soviet guards are working together at border crossings. Estonia's parliament is to begin work on legislation setting up the republic's own Defense Ministry. Yeltsin informed the Baltic governments that the short-range nuclear weapons formerly on their soil have already been shipped back to Russia. KGB operations in Latvia have been banned, and all three republics plan to take over their security services.

Lithuania's President Vytautas Landsbergis, who has been the firmest, most uncompromising Baltic leader, insists he wants all Soviet forces to go home. "Our needs would not be served by having Soviet troops here," he says. "I would like to see the withdrawal begin this year." Landsbergis conceded, however, that it might not be completed until all Soviet forces are pulled back from Germany around the end of 1994. The troops withdrawing from the West will need staging areas along their supply lines.

Latvian President Anatoli Gorbunovs was less insistent. After talks with new Cabinet ministers in Moscow, he said that his country might allow the Soviet armed forces to use its bases during an extended transition period. Other local officials suggest offering base rights to Soviet naval and air units with the idea of earning hard currency from the leases.

That question—how to earn money and make their way in the world—is the toughest one facing the Balts. Their road to independence has been hard and bloody, and the jubilation that followed their success was short-lived. They have virtually no natural resources, few products good enough for export to the West and little hard currency to pay for their needs. No matter how many new em-

Out of Control

A hotbed of nationalism that sparked World War I, the Balkans ignite a new crisis as Serbs and Croats open full-scale civil war

Not long ago, the reputation of the Balkans as the tinderbox of Europe seemed to have faded. Yugoslavia was the acceptable face of communism: estranged from Moscow, a pioneer of peaceful coexistence with the West, a country whose rugged Adriatic coastline attracted tens of thousands of vacationers. But last September that idyllic image was shattered. After three months of ethnic skirmishing, hapless Yugoslavia erupted in the first full-scale war in Europe since 1945. The fighting between federal forces and breakaway Croatia gave the world beyond a stark reminder of the region's capacity for violence.

A HISTORY OF STRIFE

The threads that have stitched together an unwieldy federation of rivalrous ethnic groups since World War II have been unraveling for years. Since 1981, the 1.7 million Albanians in the Serbian-controlled province of Kosovo have been agitating for separate status. In the spring and summer of 1990, the northern republics of Slovenia and Croatia voted to install noncommunist, Western-oriented governments, while Serbia, the largest republic, chose to retain its communist government—lately renamed socialist. Those divisive events were followed by a referendum in which 88% of Slovenia's 2.1 million citizens voted for independence.

Secessionist fever in Croatia, meanwhile, nearly erupted in war when Belgrade accused Croatian defense minister Martin Spegelj of fomenting an armed insurrection. Federal troops were called in, and a tense standoff was resolved only when Croatia agreed to demobilize—but not disarm—its police reservists.

The intractable conflict that has riven Yugoslavia's two major nationalities has festered since the country was established. The Serbs, who threw off Turkish rule in the 19th century, are Christian Orthodox; the Croats, who were subjugated by the Habsburg Empire, are Catholics. Their mutual hatred and distrust has grown more virulent as nationalist ambitions seethe throughout Eastern Europe. Only the suzerainty of socialism imposed by Josip Broz Tito after World War II managed for a time to keep the rivalry in check. Now that has crumbled.

THE FLASH OF WAR

Mid-September, the Serb-dominated Yugoslav military threw itself into the conflict with a will. Federal gunboats boomed off the Croatian coast as warplanes and artillery opened fire on targets across the secessionist republic. A massive column of federal battle tanks, armored personnel carriers and 155-mm howitzers set out from Belgrade to assault Croatia's eastern wing, which borders on Serbia. In another action, two columns of federal reservists marched into Bosnia-Herzegovina, shattering the tense calm of that buffer state with its explosive mixture of Serbs, Croats and Slavic Muslims. When an oil refinery blew up under attack in Osijek, Croatia's key city in the east, it became clear that a region long dormant had loosed a volcano of passions.

On Oct. 1, Dubrovnik, the architectural jewel of the Adriatic coast, came under siege. In November, 50,000 civilians spent days huddled in underground cellars and shelters while shells tore apart their matchless city. With potable water and food in ever diminishing supply, terrified Yugoslavs subsisted on powdered milk and the forlorn hope that the international community might finally come to their rescue.

To the north and east along the banks of the Danube River, the stench of decomposing livestock, pets and people wafted through the rubble-strewn streets of Vukovar. Through 12 weeks of fighting, 58,000 townspeople had fled. The 12,000 who remained behind cowered in the town's cellars and sewers, rolling cigarettes from tea leaves and burning strips of oil-soaked cloth for light. "This is hell," Vesna Vukovic, a Croat television reporter, moaned over the airwaves. "We cannot stand it anymore."

It was a cry of despair from a civilian population that has seen its collective lives, homes and loved ones laid waste by artillery and gunboat bombardments. The relentless barrages on Dubrovnik and Vukovar were only the most dramatic reminders of the human toll in this vengeful war between Europeans—the worst on the Continent since 1945. No one had even begun to add up the economic and physical damage to the country. Was anybody with the power to stop the carnage listening?

Only perhaps. After almost five months of hostilities, 12 failed truces and a death tally of more than 7,000, the Croatian and Serbian militias signaled in mid-November that even they might finally have had enough. In the most promising bid yet for a true cessation of hostilities, both sides agreed to the proposed dispatch of United Nations peacekeeping forces. Croatia, which had lost control of almost a third of its territory, for the first time invited U.N. troops to be stationed in areas populated by Serbs. In exchange, the Yugoslav federal army, which has acted in tandem with Serbi-

At the front: a flaming barricade erected by Slovenian militia

Noncommunist republics seeking independence or loose federation

Communist republics wishing to retain the present federation

Republics seeking compromise

$ Average monthly net wages per worker

Grains

Livestock

Manufacturing

Mining

* Serbian province which has voted to be a full republic

TIME Map by Paul J. Pugliese

an militias, announced that it would withdraw from Croatian territory if the security of the Serbian enclaves could be assured.

The move toward a resolution of the crisis seemed to take a little of the ferocity out of the fighting. In Dubrovnik, where the guns were stilled to permit the evacuation of wounded civilians and 14 European Community monitors, a tenuous cease-fire held from one hour to the next. In Vukovar the fighting also subsided, largely because the Serbs seemed to have subdued the Croatian forces, despite reports that an organized force of holdouts had taken refuge in the sewer system. Although the army continued to pound Vukovar with rockets and artillery, a Western diplomat said, "They're not doing much now but making the rubble bounce."

Silencing the guns in Vukovar may be a symbolic achievement. The quaint town in the eastern Slavonian region of Croatia is one of two large areas in the republic populated predominantly by Serbs, which gives it a significance disproportionate to its size and population. The federal army intervened in force to show that it could defend embattled Serbs; the Croats dug in to demonstrate that they could hold out on their own soil. The results proved only how futile this war really is. The ill-armed paramilitary forces fielded by the Croats learned that they could not stand up to the overwhelming military superiority of the army. As for the army, it "defended" Serb civilians so thoroughly that barely a single Serbian house is left intact.

The months of war have touched every pocket of Croatia, where the lessons learned are certain to breed hatred for generations to come. An estimated 500,000 Croats and Serbs have fled the republic since war erupted following its June 25 declaration of independence. To make matters worse, about 1.5 million Yugo-

slavs, fully 12% of the labor force, are now jobless. Many of the unemployed have signed up with local paramilitary forces.

Serbian, Croatian and federal army authorities have little faith that fighting will soon end. Although officials reached agreement on a 13th truce in mid-November, none of them exercise full control over the paramilitary forces. Major General Milav Pujic, a Deputy Minister of Defense, estimates that to hold territory one peacekeeping soldier will be needed for every 10 civilians. It remains an open question whether the international community has the manpower, the stomach or the sympathy for such a massive operation.

Lives in Limbo

In August, British journalist John McCarthy was freed in Beirut after 1,940 days of captivity

With the last of the American hostages now home, the former captives tell their harrowing tales of horror and courage

Terry Anderson may have lost 2,455 days of his life, but he has lost none of his journalistic instincts. "The worst day?" he said in response to a question from the reporters. "The worst day I had was Christmas of 1986." A veteran storyteller, Anderson first set the scene. He was in solitary. Similarly confined but within eyeshot were fellow hostages Tom Sutherland, John McCarthy and Brian Keenan. "We had nothing, no books, nothing."

Anderson unfolded the tale, offering his colleagues a bit of a scoop. "One thing we could do—and my captors may be surprised to learn this—was talk to each other." Anderson explained that he had learned sign language in high school, a one-handed alphabet that he had taught the other captives. On this bleak day Anderson was relaying silent messages to Sutherland, who would pass them on to Keenan, and so forth. Then, calamity struck. "I took off my glasses and dropped them and broke them," he said. "My eyes are very bad. Couldn't see." End of silent, cell-to-cell dialogue. End of story. "That was a bad day," he concluded.

Anderson's release on Dec. 4 seemed to unburden other ex-hostages of their "survivor's guilt" and uncork fresh memories of physical pain and mental anguish. If a single thread ran through the recollections, it was the abject despair each man experienced when confined in solitary, and the mutual appreciation each felt for his fellow hostages when they were penned together. As for their own fortitude, they left the marveling to others. "You just do what you have to do. You wake up every day, and you summon up the energy from somewhere," Anderson said without dramatic effect.

Of the three men freed the first week of December, only Anderson, 44, appeared to emerge whole, albeit somewhat thinner, somewhat balder and with a hint of a limp. Journalism professor Alann Steen, 52, who suffered permanent neurological damage when he was kicked by his captors for unwittingly prolonging an exercise period, will remain on medication for the rest of his life to control seizures and blackouts. University administrator Joseph Cicippio, 61, whose skull is still dented from the clubbing he received at the time of his capture five years ago, will live out his life with a burning sensation in his fingers and toes, the result of the frostbite he suffered during a winter spent chained on a partially exposed balcony.

It was hard to imagine surviving even a single day, as the details of the hostages' living conditions piled up: airless, windowless cells barely larger than a grave, in which the men could not stand upright. Extreme temperatures, both hot and cold. Filthy blindfolds. Steel chains that were never unlocked, save for the 10-minute daily visit to the "toilet," a fetid hole in the ground. Months without baths. Meals that never varied: bread, cheese and tea for breakfast and dinner; boiled rice and vegetable-something-or-other for lunch.

To this nightmare were added moments of indignity that scorched the soul. Father Lawrence Jenco's first glimpse of Anderson back in 1985 was through a crack in a partition. There was Anderson, blindfolded and chained to a bed, surrounded by guards who kept walking around him, tossing off mocking salutes and shouting, "Heil Hitler!" Several of the hostages were led to believe they would be released imminently, only to have their hopes callously dashed. "One night they said I was going home and dressed me in nice clothes," Jenco recalls of his 564-day captivity. "When I dressed, they said, 'Just kidding,' and laughed. I started to cry."

For different reasons and at different times, some of the hostages surrendered to despair. Anderson's former cell mates recall how in December 1987, when the journalist was forbidden to send a Christmas message to his family, he slammed his head against a wall until the blood streamed down. Sutherland, who shared a cell with Anderson through most of his 2,353-day captivity until his release in November, revealed that he had attempted suicide three times.

What pulled the men through such moments of hopelessness? For Sutherland it was thoughts of his family. For Anderson it was a Bible and a pho-

Western hostage held longest: Associated Press reporter Terry Anderson with his sister Peggy Say upon his release in December

tograph of his daughter Sulome, now six, whom he met for the first time in December. Three bare wires hanging from the ceiling evoked for the Rev. Benjamin Weir the fingers of the painting on the ceiling of the Sistine Chapel. Others discovered a faith they never knew they had. "Before I didn't believe in God, and now I do," Frenchman Roger Auque told the British press after his 319 days in captivity.

Humor leavened more than a few low moments. Each night when the guards would ask if they needed anything before going to sleep, Sutherland would suggest a fighter-bomber, Jenco would ask for a taxi, and some wise guy would inevitably pipe up with an order for a glass of wine.

Sometimes the ribbing carried a harsh undercurrent, which may have been the safest way of venting the anger the hostages could not afford to direct toward their captors. On rare occasions tensions erupted in hostility, such as the episode in September 1985, when captors invited a group of hostages to select among themselves who should go free. Anderson and David Jacobsen nearly came to blows, and Weir won—by the captors' choice.

Relations with their captors were far rockier. Nine men died in captivity. After his release, Anderson disclosed that he believes CIA station chief William Buckley perished right in the cell with him in June 1985. The pneumonia-ridden Buckley died choking on his own fluids.

Most of the time the guards and their captives had a mutual understanding. "We had to do anything they said," says Sutherland. "If they said stand up, we had to stand up. If they said sit down, we had to sit down. They wouldn't tolerate any disobedience." If hostages obeyed the rules they were left alone. Although conditions were unhygienic, the captors could be roused to action when real illness threatened. Robert Polhill received regular insulin injections for his diabetes. Cicippio was hospitalized for two months for a stomach ailment. British church envoy Terry Waite was given both an air-conditioner and medicine for his asthma. There were a few flashes of human compassion. Jenco was taken to a roof one night. Thinking he was about to be shot, Jenco says he discovered that "the guard merely wanted me to see the moon." In 1985 at Christmas—cited as the most dismal day of the year—some hostages were presented with a cake.

It is a testimony to their strength of character that many of the ex-hostages speak of the need to forgive their former captors. "I'm a Christian and a Catholic," Anderson said in December. "It's required of me that I forgive, no matter how hard it may be." Father Jenco, by contrast, argues, "Anger is a very good emotion. Even Jesus got angry." While there is little evidence of the Stockholm Syndrome, wherein captives begin to identify with their tormentors, several of the former detainees seem to have some empathy for the plight of the underpaid men who held them. Similarly, many of the ex-hostages harbor no bitterness toward the Bush Administration for its failure to secure their release sooner.

Now the newly released hostages must turn their attention to the rest of their lives. After so many years in captivity, the smallest tasks excite and bewilder. Sutherland says he washes his hands a hundred times a day. Jesse Turner says the hardest adjustment is "getting used to freedom, deciding what I'll do next." Anderson admits, "I've forgotten what it's like to have to be organized." History has flashed along at astonishing speed in their absence, and they must catch up. Sutherland already has a fax machine, which he must learn to operate. Both Turner and Anderson have daughters, born during their captivity, whom they must get to know. "I have a whole new life," Anderson says. "It's going to be happy, God willing."

Finally Face to Face

Hostile exchanges open the Arab-Israeli peace conference, but the rat-a-tat is sound bites and speeches, not guns

Outside the conference hall there were a few grudging handshakes among advisers, but also shouted epithets like "terrorist!" and "murderer!" In formal sessions Arab, Palestinian and Israeli delegates would rarely even look at one another as they laid their cases before the world, but nobody walked out. At the end of three days it was uncertain, in the most literal sense, where the talks were going: the delegates concluded the opening phase by quarreling bitterly about whether they should continue meeting in Madrid or move to some different venue.

This is a peace conference?

Absolutely, and already one for the history books. No amount of confrontational rhetoric could obscure the simple fact that Israelis, Palestinians and other Arabs, sworn blood enemies for more than four decades, were sitting around a table, talking. The speechmaking in the tapestry-hung Hall of Columns of the Royal Palace in Madrid that opened the Middle East peace conference on Oct. 30 was,

like a wedding or a baptism, a solemn rite symbolizing a new beginning. Come what may, the Middle East crisis, perhaps the longest-running and most envenomed in the world, had passed the point where the antagonists would not even talk.

Which is not to say that negotiations will succeed. The participants were talking to the U.S., their own constituents, the rest of the world, far more than to one another. If the conference started out as well as could be expected, that is because everyone has learned to expect little. President Bush warned that no agreement could be foreseen in "a day or a week or a month or even a year." Meanwhile there would be snags, deadlocks, perhaps even temporary breakdowns.

So it was not surprising that both the Israelis and their adversaries began with statements that restated old grudges. Substantive discussions will come later—maybe; the opening was devoted to posturing and symbolism. The Arabs and Israelis were there only

because Bush and U.S. Secretary of State James Baker had seen to it that they could not afford to be absent. Boycotting the talks would have given the boycotters a black eye in world opinion. Attending allowed them to play to the biggest audience ever.

Rival spin doctors advised more than 5,000 journalists how every word and gesture ought to be interpreted. Every part of the arrangement was calculated to make, or avoid, some symbolic point: no flags were allowed at the negotiating table, because the Israelis would not sit in the same room with a Palestine Liberation Organization banner.

On the outside chance the peace talks do break up, it will probably be over a symbolic point. October's opening was supposed to be followed by bilateral negotiations in Madrid between Israel and each of three enemies: Syria, a Palestinian-Jordanian delegation and Lebanon. But the Israelis demanded that the talks be moved to the Middle East. By bringing Arab negotiators to Jerusalem and then sending its own diplomats to Arab capitals, Israel hoped that its neighbors would recognize it in fact, if not officially, as a genuine nation. For exactly that reason, the Arabs resisted the idea. Eventually, the Bush Administration persuaded the negotiators to meet in Washington. But on Dec. 4, when the second round of talks was meant to take place, the Israeli delegation failed to appear; however, talks began the following week. The White House expressed disappointment at the Israeli delay, and admonished Jerusalem for erecting a new Jewish settlement in the occupied West Bank just as the negotiators were gathering in Washington. To speed the process along, the United Nations General Assembly voted on Dec. 16 to rescind a 1975 resolution equating Zionism—the movement on which Israel is founded—with racism.

In Madrid the main participants played their hands with varying degrees of skill and clumsiness:

▶The U.S. scored a considerable victory in getting the talks started at all, dramatizing its unchallenged status as the world's sole remaining superpower. Bush did not need to make that point; Soviet President Mikhail Gorbachev did it for him. The Soviet Union is nominally co-chairman of the conference, and its participation enabled some Arabs to claim that they were not just knuckling under to the U.S. But Gorbachev made it clear that Moscow would pretty much go along with whatever the U.S. wants.

The delicate U.S. task is to keep the talks moving without getting trapped into so direct a role that it would seem to be arm-twisting one side or the other. Bush and Baker tiptoed through that minefield adroitly enough. The President reassured a wary Israeli delega-

tion by speaking of "territorial compromise" instead of "land for peace," a formula that Israelis loathe. He also backed the Israeli view that the conference should lead not just to nonbelligerency but to "real peace" as well. Explained Bush: "I meant treaties. Security. Diplomatic relations. Economic relations. Trade. Investment. Cultural exchange. Even tourism." At the same time, he responded to an Arab concern by calling for everyone to "avoid unilateral acts" that might "prejudice" the peace process. Translation: Israel, stop building those settlements in the occupied territories.

Baker closed the round by sharply chiding delegates for failing to look to the future, but judging when and how to step in to bridge gaps will be the real test of the Administration's success.

▶Israel bowed to American decisions that elevated the Palestinians to near equal status, giving the Jordanian-Palestinian delegation two of everything: two conference rooms, two briefings, even two speeches at the sessions. Those concessions allowed Israel to soften its image of intransigence.

Then Israel's Prime Minister, Yitzhak Shamir, blew it, big. He has always vowed never to give up an inch of territory, and he did not change that stance; he devoted half of his 34-minute speech to a recitation of the oppression of Jews through centuries. There was little in his speech to suggest a willingness to compromise, and he followed up with a bitter blast at Syria. But Shamir was playing less to world opinion than expressing deep convictions that also work for him politically back home. He had appeased Israeli peaceniks by attending the conference while reassuring his hard-line supporters that he remains unbending on issues that count.

▶Syria was quite as intransigent. Foreign Minister Farouk al-Sharaa told the conference that Israel must give up "every inch" of the lands conquered in 1967. The next day he directed a ferocious personal diatribe at Shamir. The Syrians came across as bellicose tough guys who seemed to have no idea how to play to a worldwide audience— and maybe didn't care. They only had to please an audience of one: Hafez Assad.

▶The Palestinians were big winners. Instead of the unshaven face of Yasser Arafat, they presented an image of intelligence, professionalism and sensitivity. They sounded the most conciliatory notes and made the first substantive concessions, explicitly saying they will now accept the limited self-rule they spurned when it was offered as part of the Camp David agreement.

Haidar Abdul-Shafi, head of the Palestinian delegation, easily trumped Shamir. Though the Palestinian's talk was just as unyielding, his tone was mild. He too was playing a public relations game, appealing to the Israeli peace movement and worldwide sympathizers.

More than public relations is involved in making peace, of course. The differences are real, the fears genuine. But paradoxically, p.r. may offer some hope. If both sides figured that they could not afford to stay away from this conference, they might calculate that they also cannot afford to let it break down, and thus they must be drawn to offer concessions to keep it going. Maybe not. But if in the Middle East it is always wise to prepare for the worst, it is equally necessary to expect the unexpected.

The Twilight of Apartheid

De Klerk moves to sweep away the last legal pillars of racial inequality. But a scandal raises questions about his intentions.

President F.W. de Klerk, above, struck down the pillars of apartheid; A.N.C. leader Nelson Mandela seeks further reforms

What a difference a year makes. On Feb. 2, 1990, President F.W. de Klerk stunned his country by opening Parliament with a pledge to legalize the militantly antiapartheid African National Congress and release A.N.C. leader Nelson Mandela from jail. On Feb. 1, 1991, De Klerk surpassed expectations again by declaring his intention to bring a swift end to legally sanctioned racial segregation. He called on Parliament to repeal immediately the remaining pillars of discrimination that dictate where blacks can work and live. "There is neither time nor room for turning back," De Klerk declared. "There is only one road—ahead."

De Klerk asked lawmakers to dismantle the Group Areas Act, which segregates residential areas, and the Land Acts, which bar blacks from owning land outside designated homelands. In June Parliament repealed the Population Registration Act of 1950—the law that forced South Africans to register by racial group.

The President's Manifesto for the New South Africa drew a wildly mixed response. Outraged members of the opposition Conservative Party called De Klerk a "traitor to the nation" before staging the first mass opening-day walkout in the legislature's history. Antiapartheid protesters, meanwhile, complained that De Klerk did not go far enough. A.N.C. supporters demanded immediate voting rights for 28 million blacks, who constitute 70% of the country's inhabitants but have no representation in the national government.

De Klerk's speech capped one of the most fateful periods in the struggle against apartheid. Earlier, the A.N.C. and its major rival, the Zulu-based Inkatha Freedom Party, moved to end their bloody internecine strife. Mandela and Zulu chief and Inkatha leader Mangosuthu Buthelezi finally met for the first time in 28 years and asked their followers to "cease all attacks against one another." Feuding between the two factions has claimed as many as 8,000 lives since 1984.

Their reconciliation and De Klerk's repeal of apartheid set the stage for the next phase of the black campaign for equality. Overshadowing everything else is the problem of framing a new constitution. Major differences remain, but De Klerk's government and Mandela's A.N.C. have already agreed on some important ideas. The document, for example, must contain a bill of rights and set up a two-chamber legislature with some form of proportional representation.

SANCTIONS

In July, as a positive incentive to keep reform going, President Bush rescinded the bans on most trade with South Africa and on new investment in the country, which were enacted in 1986 over Ronald Reagan's veto. Even if the trade restrictions seem to have had little economic impact, the limitations on loans and investments did hurt. And the sanctions imposed by the U.S., the European Community, the Commonwealth and other groups of nations had

Tearing Down The Walls

1989

Sept. 6: President F.W. de Klerk initiates reform by legalizing peaceful demonstrations and opening segregated beaches

Oct. 15: The government releases six A.N.C. leaders from prison, including Walter Sisulu

1990

Feb. 2: De Klerk lifts the ban outlawing the A.N.C. and other political groups

Feb. 11: Nelson Mandela is freed from jail after 27 years

May 2: The A.N.C. and the government hold their first formal talks

June 7: De Klerk ends the state of emergency in most parts of the country

hammered home to South African whites, as probably nothing else could have, the fact that their country had become a global outlaw. The 12-nation E.C. voted in April to remove its ban on imports of certain products. The International Olympic Committee decided to let South African athletes compete in future games, ending a 21-year ban that was especially devastating to the sports-mad country. For its part, Pretoria signed the nuclear nonproliferation treaty, a significant move since it is thought to have developed the ability to make atom bombs.

Some American blacks and liberals nonetheless denounced Bush's action as premature, an opinion also voiced by Nelson Mandela. They contend that South Africa is still far from multiracial democracy, and that without the continued pressure of sanctions, full equality will never come.

WHITHER THE A.N.C.?

The A.N.C. was doomed to fall short of the absurdly high hopes inspired by Mandela's release from prison. But the organization has genuinely dismayed many South Africans with its increasingly strident demands, its role in township violence, its muddled ideas about nationalizing parts of the economy and its maddening bureaucratic sluggishness. Not long ago, A.N.C. leaders argued that the government should simply hand over power. Now it is reasonable to wonder if the organization, even with its large number of sympathizers, could win a democratic election when one is finally held. And if the A.N.C. did come to power, would it be fit to govern?

De Klerk showed impressive skill at outmaneuvering Mandela and maintaining control of the transition process. He enjoys strong support from whites and blacks alike. Indeed, the government's competence frustrates the A.N.C. Most galling has been the success that De Klerk has had in being welcomed by black African leaders the congress considers close allies.

SCANDAL

At the end of July, however, De Klerk was confronted with a major credibility crisis. Exposés in the Johannesburg *Weekly Mail* showed that the government, despite repeated denials and stonewalling, had provided covert funds via the South African police to underwrite Inkatha. By Pretoria's admission, Inkatha and an allied labor union received at least $600,000.

The scandal widened days later, when Foreign Minister Roelof ("Pik") Botha admitted that contrary to previous denials, South Africa had secretly spent more than $36 million to keep the leftist South West Africa People's Organization from winning a commanding victory in pre-independence elections in neighboring Na-

mibia in 1989. Pretoria's support of at least seven parties opposed to SWAPO may have prevented the organization from gaining the two-thirds majority it needed to introduce a socialist constitution.

The disclosure of "Inkathagate"—as the affair was quickly dubbed—undermined De Klerk's credibility at just the moment he was trying to get the A.N.C. and other black groups to the negotiating table to write a new constitution that would extend voting rights to the black majority.

Furthermore, the scandal lent credence to charges that security forces have aided armed attacks by Inkatha supporters on A.N.C. members. Since 1986 more than 6,000 people have been killed in black-vs.-black clashes, giving comfort to those who argue that inherent tribalism renders blacks unfit to be stewards of democracy. Nelson Mandela has warned that power-sharing talks could founder unless the government can ensure the impartiality of the security forces, a notion Inkathagate puts in serious doubt.

Mandela, who often described De Klerk as a man of integrity, is now clearly suspicious of his intentions. The A.N.C. demanded a full inquiry and called for a freeze on the $132 million earmarked for secret projects in this year's government budget. As details of covert funding trickled out, politicians—white and black—and newspapers across the ideological spectrum demanded quick action to salvage the government's relationship with the A.N.C., including the resignations of the three Cabinet ministers who have been linked to the scandal so far.

De Klerk insisted that funds funneled to Inkatha were for the organization's anti-sanctions efforts, not political work. The biggest attempt to contain the political fallout came from the Zulu-based movement itself. Claiming he never knew about Pretoria's $87,500 donation to his organization for two rallies in 1989 and 1990, Buthelezi repaid the amount to the government; his assistant M.Z. Khumalo took responsibility for the transaction and resigned.

Inkathagate has seriously eroded trust in Pretoria and bolstered suspicions that the President and his National Party colleagues intend to remain in power on their own terms. Ironically, Foreign Minister Botha admitted that the government's illegal spending "probably" strengthened the A.N.C.'s long-standing demand for a new interim government that includes itself and other black parties.

Freeing Mandela and scrapping the apartheid laws were, in retrospect, simple tasks compared with what must come next. A watching world still has high hopes for a peaceful transition to multiracial democracy in South Africa. But as the Inkathagate affair shows, the President is not exactly the smooth agent of political change suggested by his carefully crafted public image.

June 19: Parliament repeals the Separate Amenities Act, opening formerly whites-only public facilities

Aug. 6: The A.N.C. agrees to suspend its "armed struggle"

Sept. 24: De Klerk visits U.S., meets Bush

1991

Jan. 29: Mandela meets Buthelezi

Feb. 1: De Klerk asks Parliament to repeal all remaining apartheid laws

June 17: Parliament repeals the Population Registration Act of 1950

July 10: Bush rescinds most U.S. bans on trade with South Africa

Mid-July: "Inkathagate" scandal erupts: government admits to secretly aiding Buthelezi's Inkatha party and spending $36 million to rig Namibia's 1989 election

Dec. 20: De Klerk offers power-sharing arrangement in transitional government chosen by voters of all races

War of the Widows

Never mind that she departed in ignominy aboard a U.S. Air Force jet. Forget that she is under indictment for looting her country. Imelda Marcos was determined to go home like a hero. And what Imelda wants, Imelda usually gets. She returned to the Philippines in November: as she landed, few could ignore how eerily similar her arrival was to that of opposition leader Benigno Aquino eight years earlier. His assassination triggered the fall of Ferdinand and Imelda Marcos. But instead of the fatal gunshots that greeted him, well-wishers surged onto the plane to welcome the former First Lady.

Imelda, being Imelda, refused to join her motorcade in a safe area. Instead, she insisted on leaving through the arrival lobby in full view of the press and supporters. After frantic calls to President Corazon Aquino, Imelda had her way. A trivial victory, but Imelda watchers were already keeping score on what the press dubbed "the war of the widows." Aquino had conceded twice: she reversed her ban on Marcos' return after a Swiss judge ruled that the former First Lady must be found guilty in a Philippine court before the government could hope to recoup an estimated $350 million in "ill-gotten wealth" from frozen Marcos accounts in Swiss banks. Aquino also agreed to allow interment of the body of the late President Marcos in his home province. But Imelda insists on a hero's burial in Manila's national cemetery. She returned without the corpse—but in time to fulfill a six-month residency requirement for prospective presidential candidates. Whether she runs or not, her return signaled the unofficial start of the 1992 presidential campaign. Most analysts do not underestimate Imelda's candidacy.

On the Stand

When he first took the stand in February, Kenneth Kgase, 31, refused to testify against Winnie Mandela, the wife of African National Congress leader Nelson Mandela, out of fear for his life. In March, after being threatened with jail for his silence, Kgase decided to talk. And what he had to say in a packed Johannesburg courtroom resounded like a thunderclap. Mandela and her bodyguards, said Kgase, savagely beat him and three other young black men in her Soweto home in December 1988.

Prosecutors accused Mandela and her guards of having abducted Kgase and the three others from a Methodist shelter and of then trying to pummel them into saying they had had sex with a white minister. The minister has been cleared by his church. Kgase accused Mandela of repeatedly punching the victims, and said she struck him with a whip, "humming a tune and dancing to the rhythm." Kgase testified that some of the worst beatings were reserved for James Moeketsi

("Stompie") Seipei, 14, whom Mrs. Mandela accused of being a police informant. The youth was later found dead. Jerry Richardson, head of Mrs. Mandela's bodyguards, has been convicted of the murder.

In May, Judge Michael Stegmann found Mandela to be only an accessory to the assault but decided that she had planned the kidnapping. Denouncing her as a "calm, composed, deliberate and unblushing liar," he sentenced her to six years in prison. In July, however, Judge Stegmann granted Mandela permission to appeal her conviction, a process which could take months or even years.

Actress, Temptress, Empress

When Jiang Qing, Mao Zedong's widow and one of the most powerful women in the People's Republic, died while under house arrest in mid-May, China's rulers tried to keep her passing a secret: it was the second anniversary of the Tiananmen pro-democracy demonstrations, and they didn't want any fresh trouble. The regime need not have worried: Jiang left no political heirs to mourn her, and the empire of the proletariat that she once intended to lead rotted away long ago.

In 1966, by Mao's side, she was one of the guiding lights of the Great Proletarian Cultural Revolution, a radical upheaval that would last a decade and leave scars still visible today. "I was Chairman Mao's dog," she said at her trial in 1980. "Whomever he told me to bite, I bit." She was the ringleader of the Gang of Four, a group of ambitious radicals who coveted power. After her husband's death, she set her sights on the chairmanship of the Communist Party. She failed, but she did not go quietly. At her show trial, Jiang was unrepentant when charged with complicity in the death of 34,000 people and the unjust persecution of 729,511 others during the Cultural Revolution.

Jiang Qing was the last of her many names: born Li Jinhai in 1914, she first came to prominence as a starlet. When Shanghai was taken by Japanese troops in 1938, she headed for the interior and joined the communist survivors of the Long March. In 1939 she threw the party into crisis when she became pregnant by Mao Zedong, who was married and 21 years her senior. They eventually married, but she was not allowed to enter politics until the mid-'60s. When Mao died in 1976, Jiang was overthrown within a month by a military coup. She was condemned to death, but the sentence was commuted to life imprisonment. In May, Jiang hanged herself in a secluded villa in the suburbs of Beijing, apparently ailing from throat cancer. In her tumultuous life, she was actress, temptress, empress. She died a villain consigned to history.

A Man for All Nations

For the United Nations' African bloc, the election in November of Egyptian diplomat Boutros Boutros Ghali as the new Secretary-General to succeed the retiring Javier Pérez de Cuéllar was a semisweet victory. The Africans had engineered their continent's first turn at the helm of the world organization—and had outmaneuvered the big guns of the U.S. and Britain to achieve it. But Ghali was the "least African" candidate put forward by a bloc that dearly wanted to see the job go to a sub-Saharan black.

Ghali defies categorization. He is an Arab who is a Coptic Christian with a Jewish wife. He represents the Third World with Parisian sophistication; he is the son of a wealthy family, the grandson of a Prime Minister. At 69 he was considered too old for the demanding job and was criticized for campaigning for it too vigorously.

But Ghali brings strong qualifications to the $202,346-a-year post. He is an expert in international law, and has a 21-page curriculum vitae replete with degrees, decorations and scholarly writings in three languages. A key negotiator in the Camp David peace process, he has helped mediate many quarrels. A Western analyst in Cairo calls him a "man of vision and integrity, not anybody's pushover." But with only five years to make his mark, the incoming Secretary-General must work fast. He faces a devastating U.N. financial crisis, increasing demands for peacekeeping operations and humanitarian aid, and a whole new global agenda—an awesome challenge for an untried man.

Heroine in Chains

Members of the Norwegian Nobel Committee said in October that they could not be sure that Aung San Suu Kyi even knew she had been awarded the 1991 Nobel Peace Prize. But if she had access to a short-wave radio, she might have learned the news.

Aung San Suu Kyi, 46, the leader of Burma's democratic opposition, has been under house arrest since July 1989. As a leader using "nonviolent means to resist a regime characterized by brutality," read the Nobel citation, Aung San Suu Kyi has become "one of the most extraordinary examples of civil courage in Asia in recent decades." Although she was already under house arrest, in May 1990 her National League for Democracy party won a landslide victory in the parliamentary elections, taking 392 of the 485 seats. But the generals—who renamed the country Myanmar—refused to surrender power. Instead, they arrested scores of elected parliamentarians and Buddhist monks.

Concerned about trade, the six-member Association of South East Asian Nations has repeatedly rejected calls from the West to impose sanctions on Burma. Some Asians even see the Peace Prize as a form of neocolonial interference in Burma's affairs. Lee Kuan Yew, the former Prime Minister of Singapore, explains that ASEAN thinks sanctions will not work. "If we boycott or condemn the government," he says, "we'll lose influence with it."

The prize, which includes a gold medal and about $1 million, was presented to Aung San Suu Kyi's son in Oslo in December. The junta has told her she can leave the country only if she agrees never to return. It is a condition she flatly refuses.

Japan's Tough P.M.

Kiichi Miyazawa was 19 when he made his first trip to America. It was 1939, and tensions between Japan and the U.S. were running high, but the traveler liked what he saw. "The American boys and girls were their own masters. I was so impressed." As a young official in the Ministry of Finance after the war, Miyazawa often negotiated with American occupation forces, and during his next four decades of government service, he befriended a string of prominent Americans, such as Henry Kissinger and David Rockefeller.

In November, Miyazawa took over as Japan's new Prime Minister. Will his positive experience with Americans translate into a new era of cordial relations between the U.S. and Japan?

Not necessarily. Yes, Miyazawa is extraordinarily fond of America and has an elegant command of English. But he is also a tough negotiator with firmly held convictions. He speaks his mind. Unlike many of his less sophisticated predecessors, he will not bow silently to pressure from Washington. As Trade Minister in 1970, Miyazawa broke off talks over a textile agreement because he felt the U.S. was demanding too much. His successor completed the deal—by giving Washington exactly what it wanted.

Miyazawa's talk on trade remains blunt. The U.S. deficit with Japan has declined from a peak of $57 billion in 1987 to $41.1 billion in 1990, and Miyazawa credits both nations with engineering the impresssive 28% drop. But he says that shrinking the gap further will be difficult because the U.S. economy has become overly dependent on Japanese imports.

Miyazawa's outspokenness might lead some to call him anti-American. But while he may be tough on trade issues, he firmly believes that "Japan's alliance with the U.S. must be strengthened." He is willing to have Tokyo pay more of the cost of basing U.S. forces in Japan; he is eager to cooperate with Washington on diplomatic issues, such as Third World debt or U.N. peacekeeping operations. But he will insist that Japan be treated as a full partner in any jont effort and not merely be sent the bill afterward.

The new Prime Minister is unlikely to change the course of U.S.-Japanese relations in a dramatic way. His political philosophy, after all, is similar to that of previous leaders. But the tone of the debates between Tokyo and Washington will surely become sharper.

Return to Normalcy

At the moment of triumph, life shone with new promise. The civil war that ravaged Ethiopia for 30 years was over. And in the months since June, when Mengistu Hile Mariam, the country's hard-line Marxist dictator for 14 years, was driven from power, the competing guerrilla bands achieved a relative peace and joined in a transitional government. The death toll fell from 10,000 people a month to a few hundred. Where torture and disappearances once silenced opposition voices, Ethiopians felt free to voice their demands and even shout insults at President Meles Zanawi, a democratic exercise he withstands calmly.

The view ahead, however, is clouded. The shattered economy remains moribund, the country's 53 million citizens impoverished. The treasury is empty, half the factories are closed, and much of the land is eroded. It is something of a miracle, then, that the political center fashioned after Mengistu's flight is holding. Where most of black Africa has opted to quell tribal rivalry by imposing strict one-party rule, Meles has embarked on a daring multiparty experiment that acknowledges ethnic differences. Though the interim government is dominated by Meles' Ethiopian People's Revolutionary Democratic Front, its ruling council includes representatives from 35 different parties. In July it adopted a charter ensuring each ethnic nationality the right to self-determination. Already the Red Sea province of Eritrea has set up its own provisional government and will hold a United Nations–sponsored referendum on independence in two years.

A Very Private War

Transfixed by the war in the gulf, the world was looking the other way. But the death was just as real. In an agonizing replay of the collapse of Liberia in 1990, the fierce civil war in Somalia ended in February with the collapse of the government of Siad Barre, who fled the country in a tank only moments ahead of the rebel forces.

Barre, a onetime policeman who seized power in a military coup in 1969, sealed his own fate by depending more and more on his kinsmen to support his autocratic rule. In May 1988 the Somali National Movement, formed by the northern Isaq clan, rose in rebellion and seized several towns. The army failed to put down the revolt with vicious bombing and shelling that killed as many as 50,000 civilians and insurgents; the rebels soon controlled the countryside in the north. Meanwhile, in the country's southern region, the Ogadeni clan launched the Somali Patriotic Movement; they were soon joined by the Hawiye clan's United Somali Congress, which prevails in the center of the country and in the capital of Mogadishu.

The month-long final campaign killed more than 5,000 civilians

and forced tens of thousands to flee. Prospects for the new government—representing three clans that have feuded for centuries—seemed bleak.

Aristide's Fall

It was an old-fashioned coup. A mere eight months after taking office as Haiti's first freely elected President, Jean-Bertrand Aristide, a 38-year-old priest, was driven into exile in late September when rampaging soldiers opened fire on street crowds and threatened Aristide with death.

George Bush's first reaction was to denounce the overthrow and call for Aristide's reinstatement. But within weeks Bush backed away, citing allegations of human-rights abuses by the activist priest—charges soon bolstered by an Organization of American States team in Haiti. Most disturbing: a Sept. 27 speech in which Aristide seemed to condone Père Lebrun, a form of lynching in which a gasoline-soaked tire is set ablaze around a victim's neck. Aristide's return became more complicated when Joseph Nerette, 67, a Supreme Court judge, was hastily sworn in as provisional President by Haitian lawmakers after soldiers stormed the legislature to deter Aristide's return. Other troops took over the Port-au-Prince airport while the head of the Haitian armed forces, Brigadier General Raoul Cedras, and OAS diplomats were meeting there. The undisciplined attacks suggested that Cedras did not control the army. Now suspected as mastermind of the coup: Major Michel François, 34, head of the police in Haiti's capital and the driving force behind the violence that claimed 300 lives.

Death's Return

This is the art of darkness: in the rural town of Sriperumbudur, near Madras, a young woman offers a sandalwood garland, bows—and, suddenly, the once and likely future of India, a figure invested with the symbolic weight of generations, is obliterated in a deafening roar and a ball of flame. A man whose incandescent family had long been identified with one-sixth of the human race, Rajiv Gandhi, 46, on May 22 went the way of his mother Indira, falling to a climate of violence that has steadily overtaken the subcontinent.

With one blow, the fortunes of 844 million people became hostage to a terrible uncertainty. On the comeback trail for months, the former Prime Minister, and leader of the Congress Party, had gone a long way toward regaining public faith in his ability to rescue India from a deepening hole of debt and drift. His goal was to "bring India

into the 21st century." Indians did not love Rajiv in the universal way they adored his grandfather Jawaharlal Nehru, nor did they honor him with the grudging respect they paid his mother. But they regarded him as an essentially decent man, a reluctant politician struggling to live up to his inheritance of noblesse oblige.

Rajiv's death sickened the country with shame and impotent rage. Even before his assassination, 229 people had died in election mayhem across the country; in its wake, 26 more people died. Suspicions immediately fell on the Tamil Tigers, a band of guerrillas who have been fighting Indian peace-keeping troops in Sri Lanka. As his remains were cremated along New Delhi's Jamuna River, India, like most mourners, basically wept for itself. Said Natwar Singh, a former deputy in Gandhi's Cabinet: "What has this country of Buddha and Mahatma Gandhi come to? We were an example to the world. Now we are a warning."

El Salvador: New Year's Peace

When Salvadoran President Alfredo Cristiani addressed the United Nations General Assembly in late September, he predicted that 1991 would bring peace to his country. And high time too: a civil war involving the government and leftist guerrillas has left 75,000 dead in the past 12 years. Two days later, after 17 months of U.N.-brokered talks, the government and the rebels signed an agreement setting out a framework for reintegrating the rebels of the Farabundo Martí National Liberation Front into society and offering assurances for their safety. The agreement also pledged to transfer the police force from military to civilian control and permit former rebels to join it. Moreover, the two sides agreed to reduce the size of the army and purge officers notorious for human-rights abuses.

Cristiani's prediction of peace in 1991 came true at the last possible moment: at the stroke of the new year, the government and rebels reached a peace agreement that aimed to bring an almost immediate halt to the fighting and a final end to the civil war by autumn of 1992. According to the plan, a formal cease-fire will go into effect on Feb. 1, 1992, and "final agreements of peace" will be signed in Mexico City on Jan. 16. "This signing constitutes the beginning of a new era of rebuilding toward democracy and freedom," said Cristiani. And one of the five top rebel commanders, Salvador Sanchéz Cerén, added, "The war in El Salvador is over."

Return to the Killing Fields

A man quick to laughter and tears, Prince Norodom Sihanouk was bursting with both. An Air China jetliner from Beijing had brought him home to Phnom Penh after a tortuous personal odyssey of nearly 13 years. But the November return of Cambodia's exiled former head of state brought no certain end to his homeland's generation-long nightmare.

Under the auspices of a U.N.-brokered settlement, the Prince returned to lead a transitional Supreme National Council composed of Cambodia's four warring factions. It included, by necessity, Pol Pot's Khmer Rouge, whose Maoist-inspired ideology had devastated the country from 1975 to 1979 and resulted in more than 1 million deaths. Under an October agreement signed in Paris, the council will assume authority over international relations, but actual day-to-day governing power will remain in the hands of Hun Sen's Vietnamese-installed regime, pending elections within 18 months.

The legacy of 20 years of warfare is explosive. Land mines dot the countryside like rice seedlings, and fighting forces remain heavily armed. U.N. troops may eventually demobilize regular units, but retrieving militia weapons will be harder. Banditry has been rising since a cease-fire took effect in May. The U.N.'s peace-monitoring troops, which perhaps will number 10,000 in all, are to arrive in full force early in 1992; until then, just 268 soldiers and civilian officials are in charge.

Flight on the Adriatic

The refugees began turning up in southern Italy's fishing villages aboard commandeered vessels ranging from tugboats to freighters. In the space of six days in March, 20,000 Albanians fled worsening shortages of food and other essentials in their impoverished homeland and sought asylum across the Adriatic's Strait of Otranto. Startled local authorities in Italy did their best to provide temporary accommodations in schools and army barracks, but thousands of the Albanians were soon forced to camp out on town docks, wrapping themselves in plastic sheets for warmth.

Not for long, however. Following an emergency Cabinet session in Rome, Deputy Prime Minister Claudio Martelli declared that "this exodus cannot continue." The vast majority of Albania's visitors are "not political refugees but economic refugees," he said; as such, they failed to qualify for asylum under Italian law and were returned home by ship.

In the summer the Italian government resorted to more drastic measures in dealing with 18,000 destitute refugees in the southern port of Bari. Albanians had fought their way ashore after crossing the Adriatic on grossly overcrowded boats, only to be penned into coal docks and the local soccer stadium without adequate food or water. The angry men and women then proceeded to wreck the stadium. Later, when supplies did arrive, complained a Caritas relief worker, "the police threw food at them like in a zoo." After battling security forces for two days and suffering from exposure, most of the dispirited Albanians willingly got on board more than 50 military and Alitalia flights headed for Tirana. A few hundred holdouts, including army deserters, were allowed to stay while an Italian commission decided if they qualified for political asylum.

The Italian government's tough stand, doubtless influenced by Italy's 11% unemployment rate, was the most dramatic display to date of Western Europe's growing reluctance to receive waves of immigrants from the East.

Unity's Shadows

After years of waiting, the Berlin Wall, once the ugliest scar on a wounded country, was knocked down. All 80 million Germans are now free to read, hear and say what they please. In October 1990, the raising of the black-red-and-gold flag above Berlin made Germany a single political entity. It should have ushered in a period of rejoicing.

Yet there is little joy in Germany today. The East has awakened from a 40-year socialist sleepwalk to the devastating realization that countless lives have been wasted on the communists' failed experiment. The West achieved its dream of unity and freedom for "our brothers and sisters" only to discover that those siblings will be an expensive burden for some time. Dependence breeds resentment on both sides of a relationship.

Easterners expected substantial help from their rich western cousins, but they quickly discovered that wealth is not synonymous with generosity. Among the first west Germans they met were property owners with eviction papers or investors with dismissal notices. Of an eastern work force of 9 million, 840,000 are officially jobless and 2 million are being paid to do little or nothing on a government-subsidized system of "short-time work." Scattered eruptions of neo-Nazism point to a mounting frustration beneath the surface.

Politicians are learning just how much time and money will be needed for recovery: in 1990 they talked of closing the gap between east and west in two or three years. By spring 1991 they were saying four or five, maybe 10. But some people are optimistic. "There's nothing wrong with this country," says Rudolph Sommerlatt, 64. "Just give the middle class a chance. We have a lot to make up for the years of socialism when we could not function. We'll make it."

Blueprint for the Dream

The European Community's summit in the medieval Dutch town of Maastricht in December, aimed at forging deeper economic and political integration, was a qualified success. After two days of heated wrangling, the 12 heads of state and government produced an agreement that took a giant step toward monetary unity, a half step toward strengthening a separate European defense organization, and a baby step toward framing a common foreign and security policy. They also moved toward pursuing joint action in areas ranging from immigration to education and labor. The Community—the industrialized world's largest single market, with 340 million people—should provide much needed stability in the face of turmoil in Eastern Europe. "Further integration is now inevitable," said German Chancellor Helmut Kohl. "The course is irreversible."

The summit's crowning achievement was the commitment by 11 of the 12 (Britain excepted) to monetary union by the end of the century. After years of debate, the leaders agreed to establish a single European Currency Unit, the ECU, as early as January 1997. But each country must first meet stringent economic criteria, such as controlled government debt and limited budget deficits. All this is designed to make western Europe the world's biggest economic power, equipped to meet the American and Japanese challenge. But Britain demanded that it be allowed to decide later in the decade whether or not to adopt the ECU. Moreover, the Maastricht decisions raise the prospect of a "two-tier Europe" in which the economically powerful countries of the north will pull even farther ahead of the nations to the south.

MAN OF THE YEAR

IMAGES OF 1991

E ach December the editors of TIME assign themselves two slightly audacious tasks: to select the most influential person and most compelling pictures of the year. Sometimes mistaken for an award or honor, the title "Man of the Year" is simply a designation, identifying the person (or force) that has most influenced the course of events in the preceding year—for good or evil. Authentic heroes have been among the designees: Mahatma Gandhi, Pope John XXIII and the Rev. Martin Luther King Jr. But dictators and demagogues have had their day as well, from Adolph Hitler and Joseph Stalin to the Ayatullah Khomeini.

In selecting the Images of the Year, the editors are mindful of the power of photographs to move us in ways words cannot. Here are the pictures we will hang in our personal galleries as the symbols of 1991: the pain of war and exile, the glory of a victorious army and, dwarfing even modern man's capacity for destruction, the energy of a newly erupting volcano.

Prince of The Global Village

TED TURNER looks to the far horizon, whether relaxing at his Montana ranch or linking people via the world's largest global TV network

isionaries are possessed creatures, men and women in the thrall of a belief so powerful that they ignore all else—even reason—to ensure that reality catches up with their dreams. The vision may be the glory-driven daring of a Saddam Hussein, who foolishly tried to extend his rule by conquest and plunder, or the seize-the-day bravery of a Boris Yeltsin, who struggled to free a society from seven decades of iron ideology. But always behind the action is an idea, a passionate sense of what is eternal in human nature and also of what is coming but as yet unseen, just over the horizon.

A generation ago, social theorist Marshall McLuhan proclaimed the advent of a "global village," a sort of borderless world in which communications media would transcend the boundaries of nations. "Ours is a brand-new world of 'allatonceness' " he wrote. " 'Time' has ceased, 'space' has vanished. We now live in . . . a simultaneous happening." McLuhan underestimated the enduring appeal of the status quo. The fusion of television and satellites did not produce instantaneous brotherhood, just a slowly dawning awareness of the implications of a world transfixed by a single TV image.

It took another visionary, and the band of dreamers and opportunists he gathered around him, to demonstrate that McLuhan was wrong only temporarily. In 1991, one of the most eventful years of this century, the world witnessed the dramatic and transforming impact on those events of live television by satellite. The very definition of news was rewritten—from something that *has happened* to something that *is happening* at the very moment you are hearing of it. A war involving the fiercest air bombardment in history unfolded in real time—before the cameras. The Soviet Union overthrew its leaders and their doctrine—before the cameras. To a considerable degree, especially in Moscow, momentous things happened precisely *because* they were being seen *as* they happened.

These shots heard, and seen, around the world appeared under the aegis of the first global TV news company, Cable News Network. Contrary to the dictum of former U.S. House Speaker Tip O'Neill that "all politics is local," CNN proved that politics can be planetary, that ordinary people can take deep interest in events remote from them in every way—and can respond to reportage framed in global rather than purely nationalistic terms.

Back in CNN's infancy Ted Turner sensed the wonders to come. "I am the right man in the right place at the right time," he said. "Not me alone, but all the people who think the world can be brought together by telecommunications." The years since, and most especially the year 1991, have demonstrated how emphatically he was right. For influencing the dynamic of events and turning viewers in 150 countries into instant witnesses of history, Robert Edward Turner III is TIME's Man of the Year for 1991.

History as It Happens

On the night that the bombs began to fall on Baghdad, Gilbert Lavoie, press secretary to Canada's Prime Minister, Brian Mulroney, telephoned his counterpart Marlin Fitzwater at the White House. "Marlin said, 'Hi, what are you doing?'" Lavoie recalls, "and I said, 'I'm doing the same thing you are—watching CNN.'"

So was virtually every other senior official in virtually every government. In that respect, at least, the night of Jan. 16, 1991, was actually rather ordinary. From Rome to Riyadh, London to Lagos, Beijing to Buenos Aires, Cable News Network is on more or less continuously in the suites of a vast array of chiefs of state and foreign ministers. It has become the common frame of reference for the world's power élite. Boris Yeltsin and Mikhail Gorbachev, George Bush and Saddam Hussein, Yitzhak Shamir and Hafez Assad—the headline sparring partners of the year just past—are all alert watchers. What a computer message can accomplish within an office, CNN achieves around the clock, around the globe: it gives everyone the same information, the same basis for discussion, at the same moment. That change in communication has in turn affected journalism, intelligence gathering, economics, diplomacy and even, in the minds of some scholars, the very concept of what it is to be a nation.

Only a glint of thought to its founder, Ted Turner, a dozen years ago, CNN is now the world's most widely heeded news organization. British Foreign Secretary Douglas Hurd won't stay in hotels that don't offer the network. When the name of his country was inadvertently omitted from a news quiz about nations participating in November's Middle East peace talks, Jordan's King Hussein was watching and was so irritated that he had palace officials immediately call CNN's Amman office to complain.

Singapore stockbrokers protested their government's politically inspired ban on private satellite dishes, arguing that access to instantaneous war news on CNN was vital to anticipate fluctuations in world financial markets. The terrorists who held Terry Anderson hostage in Lebanon used CNN as the vehicle to release a videotape of his appeal for help. CNN can be seen at the El Kabir Hotel in Tripoli, favored by Muammar Gaddafi's network of radical extremists. It can also be seen at the Vatican, where Archbishop John Foley, president of the Pontifical Council for Social Communications, rises by 6 a.m. to watch and "know what to pray about."

CNN has become the fourth most respected brand name in the U.S., according to a recent poll of 2,000 people, ranked just behind

the Disney parks, Kodak and Mercedes-Benz and ahead of Rolex, Levi's, IBM and AT&T. (ABC, NBC and CBS were not offered by the opinion seekers.) As a source of knowledge in turbulent times, CNN may be without peer. "Ted Turner is probably the pre-eminent publisher in America today, maybe in the world," says Don Hewitt, founding producer of *60 Minutes* on CBS. "When there was a disaster, it used to be that people went to church and all held hands. Then television came along, and there was this wonderful feeling that while you were watching Walter Cronkite, millions of other Americans were sharing the emotional experience with you. Now, the minute anything happens, they all run to CNN and think, 'The whole *world* is sharing this experience with me.'"*

CNN's coverage of the war in the gulf and the failed Soviet coup fostered a new kind of headlong television diplomacy

For most of the gulf war, CNN was the prime source of news, information and up-to-the-minute political intelligence for the U.S. government. President Bush is known to have said to other world leaders, "I learn more from CNN

---

*CNN is owned by a consortium in which Time Warner, TIME's parent company, has a 21.9% stake.

than I do from the CIA." That is apparently not a joke. Secretary of State James Baker and Secretary of Defense Dick Cheney turned to CNN to find out what was happening in diplomacy or combat because its speed and accuracy in newsgathering outstripped the work of the National Military Intelligence Center and the CIA. Those agencies remain geared to cycling paperwork up through chains of command, at a pace often too slow during a fast-breaking crisis.

Perhaps the biggest impact of CNN has been on diplomacy. There, too, the stately march of paper via protocol has been supplanted by spontaneity and pragmatism. The public press conference has outstripped the private letter. No longer is the performance just for show while the real deal is done behind closed doors. CNN's reach makes it a kind of worldwide party line, allowing leaders to conduct a sort of conference call heard not only by the principals but also by their constituents across the planet.

When U.S. troops invaded Panama in December 1989, the Soviet Foreign Ministry read its condemnation to a CNN crew before passing it through diplomatic channels. During the buildup to the gulf war, Turkish President Turgut Ozal was watching a CNN telecast

governments to do their bloody deeds, if they dare, before a watching world. Sometimes they dare not, especially when CNN can reach even a relatively few citizens within the oppressed land and serve as a beacon of freedom. During the failed Soviet coup in August, as key state news organs were being taken over by supporters of its leaders, Russian President Boris Yeltsin showed himself in public atop a tank to rally a crowd nearby—and a far larger one throughout his nation. He knew that CNN might still be seen by about 100,000 Muscovites and some thousands of residents in other cities, a tiny percentage of the population but enough to spread by word of mouth that the battle for freedom was not lost. The image of a defiant Yeltsin sent the same signal to the rest of the world and heightened pressure on President Bush to denounce the coup. Historians will debate how much impact this televised imagery had on the outcome. But it is noteworthy that a diplomat representing one of the newly independent Baltic republics jubilantly called people at CNN days later and thanked them for helping to give his country its freedom.

In all these cases, many of the same gut-wrenching images could be seen on other networks. But CNN was apt to carry them first

OCTOBER '91 Clarence Thomas claimed to be the victim of an "electronic lynching"

FEBRUARY '90 Nelson Mandela, the living symbol of black confinement, strode free at last

DECEMBER '89 When the U.S. invaded Panama, the hated rule of Manuel Noriega fell in panic

NOVEMBER '89 The fall of the Berlin Wall: No longer could a whole nation be a prison to its people

of a press conference and heard a reporter ask Bush if Ozal would cut off an oil pipeline into Iraq. Bush said he was about to ask Ozal that very question. Moments later, when the telephone rang, Ozal was able to tell Bush that he was expecting the call.

The final effort at a peaceful settlement of the gulf war epitomized the transition from the old diplomacy to the new. Secretary of State Baker met for six hours with Iraqi Foreign Minister Aziz but could not persuade him to accept a manila envelope containing a private letter from Bush to Saddam Hussein. As the meeting ended, both sides readied press conferences blaming each other. Aziz let it be known he would wait for Bush to appear, thus having the last word. White House press secretary Marlin Fitzwater quickly telephoned CNN correspondent Charles Bierbauer. Tell your bosses in Atlanta and your man with Aziz in Geneva, said Fitzwater, that Aziz is going to have to speak first, "if we have to wait until Christmas." Bush won. Says Fitzwater: "The whole thing took about five minutes to settle. CNN was the midwife on both ends."

CNN has also become a kind of global spotlight, forcing despotic

around the world and, certainly, to air them more frequently and at greater length. Moreover, the very existence of CNN has compelled rivals, inside and outside the U.S., to pursue more international news and air more of it live.

Among the most avid watchers of CNN, although they don't always like to admit it, are other journalists. In almost every major U.S. newsroom, and in many elsewhere in the world, the channel is perpetually on and someone is watching, or at least glancing over frequently. Once upon a time, newspapers broke the news to the public. Then TV took over that role, and ever since, newspapers have tried to redefine themselves by becoming more analytical. Now, even most TV reporters try to pride themselves on doing a story analytically and in depth; it is a foregone conclusion that CNN will do the story first.

At many events it covers, from summits to celebrated trials, CNN itself becomes a major news source. During the Arab-Israeli peace conference in Madrid last November, where access was severely limited, most of the 4,600 journalists had to follow the proceedings on

CNN. A common temptation is to skip other reporting and just re-hash what shows up on the screen. Sometimes even the most serious reporters are forced to rely on CNN's better access. As retired Air Force General Michael Dugan quipped about his work as military analyst for CBS, "What CBS did during the gulf war was watch CNN." The same might be said of most other broadcast and print news teams.

The plight of newspapers in a video age has rarely been more vivid than during the early days of the gulf war and the Soviet leadership crisis. News columns looked as though they had been put together simply by watching CNN the night before. Analyses were interesting but often nearly 24 hours out of date and no longer relevant.

For some social theorists, CNN has become far more than a news medium. It is now considered prime evidence for the evolution of a borderless world. As corporations become multinational and free trade transcends tariffs, as Europe develops a single currency and other regions build spheres of economic cooperation, as pop culture and air travel and migration and, yes, television make the world psy-

politics. But its intellectual thinness is evident in the way it covers foreign affairs—with the same tired emphasis on revolutions, wars, famines and disasters found in the traditional half-hour nightly network news shows, despite having the airtime to give a more rounded picture.

Perhaps the largest factor in CNN's prosperity is, paradoxically, sound business management. The network demonstrated to its fat rivals that news could be delivered much more cheaply. CNN salaries were lower but its people were hungrier and harder working. It did not get trapped into make-work union rules. It pioneered the practice of cross training, in which employees must learn and perform multiple skills. It reduced the camera-crew size from four to two, a standard that is now emulated throughout the industry.

The most expensive thing CNN does is the most necessary to its survival: broadcasting live and at length from remote locations. The network pioneered the use of costly "flyaway" satellite uplinks—packages of technology that can be disassembled into suitcase-size components weighing less than 100 lbs. each and capable of being checked as luggage onto an ordinary passenger jet.

OCTOBER '89 The earth quakes in San Francisco, and a nightmare interrupts California dreamin'

JUNE '89 Helpless to intervene, the world watched the blood flow as the Chinese cracked down in Tiananmen Square

DECEMBER '88 Blowing up Pan Am Flight 103, vengeful terrorists sent a message: NO ONE IS SAFE

JANUARY '86 The *Challenger* explodes: A flash, silence and a reminder that all technology is imperfect

chologically smaller, these theorists contend that the concept of nationalism recedes. Says Joshua Meyrowitz, professor of communication at the University of New Hampshire: "National sovereignty wasn't based only on power and barbed wire; it was based also on information control. Nations are losing control over informational borders because of CNN."

Scholars frequently belittle CNN for its unscholarly haste and supposed shallowness. In place of slowly mulled research from experts marinated in their fields, CNN delivers raw news. It features live events, bulletins and studios full of talking heads, often with scant analysis. CNN came into being just as the Big Three American networks were moving away from their tradition of retaining in-house experts, and the new network set the pace. CNN anchors are apt to be more trained in the mechanics of television than in the nuances of the many subjects they discuss. The reporting ranks number mostly workaday generalists.

CNN nonetheless does a good job on business, technology, entertainment and sports, and capably covers the White House and U.S.

In his disjointed but richly anecdotal book *Live from Baghdad* (Doubleday; $22), Robert Wiener, producer of CNN's wartime coverage from Iraq, offers these concluding words: "To broadcast, for the first time in history, live pictures to the entire world of a war in progress from behind enemy lines. Murrow would have loved it!" Indeed, Edward R. Murrow, himself a wartime broadcaster from London rooftops, would have. And so did the whole watching world. The sense of shared experience is the vital starting place for building a consensus on every matter of global concern, from nuclear disarmament to environmental cleanup, from hunger to health care.

What CNN viewers have seen in the past year is the awakening of a village consciousness, a sense that human beings are all connected and all in it together, wherever on the planet they may be. How else to explain Kenyans who lined up six-deep in front of electronics stores to watch footage of a war they had no soldiers fighting in? The full potential of the medium that Ted Turner bet the house on is just beginning to be realized. What we are seeing is not just the globalization of television but also, through television, the globalization of the globe.

The Taming of Ted Turner

Ted Turner's life may best be understood as a startling series of narrowly missed disasters. When he skippered his yacht in Britain's prestigious Fastnet race in 1979, he was so absorbed in victory that he did not even know a gale was killing 15 yachtsmen in the boats behind him. The Atlanta Braves, which Turner bought in 1976, snuffled along in the gutter for years, then went from last place to first in their division this year and lost the World Series by only a bat's whoosh. And CNN, once derided as the "Chicken Noodle Network" for its low wages and amateurish presentation, is now the video medium of record.

But these public triumphs are nothing compared with what he achieved on Nov. 19 of this year: Turner, alive and well, stabilized by medication and psychiatric counseling, beloved by Jane Fonda, celebrated his 53rd birthday. Fifty-three was the age at which Turner's father shot himself, and it was an age that many people who know Turner did not expect him to reach. While most Americans think of Turner as the loud cheerleader of the Braves, the corporate Don Quixote who went after CBS or the peace-loving impresario of the Goodwill Games, those close to him have always known Turner was haunted by a self-imposed deadline.

For Turner, life has been a struggle to master what he calls his "greatest" fear—the fear of death. "Because if you can get yourself where you're not afraid of dying, then you can . . . move forward a lot faster," he says. If Turner can sound lighthearted about his death obsession, it is because he does feel much better about life these days. One of the main reasons is that at the urging of his second wife Janie, he began to see an Atlanta psychiatrist, Dr. Frank Pittman, in 1985. Pittman did two important things for Turner. The first was to put him on the drug lithium, which is generally used to treat manic depression, including a milder tendency toward mood swings. Turner's colleagues and J.J. Ebaugh, the woman for whom he left Janie, suddenly saw an enormous change in his behavior. "With lithium," says Ebaugh, "he became very even tempered. Ted's just one of those miracle cases. I mean, lithium is great stuff, but in Ted's particular case, lithium is a miracle."

Turner agrees that the medication helped calm him down. But Pittman's second contribution was to help Turner exorcise his father. To understand why Turner and the father he worshipped had no ordinary filial competition, consider this: when young Turner did something bad, his father, Ed, beat him with a wire coat hanger. When young Turner did something very bad, Ed once ordered his son to beat him. "He laid down on the bed and gave me the razor strap and he said, 'Hit me harder,' " Turner told interviewer David Frost.

Ed Turner, who became a millionaire in the billboard business, was determined to give his son both ambition and the self-doubt that keeps ambitious people going. Ted's father sent the boy to a military academy from the fifth grade on, punished him at home for such omissions as failing to read a new book every two days, and charged him rent during summer vacations. When Ed committed suicide, Turner says, "that left me alone, be-

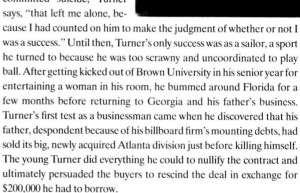

cause I had counted on him to make the judgment of whether or not I was a success." Until then, Turner's only success was as a sailor, a sport he turned to because he was too scrawny and uncoordinated to play ball. After getting kicked out of Brown University in his senior year for entertaining a woman in his room, he bummed around Florida for a few months before returning to Georgia and his father's business. Turner's first test as a businessman came when he discovered that his father, despondent because of his billboard firm's mounting debts, had sold its big, newly acquired Atlanta division just before killing himself. The young Turner did everything he could to nullify the contract and ultimately persuaded the buyers to rescind the deal in exchange for $200,000 he had to borrow.

Turner proved far more adept even than his father at the billboard business. So as the money rolled in, he turned to sailing and broadcasting in pursuit of his father's elusive benediction. By 1982, when he was 43, he had successfully defended the America's Cup, launched the first nationally televised cable-TV station and the first

EITHER LEAD, FOLLOW OR GET OUT OF THE WAY

24-hour news network, and made the first edition of the *Forbes* 400 list—enough success, he says, to have begun to lay "the ghost" of that paternal judgment "to rest." But until six years ago, he was still an emotional cripple, doing his best to imitate his father. He drank, but not well ("Two drinks and Ted was gone," says a friend), and earned early notoriety for showing up at the America's Cup press conference knee-walking drunk. He was such a determined womanizer that he made clear to Janie before their marriage in 1964 that he had no intention of becoming monogamous, according to several intimates.

In his sailing days he was rarely home, and during one period he missed three consecutive Christmases. When he did spend time with his family, says his eldest son Teddy, he behaved as though "kids were a necessary evil." He forbade crying, snapped at the slightest imperfection and ran his weekends at his South Carolina plantation on a militaristic schedule of dawn-to-dusk hunting.

What Turner recognized in the mid-'80s was that his roller-

At 43, Turner was a champion sailor and cable mogul. Then he began his real achievement — exorcising his father's legacy.

coaster emotional life, which had served him well in his risk-taking entrepreneurial days, was not particularly useful in running an international company with long-term ambitions and an estimated worth well in excess of $7 billion. The businessman who three times in his life had leveraged almost everything he owned and borrowed heavily—to buy back his father's billboard company, to start CNN and to purchase MGM—says he came to believe he did not "have to take desperate gambles anymore."

It was not just that Turner had more to lose; he was also convinced that through some cyclical inevitability he was doomed to lose what he had. In 1986 Turner's premonition came close to happening: his acquisition of MGM/UA for $1.7 billion buried him so deeply in debt that he had to be bailed out by a consortium of cable operators (including Time Warner, which owns TIME) that invested

Turner loved winning more than sailing. He said the sport was cold and wet.

Tomahawk choppers Turner and Jimmy Carter share a dedication to the Braves, world peace and the environment

$568 million in the company in exchange for minority ownership. Turner remained chairman, but he was forced to give cable operators seven seats on the 15-member board and veto power over any decision that would cost the company more than $2 million. It was a major setback, but once he had resigned himself to the company's shotgun marriage, it came almost as a relief: it forced stability on Turner just as he was growing weary of his own high-wire act. And then, of course, there was J.J. Ebaugh, possibly the first woman Turner truly loved.

He met her in 1980 in Newport, R.I., when she was dating Tom Blackaller, a legendary sailor whose boat, *Clipper,* shared a dock with Ted Turner's *Courageous.* The adventuresome California blond, who could drive race cars, pilot sailboats and fly airplanes, caught his eye. Although he did not own an airplane, he hired Ebaugh as a pilot, and she moved to Atlanta in 1981, bringing along a used one she had bought for him. When she announced she was leaving him in 1986, Turner wooed her back by promising to change his ways. In counseling, the man about whom it is said that talking to him is like listening to a radio began to tame his mouth.

The more flexible Turner made a variety of sacrifices. He left his wife and gave up philandering. After moving in with Ebaugh in 1986, he also agreed to spend more time with her in California and even bought a cliff-hanging house in Big Sur. The couple split up two years later. By the time he started dating Fonda in early 1990, Turner was so reformed that he agreed to spend half his time in Los Angeles while Fonda's son Troy was still in high school there. When Fonda decided she would quit drinking a year ago, Turner announced he would too. He has given up hour-to-hour management of his company. He now eats much of the health-food menu her cook prepares and has lost 10 lbs. He follows her on hikes and bike rides; she follows him hunting and fly-fishing and to baseball games.

Turner is also showing signs that he wants to enjoy his family. Four years ago he began organizing regular family vacations; he is openly affectionate with his children and checks in regularly with Fonda's two kids.

But Turner has reinvented himself most by shifting his longtime preoccupation with self-destruction away from himself and onto the world. He has always been an environmentalist—as long, in fact, as he has been a hunter. He now plans to turn his Flying D ranch near Bozeman, Mont., into what amounts to a privately owned national park: he has uprooted miles of barbed-wire fence, let pastures return to native grasses and started raising a herd of buffalo he hopes will swell to 4,000.

For the past six years, Turner has also made a public career of saving the planet. His heroes used to be Alexander the Great and Napoleon; now they are Martin Luther King and Gandhi. In 1986, to promote world peace, he staged the Goodwill Games in Moscow, on which he lost $26 million, and staged them again last year in Seattle, losing an additional $44 million.

It is possible to detect in his quest the messianic reflex that overcomes people with big checkbooks and egos to match. He has issued what some are calling the "Ted Commandments," a list of 10 voluntary initiatives that would make the world a better place. (It includes "I promise to have no more than two children"—a belated pledge, since he has five.) He has told intimates he hopes to receive the Nobel Peace Prize.

His new crusade is also a sure, efficient way of outliving his father. For the one lesson Turner drew from that suicide is that people should never set goals they can reach. "My father told me he wanted

Jane Fonda has given up movies to create a new life with Turner

to be a millionaire, have a yacht and a plantation," says Turner. "And by the time he was 50 he had achieved all three, and he was having a very difficult time." Turner has carefully arranged to avoid that situation. "I'm not going to rest until all the world's problems have been solved. Homelessness, AIDS. I'm in great shape. I mean, the problems will survive me—no question about it."

In the meantime, as a grand rebuke to his father's final repudiation of life, Turner plans to write about his own. He put a stop to an autobiography written with a collaborator five years ago because he felt the first draft made him sound like a rube and the second draft made him sound boring. Now, at last, Turner believes he will like the sound of his own voice.

Inside the World of CNN

t is Wednesday afternoon, the woman who has accused William Kennedy Smith of rape has just begun to testify, and producer Bob Furnad is having a Maalox moment. After two days of mostly pallid testimony by other witnesses, prosecutor Moira Lasch has suddenly called the accuser to the stand. But Furnad, who is running the control room, has just learned that Terry Anderson, the last American hostage to be released, is scheduled to make his first appearance in Damascus at 3:30 p.m.—smack in the middle of CNN's trial coverage. What should Furnad do: continue to cover the long-awaited testimony of the accuser in the most publicized rape trial in history, or cut away to Terry Anderson's press conference?

The decision is made quietly, almost imperceptibly: no matter what is happening at the trial, CNN will cut away to Anderson. When it does, only seven minutes of the accuser's testimony is lost; her emotional account of the event is yet to come. Count it another CNN success.

The Smith trial illustrated the essence of the news channel: the coverage was live, dramatic, exhausting, messy and irresistible. It also proved to be a tricky test for the people who decide what mix of news CNN will beam to its global audience. As the all news network's impact has grown, those decisions have become more crucial. To the extent that the images CNN chooses to show—Boris Yeltsin defying coup plotters or a reporter sifting through bomb damage in Baghdad—are important in shaping people's attitudes and governments' policies, a small handful of news executives in Atlanta are among the world's most influential journalists.

Ted Turner may be the only one who ever thought CNN could come so far so fast. When Turner first launched the upstart 24-hour news operation in 1980, under the guidance of its brilliant but volatile president Reese Schonfeld, it had a staff of 300 and a newsroom tucked into the basement of a converted country club. Technical flubs were common: on the very first hour of CNN's first day, a story about baseball star Reggie Jackson was cut short when the transmission from New York suddenly went dead.

Today CNN has a staff of more than 1,700, a global reach in excess of 75 million homes, and a budget that keeps growing while the three broadcast networks cut back. Its headquarters are spread over several floors in a hotel-and-shopping complex in downtown Atlanta, formerly called the Omni and now dubbed CNN Center. The network has established its credibility, and it makes money: a profit of $134 million in 1990, and most likely more in 1991.

Yet the critical decisions are still made in seat-of-the-pants fashion, chiefly by three top executives. The veteran of the trio is Ed Turner, a charter member of the CNN staff, who is responsible for its worldwide network of 95 correspondents. He is the soul of CNN: serious, pragmatic, not flashy but fiercely competitive.

If Turner is in charge of getting news into the building, Furnad, senior executive producer, is the man responsible for getting it on the air. An 18-year veteran of ABC News who joined CNN in 1983, Furnad is a feisty field general who can berate his troops for a technical slipup one minute, praise them warmly the next.

Overseeing the entire network is Tom Johnson, the former publisher of the Los Angeles *Times* who was installed by Ted Turner as CNN's third president in August 1990. Johnson, 50, is an affable Georgia native with a Rolodex full of political contacts, dating from his years as an aide to President Lyndon B. Johnson.

Some CNN insiders feel Johnson's leadership has been lacking. There is much talk these days at the news channel about the need to forge a new direction for the '90s, and a suspicion that Johnson has not found one. CNN is still struggling to find a way to consistently attract more than a relatively small core of news junkies. Toward that end, Johnson is trying to stress more perspective and analysis in CNN's reporting, and to find more "anchors who are journalists." CNN has also set up a 60-member election unit, which will produce a daily half-hour program of campaign news starting in January.

Conscious of CNN's role as the de facto network of record, Johnson and his colleagues are especially sensitive to matters of fairness and balance. They have been diligent about running in full the candidacy announcement of every major-party presidential aspirant.

Even in handling the Smith trial, an instinct for fairness carried CNN through the slow stretches. Viewers may have been alternately bored and titillated, but they were not shortchanged. For all the salacious material, CNN's coverage was sober, well judged and informative. That it was a ratings hit as well (the average audience was 1.9 million homes, nearly five times normal) should come as no surprise—or be cause for dismay. After years of churning out the news, CNN has earned the right to its blockbusters.

SOUTHERN IRAQ

"I saw the look on my boy's face, and I know he will never be the same."

DANIEL KOZAKIEWICZ on reaction of his son, Sergeant Ken Kozakiewicz, to a buddy's "friendly fire" death

NEAR AN NASIRIYA, IRAQ

"Every soul shall have / A taste of death."

THE KORAN, SURA 3:185. An Iraqi soldier, incinerated in his truck on a road near the Euphrates River

KENNETH JARECKE—CONTACT FOR TIME

KUWAIT

"We don't belong here. This has nothing to do with us. It is all Saddam. He is crazy."

IRAQI PRISONERS, guarded by U.S. Marines, head for Saudi border

TONY O'BRIEN—JB PICTURES

KUWAIT OIL FIELD

"The ground is so hot, if you kneel on it, you get blisters … Your clothes heat up and your zipper burns."

CANADIAN ROUGHNECKS, looking like molten bronze figures against 4,000°F oil fires that turned sand into liquid glass, struggle to cap a gushing well

115

ISIKVEREN, TURKEY

"Every day 20 children are buried between the tents. Older people are dying too; so are younger adults. They are dying, dying even as I speak."

The Kurds' plight, in the words of **DR. GERARD SALERIO** of France's Doctors of the World. Here, refugees in morning mist bury children who died overnight

MOUNT PINATUBO, PHILIPPINES

"It started with little stones, then it became pitch dark, and the rain and sand began to fall. I thought it was the end of the world."

HIGH SCHOOL STUDENT in city of Angeles, near now abandoned Clark U.S. Air Base, after the 5,842-ft. Pinatubo, dormant for 611 years, blew its top—an eruption that, with accompanying earthquakes and torrential rains, took 330 lives

119

NEAR CHITTAGONG, BANGLADESH

"In the twinkling of an eye it ended! None could see When life was, and when life finished!"

RABINDARANTH TAGORE, *Sea-Waves*. In the wake of May's cyclone, whose 145-mph winds and 20-ft. waves left 125,000 dead, a lone survivor wanders on a corpse-littered shore

120

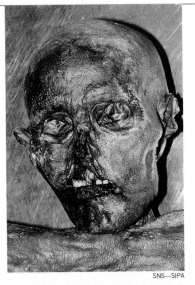

SNS—SIPA

SIMILAUN GLACIER

"What drove him there—
hunting for game, searching
for minerals, visiting
a friend in the next valley?"

Innsbruck archaeologist KONRAD SPINDLER on
discovery of a Bronze Age "Iceman,"
up to 4,800 years old, in a retreating glacier
in Austria's Alps

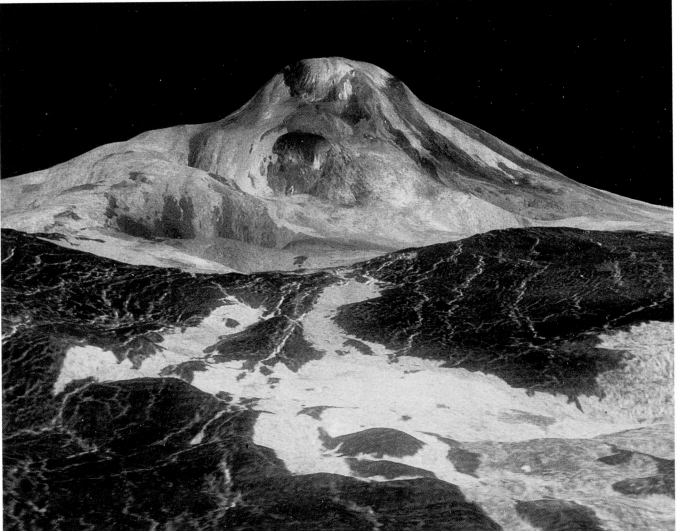

NASA—JPL

MAAT MONS PEAK, VENUS

"Venus, thy eternal sway, All the race of men obey."

EURIPIDES, *Iphigenia at Aulis.* The lava flow on Venus's second tallest peak (roughly
0,000 ft.), shown in radar images from the Magellan

The Year of Living Painfully

By JOHN GREENWALD

For U.S. consumers and companies, 1991 was the year the bill for the financially heedless 1980s came due in full. It was a year in which a supposedly short and shallow recession turned into a seemingly intractable slump. It was a year that saw the American banking system look shakier than at any other time since the Great Depression. It was a year that witnessed the humbling of mighty IBM and the continued shake-out of the nation's airlines. It was a year of breathtaking scandals, in which an obscure foreign lender called the Bank of Credit & Commerce International emerged as the most corrupt corporate enterprise ever and mighty Salomon Brothers stood exposed as a Wall Street outlaw. And through it all, 1991 was a year in which many Americans felt squeezed between layoffs and falling incomes on the one hand and the rising cost of such items as taxes and health care on the other.

There was some good news too, of course. Tempered by stable oil prices in the wake of the gulf war, the inflation rate hovered near a moderate 3% for most of the year. Interest rates on home mortgages fell to levels not seen since 1977 as the Federal Reserve Board eased credit in an effort to spur the economy. And securities firms began hiring employees for the first time since the 1987 crash as bull markets in stocks and bonds roped in welcome new business.

But the ailing economy set the tone for the year. While many experts initially argued that the recession that began in July 1990 had ended last May, the ensuing months brought little sense of relief. Burdened by debt and faced with stiff competition, U.S. firms continued mass layoffs of white-collar workers in industries ranging from banking to computers. By Thanksgiving, consumer confidence had plunged to an even lower level than surveys had found during the severe 1982 recession.

The economic malaise was paralleled by disturbing signs that governments everywhere were losing control of financial institutions. The world's banking authorities stood by as B.C.C.I. grew into a global money launderer and gunrunner that stole billions of dollars from its own depositors and insinuated its way into the power élites of many countries. B.C.C.I.'s secret control of Washington's First American Bankshares brought down First American chairman Clark Clifford, the doyen of Democratic power brokers, who denied knowing of the ownership but resigned in disgrace and shuttered his venerable Washington law office.

On Wall Street, Salomon Brothers admitted in August that it had unlawfully tried to monopolize the government bond market, a confession that cost cigar-chomping chairman John Gutfreund his job. Meanwhile, deposed junk-bond king Michael Milken paid the price for years of securities-law violations when a federal judge sentenced him to 10 years in prison.

The economy's plight was worsened by a U.S. banking system that remained awash in both bad loans and a reluctance to extend new credit. To protect depositors, Congress in November granted $70 billion of new borrowing authority to the all but broke Federal Deposit Insurance Corporation. Still, the money could prove little more than a stopgap, since a few failures like the $22 billion collapse of the Bank of New England last January threatened to deplete the fund rapidly. And mindful of the savings and loan fiasco, lawmakers rejected a Bush Administration plan to let banks set up nationwide branches and become one-stop financial centers.

When banks weren't collapsing, they were busy consolidating to cut costs and expand into new markets. In a can-you-top-this flurry of megadeals last summer, Chemical Banking agreed to aquire Manhattan rival Manufacturers Hanover for $2.3 billion in stock, only to see the purchase swiftly overshadowed by the $4.5 billion merger of California behemoths BankAmerica and Security Pacific.

Just as dramatic was the identity crisis that struck IBM. With its dominant share of the markets for mainframe computers and personal computers stuck in long-term decline, IBM stunned the industry in July by joining forces with archrival Apple in a pact to develop powerful new PCs. Then in November Big Blue unveiled the most radical shake-up in its 78-year history. IBM said it would spin off virtually all its divisions into smaller, more entrepreneurial units.

Other blue chip companies suffered crises of their own. Detroit's woes deepened as the recession kept consumers out of dealers' showrooms. Analysts expected General Motors, Ford and Chrysler to show a combined loss of nearly $6 billion for 1991. Airlines were particularly hard hit: Pan Am, Eastern and Midway went out of business after landing in bankruptcy court. Beleaguered Sears was overtaken by the Wal-Mart discount chain as the No. 1 store where America shops. And American Express left home without its cachet when defaults by holders of its Optima card forced the firm to write off $155 million of bad loans.

There were seismic upheavals among individually owned empires as well. British media mogul Robert Maxwell died while yachting off the Canary Islands in November, just eight months after he had rescued the New York *Daily News*. An autopsy found that he had probably suffered a heart attack, but allegations that Maxwell had improperly shifted funds between his holdings raised questions about the cause of his death and left his debt-laden empire in disarray. Donald Trump watched creditors carve up his real estate empire and lost the famed Plaza Hotel to his ex-wife Ivana in the most breathlessly reported divorce of the year.

Overall, Americans struggled in 1991 to live within means that too often were shrinking. That made the troubled economy the country's top concern as the old year ended and the U.S. headed into the 1992 election season.

The Dirtiest Bank Of All

How B.C.C.I. and its "black network" became a financial supermarket for crooks and spies— and how the U.S. tried to cover up its role

Bank-fraud cases are usually dry, tedious affairs. Not this one. Nothing in the history of modern financial scandals rivals the saga of the Bank of Credit & Commerce International, the $20 billion rogue empire that regulators in 62 countries shut down July 5 in a stunning global sweep. Never has a single scandal involved so much money, so many nations or so many prominent people.

Superlatives are quickly exhausted: it is the largest corporate criminal enterprise ever, the biggest Ponzi scheme, the most pervasive money-laundering operation and financial supermarket ever created for the likes of Manuel Noriega, Ferdinand Marcos, Saddam Hussein and the Colombian drug barons. B.C.C.I. even accomplished a Stealth-like invasion of the U.S. banking industry by secretly buying First American Bankshares, a Washington-based holding company with offices stretching from Florida to New York, whose chairman was former U.S. Defense Secretary Clark Clifford.

But B.C.C.I. is more than just a criminal bank. From interviews with sources close to B.C.C.I., TIME has pieced together a portrait of a clandestine division of the bank called the "black network," which functioned as a global intelligence operation and a Mafia-like enforcement squad. Operating primarily out of the bank's offices in Karachi, Pakistan, the 1,500-employee black network used sophisticated spy equipment and techniques, along with bribery, extortion, kidnapping and even, by some accounts, murder. The black network—so named by its own members—stopped at almost nothing to further the bank's aims the world over.

The more conventional departments of B.C.C.I. handled such services as laundering money for the drug trade and helping dictators loot their national treasuries. The black network operated a lucrative arms-trade business and transported drugs and gold. According to investigators and participants in those operations, it often worked with Western and Middle Eastern intelligence agencies. The strange and still murky ties between B.C.C.I. and the intelligence agencies of several countries were so pervasive that even the White House became entangled. The National Security Council, for example, used B.C.C.I. to funnel money for the Iran-*contra* deals, and the CIA maintained accounts in B.C.C.I. for covert operations. Moreover, investigators told TIME that the Defense Intelligence Agency maintained a slush-fund account with B.C.C.I., apparently to pay for clandestine activities.

But the CIA may have used B.C.C.I. as more than an undercover banker: U.S. agents collaborated with the black network in several operations, according to a B.C.C.I. black-network "officer" who is now a secret U.S. government witness. Sources told investigators that B.C.C.I. worked closely with Israel's spy agencies and other Western intelligence groups as well, especially in arms deals. The bank also maintained cozy relationships with international terrorists, say investigators who discovered suspected terrorist accounts for Libya, Syria and the Palestine Liberation Organization in B.C.C.I.'s London offices.

The bank's intelligence connections and alleged bribery of public officials around the world may explain the biggest mystery in the B.C.C.I. scandal: why banking and law-enforcement authorities allowed the bank to spin out of control for so long.

In the U.S. investigators have said openly that the Justice Department not only reined in its own probe of the bank but was also part of a concerted campaign to derail any full investigation. In July Robert Morgenthau, the Manhattan district attorney who first launched his investigations into B.C.C.I. in 1989, said, "We have had no cooperation from the Justice Department since we first asked for records in March 1990. In fact, they are impeding our investigation, and Justice Department representatives are asking witnesses not to cooperate with us."

B.C.C.I. was started in 1972 with the putative mission of becoming the Muslim world's first banking powerhouse. Though it was incorporated in Luxembourg and headquartered in London, had more than 400 branches and subsidiaries around the world and was nominally owned by Arab shareholders, B.C.C.I. was always a Pakistani bank, with its heart in Karachi. Agha Hasan Abedi, the bank's founder and leader until his ouster in 1990, is a Pakistani, as are most of the bank's former middle managers. And it was in Pakistan that the bank's most prodigiously corrupt division was spawned.

The Soviet invasion of Afghanistan in 1979 and the resulting strategic importance of neighboring Pakistan accelerated the growth of B.C.C.I.'s geopolitical power and its unbridled use of the black network. Because the U.S. wanted to supply the *mujahedin* rebels in Afghanistan with Stinger missiles and other military hardware, it needed the full cooperation of Pakistan, across whose border the weapons would be shipped. By the mid-1980s, the CIA's Islamabad operation was one of the largest U.S. intelligence stations in the world. "If B.C.C.I. is such an embarrassment to the U.S. that

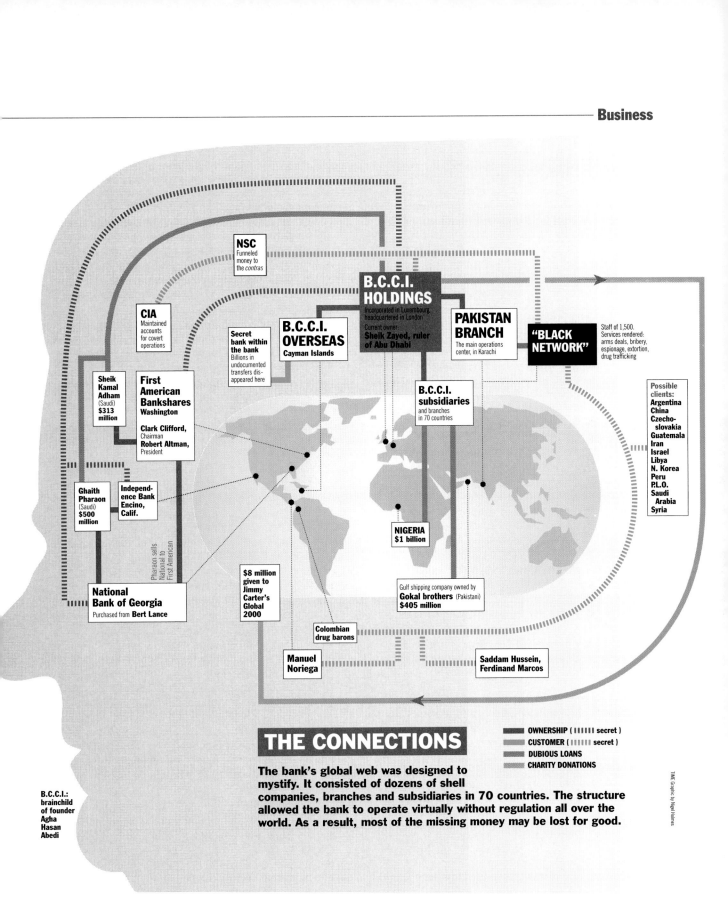

NSC
Funneled money to the *contras*

B.C.C.I. HOLDINGS
Incorporated in Luxembourg, headquartered in London
Current owner:
Sheik Zayed, ruler of Abu Dhabi

CIA
Maintained accounts for covert operations

Secret bank within the bank
Billions in undocumented transfers disappeared here

B.C.C.I. OVERSEAS
Cayman Islands

PAKISTAN BRANCH
The main operations center, in Karachi

"BLACK NETWORK"

Staff of 1,500. Services rendered: arms deals, bribery, espionage, extortion, drug trafficking

Possible clients:
Argentina
China
Czecho-
slovakia
Guatemala
Iran
Israel
Libya
N. Korea
Peru
P.L.O.
Saudi
Arabia
Syria

Sheik Kamal Adham
(Saudi)
$313 million

First American Bankshares
Washington

Clark Clifford,
Chairman
Robert Altman,
President

B.C.C.I. subsidiaries
and branches in 70 countries

Ghaith Pharaon
(Saudi)
$500 million

Independ-ence Bank
Encino, Calif.

Pharaon sells National to First American

National Bank of Georgia
Purchased from **Bert Lance**

$8 million given to Jimmy Carter's Global 2000

NIGERIA
$1 billion

Gulf shipping company owned by
Gokal brothers (Pakistani)
$405 million

Colombian drug barons

Manuel Noriega

Saddam Hussein, Ferdinand Marcos

THE CONNECTIONS

OWNERSHIP (‖‖‖‖ secret)	
CUSTOMER (‖‖‖‖ secret)	
DUBIOUS LOANS	
CHARITY DONATIONS	

The bank's global web was designed to mystify. It consisted of dozens of shell companies, branches and subsidiaries in 70 countries. The structure allowed the bank to operate virtually without regulation all over the world. As a result, most of the missing money may be lost for good.

B.C.C.I.:
brainchild of founder
Agha Hasan Abedi

TIME Graphic by Nigel Holmes

forthright investigations are not being pursued, it has a lot to do with the blind eye the U.S. turned to the heroin trafficking in Pakistan," says a U.S. intelligence officer.

The black network was a natural outgrowth of B.C.C.I.'s dubious and criminal associations. Its original purpose was to pay bribes, intimidate authorities and quash investigations. But according to a former operative, sometime in the early 1980s the black network began running its own drugs, weapons and currency deals. "B.C.C.I. was a full-service bank," says an international arms dealer. "They not only financed arms deals that one government or another wanted to keep secret, they shipped the goods in their own ships, insured them with their own agency and provided manpower and security. They worked with intelligence agencies from all the Western countries and did a lot of business with East bloc countries."

U.S. intelligence agencies were well aware of such activities. "B.C.C.I. played an indispensable role in facilitating deals between Israel and some Middle Eastern countries," says a former State Department official. "And when you look at the Saudi support of the *contras,* ask yourself who the middleman was: there was no government-to-government connection between the Saudis and Nicaragua."

Yet the bank's arms business was benign compared with the black network's other missions. Sources say B.C.C.I. officials, known as protocol officers, were responsible for providing a smorgasbord of services for customers: paying bribes to politicians, supplying "young beauties from Lahore," moving drugs and expediting insider business deals. When it came to recruiting and persuading, the black network usually got its way. "We would put money in the accounts of people we wanted to seduce to work for us," says a source we'll call Mustafa, "or we would use terror tactics," including kidnapping and blackmail. "We were after business cooperation or military or industrial secrets that we would use or broker, and we targeted generals, businessmen and politicians. In America it was easy: money almost always worked, and we sought out politicians known to be corruptible."

The black network's mission eventually became the pursuit of power and influence for its own sake, but its primary purpose was to foster a global looting operation that bilked depositors of billions of dollars. Price Waterhouse, the accounting firm whose audit triggered the worldwide seizure of B.C.C.I. assets in July, said the disarray is so extreme that the firm could not even put together a coherent financial statement. But investigators believe $10 billion or more is missing, fully half of B.C.C.I.'s worldwide assets.

How did it happen? B.C.C.I.'s corporate structure allowed the bank to operate virtually without regulation all over the world. The bank's organizational web consisted of dozens of shell companies, offshore banks, branches and subsidiaries in 70 countries. It was incomprehensible even to its own financial officers and auditors. The bank's extensive use of unregulated Cayman Islands accounts enabled it to hide almost anything. The bank's unique method of accounting—longhand in paper ledgers, written in Pakistan's Urdu language—makes it likely that most of the missing money will never be traced. Nor is it likely that anyone will ever know just how much Abedi, who has incorporated a new bank, called the Progressive Bank, in Karachi, stole from the rest of the world.

B.C.C.I.'s downfall was inevitable because it was essentially a planetary Ponzi scheme, a rip-off technique pioneered by American flimflam man Charles Ponzi in 1920. B.C.C.I. gathered deposits, looted most of them, but kept enough new deposits flowing in so that there was always sufficient cash on hand to pay anyone who asked for his money. During the years of its most explosive growth, in the late 1970s and mid-1980s, B.C.C.I. became a magnet for drug money, capital-flight money, tax-evading money and money from corrupt government officials. B.C.C.I. quickly gained a reputation as a bank that could move money anywhere and hide it without a trace.

As B.C.C.I.'s influence grew, a corrupt core of middle management evolved, usually branch officers in foreign countries who were given wide latitude to do as they pleased. Increasingly, that meant serving a core clientele of what investigators estimate to be 3,500 corrupt business people around the world.

The more B.C.C.I. became a conduit for money laundering, the more deposit gathering became the bank's chief goal. At annual meetings, founder Abedi would harangue his employees for days on the importance of luring deposits. That was probably because billions of dol-

B.C.C.I.: Rise and Fall

1972

Declaring his intention to form the Third World's first multinational bank, Pakistani financier Agha Hasan Abedi organizes the Bank of Credit & Commerce International. Bank of America puts up $2.5 million, or 25%, of the bank's capital, Arab investors the rest.

1975-76

U.S. regulators reject a B.C.C.I. bid for two New York banks when Abedi fails to disclose requested details about his company.

1977

Abedi helps Saudi billionaire Ghaith R. Pharaon begin his acquisition of the National Bank of Georgia from Bert Lance.

1978

B.C.C.I. makes a hostile bid for Financial General Bankshares of Washington. When the SEC seeks to block the bid, B.C.C.I. hires Clark Clifford to help.

1980

Financial General agrees to sell to a group of Middle East investors, the same investors who own B.C.C.I. Uneasy, regulators delay approval.

1981

Regulators grant approval after Clifford assures them that no link will exist between B.C.C.I. and the U.S. banking company.

1982

Clifford and law partner Robert Altman become chairman and president of the bank holding company, now renamed First American Bankshares, while remaining B.C.C.I.'s chief U.S. attorneys.

lars were vanishing. At the highest levels, B.C.C.I. officials whisked deposits into secret accounts in the Cayman Islands. These accounts constituted a hidden bank within B.C.C.I., known only to Abedi and a few others. From those accounts, B.C.C.I. would lend massive amounts to curry favor with governments or to buy secret control of companies.

U.S. regulators discovered that such loans had enabled B.C.C.I. to buy clandestine control in three American banks: First American Bankshares in Washington, National Bank of Georgia (later purchased by First American) and Independence Bank of Encino, Calif. The latter two were bought officially by Abedi's front man, Ghaith Pharaon, the putative Saudi tycoon who received an estimated $500 million in B.C.C.I. loans in the 1970s and '80s. Those loans were secured only by shares of stock in the companies Pharaon purchased, which meant that they were designed never to be repaid.

W hat Abedi got in return for such loans was de facto ownership of three American banks, since he held their shares as collateral for loans not intended to be repaid. More important, this "nominee" shareholder arrangement meant that B.C.C.I. itself remained invisible to U.S. banking regulators. Following its discovery early in 1991 that B.C.C.I. owned both First American and Independence Bank, the Federal Reserve ordered B.C.C.I. to sell them off.

B.C.C.I.'s deposits also disappeared through the black network, which used the money to pay bribes and conduct its weapons and currency deals. According to a former officer, B.C.C.I. bought virtual control of customs officials in ports and air terminals around the world. In the U.S. millions of dollars flowed through B.C.C.I.'s Washington office, allegedly destined to pay off U.S. officials.

The bribes and intelligence connections may offer an explanation for the startling regulatory inaction. The Justice Department hindered an investigation by Massachusetts Senator John Kerry, whose Subcommittee on Terrorism, Narcotics and International Operations was the first to probe B.C.C.I.'s illegal activities. "We have had a lot of difficulty getting any answers at all out of Justice," said Kerry last summer. "Somebody consciously or negligently took their eyes off the ball in this investigation."

According to Jack Blum, Kerry's chief investigator in 1988-89, the lack of cooperation was so pervasive and so successful in frustrating his efforts to investigate B.C.C.I. that he says he believed it was part of a deliberate strategy. Said Blum: "There's no question in my mind that it's a calculated effort inside the Federal Government to limit the investigation. The only issue is whether it's a result of high-level corruption or if it's designed to hide illegal government activities."

The Justice Department denied any reluctance to investigate. Said spokesman Dan Eramian: "We believe there has been good cooperation between law-enforcement [agencies] in this investigation. We're often accused of dragging our feet, and part of that we believe is partisan in nature."

Last August Kerry held the first public testimony on the B.C.C.I. affair as part of a global offensive against the rogue bank. The sessions brought the shadowy institution irrevocably into the public arena. Among the developments:
▶ A New York State grand jury indicted B.C.C.I. and its two principal officers for fraud, bribery, grand larceny and money laundering after a two-year investigation led by Manhattan district attorney Robert Morgenthau. B.C.C.I., said Morgenthau, had looted depositors of more than $5 billion in "the largest bank fraud in world history." Named as defendants were Abedi and Swaleh Naqvi, who had been the bank's chief operating officer. But bringing the pair to trial could prove impossible. Pakistan said it refuses to extradite the ailing Abedi, 68, who is a hero in his homeland for organizing the Third World's largest bank.
▶ The Federal Reserve Board fined B.C.C.I. $200 million for illegally acquiring control of three prominent U.S. banking institutions. Chief among them was First American Bankshares, Washington's largest bank holding company, which was headed by former Defense Secretary Clark Clifford and his law partner Robert Altman. Clifford and Altman, who served as attorneys for B.C.C.I. throughout the 1980s, have denied knowing it owned First American. But in August the Federal Reserve Board forced them to resign their First American posts..

1983
B.C.C.I. purchases a Colombian bank with branches in Medellín and Cali, centers of drug traffic.

1985-87
B.C.C.I. launders $32 million of drug money; $500,000 from Manuel Noriega passes through First American.

1986
First American buys Pharaon's National Bank of Georgia.

1988
A Florida grand jury indicts B.C.C.I. for laundering drug money. During the investigation, a B.C.C.I. official says Abedi owns First American.

1989
Reeling from the Florida case and bad loans, B.C.C.I. loses $498 million. Despite evidence of B.C.C.I. control, regulators permit First American to buy a Florida bank.

1990
B.C.C.I. pleads guilty in Florida and pays $15 milion. Sheik Zayed bin Sultan al-Nahayan of Abu Dhabi, a longtime investor in B.C.C.I., acquires control of the troubled bank and orders an audit, which finds that an estimated $4 billion is missing. First American Bankshares loses $182.5 million for the year.

1991
The Federal Reserve probes whether B.C.C.I. owns First American and orders the banking firms to halt all transactions with each other. The Fed asks the Justice Department to consider possible criminal charges. A grand jury in New York City examines evidence of money laundering and fraud. Before year-end, B.C.C.I. enters a guilty plea, forfeiting $550 million for fines, penalties and litigation costs, as well as restitution to 1.2 million depositors worldwide.

The other two secretly owned banks were the National Bank of Georgia and CenTrust Savings. Pharaon used B.C.C.I. funds to become a partner of financier David Paul, who built CenTrust into a giant house of cards before it collapsed in 1990 at a cost to taxpayers of $2 billion.

TIME learned that Pharaon helped keep CenTrust open for a year longer than its bankrupt condition warranted after acquiring a total of 1.5 million CenTrust shares, or more than 5% of the S&L's stock, in 1988 and 1989. CenTrust was so shaky by late 1988 that regulators for the Federal Home Loan Bank Board in Atlanta had decided to shut it down. Pharaon and Paul, who became a target of a Miami grand jury investigation of CenTrust, struggled to keep the institution's doors—and coffers—open.

Pharaon assured regulators that he was backed by oil-rich Arabs who would keep CenTrust solvent. When that tack failed to deter officials, Pharaon and Paul flew CenTrust's corporate jet to Washington to give similar promises to M. Danny Wall, who chaired the Home Loan Bank Board at the time. After the session, regulators said CenTrust could remain open by selling bonds to shore up its capital. But when few investors bought the offering, Pharaon ponied up $30 million to keep CenTrust afloat. Once regulators let CenTrust stay in business, B.C.C.I. whisked the $30 million back into its own accounts. By the time CenTrust formally went bust in 1990, the yearlong delay in closing the thrift may have cost American taxpayers as much as $1 billion in extra bailout expenses.

▶Kerry released part of a 1986 CIA memo warning the Treasury and State departments that B.C.C.I. had secretly owned First American since 1982. Yet the Reagan Administration apparently did nothing in response to the document. CIA Deputy Director Richard J. Kerr confirmed that the agency had used B.C.C.I. to move money around the world; other sources confirmed that the Defense Intelligence Agency, which monitors other nations' armed forces, had trans-

ferred funds through the bank. Sources said that the CIA had closed all agency accounts by 1989.

▶Peru launched a government-wide probe of charges that B.C.C.I. gave two central-bank officers $3 million in bribes in return for their depositing $200 million of Peruvian funds in secret B.C.C.I. accounts in Panama. Officials denied the allegations, which were part of the Manhattan indictment against B.C.C.I. But they said they had deposited money with B.C.C.I. because threats by former President Alan García Pérez to reduce Peru's foreign-debt payments had scared off other banks.

▶A London court halted the liquidation of B.C.C.I.'s British branches until December to give Sheik Zayed bin Sultan al-Nahayan, the ruler of Abu Dhabi who acquired control of B.C.C.I. in 1990, a chance to rescue depositors and develop a plan to reopen a cleansed and scaled-down version of the global bank. Zayed immediately put up $84 million to help rescue the 120,000 British customers who had entrusted $400 million to B.C.C.I.

Like an oil spill, the B.C.C.I. affair has been slowly tarring a growing list of prominent U.S. politicians. In late October, President Bush was embarrassed when it was revealed that 33-year-old ex–White House aide Edward Rogers had accepted a $600,000, two-year contract to help defend B.C.C.I. insider Kamal Adham from criminal probes. Though Rogers' contract with Adham was not illegal, it showed extremely poor judgment. President Bush publicly admonished the former aide, and Rogers resigned the account.

Others tainted by the scandal include former President Jimmy Carter, who accepted millions in contributions from B.C.C.I. for his presidential library and his charitable foundation; former Atlanta Mayor Andrew Young, who borrowed money from B.C.C.I. and did not pay it back; former Prime Minister of India Indira Gandhi, who once presented a prize established by B.C.C.I.; and former Treasury Secretary John Connally, who bought a Texas bank with Ghaith Pharaon. Even

Fall of a Patriarch

"There is no function of any kind on the part of B.C.C.I. I know of no present relationship. I know of no planned future relationship."
—Clark Clifford, 1981

Those words must have long haunted the former Defense Secretary, who resigned under pressure last August as chairman of First American Bankshares, Washington's largest bank holding company. A decade ago regulators, relying on Clifford, permitted a group of Middle Eastern investors to acquire First American. Those purchasers, however, turned out to be alleged fronts for the notorious B.C.C.I. The secret ownership demonstrated B.C.C.I.'s knack for infiltrating power élites even as it served as a cash conduit for terrorists, gunrunners and drug thugs.

The departure of Clifford, a venerated Democratic Party elder, and bank president Robert Altman, who also resigned, came after intense prodding by the Federal Reserve Board. The regulators had

been seeking to restore public confidence in First American (assets: $11 billion), which has been plagued by troubled real estate loans in the Washington area. Last spring the Fed tapped former Republican Senator Charles Mathias of Maryland to head a committee to oversee First American. While Clifford, 84, and law partner Altman, 44, retained their titles, investigators told TIME that the Mathias group gradually took over. "It started to get nasty," said one.

By then the Federal Reserve, which last July fined B.C.C.I. $200 million for its secret American bank acquisitions, had decided Clifford and Altman had to go and picked former Attorney General Nicholas Katzenbach to succeed Clifford as chairman. Clifford and Altman still face a daunting battery of probes. Grand juries in Washington and New York City are studying how much both men knew about B.C.C.I.'s secret ownership of First American.

Secretary of State James Baker's name indirectly came up after acting CIA Director Kerr testified before a Senate panel in October. Kerr revealed that in 1985 the CIA told the Treasury Department, then headed by Baker, that B.C.C.I. secretly owned First American Bank, the largest bank in the nation's capital—a critical piece of information that Treasury never pursued. TIME learned that last May, B.C.C.I. paid $1.3 million in fees to the Washington law firm of Patton, Boggs and Blow, a lobbying powerhouse that includes Ron Brown, chairman of the Democratic Party, among its partners.

Last summer evidence suggested that the Department of Justice was continuing to hamstring its own investigation and interfere with the aggressive inquiries being pursued by Manhattan district attorney Morgenthau. The Justice Department pursued an odd mixture of passive and aggressive behavior: incuriously passive in its own pursuit of B.C.C.I. but intensely aggressive in turf battles with Morgenthau's investigators.

In July then Attorney General Dick Thornburgh pledged cooperation. But investigators have since complained that the promise was not kept. Kerry battled a Justice Department decision to prohibit him from taking testimony from former U.S. Customs Service agent Robert Mazur. Mazur, who led the undercover sting operation that produced the first indictments of B.C.C.I. in 1988, quit the agency to work for the Drug Enforcement Administration. When he finally testified in late November, Mazur said that hundreds of leads concerning secret B.C.C.I. ownership of U.S. banks and alleged payoffs to U.S. politicians had been ignored. "A lot of follow-up in contacting witnesses and reviewing records was lost that might have benefited the case," he declared.

"There is a feeling that somebody in Washington is trying to cut a deal on B.C.C.I.," said a senior official last fall, "that they really don't want the U.S. Attorney's office to actually return indictments because that would muck up their ability to do some kind of a package deal, where we cut off the hands of a few Pakistanis and paint it as if they were really all the big folks. They'll absolve the Sheik (Sheik Zayed, the ruler of Abu Dhabi, who oversees the shuttered B.C.C.I. empire) and then let the bank reopen overseas" to repay its foreign debts.

There is logic to this complaint: B.C.C.I. losses are put at $12 billion, and officials in this country and Britain pleaded with Zayed, one of the world's richest men, to make good on the losses. Meanwhile, in Abu Dhabi, Zayed placed under house arrest many of the bank officers wanted for questioning by U.S. officials.

Justice Department officials bristled at the suggestion that their work was impeded by anyone, in or out of government. Said Robert S. Mueller, head of the Justice Department's criminal division: "The investigation is not being held up, it's being coordinated. We've got some blemishes, but we have not covered up." Mueller revved up the investigation last July by adding more manpower and said his department was trying its best to work with other probers.

Indeed, in mid-November the Justice Department indicted B.C.C.I. founder Abedi, former bank president Naqvi and front man Pharaon. They were charged with illegally taking over Independence Bank of Encino, Calif., and with fraud that contributed to the billion-dollar downfall of the CenTrust thrift. Since the U.S. stands little chance of extraditing Abedi from Pakistan and Naqvi faces charges in Abu Dhabi, Pharaon's indictment may be the most productive of the three. The Saudi national is unlikely to leave his haunts in Europe or Latin America.

The question that lingered for months was why the Justice Department limited its inquiry and allowed the law-enforcement community to believe the B.C.C.I. case was too sensitive to be handled routinely. Former B.C.C.I. officers said the bank's extensive U.S. intelligence connections and allegations of political payoffs help explain the Justice Department's foot dragging. In Congress, only a handful of legislators demanded action.

By late December, however, Morgenthau's office had changed its tune, announcing that it had made progress in the case with the assistance of the Department of Justice. B.C.C.I. and three related corporations agreed to plead guilty to six of 12 criminal counts and to forfeit its U.S. assets, estimated at $550

B.C.C.I. wooed former leaders Carter and Gandhi; it performed financial favors for Peru's Alan García, bottom

million, to an account to be controlled by the U.S. government. Among other things, this money will go toward paying a $10 million fine to New York State, making restitution to B.C.C.I.'s 1.2 million depositors worldwide, assisting First American Bankshares and the Independence Bank, and reimbursing the Manhattan district attorney's office for the costs of its investigation. While this is a hopeful beginning, it will undoubtedly take years to fully reconstruct the illegal activities of B.C.C.I.—the largest criminal operation in history.

A Slump That Won't Go Away

Thanks to the borrow-and-spend binge of the '80s, the U.S. remains burdened with problems that will frustrate growth for years to come

In the afterglow of the allied victory in the gulf war last spring, the U.S. economy seemed ready to shake off its malaise. Consumer confidence rose sharply, and sales of cars and homes began to shift into high gear. But in the clear light of winter, that hopeful moment seems long gone. Despite assertions from Washington and most economists that the recession ended last May, the recovery may be the weakest in postwar history, and many sectors could even be sliding backward. "The situation is far worse than the government would like us to believe, and things are going to remain this difficult for some time," says Bernard Brennan, chairman of Montgomery Ward. "I think we're naive to assume that we're out of the recession. It's even probable that the next phase could be worse than the first."

That gloomy assessment reflects one of the great ironies of current events. At the moment when democracy and free enterprise have triumphed over communism in the Soviet Union and Eastern Europe, the U.S. is paying the price of capitalism run amuck. Maimed by the prodigious explosion of debt that characterized the 1980s, the overburdened economy is undergoing a painful consoli-

dation and a shift in values away from the fast-money, speculative practices that came at the expense of financial soundness and long-term growth.

The '80s left behind structural burdens that are likely to rob the U.S. of robust growth for several years. Among them: record federal deficits ($285 billion for the past fiscal year) and an orgy of overbuilding that has sent the commercial real estate industry into an out-and-out depression. Beset by the speculative hangover, the economy has expanded just 2.6% from 1989 through mid-1991. Economists predict that the economy will bump along at a sluggish pace of less than 3% a year through 1995.

The fallout from the '80s has given consumers, who account for two-thirds of all spending, an abiding fear of being laid off as companies retrench. Since the recession began in July 1990, more than 1.6 million jobs have been lost. While the Labor Department reported that the unemployment rate in November remained at 6.8%, many economists and investors saw little to cheer. Among other grim signs, the labor statistics showed that the number of discouraged workers, those who have quit looking for jobs and are no longer counted among the unemployed, had risen 100,000 in the third quarter, to 1.1 million.

The unemployment report came after American Express said it would lay off 1,700 workers and take a $265 million write-off because of defaults among holders of its Optima credit card. Ames Department Stores, meanwhile, said it would close 77 of its 448 stores and lay off about 4,500 employees early 1992.

Spending is caught in what might be called a lending gridlock. Bankers, many of them saddled with bad loans and hampered by overzealous regulation, have been unwilling to lend. But even when they do make money available, many overleveraged consumers and companies are reluctant to borrow more.

Foundation, taxes will absorb a record 35.1% of Americans' income in 1991, up from 34.1% the previous year.

A combination of fear, prudence and even trendiness has turned American consumers into chronic stay-at-homes. "This recession has become a state of exhaustion from the delusions of the 1980s," says Audrey Freedman, a management counselor for the Manhattan-based Conference Board. "There is a general public turning away from confidence in government, the private sector and enterprise itself. We're just tired."

Not everyone is worn out, of course. Foreign demand for U.S. products, spurred by the strength of foreign currencies in relation to the weak dollar, has created a boomlet for some manufacturing firms. "If we didn't read about it in the newspapers, we wouldn't know a recession has been going

The economy's few bright spots are flickering at best. Buoyed by exports of capital goods, some manufacturers have been adding jobs at a time when most other industries have been cutting back. The government reported that orders for U.S. factory goods rose 1.9% in October but failed to make up for declines of 2.3% and 2% in the previous two months. If manufacturing falters, the last best hope will be housing, which has benefited from a drop in fixed-rate mortgage costs. The Commerce Department said sales of new single-family homes rose 2.2% in October, the seventh gain in nine months.

Burdened by the runaway federal deficit, Washington cannot cut taxes or increase spending to stimulate business growth, as it did in every other major downturn since World War II. Nor has the Federal Reserve Board's actions to lower interest rates provided much of a lift outside the housing market, even though the prime rate has fallen from 10.5% two years ago to 7.5% at year's end.

One reason this recession has so profoundly hampered spending is that the middle class has been hard hit. Nearly 600,000 of the lost jobs belonged to middle managers and other white-collar workers as companies slashed their payrolls because of slow sales, crushing interest charges and tough foreign competition.

"There is no historical precedent for this," says Dan Lacey, an Ohio-based employment consultant. "This does not represent a recession," he says of the downsizing, "but a permanent shift in management thinking that is both structural and profound." Shellshocked consumers have plenty to worry about besides losing their jobs. Debt burdens are so heavy that Americans are filing for bankruptcy at a record annual rate of 880,000; the number could swell to 1 million for the entire year. At the same time, household tax burdens are rising because of increased levies by deficit-ridden state and local governments and last year's federal budget agreement, which boosted alcohol, tobacco and payroll taxes. According to the Tax

on," says George Schueppert, chief financial officer of CBI Industries, an energy-equipment company that has totted up $1.5 billion worth of new orders this year, largely from Asia and Latin America. But merchandise exports amount to just 7% of American GNP and can scarcely drag the economy out of the doldrums single-handedly. Moreover, the manufacturing boom could quickly go bust if nervous domestic consumers don't start opening their wallets soon.

Few industries have been whipsawed by stop-and-go shopping as severely as U.S. automakers. Despite a surge in July, their sales for the model-year that ended in September totaled just 12.5 million units, the lowest level since 1983. With domestic auto plants now running at an average of just 65% of capacity, Detroit claims that no carmakers—not even the Japanese—are operating profitably in the U.S.

This may be the painful consequence of the heedless and high-flying '80s. "We live in the box we've got ourselves in," says Lyle Gramley, chief economist for the Mortgage Bankers Association of America and a former Fed governor. "We are paying the price for what we did in the past with this enormous federal deficit. The price goes beyond the poor functioning of the economy now. Here we are, this great, wealthy, affluent nation, and we cannot afford to rebuild our highways or bridges. We cannot afford to have a really serious war on drugs. We cannot afford to improve our educational system. This is absurd."

Reinvigorating the economy will require substantial new investments in all the areas that Gramley mentions. That has already triggered a politically volatile debate about shifting funds from defense to education and other programs to foster long-term growth. But having triumphantly demonstrated the power of capitalism to doubters abroad, the U.S., ironically, now faces the test of showing that the American brand of private enterprise can still solve problems at home.

Swaggering Into Trouble

Financial powerhouse Salomon Brothers digs a huge hole for itself by cheating in the most sacrosanct of markets

As the most powerful government bond dealer on Wall Street, Salomon Brothers has long been known for its swagger and a rough-and-tumble culture that reveled in practical jokes. But the scandal that stunned the giant firm last summer was no laughing matter. With the company's stock collapsing in the wake of disclosures that Salomon had repeatedly tried to corner the market for Treasury securities, chairman John Gutfreund and president Thomas Strauss resigned at an emergency board meeting on Sunday, Aug. 18. Omaha billionaire Warren Buffett, whose Berkshire Hathaway owns 14% of Salomon's preferred stock, said he would be willing to become an interim chairman, and immediately set about recasting Salomon in a more conservative mold.

The trouble began Aug. 9, when Salomon said it had suspended managing directors Paul Mozer and Thomas Murphy and two other employees for violating federal rules against acquiring more than 35% of Treasury notes and bonds at a government auction. The ceiling is designed to prevent large firms from purchasing enough of an issue to dictate the price of the securities when they resell them to smaller buyers. Had Salomon's infractions stopped there, the firm might have contained the damage. But Salomon dropped a bombshell on Aug. 13, when it admitted that Gutfreund, Strauss and others had learned last April of a trading violation but had failed to report it. The firm later found still more irregularities but apparently did not disclose them until faced with a government investigation.

The Justice Department and federal regulators launched investigations of the firm. Shareholders feared Salomon could even be barred from dealing in Treasury securities, a devastating penalty that could dry up most of the firm's profits. Such concerns caused the price of Salomon stock to plunge.

Gutfreund's resignation marked the end of one of Wall Street's most fabled careers. A gruff-talking bond trader, Gutfreund, now 62, became chairman of Salomon in 1978. According to *Liar's Poker,* a 1989 best seller by Michael Lewis, Gutfreund exhorted traders to come to work each morning

Gutfreund ruled Salomon for 13 years; Buffet, above, offered to step in as interim chairman

"ready to bite the ass off a bear." When the traders were not executing humongous deals, they delighted in such pranks as replacing the contents of a male colleague's suitcase with lingerie.

Ironically, it was a practical joke gone awry that helped bring Salomon down. In an elaborate form of hazing, Mozer reportedly persuaded a Salomon customer last February to submit a bogus $1 billion order for 30-year Treasury bonds. The idea was to shock the novice trader who received the order. But the prank backfired: the deal went through, and the unauthorized purchase landed on Salomon's books. Furthermore, Salomon rigged bids to exceed the 35% trading ceiling in at least three Treasury auctions. In December 1990, for example, the firm bought 35% of an $8.5 billion, four-year-note sale and also submitted a $1 billion bid that was ostensibly for a customer but was really for its own account. The combined transactions gave Salomon a 46% share of the overall deal. Such hubris has cost the firm dearly. Salomon already faces 43 civil lawsuits stemming from Treasury auction violations, and some of its former customers are suing the company.

To counter all the bad news, Buffett and his new chief operating officer, Deryck Maughan, have set out to make Salomon Brothers a "model" for Wall Street. To cut costs the new management team took back $110 million earmarked for bonuses; laid off nearly 140 highly paid investment bankers, stock traders and analysts; and established comprehensive rules for trading. In a sign that some of Buffett's reforms have had the desired effect, the World Bank announced in early December that it would return its business to Salomon after a three-month suspension. The move by the World Bank, the largest borrower of dollars outside of the U.S. government, may be just the vote of confidence the ailing Salomon needs to regain some of its former luster, if not its swagger.

Looking for Security

As banks face a shakeout, some small institutions disappear while big banks grow bigger

Amid the sudden-death dealmaking of the past decade, the world of banking seemed like an island of calm reserve. But this year, with too many banks chasing too little business in a slumping economy, the industry experienced a dramatic restructuring.

In January, Boston-based Bank of New England Corp. collapsed. To prevent a run on deposits that could spread throughout troubled New England and beyond, federal regulators rushed to bail out the region's fourth largest banking company (assets: $22 billion) and even stood behind deposits of more than $100,000, the limit covered by federal insurance. But that policy raised complaints.

When the small, black-owned Freedom National Bank (assets: $121 million) failed in November 1990 in New York City's Harlem, the Federal Deposit Insurance Corporation saw no risk of a widespread panic and let holders of large deposits suffer heavy losses. Stunned charities, churches and other customers lost $11 million in accounts that exceeded the $100,000 limit. Such favored treatment for the customers of big banks became a heated issue as consumers and politicians braced for a possible wave of new banking failures. Said John Jacob, president of the National Urban League, which lost more than $200,000 at Freedom National because of the government's double standard: "I think it is grossly discriminatory against banks that happen to be small."

For American savers, already reeling from the savings and loan debacle, the banking crisis inspired rising anxiety about the safety of their money. In a TIME/CNN poll of 1,000 adults surveyed last January by the firm Yankelovich Clancy Shulman, just 7% said they felt very confident about the soundness of U.S. banks, while 59% said they were only somewhat confident or not confident at all. Bigness is not necessarily reassuring: 52% said they had more faith in local banks than in larger ones, while 36% felt safer with their money in major institutions.

The Bank of New Eng-

land collapse may have ended prospects for a long-sought reform to limit federal-insurance coverage. The Administration wants to restrict depositors to a total of $100,000 in federal insurance in any one bank; in the S&L bailout, some big customers are being repaid the full $100,000 for each of several accounts in a single institution. Yet any move to cut back this blanket coverage could lead to the type of panic that the FDIC sought to avert in New England.

For some, big proved beautiful. In July, Chemical Banking agreed to acquire Manufacturers Hanover in a $2.3 billion stock swap. The merger of the two huge but weak Goliaths, both burdened by hefty portfolios of ailing loans, created a bank with assets of $135.5 billion. But the merger will inflict sharp pain on employees and the troubled New York economy. Chemical and Manufacturers said they would eliminate $650 million a year in costs through a series of deep cutbacks. The banks plan to pare 6,200 jobs, or nearly 15% of their combined work force, and shut 70 of their 436 branches in the New York City area. Manufacturers Hanover, which financed construction of the Brooklyn Bridge, will see its name vanish into corporate history.

While banking experts generally praised the deal, they cautioned that executives could find themselves balking at the drastic cuts that will be needed for substantial cost savings. And the banks' underachieving loans, which range from troubled real estate mortgages in New York City to unpaid Third World debt, will erode their profits for years to come. But the banks plan to rev up quickly. Among other things, they intend to raise $1.25 billion by selling stock. If Congress approves interstate banking, the new Chemical could shop for banks and savings and loans throughout the New York City region.

In August, San Francisco-based BankAmerica upped the ante by merging with its smaller Los Angeles rival Security Pacific in the largest such deal in banking history. With $193 billion in assets, the enlarged BankAmerica now ranks a close second to New York's Citicorp among U.S. banks. The merger could eventually reap savings of $1 billion annually for the two institutions as they combine functions and reduce overhead. This may mean layoffs of up to 10,000 workers, or 11% of the work force. But the merger with the revitalized BankAmerica was a necessary maneuver for CEO Robert Smith's troubled Security Pacific, which has been weakened by bad real estate loans. BankAmerica will now be a force in 10 Western states and is reportedly considering a bid for New England's Shawmut National as well.

For the U.S. banking system, 1991 has been the maximum stress test. How the government responds to the shakeout will determine the shape of U.S. banking for the rest of the 1990s—and beyond.

Customers queue to collect their money following the collapse of Harlem's 26-year-old Freedom National Bank in New York City

133

Love at First Byte

Giving up their blood rivalry,
Apple and IBM join forces to develop bold new hybrids in personal
computers. The chemistry may be just right.

From opposite ends of the U.S., they carried on the computer industry's fiercest rivalry. Based in suburban New York, International Business Machines has long dismissed Apple Computer as a bunch of rabble-rousers. Miles away, in both distance and culture, Silicon Valley–based Apple (1990 revenues: $5.6 billion) attacked IBM ($69 billion) as an impersonal bureaucracy, mocking the company in TV ads as Big Brother. The warring companies forced computer users to choose sides. Those wanting easy-to-use software favored Apple, while others threw their lot behind IBM because its PCs were backed by a wider assortment of programs.

But in a rapidly changing industry, IBM and Apple have found much in common. After years of dominating their own spheres of influence, they now face similar woes: declining market share, relentless low-cost competitors and aging technology. While IBM and Apple remain the biggest players, with a combined market share of 38%, their rivalry has lost its potency, as brand loyalty has given way to price competition.

The two companies decided in early July to put their differences aside. IBM and Apple plan to join forces and share technology in a potentially powerful partnership that could reshape the computer industry. Among the elements:

▶ The two companies will form a joint venture to develop an advanced operating system, the basic controlling software of computers, which IBM and Apple will use in their machines and sell to other companies.

▶ Apple's user-friendly Macintosh system will be integrated into IBM's product line, including the large computers that serve as the heart of corporate systems.

▶ Apple will gain access to IBM's advanced high-speed microprocessors, which will be incorporated into future editions of the Macintosh and other machines.

▶ The two computer makers will seek to develop a new generation of high-powered multimedia hardware and software, which could be marketed under both brand names.

Rather than choose sides, customers now insist that computers work together in networks, regardless of the make or model. That has harmed

Steven Jobs co-founded Apple

John Sculley, Apple's CEO

IBM chairman John Akers

Apple, since its operating software is not the most compatible. But it has been no blessing for IBM either, because its operating system is so common that customers often prefer to buy clone machines that work like IBM's but cost less. Customers have become more concerned about price than brand names or even high performance.

Indeed neither IBM nor Apple has been able to halt customer defections. IBM's market share in PCs has dropped by half, to 23%, while Apple's has declined to 15%, from 18%. The changing marketplace has forced both companies to make some painful adjustments. In the largest layoff in the company's history, Apple pared 1,500 jobs, or about 10% of its work force, this summer. IBM, which during the January-March period reported the first quarterly loss in its 80-year history, plans to reduce its 353,000 labor force by 20,000 in 1992, following a similar cut in 1991.

Another problem that drove IBM and Apple into each other's arms is their growing friction with some powerful partners, most notably Microsoft, the software giant run by William Gates III. Microsoft was the creator of MS-DOS, the software that runs the IBM PC, but the two companies have had a falling out over the next generation, called OS/2, which runs IBM's line of PS/2 computers. The new IBM-Apple venture, which will develop its own software, could spell the end of OS/2 and any remaining relationship with Microsoft. The alliance scorns another powerful company, Intel, which has supplied the microprocessors for IBM's machines and has commanded an almost monopoly position as a maker of IBM-compatible chips. Possibly to foster more competition, the new partnership says it will buy advanced processors from Motorola.

The IBM-Apple combination has its risks. Most PC joint ventures have foundered, and this one will have to stand the test of vastly differing corporate cultures. Consumers could be disillusioned with both companies at first, viewing Apple as selling out and IBM as consorting with free spirits from the West Coast. But if the collaboration works, consumers will not have to worry about divided loyalties and incompatible programs. They won't be in Apple's orbit or IBM's but in the best of both computer worlds.

134

American

PURCHASES	COST in millions
1986 Air Cal, a West Coast carrier	$225
1989 TWA's Chicago operations and routes to London	$195
Eastern's routes to 20 Latin American destinations	$310
1990 Continental's Seattle-Tokyo route	$150
1991 Six TWA routes from the U.S. to London	$445

United

PURCHASES	COST in millions
1985 Pan Am's trans-pacific routes to Tokyo and other cities	$750
1990 Six Delta gates in Orlando	N.A.*
1991 Pan Am equipment and routes from six U.S. cities to London	$400
Leased seven Qantas 747s	$33.5 (estimate)
Negotiating purchase of Pan Am routes to Latin America	N.A.

*Not available

Delta

PURCHASES	COST in millions
1987 Western Airlines	$800
1991 18 Eastern gates in Atlanta	$41.4
10 Eastern L-1011 jetliners, plus parts	$67.5
Three Eastern gates at Los Angeles International Airport	$21.7
Nine Eastern landing slots at Washington National Airport	$5.4
Seven Eastern landing slots at La Guardia Airport	$3.5
Pan Am's Frankfurt hub, 45 aircraft and routes from Miami and Detroit to London	$260

Northwest

PURCHASES	COST in millions
1986 Republic Airlines	$884
1991 25% of Hawaiian Airlines, including routes to Australia and Japan	$20
Eastern's hub at Washington National Airport	$35
Negotiating to operate or buy Trump Shuttle	N.A.
Bidding for a 49% interest in Qantas airline	N.A.

Get 'Em While They Last

As weak airlines falter, four giant U.S. carriers are picking up the pieces and racing toward global dominance

Think of Delta Air Lines, and the hubs that come to mind are Atlanta, Salt Lake City and Dallas. But now Delta customers can dream of more exotic destinations: Brussels, Vienna, Rome, New Delhi, Moscow. In July, Delta snapped up most of failing Pan Am's assets, including transatlantic routes serving Europe, Asia and Africa, and its northeastern shuttle—for just $260 million, about what the shuttle alone would have cost a year ago. By the end of the year, Delta had put up $115 million to keep Pan Am flying in exchange for 45% of the company. But airlines eat cash: in December, after 64 years, Pan Am was grounded for good. United Airlines' subsequent purchase of the fallen carrier's Latin American operations positions it to become the only airline with a major presence in the North Atlantic, the Pacific and Latin America.

Twelve years into the chaos of airline deregulation, which has seen dozens of new carriers enter the business and fail, U.S. airlines are holding their last big sale. The industry lost a record $2.4 billion in 1990, sending Eastern to the scrap heap and four major carriers—Continental, Pan Am, Midway and America West—into bankruptcy. The last shaky carriers—like TWA—may soon follow.

Swaggering through the ruins, a handful of robust carriers are picking over the choicest goods and becoming worldwide powerhouses in the process. Says Russell Thayer, an airline consultant: "Consolidation has reached critical mass in the industry. The big three—American, United and Delta—are going global at a tremendous rate, while Northwest is scrambling to catch up with them. Within a year, we may be down to four or five large carriers."

Since the summer of 1990, a flurry of crushing financial blows has turned an already brutal culling process into a full-scale rout. The airlines were loaded with debt after a decade of mergers, frantic expansion and multibillion-dollar orders for new aircraft. The approach of the gulf war brought a sharp run-up in oil prices, adding $2 billion, or 12.5%, to the industry's jet-fuel costs. Then, in a desperate bid to fill seats as the recession deepened and war jitters sidelined travelers, U.S. airlines slashed fares. By last April, 95% of all U.S. air passengers were traveling on the cheap, according to the *Airline Monitor,* an industry-research monthly. Despite a heady 30% increase in its passenger traffic from April to June, Phoenix-based America West was forced to seek bankruptcy protection in June.

As struggling carriers shed weight in their struggle to stay aloft, American, United, Delta and Northwest (combined U.S. market share: 70%) moved to expand into new markets by snapping up the best parts. American and United are pushing into Latin America. In the transatlantic market, where TWA and Pan Am have steadily lost ground over the years to heavily subsidized European flag carriers, American, United and Delta will present much more formidable competition. One measure of their clout: each airline is larger than all the European carriers combined.

As American-based powerhouses, they enjoy another advantage in international markets: traffic originating in the U.S. accounts for nearly half the world business. If the big bruisers from the U.S. succeed in expanding their international market share, the domestic operations of American carriers will grow even stronger as they feed passengers into their route systems. Opportunities also abound in the Pacific, the fastest-growing airline market in the world. But Northwest, which recently gave way to United as the largest U.S. carrier to Asia, is hard pressed to match its stronger rivals. Its parent firm is burdened with heavy interest payments, and the airline lost $62 million on revenues of $1.6 billion during the first three months of this year.

While the U.S. may gain in some ways as its big carriers expand their international market share, travelers will see fewer of the rock-bottom prices they enjoyed during the past decade of desperate competition. And as smaller regional airlines continue to disappear, the huge carriers may also be tempted to drop service to some of their less profitable destinations.

Maxwell's Plummet

Ever since Robert Maxwell slipped mysteriously into the Atlantic Ocean on Nov. 5, his media empire has been crumbling rapidly. While Maxwell's sons Kevin, 32, and Ian, 35, scrambled to prevent the conglomerate's collapse, creditors in half a dozen countries have been busy sorting out the tangled web of 400 interlocking companies that were woven together by the late tycoon.

But efforts to rescue the family business suffered one setback after another, including stunning revelations of possible fraud and double-dealing. Unable to keep the conglomerate, parts of which are publicly traded, from unraveling, Maxwell's sons called it quits in early December and put the family's privately held enterprises into receivership. Later that month, Maxwell Communication, one of the company's flagship operations, filed for bankruptcy-court protection in the U.S. Although the filings will buy the family time, they will do little to end the international row over Maxwell's assets. The Maxwell empire, which ranges from such highly visible publications as New York City's *Daily News* and London's *Daily Mirror* to tiny entities like Nimbus Records, is the subject of investigations on both sides of the Atlantic, notably a criminal probe by Britain's Serious Fraud Office. Some 30 banks and other creditors are lining up in what promises to be a bruising humbug. Investigators are particularly curious to know how much Maxwell's sons knew of his draining an estimated $1.46 billion this year from public companies and pension funds.

Maxwell was deep in hock and struggling to keep his conglomerate afloat before his death. The Czechoslovak-born press baron had run up $4.5 billion in debts to buy everything from American book publishers to British soccer teams. But even before Maxwell was interred, reports of financial skulduggery in his shop began to surface. First came the startling revelation that the company was broke. Then came the discovery that Maxwell had pledged the same assets as collateral for various loans. And in December it was revealed that the media magnate had secretly—and improperly—"borrowed" $767 million from worker pension funds at the two public concerns under his control. The money is missing and unaccounted for.

The latest revelations revived speculation linking Maxwell's death to the dire financial condition of his media empire. Although the preliminary autopsy report claimed the 300-lb. 68-year-old died of "natural causes," the exact circumstances of his death are still unknown.

The Maxwell family's conglomerate is loosely organized into three clusters. The two publicly listed companies include the Mirror Group, which publishes the *Daily Record,* the *Sunday Mail* and *Racing Times,* as well as the Mirror newspapers. Maxwell Communication controls such concerns as Macmillan books and P.F. Collier encyclopedias. The Robert Maxwell Group is privately held and owned 100% by the family. Its operations include the Oxford United Football Club and publications like the *European,* as well as stakes in newspapers in Israel, Hungary and Kenya.

But all three holding companies are also directly and indirectly linked to dozens of other family-controlled enterprises. Maxwell's creditors were unaware of the nature of the corporate structure because the man whose wealth was estimated at $1.8 billion incorporated family trusts in Lichtenstein, where tax laws and disclosure rules are virtually nonexistent. Not even Maxwell-family members were aware of the web's scope. As a result, the senior Maxwell was able to pile debt upon debt. Dozens of banks—including Swiss Bank, Midland and Lloyd's—were left holding the bag.

Months before Maxwell vanished from his 180-ft. yacht, there was a growing fear that he was having trouble meeting his repayment schedule. Despite his eroding financial condition, however, he was able to pass annual audits by accountants Coopers & Lybrand Deloitte. That enabled Maxwell to add on more debt in March when he purchased the *Daily News* from the Tribune Co. by assuming as much as $35 million in obligations.

As concerns about Maxwell's financial strength mounted, stock in Maxwell Communication weakened. After reaching a high of $4.28 a share in April, the price plunged to $2.18 by Nov. 5, the day he disappeared. After he was reported missing, the stock dropped as low as $0.63. The decline in stock value was of special concern to Maxwell's creditors, since most of the family's 68% stake in the company was pledged as collateral for loans. That stake, valued at nearly $2 billion in May, is now worth only $440 million.

Maxwell did recognize that some assets would have to be sold to help pay off debt. So far, his sons have been able to raise more than $700 million by selling off assets at fire-sale prices. For now, it will be up to the courts to sort out the mess. The Maxwells acted to place the Robert Maxwell Group into receivership after all attempts to raise fresh outside capital proved hopeless. John Talbot, the administrator appointed by the High Court to oversee the family's private holdings, said Maxwell's remaining assets were likely to be put up for sale. That includes the Maxwells' stock in Maxwell Communication as well as their 51% stake in the Mirror Group. The final collapse of his empire suggests that Robert Maxwell was less a media mogul than a master of a shell game.

Trump Trips Up

American Express never really wanted a 282-ft. yacht. Bankers Trust isn't sure what it will do with the Grand Hyatt in Manhattan, nor is Manufacturers Hanover exactly giddy about owning the Regency Hotel in Atlantic City. But then Citicorp is not exactly cut out to be a retailer or an airline operator, either.

Meet Donald Trump's bankers. Last April a gaggle of major financial institutions had to admit, after lending Trump billions of dollars, that there's a lot less to the Donald and his empire than the banks had believed. Already more than $3.8 billion in the hole and sliding perilously close to bankruptcy, the brash New York developer had no choice but to dismantle his vast holdings. And yet, Trump, the consummate gambler, seems to have come up with a strong hand. "I have a great relationship with the banks," Trump insisted, pooh-poohing any notion that he was cornered. "The 1990s are a decade of deleveraging. I'm doing it too."

While he gave up his *Trump Princess* yacht, the Regency, his half-interest in the Hyatt and his 27% interest in the Alexander's store chain, Trump retained the Plaza Hotel, the Trump Tower, a valuable tract of Hudson River waterfront and his estate in Palm Beach, Fla. At year's end, the fate of the Trump Shuttle, which he purchased from Eastern in 1989, was unclear. After both Northwest Airlines and American Airlines pulled out of possible deals, USAir reached a preliminary agreement in December to fly the shuttle for up to ten years, with an option to buy it after five years. Indeed, Trump has bet most heavily on his Atlantic City casinos: the Trump Taj Mahal, the Trump Castle and the Trump Plaza Hotel and Casino. As he once said of the casino business, "Most of all, I like the cash flow."

Trump's financial humbling is rooted in the speculative frenzy of the '80s. Behind every mover and shaker were banks and investment houses looking to score. Trump won the confidence of investors early, and when the Northeastern real estate boom took off, he found he had unlimited credit. While millions of casual observers were dazzled by the glitter of his empire, few understood that Trump's fortune was built on a mountain of debt. The moneymen who did understand seemed not to care. Whatever Donald wanted, Donald got. Citibank loaned him $1.1 billion; Bank of America $400 million; Bankers Trust about $164 million, much of it undersecured. Says a knowledgeable source close to Trump's bankers: "They ought to be shot. They didn't ask questions." Even as Trump's fortunes continued to decline, the bankers tried to look the other way.

Now they are facing facts. But don't count the Donald out yet. Brinkmanship is the stuff that gamblers are made of, and is Trump's raison d'être.

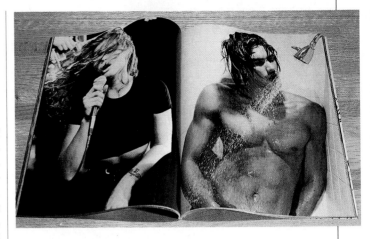

Calvin Heats Up

"Jeans," intones Calvin Klein, "are about *sssexx.*"

He first discovered that truth in 1980, when 15-year-old Brooke Shields cooed that nothing came between her and her Calvins, "nothing." That ad campaign ruffled a lot of feathers, sold a lot of jeans and spawned a hypothalamus-numbing host of imitators.

Though Klein has been distracted by selling perfumes with names like Obsession, he's once again focusing on the jeans war, and his opening salvo was a 116-page ad supplement that accompanied the October issue of Vanity Fair. It is touted as the largest ad supplement for a consumer magazine in U.S. history, and industry sources say Klein spent more than $1 million to produce and place it.

Totally textless, utterly black and white, the glossy portfolio photographed by Bruce Weber is a jumbled pastiche of naked bodies, black leather jackets, Harleys and tattoos. Biker chicks straddle their "hogs" and rough up their men. Rippling hunks wield electric guitars like chain saws, grab one another, sometimes themselves. Oh, yes, there are even a few incidental photographs of jeans, most of which are being wrestled off taut bodies or used as wet loincloths.

"The book," says Klein, "is a fantasy about a rock concert. You see the band onstage, backstage, after the show. The wild and crazy groupies. The people living in the motorcycle world. It's about excitement. Hot and sweaty rock 'n' rollers who wear nothing but jeans and skin. It's about denim. People love it."

It's also about money. And troubled retailers and advertising executives love that. *Women's Wear Daily* reported that Klein plans to spend about $10 million on jeans advertising this year. In September he staged his first all-jeans fashion show in New York City. Magazine publishers, buffeted by an industry-wide decline of 10.4% in ad pages, are also heartened. Images from the supplement will be appearing as ads in various magazines for months. Is Klein's splash going to grow into a full-blown trend? *Elle* slapped a videotape, a scented card and an order form for Estée Lauder's SpellBound perfume onto 14,000 copies of its September issue. "It's terrific. The excitement factor works," said *Elle's* publisher, Lawrence Burstein.

Not everyone is enthralled. Some find the material offensive, the message obscure, the numbers questionable. "Are sales going to offset the cost of Calvin's 116 pages? I suspect not," says a magazine-publishing executive. 'His supplement is more of an ego piece." But Klein has no doubts. "People get the message," he enthuses. "It's big, it's sexy and it's so *right*."

No Rain, No Gain

From the rich farmlands that yield half the nation's fruits and vegetables to the usually snow-drenched Sierra Nevadas to the lush gardens of Bel Air, Californians grappled with the state's worst-ever drought in 1991, now in its fifth year. Farmers, who contribute $17.6 billion to California's $750 billion-a-year economy, suffered a double blow in February. The state department of water resources, which normally supplies water to farming areas in the fecund San Joaquin Valley, suspended all agricultural deliveries of the water it controls. Meanwhile the Federal Government warned of up to 75% cutbacks in the low-priced water from its reservoirs. City governments called emergency sessions to consider strict rationing. In the first unforeseen crisis of his new administration, Governor Pete Wilson stopped just short of declaring a state of emergency, instead creating a "drought action team" to draft a water plan. Cautioned Wilson: "This is a threat to our livelihoods, not our lives."

For California's nonfarm economy, the drought's long-term effects will probably be more important than the immediate ones. "We will survive the drought," says Gary Burke, president of the Santa Clara County Manufacturing Group. "But what effect will the drought have on companies' plans to expand and new businesses' decisions to locate in Santa Clara?"

He has a point. While emergency actions by industry and government may ease the crisis, California will have to adopt a better system for allocating water to attract skittish businesses and stabilize its agriculture industry. Analysts across the political spectrum prescribe a market system in which those who have water can easily sell it to those who need it more. Many agree on the root of the problem: California water is much too cheap. The federal authorities that sell it lose millions of dollars a year by charging farmers far less than it costs to provide new supplies.

GM Skids

The Christmas week speech from the chairman of General Motors traditionally sounds like an address from a head of state. Small wonder: the company is so large (1990 revenues: nearly $127 billion) that if it were an independent nation, its economy would rank among the world's Top 20. By closed-circuit TV from GM headquarters in Detroit, the 1991 broadcast reached 395,000 employees, who stopped work and put down their tools in 130 factories across the U.S. But the message from chairman Robert Stempel was unlike any other from a GM chief in the corporation's 83-year history.

As of Jan. 1, he said, the company would embark on a multiyear program that would close 25 North American plants and reduce its present work force by 19%—or 74,000 employees. Under Stempel's retrenchment plan, GM would abandon for the foreseeable future its hopes to regain its lost share of the U.S. market, which has fallen in the past decade from 45% to slightly more than 35%; indeed, by 1995 the company would be only half the size it was a decade earlier. "We are asking you to help remake the world's largest automobile company," Stempel pleaded with GM workers. "We can't wait."

GM has been struggling to halt its downward slide since the oil crisis of the late 1970s, when fuel-efficient foreign cars gained in popularity and Americans tired of the nagging quality problems of U.S.-made cars. Although Detroit's Big Three—GM, Ford and Chrysler—all closed plants during the 1980s and improved their cars, GM continued to suffer from inefficiencies. For instance, it built far more cars than consumers wanted and used more workers to make each car than any other auto company. Such excess, aggravated by the recession, resulted in losses estimated at $450 million a month this year. The immediate goal of his plan, Stempel declared, was to restore profitability in North America, where GM faces huge losses in 1991. Said he: "We cannot blame our problems on the war, the plunge in consumer confidence or the recession. Rather we must make fundamental changes in the way GM does business if we are to improve our performance." Analysts predicted, however, that the changes would not result in profits before 1993.

Mr. Sam Stuns Goliath

With its commanding view of Chicago's skyline, the executive floor of the 110-story Sears Tower is a monument to the company's glorious century as America's favorite store. But when Sears' 13 directors gathered last February, they faced overwhelmingly bad news: Sears, officially, is no longer America's largest retailer. The new king: Wal-Mart, a onetime backwoods bargain barn that has pulled past Sears in North American sales. K Mart, advancing steadily but less spectacularly, edged up just behind Sears, leaving the former leader an uncertain No. 2.

While Sears directors worried in Chicago, Wal-Mart founder

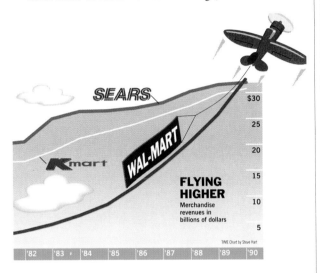

FLYING HIGHER
Merchandise revenues in billions of dollars

TIME Chart by Steve Hart

Sam Walton, 72, was working in his spartan little office in Bentonville, Ark. (pop. 11,000). Starting at 7 every morning, employees scurry through the drab two-story building whose Formica desks and battleship-gray walls belie the company's immense profitability. Wal-Mart has plenty of room to grow—shoppers in 15 states have yet to see one store. The chain got started in 1962 much the way Sears did decades earlier, by targeting underserved rural areas. Stocking everything from cosmetics to lawn furniture, Wal-Mart developed a loyal core of customers. Walton—Mr. Sam to his 350,000 employees—invested in a state-of-the-art satellite system that maintains round-the-clock inventory control.

Wal-Mart's relentless efforts have yielded remarkable results. Just 10 years ago, company sales of $2.4 billion were less than 12% of Sears'. But in the past three years, while Sears' North American retail sales have grown only 14%, from $28 billion to $32 billion, Wal-Mart's have doubled, from $16 billion to $32.6 billion.

Critics say Sears management has lost touch with its customers and its mission. As a result, several retail expansions during the past few years have failed. Last February, Sears' chief executive, Edward Brennan, 57, announced that 9,000 more Sears employees must be laid off by December, bringing total job cuts this year to 33,000, more than 8% of the firm's 394,000 merchandising staff.

One exception to Sears' dismal pattern is the success of the Discover credit card. Cardholders can use Discover to shop at stores other than Sears, including Wal-Mart. Most businesses might refuse to accept a credit card issued by their competition. Not Sam Walton. He wants to make shopping at Wal-Mart as easy as possible—and if Sears wants to help, well, that's fine with him.

Hitting the Credit Limit

In the race to create vast financial supermarkets, American Express was among the first in line. Backed by a blue-chip image and the clout of its green charge cards, the Manhattan-based conglomerate went on a spending spree in which it acquired brokerage firms, insurance companies and a real estate business in an ambitious bid to offer a grocery list of investment services under one roof.

Initially, the strategy produced one success after another, contributing to American Express's almost mythic reputation. But recent misfortunes and poor decisions have prompted a reappraisal of Amex. Acquisitions that looked like masterstrokes only a few years ago are now facing criticism; the decision-making process that was once considered flawless is suddenly being second-guessed; businesses that were thought to be impervious to economic downturns have proved to be vulnerable.

The latest shock is the poor performance of the Optima card. Launched four years ago as Amex's response to Visa and Master-Card, the card was perceived as a winner. But the company announced in October that Optima (total card members: more than 3 million) had suffered much higher defaults than expected. The result: $155 million in Optima write-offs during the third quarter, which will produce a loss—the first one ever—of $88 million for the company's Travel Related Services division.

Moreover, the company is conducting an internal investigation to see whether Optima executives falsified records to hide the true degree of cardholder defaults. The Federal Deposit Insurance Corporation is probing the matter as well, because the American Express Centurion Bank, which issues Optima, filed incorrect documents with federal regulators as a result of the apparent cover-up. Amex investors, meanwhile, have filed a class action claiming that the company misrepresented the card's performance.

Amex is slowly learning to be humble. Earlier in 1991 the company's weakened financial condition forced it to search for outside capital. Warren Buffett, the Omaha-based billionaire, stepped in with a $300 million investment. While chairman James Robinson may not have fully repaired Amex just yet, the company seems to have come to grips with the likelihood that the 1990s will be a time of less-than-platinum performance.

TIME

THE SIMPLE LIFE

Rejecting the rat race, Americans get back to basics

Back to Basics

By GEORGE RUSSELL

In the Eighties, the country went on a spree of getting and spending the like of which the U.S. had never seen. By the beginning of the Nineties, Americans were sobering up quickly; in a remarkably short period of time, something like an unofficial national stocktaking was underway. On the home front, therefore, 1991 was a year in which American society retook its measure, a year of redefinition, in almost every sense of the word.

Looking back on the acquisitive Eighties, people did not like what they saw—or what they had become: a nation of over-committed, over-scheduled, over-indebted, two-career strivers. At best, occasional parents. Not-all-that-good neighbors. Much of the excess, and the subsequent self-searching, came from the oft-despised Yuppie class, but assigning a sociology to this particular backlash did not do it justice. It was, above all, an affirmation of values. Americans had the feeling that much of what makes life worth living, in terms of family, community and spirituality, had been trampled in the race for the six-figure income and the BMW.

In its middle age, the baby-boomer generation decided it was time to drop—not out, but back. Maybe the career was not so important; maybe the kids were. Maybe having kids was. The new attitude was not one that would inspire a consumer-led recovery from recession (and as a result, the economy kept sputtering). But it could lead to a very substantial realignment of national priorities, in everything from defense to food labeling, a realignment that politicians would ignore at their peril.

Just as they seemed to agree that money and status were no longer the paramount measures of their private achievements, Americans were in no mood to continue substituting expenditure for results in the public sphere. America's public squalor had never come cheap: in health care and in education, to name but two areas, the U.S. had poured out billions to achieve disaster. A determination was growing that this simply would no longer do. A form of grassroots subversion began sweeping school districts across the country: if monopoly was bad for the private sector, maybe it was bad for the public sector too. Why not let free-market forces help to decide, for example, which schools students chose to attend? The main point, though, was more fundamental: We can do better. President Bush leaped on the bandwagon: American students would lead the world in science and math by the new millennium. In 1991 we had not yet agreed how that would happen.

In fact, we had not even agreed on We. Europeans have long concurred that geography is destiny, but in the United States, past, present and future are battlefields of demography. In an immigrant nation it could hardly be otherwise—and in the U.S., the demographic scales were tipping with increasing emphasis in favor of new arrivals from Asia, Latin America and elsewhere in the Third World.

As the newcomers poured into the institutions most sensitive to the changing texture of population—schools and universities—ideas too seemed to come under a kind of demographic assault. Were Christopher Columbus and George Washington avatars of genocide rather than heroes of American culture? Was American culture even worth applauding? White middle-class American parents occasionally scratched their heads as they faced a flood of jargon that named the sins of generations present and past: Eurocentrism, homophobia, even species-ism.

What was really going on? American society was doing what it had always done in the past: stretching its self-image to accommodate the latest guests at the democratic feast. (Columbus himself only became an American hero in the 1820s, as southern Europeans arrived to challenge the dominant WASPs.) As in any time of such profound ferment, a certain amount of unappetizing froth also floated to the surface. Some of it took the form of objectionable personality types, perennial victims who now had The Culture to blame for their myriad woes, and neo-Puritans who policed the boundaries of "political correctness" for impermissible deviations from the party line.

In a nation governed by laws rather than by men, it was inevitable that the passion for redefinition that dominated 1991 should also shake some of the comfortable assumptions of ethics and justice. A nation glued to the televised confirmation hearings of Supreme Court Justice Clarence Thomas was unlikely ever again to take for granted the issue of sexual harassment. On campuses, where the sexual revolution was in its Thermidor in the wake of AIDS, the same kind of heated reconsideration was focused on the issue known as "date rape." When does no mean no? The very fact that the question had to be asked meant that a rethinking of legal assumptions regarding women's rights to romance without violence was overdue.

Other legal pillars trembled. A fanatical Michigan doctor named Kevorkian, armed with a bagful of poisons, claimed he was performing a public service by helping women in agony to commit suicide. A book on how to kill one's self stayed endlessly on the best-seller lists. Do people have an inalienable right to cut short their own pursuit of happiness? In 1991 new answers to that question seemed alarmingly close to the surface.

Could there ever be a bigger legal issue than God? As the year wound to an end, the separation of church and state—one of the fundamental American verities, and one of the most contentious—also seemed ripe for reconsideration, in the form of a case before the Supreme Court concerning graduation prayer. For the first time in 40 years, it seemed that the court might narrow the wall between religion and public life. In a year given over to the rethinking of basic principles, nothing was sacred, it seemed, except perhaps for sacredness.

Who Are We?

A growing emphasis on the nation's "multicultural" heritage exalts racial and ethnic pride at the expense of social cohesion

Exactly 215 years ago, some subjects of Britain's King George III adopted a Declaration of Independence that asserted the necessity for a sovereign and free United States of America. The ground moved under that hall in steamy, summertime Philadelphia; an idea was proclaimed that would shake and reshape the world. Yet the entire world was hardly represented. All 56 of the signatories were white males of European descent, most of them wealthy property holders. Like some of his co-revolutionaries, Thomas Jefferson, who was primarily responsible for the soaring language of the document ("We hold these truths to be self evident, that all men are created equal . . ."), owned black slaves. In this context, what could "equal" mean? And why were only "men" created that way?

Americans over 40 might be startled by a description of the

1492·COLUMBUS

Multiculturalists stress that America was inhabited before Columbus and say Europeans despoiled the continent

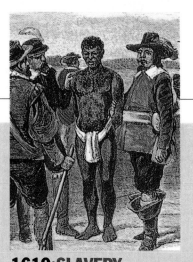

1619·SLAVERY

California's new curriculum urges students to imagine how victims felt on being sold into bondage

1621·THANKSGIVING

Harmony or harm? Critics say the holiday is an idealization of the destructive effects of colonial culture on nonwhite peoples

Glorious Fourth that points out the racial, sexual and social characteristics of the Founding Fathers, never mind taking a swipe or two at Jefferson. But most of today's schoolchildren would not be surprised. It is now fairly commonplace to learn American history in the context of who has oppressed, excluded or otherwise mistreated whom. All across the country, students are imbibing a version of the past and present that their parents would not recognize.

Some of the fundamental images of the American gallery of national icons have received a dramatic reworking. Gone, or going fast, is the concept of the melting pot, of the U.S. as the paramount place in the world where people came to shed their past in order to forge their future. Gone too is the emphasis on the twin ideals that form the basis of the American experiment: that rights reside in the individual rather than with social or ethnic classes and that all who come to these shores can be assimilated by an open society that transforms disparate peoples into Americans. Instead there is a new paradigm that emphasizes the racial and ethnic diversity of American citizens, of the many cultures that have converged here, each valuable in its own right and deserving of study and respect.

In the critical optic of this new "multicultural" perspective, American history as it was once written—those often tedious treks from Christopher Columbus to Dwight Eisenhower—leaves out too much, namely nearly everyone who was not a white male. Some adherents go further, questioning whether the Western ideas and ideals that gave birth to America discriminate against people from other traditions. A more radical school argues that those values are no more than the ethnic expression of "Eurocentric" culture and should be taught only as such.

These are not merely academic disputes. Especially in diverse, secular societies such as the U.S., a shared sense of the past plays a pivotal role in the way values and vision are transmitted from one generation to the next. The issues now being raised—although they are presented under the bland guise of syllabus reform—are thus too important to be left to teachers, school administrators and social commentators alone. Everyone deserves a say.

Put bluntly: Do Americans still have faith in the vision of their country as a cradle of individual rights and liberties, or must they relinquish the teaching of some of these freedoms to further the goals of the ethnic and social groups to which they belong? Is America's social contract—a vision of self-determination that continues to reverberate around the world—fatally tainted by its origins in Western European thought? What kind of people do Americans now think they are, and what will they tell their children about that?

Now the multicultural crusade is in the glare of public attention, thanks to the release of a report recommending changes in the way social studies is taught in New York State public schools. State Education Commissioner Thomas Sobol, responding to complaints from a number of minority groups, chose a panel of 24 educators to review the curriculums in history and related courses. One of their tasks was to suggest innovations that would improve students' understanding of "the cultures, identities, and histories of the diverse groups which comprise American society today."

There is no inflammatory rhetoric in the new report, which throws in periodic tributes to the concept of national unity: "With efforts to respect and honor the diverse and pluralistic elements in our nation, special attention will need to be given to those values, characteristics, and traditions which we share in common."

But the document is curiously silent on what those shared values are. It even seems hesitant to acknowledge the fact of U.S. citizenship; wherever possible, it advocates an awareness of global "interdependence" as a fundamental educational concern. In its constant elevation of group and ethnic interests, it represents a radical departure from the way Americans have traditionally viewed the passing on of knowledge in the common school as a means of creating citizens out of a polyglot and diverse pool of young citizens-to-be.

This fact did not account for the report's initial notoriety. A few examples of suggested reforms got most of the attention. Among them:
▶ Students would be discouraged from calling Africans who were brought to the U.S. in bondage "slaves." Instead they would be referred to as "enslaved persons," which would "call forth the essential humanity of those enslaved, helping students to understand from the beginning the true meaning of slavery."

1836·THE ALAMO
Glorified by Texans, the story of the Alamo typifies long-established disregard for Hispanic influence in America, multiculturalists say

1863·THE CIVIL WAR
A battle to end slavery? The New York report urges viewing "race" as a cultural, not physical, description

1864·THE WILD WEST
The westward migration of Americans was a violent process; multiculturalists charge that western myths downplay the holocaust of native cultures that drove the expansion

▶ Thanksgiving would be discussed not only as a feast day for whites but as a less joyous occasion for Native Americans.

▶ The habit of looking at geography from a European point of view would cease. "The Far East" and "the Middle East" would disappear, replaced by "East Asia" and "Southwest Asia and North Africa."

▶ Describing certain Americans as "minorities" would also be phased out: "If social studies is to be taught from a global perspective, many of the so-called minorities in America are more accurately described as part of the world's *majorities.*"

All these proposals have the merit of being specific and thus open to debate. The improvement wrought by "enslaved person" over "slave" may not strike everyone as immediately apparent; to Americans who know their own history, "slave" is a word heavily charged with the connotations of brutal, involuntary degradation. As to the matter of Thanksgiving, Edmund Ladd, 65, a Zuni Pueblo Indian and an anthropologist in New Mexico, says, "We celebrate Thanksgiving, Christmas and all the holidays that are Anglo-induced because that's the day we don't have to go to work. Thanksgiving is an excuse for us to get together." The adoption of "East Asia" raises the question "East of where?" It is difficult to imagine what a "global perspective" might be, given the report's vague prose.

How did things—not just in New York but in school systems across the nation—get to the muddy pass epitomized by the Sobol report? Principally because an abstract theory happened to catch and ride a new wave of actuality. The idea of multicultural education in its most extravagant current form was born during the 1960s, when colleges instituted special programs in black studies, then similar enclaves of women's studies, which were followed by successive demarcations of subject matter along racial or ethnic boundaries.

To the surprise of many doubters, the work and the students turned out by such programs were often first rate. These supposedly marginal areas of academic inquiry produced information—about the achievements of women, facets of life outside the U.S. mainstream, the work of minority artists, Americans whom history had ignored—that rattled the complacency of orthodox humanities de-

partments. And many of the graduates of these programs remained in academe, either studying for advanced degrees or earning tenure as teachers.

While they moved up the rungs, something else was going on. The 1965 Immigration Act passed by Congress had reversed a policy, in place for four decades, of favoring Europeans and making things tough for other applicants. Suddenly people from throughout the Third World found it easier to enter the U.S., rapidly changing the demographics of the nation. Between 1980 and 1990, the white non-Hispanic majority in Los Angeles County turned into a minority.

The new immigrants came for the same reasons that had propelled their predecessors: to escape poverty, hopelessness or oppression, to seek economic opportunities and to live in freedom. This huge influx of people can be seen as the latest affirmation of American values, of the global allure exercised by the ideals on which the nation was founded.

But that is not the vision conveyed by many of the multiculturalists, those veterans of the '60s and their younger colleagues, who looked at the people arriving in their classrooms and noticed that many of them, in some cases nearly all of them, had no connection whatsoever with Europe.

Why, then, were these children being forced to learn a history that derived almost exclusively from Western thought and examples? This was a good question that was probably answered too quickly by teachers and administrators on the front lines: No reason, no reason at all.

At this point the debate over multicultural viewpoints stumbled into a philosophical muddle from which it has yet to emerge.

North America was populated by a number of indigenous peoples long before the Europeans arrived, but the society that evolved and that persists today was modeled on Western examples. More specifically, the influence of the British, who held and ruled the original 13 colonies, is inescapable. The language, the system of representative government, the structure of law and the emphasis on individual liberty were all adopted from the Enlightenment ideals

144

1869·THE CONTINENT SPANNED

The rail link was the product of Chinese immigrant labor. The New York report says such people should be known no as minorities but as "part of the world's majorities."

1905·IMMIGRANTS

Forget the "melting pot." Ethnic groups should celebrate their differences, revisionists say.

1911·SUFFRAGETTES

72 years of protest earned women the vote. The New York report says their contributions are still "marginalized."

being formulated in what was once known as the mother country. Other basic American principles, such as the idea of the separation of powers, which is fundamental to the American Constitution, derive from the French philosopher Montesquieu.

It is an article of faith among most multiculturalists that no system of values is innately superior to any other; all cultures are created equal. As a way of looking at the world, this notion has considerable merit. It is, among other things, a useful corrective to chauvinisms and insularities. But to describe the Western tradition as just one of many equally important contributors to the American identity is to make hash of history, and of one of history's boldest experiments.

Faced with the pervasive traces of Western thought embodied in American life, some multiculturalists claim that this Eurocentric bias discriminates against those from different traditions. But for openers, Eurocentric is decidedly a fuzzy term, lumping together a vast diversity of nationalities and peoples, past and present. In what person or doctrine can Eurocentrism be embodied? Savonarola? Jane Austen? Deism? Communism? Insofar as it means anything specific, Eurocentric looks suspiciously like a code word for "white." In attempting to combat racism, radical multiculturalists seem all too willing to resort to racism of another stripe.

Furthermore, the oppressive effects of Western thought on nonwhites is not as clear-cut as most multiculturalists assume. Who or what is the villain here? Galileo? Einstein? The Magna Carta? The Bill of Rights? Was Martin Luther King Jr. diminished, made to feel inferior, when he read Henry David Thoreau along with Gandhi on civil disobedience? Or for that matter when he contemplated the Reformation launched by his 16th century German namesake?

Ultimately, multicultural thinking, for all its nods toward pluralism and diversity, can lead to several regressive orthodoxies. One is the notion that truth is forever encapsulated within collective identities, that what white males or females or blacks or Hispanics or Asians know about their experiences can be communicated only im-

perfectly to people beyond their pale. Those without the experience can never really know its essential features. The authority of any statement is locked within the skin of the speaker.

The Western tradition contains a refutation of this take-my-word-for-it approach. It can be seen in the Greek and Roman philosophers, then again most vividly in the writers of the European Enlightenment—Voltaire, Locke, Berkeley, all DWEMs (dead white European males), but perhaps worth a hearing in spite of this handicap. In one way or another, they argued that the validity of any statement can be tested independently of, and in no logical way depends upon, the person who makes it. This idea, totally color-blind, is one of the greatest instruments for human freedom ever conceived. It made democracy possible, since it enabled each citizen to reach reasoned judgments, and its spirit pervades the documents that established the U.S.

Perhaps most unsettling, radical multiculturalism turns upside down the principles that drew, and continue to draw, people to America: the freedom to create a new personal identity, and the chance to become part of a nation of people who have done the same thing. There is a contradiction between these commands to be oneself while also being part of a common culture, a creative tension that has produced a literature populated by loners, rebels and misfits. Also, come to think of it, a lot of stress and nervous breakdowns. No one ever said it was easy to be an American, to learn the rules anew each day, every day.

Whatever else it may accomplish, the current debate highlights the enduring volatility of the American experiment. There is no guarantee that the nation's long test of trying to live together will not end in fragmentation and collapse, with groups gathered around the firelight, waiting for the attack at dawn. No guarantee, that is, except the examples its citizens have set—examples not as frequent as their ideals mandate, but precious nonetheless—of getting out of the skins of their prejudices and meeting each other as the equals they truly are.

And a very Happy 215th Birthday to us all, whoever we think we are.

The Simple Life

Goodbye to having it all. Tired of trendiness and materialism, Americans are rediscovering basic values.

NOW Karen Glance jumped the fast track to operate a food market in her St. Paul neighborhood

THEN The former apparel-industry executive used to travel almost every day

T hese are the humble makings of a revolution in progress: macaroni and cheese. Timex watches. Volunteer work. Insulated underwear. Savings accounts. *Roseanne.* Domestic beer. Local activism. Sleds. Pajamas. Sentimental movies. Primary colors. Mixed-breed dogs. Bicycles. Cloth diapers. Shopping at Wal-Mart. Small-town ways. Iceberg lettuce. Family reunions. Board games. Hang-it-yourself wallpaper. Push-it-yourself lawn mowers. Silly Putty.

See the pattern? It's as genuine as Grandma's quilt. After a 10-year bender of gaudy dreams and godless consumerism, Americans are starting to trade down. They want to reduce their attachments to status symbols, fast-track careers and great expectations of Having It All. Upscale is out; downscale is in. Yuppies are an ancient civilization. Flaunting money is considered gauche: if you've got it, please keep it to yourself—or give some away!

In place of materialism, many Americans are embracing simpler pleasures and homier values. They've been thinking hard about what really matters in their lives, and they've decided to make some changes. What matters is having time for family and friends, rest and recreation, good deeds and spirituality. For some people that means a radical step: changing one's career, living on less, or packing up and moving to a quieter place. For others it can mean something as subtle as choosing a cheaper brand of running shoes or leaving work a little earlier to watch the kids in a soccer game.

The pursuit of a simpler life with deeper meaning is a major shift in America's private agenda. "This is a rapid and extremely powerful movement," says Ross Goldstein, a San Francisco psychologist and market researcher. "I'm impressed by how deep it goes into the fabric of this country." Says noted theologian Martin Marty of the University of Chicago: "We are all warned against thinking in terms of trends that correspond with decades, but this one is a cinch. I think that people are going to look back at today as a hinge period in the country's history." Some social observers have already dubbed the 1990s the We decade.

The mood is palpable. In a TIME/CNN poll of 500 adults, 69% of the people surveyed said they would like to "slow down and live a more relaxed life," in contrast to only 19% who said they would like to "live a more exciting, faster-paced life." A majority of those polled, 61%, agreed that "earning a living today requires so much effort that it's difficult to find time to enjoy life." When asked about their priorities, 89% said it was more important these days to spend time with their families, and 56% felt strongly about finding time for personal interests and hobbies. But only 13% saw importance in keeping up with fashions and trends, and just 7% thought it was worth bothering to shop for status-symbol products.

The movement is pervasive. "This is not something simply happening to the burnouts from Wall Street," says sociologist Stephen Warner of the University of Illinois at Chicago. "There is an American phenomenon going on that crosses all social lines. It's true of immigrant groups too, as well as the underprivileged."

Yet the shift in priorities has a surface gloss of stylishness also. Call it thrifty chic. Penny-pinching is back in vogue, even among the rich. Jackie O. shops at the Gap. Christie Brinkley wears plain white men's T shirts. Outside B.J.'s Wholesale Club in Medford, Mass., a white stretch limo waits at the curb while its passengers roam the cavernous discount warehouse. At Tom's Barber Shop in Jacksonville, lawyers and executives sit down next to truckers and shipyard workers for a $6 trim.

The beginnings of the new mind-set probably go back as far as the stock-market crash of 1987, which had little immediate effect on

At the same time, the baby-boom generation, which accounted for much of the spending binge of the '80s, is reaching middle age. Here come 75 million aching backs. A generation of reluctant grown-ups is raising children, caring for aging parents and beginning to think about retirement. Instead of pumping iron, preening and networking, they are worrying about orthodontists, skateboards and college tuitions. The backyard now has more appeal than the boardroom.

So forget those champagne wishes and caviar dreams, the right car, vodka, watch, cuisine and music system. Consumers no longer feel they absolutely must have the latest luxury product. Who would be impressed, anyway? "People don't think being square is synonymous with being a sucker anymore," says Dan Fox, marketing planning director of the Foote, Cone & Belding ad agency. Besides, they no longer seem to get a kick from spending borrowed money. Consumer installment credit dropped $342 million, or 0.6%, in December 1990 in what would ordinarily have been a busy shopping season, and a huge $2.4 billion in January.

Not everyone believes America has changed its stripes, however. "If the present generation has learned anything, it is that talk is cheap. But are they really doing anything different?" asks Stanford economist Victor Fuchs. "The baby boomers are just growing up and playing out a predictable life-cycle change." Elmer Johnson, a Chicago lawyer and former executive vice president of General Motors, sees "a hardness of heart that has not yet begun to be broken."

Yet a lot of business people who stake their livelihood on shifts in consumer behavior see thousands of small changes that they believe are adding up to something. At a Brookstone store in Boston, a man exchanges a gift, trading in a $99 executive fountain pen ("I'll never use it") for a car-care kit. Suddenly people want to buy toys that don't take batteries. Sales of dolls are up. Power dressing is out.

The change in consumer psychology is shaking many merchants to their roots. Traditional department stores ranging from Saks Fifth Avenue to Neiman Marcus have suffered from poor business as customers flock to discounters and back-to-basics stores, notably the Limited, the Gap, Wal-Mart and K Mart. The 75-store Sharper Image chain, which made its reputation in the '80s with high-tech gadgets, has been blurring its image to include more low-cost, practical goods. Example: a $19.95 aluminum-can crusher for recyclers.

In fact, that's another reason for rejecting rampant materialism: its impact on the environment. "Whenever I use something or buy something now, I'm thinking, Where is this going to end up?" says Debbie Worthley, 46, a student adviser at the University of Vermont. "I'm not as interested in buying gadgets as I was a few years ago." Seventh Generation, a two-year-old Colchester, Vt., mail-order firm that specializes in goods for the environmentally

the overall economy but gave many people an uneasy feeling about the Roaring Eighties. The spectacular failures of such '80s heroes as Michael Milken and Donald Trump have discredited the era's role models as well. Many people were awakened by individual experience: the plight of a homeless neighbor, the collapse of a bank, a friend's job loss.

The recession and gulf war cemented the trend. First, the economic downturn struck some people as a just punishment for a dizzy era of excessive borrowing and spending. Many consumers saw the recession as a warning that their behavior had to change. Cutting back and putting away the plastic seem only prudent. Then the life-and-death reality of the war came along and made the pursuit of glitz and status seem even more trivial. More Americans saw their country pulling together with a higher purpose and a can-do spirit, and many of them liked the feeling.

In scaling down their tastes, most Americans are making a virtue out of necessity. Contrary to perceptions, the past decade was an era of downward mobility for the majority of U.S. families, who kept up their spending by borrowing and relying on two incomes. Only the wealthiest 20% of Americans significantly increased their real income during the Reagan era, and the poor slipped further behind. After adjustment for inflation, the national standard of living has actually fallen since 1973; the real average hourly pay for U.S. workers has gone from $8.55 then to $7.54 today. Says Barry Bosworth, an economist at the Brookings Institution: "Americans are not becoming pessimistic. They are becoming realistic. It is right to think of cutting back."

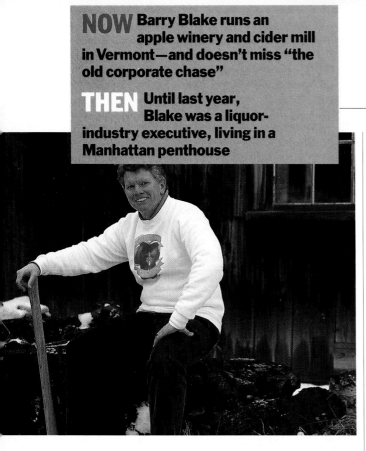

conscious, has an essay in its catalog titled "Why You Should Buy Less Stuff." Recycling has taken hold as a voguish and satisfying pursuit. People who used to meet at trendy bars now trade bons mots while sorting their garbage into the appropriate bins at the public dump.

The buzz word among marketers is "value" products, meaning quality at a low price. The Campbell Soup Co. has introduced discount frozen foods, including Swanson budget dinners (average cost: $1.39). In the hope of stemming a decline in business that typically reached 20% in the past year, restaurants are adding such moderately priced classics as fried chicken, meat loaf and bread pudding. Restaurateurs have coined a phrase for it: casualization.

The pop-culture machine is rushing to catch up with the times. Gilded '80s shows such as *Dynasty* and *Falcon Crest* are gone, swept away by a wave of proudly downscale fare, including *Roseanne, The Simpsons* and *Married . . . with Children*. Campy hobnobber Robin Leach of *Lifestyles of the Rich and Famous* has been replaced in the hearts of viewers by chatty Jeff Smith of *The Frugal Gourmet* and nonaerobic carpenter Norm Abram of *The New Yankee Workshop*. Love stories, melodramas and family films have taken over Hollywood. *Home Alone, Ghost* and *Pretty Woman,* for example, collectively reaped more than $500 million in total revenues in 1990. Get set for an onslaught of films about people waking up and smelling the coffee.

For many Americans the most startling realization is how much they have given up for their career. In her new book, *Down-Shifting,* author Amy Saltzman maintains that baby boomers have grown increasingly skeptical about the payoff for devoting so much time to the fast track. As their huge generation crowds toward the top of the corporate pyramid, many are getting stalled. At the same time, companies have been slashing the ranks of middle managers.

For Karen Glance, 36, it came down to all those little packets of shampoo. She remembers the morning she opened her bathroom cabinet in St. Paul and counted 150 that had followed her home from hotels in dozens of cities. Says the former apparel executive: "I was a workaholic, a crazy, crazy woman. I was on a plane four times a week. I just wanted to get to the top. All of a sudden, I realized that I was reaching that goal but I wasn't happy. A year would go by, and I wouldn't know what had happened."

A few months ago, Glance was shopping in a neighborhood grocery store when she learned that its owner was about to retire. Something fell into place. She looked around the old-fashioned shop, where clerks still climb ladders to retrieve goods from the upper shelves, and she decided on the spot to buy the place. The new proprietor of the Crocus Hill market may never come anywhere near to matching her old $100,000-plus yearly income, but she couldn't care less. Says Glance: "It really comes down to saying, 'Slow down. The value of life might not be in making money.'"

Mostly, though, what people want now is more time around home and hearth. Most parents of small children work outside the home. More than 7 million Americans hold down two or even three jobs to make ends meet. "Nobody seems to have any damn time anymore," says Stuart Winby, a Hewlett-Packard executive. "People can't manage their home, work and personal life." As a result, many working mothers (and some fathers) are giving up full-time careers to devote more time to homelife.

Some couples are even thinking twice about divorce in light of the problems it can pose for children, the financial damage it does to families and other consequences. The U.S. divorce rate, which reached a high of 5.3 per 1,000 people in 1979, is now 4.7 and may still be falling.

Of all those rejecting the rat race to spend more time with their families, perhaps the most famous is Peter Lynch. While the 47-year-old investment superstar was busy building the Fidelity Magellan mutual fund into a $13 billion behemoth, his youngest daughter got to be seven years old, and he felt he hardly knew her. He stunned Wall Street when he decided to give up his 14-hour workdays. With a nest egg estimated at $50 million, Lynch could afford to quit. But many ordinary people evidently felt a connection with what he did, for he received more than 1,000 letters of support for his move. These days, while other investment managers are scanning their market data at dawn, Lynch is making school lunches. Says he: "I loved what I was doing, but I came to a conclusion, and so did some others: What in the hell are we doing this for? I don't know anyone who wished on his deathbed that he had spent more time at the office."

The stay-at-home urge, also known as cocooning, has produced a boom of its own. Consumers spent more than $9 billion renting videotapes in 1990, up 13% from the previous year and nearly twice

NOW Dr. Holmes Morton studies and treats congenital diseases common among Amish children

THEN His medical colleagues told him he was throwing away a lucrative career by moving to Amish country

the $5 billion they paid to see new releases at theaters. Home entertaining is decidedly back to basics. Remember onion dip? The Mom Rule has re-emerged as America's primary meal-planning guide: if she never heard of it, don't serve it. With a couple of children in tow, mothers and fathers simply don't have time to hunt for goat cheese and sun-dried tomatoes in the supermarket.

Far from becoming hermits, though, many Americans are reaching out to strengthen their ties beyond the home. Instead of defining themselves mostly by their possessions and work, more Americans in big cities as well as small towns are getting involved with their communities.

NOW Instead of picking stocks from dawn to dusk, Peter Lynch gets up early to make school lunches for his daughters

THEN He built the largest mutual fund in the country, worth $13 billion—but had no time for his family

Lately, charitable agencies and community groups have seen an upsurge in the willingness of Americans to help the less fortunate. In 1989 citizens gave a record $114.7 billion to charitable causes across the U.S., a 10% increase from the previous year, despite the stagnating economy. Rather than exchange Christmas presents, many have started making contributions in the names of their friends. Even more impressive, more than 98 million Americans—about half of all adults—volunteered their time to charitable organizations in 1989, a 23% increase from two years earlier.

In their search for more enduring gratification in life, many people are seeking spirituality, if not a born-again commitment to organized religion. "Spirituality is in," says theologian Marty, "so much so that I get embarrassed by it." Says Milton Walsh, a Roman Catholic priest who is pastor of St. Mary's Cathedral in San Francisco: "People want some kind of direction and purpose, the basic 'Who am I? Where am I going?' "

By some analyses the 1990s will be an anxious era of dues paying for the excesses of the '80s. That may be true in a public sense, but in private lives, how much fun was the past decade? For most Americans it was a time of struggling to keep up with everyone who seemed to be making it big. Now that the bubble of financial speculation has burst, people should—and do—feel entitled to accept more modest aspirations.

Now that the conversation has changed to more humane topics, how will it affect the economy? Over the long haul, prudent consumers who feel optimistic about the future could help build a stronger foundation for the economy. For one thing, the U.S. personal-savings rate, which dropped from 9% in the mid-1970s to a low of 2.3% in late 1987, is now about 4% and climbing. That will provide a larger pool of investment capital and could help the U.S. regain its competitive footing. The poor may also eventually benefit if the notion of a kinder, gentler America is translated into concrete action.

But the final question is this: Is the simple life just a passing fancy, a stylish flashback of the 1960s? Not so, say people who have studied both eras. Contends Berkeley sociologist Robert Bellah: "It's no longer messianic, the way it was in the '60s, but relatively pragmatic. That may give the present mood a greater staying power." That's good, because the American generation now reaching middle age has a lot of promises to keep—not to mention mortgages to carry, tuition to pay and lawns to mow. No wonder they want to keep it simple.

Finger Pointers and Crybabies

Twin malformations are cropping up
in the American character: a nasty intolerance and a desire
to blame everyone else for everything

The busybody and the crybaby are getting to be the most conspicuous children on the American playground.

The busybody is the bully with the ayatullah shine in his eyes, gauleiter of correctness, who barges around telling the other kids that they cannot smoke, be fat, drink booze, wear furs, eat meat or otherwise nonconform to the new tribal rules now taking shape.

The crybaby, on the other hand, is the abject, manipulative little devil with the lawyer and, so to speak, the actionable diaper rash. He is a mayor of Washington, arrested (and captured on videotape) as he smokes crack in a hotel room with a woman not his wife. He pronounces himself a victim—of the woman, of white injustice, of the universe. Whatever.

Both these types, the one overactive and the other overpassive, are fashioning some odd new malformations of American character. Zealotry of either kind—the puritan's need to regiment others or the victim's passion for blaming everyone except himself—tends to produce a depressing civic stupidity. Each trait has about it the immobility of addiction. Victims become addicted to being victims: they derive identity, innocence and a kind of devious power from sheer, defaulting helplessness. On the other side, the candlesnuffers of behavioral and political correctness enact their paradox, accomplishing intolerance in the name of tolerance, regimentation in the name of betterment.

CRYBABIES: ETERNAL VICTIMS

This is the age of the self-tort crybaby, to whom some disappointment—a slur, the loss of a job, an errant spouse, a foul-tasting can of beer, a slip on the supermarket floor, an unbecoming facelift—is sufficient occasion to claim huge monetary awards.

It is also the age of the all-purpose victim: the individual or group whose plight, condition or even momentary setback is not a matter

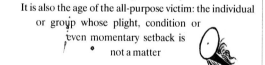

that needs be solved by individual effort but constitutes a social problem in itself. "We're not to blame, we're victims" is the increasingly assertive rallying cry of groups who see the American Dream not as striving fulfilled but as unachieved entitlement. Crybabyhood is all blame, no pain, for gain. And all too often it works.

A double-barreled social phenomenon now threatens the real exercise of civil liberties. The first barrel is "victimology." The other is what George Washington University sociologist Amitai Etzioni calls the "rights industry"—the creation by individuals and special-interest groups of freshly minted freedoms and prerogatives that must be upheld even when they are foolishly asserted, and whose transgression is—always—a matter for outcry.

Just about everybody can claim a position in the rights brigade: those who smoke and those who don't; those who demand shelter for the homeless and those who support the right of the homeless to refuse shelter; those who claim rights for fetuses and those who want the right to make their own choice for abortion; those who want their teenagers taught to use condoms and those who insist on the right to keep their kids ignorant of such things; campus hoodlums who insult their fellow students and college administrators who promulgate censorious "rules of conduct" to prevent their students from giving offense to this or that ethnic group, sexual preference or body type. Their "rights" give their claims—whatever they may be—an absolute air, and any attempt to thwart their claims turns them into victims.

Under the corrosive influence of victimology, the principle of individual responsibility for one's actions, once a vaunted American virtue, seems like a relic. The challenge: to knit a contentious American society together rather than allow it to become balkanized by competing interests. The new area of litigious behavior that has blossomed—and might be called emotional tort law—is fertilized by new rules of comparative negligence that allow a plaintiff to recover damages in a lawsuit even if he is partly at fault. Perhaps one step toward more civility and community would be a modification of the famous injunction in *Henry VI:* first let's restrain—not kill—all the lawyers. Then add a second proposal that Shakespeare never had to think of: let's gag all the crybabies. Better yet, let them gag themselves.

BUSYBODIES: NEW PURITANS

Consider, for a moment, these twin signs of our scrambled times:

▶In Los Angeles, Jesse Mercado was dismissed from his job as a security guard at the *Times* despite an excellent performance record. The reason? Mercado was overweight.

▶In Wabash, Ind., Janice Bone lost her job as an assistant payroll clerk at the Ford Meter Box Co. The reason? The firm, which will not let its employees smoke either on the job or at home, insisted that she take a urine test, which proved positive for nicotine.

Welcome to the prying side of America in the 1990s. The U.S. may still be the land of the free, but increasingly, it is also the home of the dedicated new puritans, humorlessly imposing on others arbitrary (meaning their own) standards of behavior, health and thought. To a number of concerned observers, the busybodies—conformity seekers, legal nitpickers and politically correct thought police—seem to have lost sight of a bedrock American virtue: tolerance, allowing others, in the name of freedom, to do things one disagrees with or does not like, provided they do no outright harm to others.

One key battleground in the tolerance war is life-style. These days, smoking, drinking or noshing on high-cholesterol snacks isn't just a health risk. It can endanger your job as well. Concerned about the ever rising cost of health insurance, at least 6,000 U.S. companies, including Atlanta-based Turner Broadcasting, refuse to hire smokers, and in some cases fire those who don't beat the habit, even when it is practiced off the job.

The nation's lawmakers are beginning to listen: 19 states, including New Jersey, Colorado and Oregon, have passed some form of legislation that bars employers from discriminating against workers because of their life-style.

The corporate life-style police are at least motivated by real financial concerns. All too often, other busybodies are motivated by sheer bloody-mindedness: a persistent neo-Prohibitionist movement has added to the woes of the nation's wine industry by demanding ever more prominent and explicit health-warning labels on bottles; animal-rights zealots seem to have greater respect for fauna than for their fellow humans.

Finally, of course, there are the academic enforcers of politi-

cal correctness, or p.c., whose efforts have received widespread publicity but who remain, in many cases undaunted. Hardly a week goes by without some new example of attempts to enforce conformity on campus. The weary truth is that busybodyness is, as black radical H. Rap Brown once said of violence, as American as cherry pie. The Puritans, who begat it all, had "a desperate and intolerant wish to cleanse the world of its impurities," editor Lewis Lapham of *Harper's* has written, and their ambition was to build a New Jerusalem on earth despite all of life's uncertainties. In both spiritual and secular guise, that has been a recurring theme in U.S. history, from the great awakening of the early frontier days to the noble experiment of Prohibition.

To sociologist James Jasper of New York University, today's would-be censors and neo-puritans belong to two disparate groups. One consists of those, frequently working class in origin, who feel their status threatened by differing life-styles—hence their hostility to drugs and casual sex and their sympathy for the goals of decency-obsessed media baiters like the Rev. Donald Wildmon or Senator Jesse Helms. The other group, Jasper says, consists of cause-oriented activists, such as animal rightists and environmentalists, who are intent on making people think about the consequences of letting endangered species die out or contaminating the atmosphere with hair spray.

Both groups have contributed to what sociologist Jack Douglas calls "a degree of self-centered moralism that is unprecedented in American history." Among other things, Douglas notes, the new forms of personal intolerance occur at a time when the common bonds of U.S. society—our shared values, our political understandings—seem weaker than ever. "Maybe," political analyst Sherry Bebitch Jeffe glooms, "America is too large and diverse to be one country under democracy any longer."

BLAME GAME

IN LOS ANGELES, at least three cops who witnessed the notorious videotaped beating of a black motorist last March have filed for worker's compensation, claiming that they suffered anxiety and stress.

IN TAMPA, FLORIDA, Dennis Diaz, accused of failing to pay $30,000 in child support, complained that his right to privacy was violated in 1989, when the state posted his name and photograph along with those of other delinquent fathers.

IN VENTURA, CALIFORNIA, Donna Roberts charged that a veterinarian severely injured her pet iguana in 1989; she sued for $1 million in damages, contending that the animal suffered a broken back and that she endured emotional stress. The case is pending.

IN CANNES, FRANCE, black writer-director Spike Lee, miffed because his film *Do the Right Thing* did not win first prize at the annual film festival in 1989, implied that the judges' decision was racist.

IN MARTINEZ, CALIFORNIA, crew members of a U.S. Navy train that severed an antiwar protester's legs in 1987 sued him, alleging post-traumatic stress disorder. The protester went on to win a settlement in his own suit against the government.

IN CINCINNATI, OHIO, Edward H. Winter sued a local hospital for "wrongful living." Winter argued that nursing personnel violated his rights when they saved his life after he experienced an episode of extremely rapid heartbeat—despite his instructions that no such effort should be attempted. Winter died about two years later; a judge last week threw out the case, which had been pursued by Winter's estate.

TRIVIAL PURSUIT

IN LAWRENCEVILLE, GA., police officer Robbie Smith, 25, was removed from his patrol duties and exiled to a dispatch unit last May because a "heavy metal" tattoo on his forearm was said to portray the wrong image for an officer.

IN SANTA ANA, CALIF., Helen Garrett, 51, kissed a male friend goodnight on the steps of her condominium home and the next day received a notice from the condo association saying she was "seen parking in circular driveway kissing and doing bad things for over 1 hour." The note warned of a possible fine if she repeated the infraction. Witnesses had confused Garrett and friend with two parking teens.

IN OLYMPIA, WASH., Senator James West, a Republican, last year introduced a bill in the Washington state legislature that would have made sexual intercourse illegal for unmarried teens under 18. The legislature's senate health care and corrections committee gave the restrictive bill serious consideration as an AIDS-prevention measure.

IN BENNINGTON, VT., writer Edward Hoagland was fired from his teaching job at Bennington College after students expressed outrage over three sentences he published in an *Esquire* article that they thought reflected anti-gay notions. The administration reinstated Hoagland last month.

IN ARAPAHOE COUNTY, COLO., the sheriff's department will hire only non-smokers and forbids its few remaining smokers to light up anywhere on the job, even while out on a case.

IN LEBANON, TENN., the Cracker Barrel Old Country Store and Restaurant chain briefly adopted a policy ousting employees who failed "to demonstrate normal heterosexual values." At least nine gay workers were fired before the company rescinded the rule a few weeks later.

When Is It RAPE?

He says she wanted it. She calls it a crime. A battle of the sexes rages.

Be careful of strangers and hurry home, says a mother to her daughter, knowing the world is a frightful place but not wishing to swaddle a child in fear. Girls grow up scarred by caution and enter adulthood eager to shake free of their parents' worst nightmares. They still know to be wary of strangers. What they don't know is whether they have more to fear from their friends.

Most women who get raped are raped by people they already know—like the fellow in biology class, or the guy in the office down the hall, or their friend's brother. The familiarity is enough to make them let down their guard, sometimes even enough to make them wonder afterward whether they were "really raped." What people think of as real rape—the assault by the monstrous stranger lurking in the shadows—accounts for only 1 out of 5 attacks.

So the phrase acquaintance rape was coined to describe the rest, all the cases of forced sex between people who knew each other, however casually. But that was too clinical for headline writers, and so the popular term is the narrower date rape, which suggest an ugly ending to a raucous night on the town.

These are not idle distinctions. Behind the search for labels is the central mythology about rape: rapists are always strangers, and victims are women who ask for it. The mythology is hard to dispel because the crime is so rarely exposed. The experts guess—that's all they can do under the circumstances—that while 1 in 4 women will be raped in her lifetime, less than 10% will report the assault, and less than 5% of the rapists will go to jail.

Women charge that date rape is the hidden crime; men complain it is hard to prevent a crime they can't define. Women say it isn't taken seriously; men say it is a concept invented by women who like to tease but not take the consequences. Women say the date-rape debate is the first time the nation has talked frankly about sex; men say it is women's unconscious reaction to the excesses of the sexual revolution. Meanwhile, men and women argue among themselves about the gray area that surrounds the whole murky arena of sexual relations, and there is no consensus in sight.

In court, on campus, in conversation, the issue turns on the elasticity of the word rape. At one extreme are those who argue that, for the word to retain its impact, it must be strictly defined as forced sexual intercourse: a gang of thugs jumping a jogger, a psychopath preying on old

Would you classify the following as rape or not?		RAPE	NOT RAPE
A man has sex with a woman who has passed out after drinking too much	FEMALE	88%	9%
	MALE	77%	17%
A married man has sex with his wife even though she does not want him to	FEMALE	61%	30%
	MALE	56%	38%
A man argues with a woman who does not want to have sex until she agrees to have sex	FEMALE	42%	53%
	MALE	33%	59%
A man uses emotional pressure, but no physical force, to get a woman to have sex	FEMALE	39%	55%
	MALE	33%	59%

		YES	NO
Do you believe that some women like to be talked into having sex?	FEMALE	54%	33%
	MALE	69%	20%

From a telephone poll of 500 Americans adults taken for TIME, CNN on May 8 by Yankelovich Clancy Shulman. Sampling error is plus or minus 4.5%. "Not sures" omitted.

women in a housing complex. To stretch the definition of the word risks stripping away its power. In this view, if it happened on a date, it wasn't rape.

Others are willing to concede that date rape sometimes occurs, that sometimes a man goes too far on a date without a woman's consent. But this infraction, they say, is not as ghastly a crime as street rape, and should not be taken as seriously. This attitude sparks rage among women who carry scars received at the hands of men they knew. Date rape is not about a misunderstanding, they say. It is not a communications problem. It is not about a woman's having regrets in the morning for a decision she made the night before. It is not about a "decision" at all. Rape is rape, and any form of forced sex— even between neighbors, co-workers, classmates and casual friends —is a crime.

A more extreme form of that view comes from activists who see rape as a metaphor, its definition swelling to cover any kind of oppression of women. Rape, seen in this light, can occur not only on a date but also in a marriage, not only by violent assault but also by psychological pressure. No wonder, then, that the battles become so heated. When innuendo qualifies as rape, the definitions have become so slippery that the entire subject sinks into a political swamp.

In May the Supreme Court waded into the debate with a 7-to-2 ruling that protects victims from being harassed on the witness stand with questions about their sexual history. The Justices, in their first decision on rape-shield laws, said an accused rapist could not present evidence about a previous sexual relationship with the victim unless he notified the court ahead of time.

Until the 1960s it was virtually impossible to prove rape without an eyewitness; judges were often required to instruct jurors that "rape is a charge easily made and hard to defend against; so examine the testimony of this witness with caution." A new twist in society's perception came in 1975, when Susan Brownmiller published her book *Against Our Will: Men, Women, and Rape.* In it she attacked the concept that rape was a sex crime, arguing instead that it was a crime of violence and power over women: "It is nothing more or less than a conscious process of intimidation, by which all men keep all women in a state of fear."

Out of this contention was born a set of arguments that have become politically correct wisdom on campus and in academic circles. This view holds that rape is a symbol of women's vulnerability to male institutions and attitudes. This line of reasoning has led some women, especially radicalized victims, to justify flinging around the term rape as a political weapon referring to everything from violent sexual assaults to inappropriate innuendos.

Taken to extremes, there is an ugly element of vengeance at work here. Rape is an abuse of power. But so are false accusations of rape, and to suggest that men whose reputations are destroyed might benefit because it will make them more sensitive is an attitude that is sure to backfire. On campuses, where the issue is most inflamed, male students are outraged that their names can be scrawled on a bathroom-wall list of rapists and they have no chance to tell their side of the story.

A single question is at the heart of the debate: if rape is sex without consent, how exactly should consent be defined and communicated, when and by whom? Those who view rape through a political lens tend to place all responsibility on men to make sure that their partners are consenting at every point of a sexual encounter. At the extreme, sexual relations come to resemble major surgery, requiring a signed consent form.

Historically, of course, this has never been the case, and there are some who argue that it shouldn't be—that women too must take responsibility for their behavior, and that the whole realm of intimate encounters defies regulation from on high. No one defends the use of physical force, but when the coercion involved is purely psychological, it becomes hard to assign blame after the fact. Journalist Stephanie Gutmann is an ardent foe of what she calls the date-rape dogmatists. "How can you make sex completely safe?" she asks. 'What a horribly bland, unerotic thing that would be!"

What is lost in the ideological debate over date rape is the fact that men and women, especially when they are young and drunk and aroused, are not very good at communicating. The man may envision a celluloid seduction, in

Do you believe a woman who is raped is partly to blame if:			
	AGE	YES	NO
She is under the influence of drugs or alcohol	18–34	31%	66%
	35–49	35%	58%
	50+	57%	36%
She initially says yes to having sex and then changes her mind	18–34	34%	60%
	35–49	43%	53%
	50+	43%	46%
She dresses provocatively	18–34	28%	70%
	35–49	31%	67%
	50+	53%	42%
She agrees to go to the man's room or home	18–34	20%	76%
	35–49	29%	70%
	50+	53%	41%

Have you ever been in a situation with a man in which you said no but ended up having sex anyway?	ASKED OF FEMALES	YES	NO
		18%	80%

which he is being commanding, she is being coy. A woman may experience the same event as a degrading violation of her will. That some men do not believe a women's protests is scarcely surprising in a society so drenched with messages that women have rape fantasies and a desire to be overpowered.

The use of new terms, like acquaintance rape and date rape, while controversial, has given men and women the vocabulary they need to express their experiences with both force and precision. Those who hope to raise society's sensitivity to the problem of date rape would do well to concede that it is not precisely the same sort of crime as street rape, that there may be very murky issues of intent and degree involved.

On the other hand, those who downplay the problem should come to realize that date rape is a crime of uniquely intimate cruelty. While the body is violated, the spirit is maimed. How long will it take, once the wounds have healed, before it is possible to share a walk on a beach, a drive home from work or an evening's conversation without always listening for a quiet alarm to start ringing deep in the back of the memory of a terrible crime?

Prescribing Change

With endless energy, eagle-scout scruples and a head for headlines, David Kessler revives the battered FDA

The food and drug industry lawyers had heard it all before. Now, here was the freshly minted FDA commissioner, still wet behind the ears at 39, giving them the usual dose of tough talk. "Ladies and gentlemen," David Kessler began, "I am here today to tell you that I place a high priority on enforcing the law." The attorneys, convened in a Palm Beach, Fla., hotel, nodded obligingly. "This is not the idle talk of a new commissioner," Kessler continued, to more polite nods. Then came the surprise. "Today the U.S. Attorney's office in Minneapolis is filing on FDA's behalf a seizure action against Procter & Gamble's Citrus Hill Fresh Choice orange juice," he said. "The use of the term 'fresh' is false and misleading, and it is confusing to consumers." The nodding stopped, the lawyers grew silent, and many began to wonder, "Who *is* this guy?"

The guy who stunned the food industry that April morning, and many times after, is almost certainly the most capable person ever put in charge of the Food and Drug Administration. When Kessler was appointed in December 1990 he faced an agency that for more than a decade had been bled of funds by the White House and burdened with new responsibilities by Congress. AIDS activists were picketing the front doors. Five employees had been convicted of accepting bribes. And a federal report had just concluded that the agency's meager resources were incapable of ensuring the safety of foods or the efficacy of new drugs.

But to Kessler, inheriting this mess is the opportunity of a lifetime, one he's been rigorously training for since college. A Harvard-educated physician and a University of Chicago–trained lawyer, he defied geography and sleep deficits to achieve both degrees simultaneously. He studied management at New York University and politics as a Senate staffer. For nine years, he ran the hospital at the Albert Einstein College of Medicine. When he was tapped for the FDA post, he was serving on a federal commission analyzing that very agency. "A lot of my background comes together here," he says. "I feel comfortable, enormously comfortable here."

Kessler always has a plan, and targeting a food-manufacturing giant such as Procter & Gamble was certainly part of one. Says Washington attorney and longtime friend Stuart Pape: "Going after large companies and being tough have been part of a well-considered strategy to increase the credibility and morale of the agency."

Inside the FDA, Kessler has been just as aggressive. He's cut the time frame for legal action against a violator from 50 to 25 days. He has also begun to streamline the organization, consolidating 23 department heads into five new positions. For these spots, Kessler has recruited from the private sector a number of high-powered management consultants and Washington attorneys. Most are in their early 40s, and some of them will be earning less at the FDA than they paid in 1990 in taxes.

To old friends, Kessler's first target is wonderfully appropriate. The man has always had an obsession with food, and he has certainly never been a nuts-and-berries purist. "I was a fat kid," he says. In college he was the only student in his dorm who brought an entire refrigerator from home. He kept it stocked with sodas, bagels, cream cheese and cold cuts. At Amherst he organized a pie-throwing party after negotiating a deal for 200 strawberry-rhubarb pies. In law school he trained on pizza, Chinese food and ice cream. He still has a passion for take-out, and he starts each day with a diet cola. In December 1990, at 205 lbs., Kessler was concerned that he'd cut too large a figure for a top health officer. So with characteristic discipline, he decided to reduce his calorie intake (by skipping lunch) and start exercising (usually running at 1 a.m.). Now, after altering his suits twice, he's a bony 155. Says his wife Paulette, an attorney: "He just has incredible willpower, and he's very focused."

Kessler is one member of the '60s generation who never lost the naive conviction that an individual can change the world. Deceptive food labeling troubles him because it is dishonest and unfair. And, without warning, he can break into a mini-sermon about the FDA: "There are 8,000 wonderful people here. They came here because they wanted to protect and promote the public health, and my job is to let them do their job."

While White House and Congress are pleased by his performance so far, other FDA watchers are skeptical that he will succeed in transforming his agency. "You can deal with orange juice easily, but pretty soon you've got to deal with the real inadequacies," says Charles Edwards, a former FDA commissioner who chaired the government panel that examined the agency's shortcomings. The food industry believes Kessler is pushing too far, too quickly. But Kessler remains confident. "There's nothing that isn't manageable," he says. So far, he's done a good job of making that sound credible.

Father to the Man

How Robert Bly transformed his struggle with an alcoholic dad into a mass-therapy mythology

Failure is the toughest American wilderness. Robert Bly, who is now a leader of the men's movement and author of *Iron John,* spent some years in the territory. His wilderness lies three hours west of Minneapolis, out toward the South Dakota border, in flat farm country around Madison (pop. 2,000), Minn.

Bly was the high school valedictorian who went to hell, who might have amounted to something as a farmer but instead lived on a spread his father gave him. He raised four children but otherwise, in Madison's eyes, produced nothing except obscure poetry for 25 years. He drove old cars and wore old clothes, and when Vietnam came around, he talked like a communist. His father, Jacob Bly, was a respected farmer who turned alcoholic. Robert had to fetch him out of the bars downtown sometimes.

A double humiliation: his father's alcoholism, his own failure. But whatever Madison may have once thought, Bly is a gifted poet, critic and showman who has transformed his long struggle into a strange, mythicized American phenomenon of celebrity and mass therapy. Bly is the bardic voice of that interesting but vaguely embarrassing business, the men's movement, which strikes many men as somehow unmanly. Well, says Bly, that shame is something they will have to get over.

Bly's book *Iron John* has been on the best-seller list 55 weeks ; he addresses men's gatherings around the country, speaking a fairy-tale code about each male's lost "Wild Man," that hairy masculine authenticity that began getting ruined during the Industrial Revolution, when fathers left their sons and went to work in the factories. The communion between father and son, the traditional connection, lore passing from father to son, vanished. And with it went the masculine identity, the meaning and energy of a man's life, which should be an adventure, an allegory, a quest. Bly, with some validating help on television from Bill Moyers, has brought the masculine psyche onto the stage of Oprah-consciousness. There it is either enjoying its 15 minutes of fame or remaking Americans' understanding of men, and therefore of men and women and of life itself.

"You cannot become a man until your own father dies," Bly says. Bly's father died three years ago at the age of 87 in a Minnesota nursing home. Bly is 65, so by his own reckoning, he did not become a man until he was 62. He was a long time working on it.

Bly says it was around 10 years ago that he began writing the *Iron John* story. The book is an explication of the tale of a boy who frees a Wild Man, Iron John, whom the boy's father, the king, has locked in a cage. Iron John takes the boy into the forest and step by step teaches him the secrets of being a man. In the fullness of maturity, he becomes a man and marries his princess.

Bly tires of repeating that the men's movement is not against women. Nor does the Wild Man imply savagery, brutality, aggression, obtuseness, smashing beer cans against the forehead or shooting small animals for the pleasure of watching them die.

Bly's ice-blue Norwegian eyes and white hair give him a theatrical air. His complexion sometimes radiates up to an alarming red, and he puffs a little after marching up the stairs. A large cast of characters of many ages flickers around his eyes and face. He strikes one as a struggling man, something like a difficult older brother.

He sees the men's movement—and his own celebrity—from the inside. It is a deeply formed, logical part of his own biography. It is an outcome of his years as a student at Harvard just after World War II, studying poetry with Archibald MacLeish, and then of a long depressed period, when he lived alone in New York City, subsisting on three-day-old bread, reading Rilke in the New York Public Library. After a stretch at the Iowa Writers' Workshop, he married Carol McLean, a writer he had met at Harvard. (They divorced in 1979, and he is now married to Ruth Ray, a Jungian analyst.) In 1955 Robert and Carol Bly "went to hide out at the farm" on the edge of Madison; Bly published his first book of poetry, *Silence in the Snowy Fields,* in 1962. "The land was flat and boring," he says. "That was my whole problem in writing poems about that country. I called it *Silence in the Snowy Fields* because at least it was a little more interesting with snow on it."

Bly may not be alive to certain absurdities in the men's movement that others see. Ask him about the drumming, for example, which strikes some as a silly, self-conscious attempt at manly authenticity, almost a satire of the hairy chested, and he pours forth a thoughtful but technical answer: "The drum honors the body as opposed to the mind, and that is helpful. It heats up the space where we are." As a spiritual showman (shaman), Bly seeks to produce certain effects. He is good at them. He could not begin to see the men's movement, and his place in it, as a depthless happening in the goofy circus of America. It is odd that Bly is not more put off by the earnest vulgarity of the enterprise.

"I hate being a pop figure," he says and winces. But he has made the transition from private trauma to public stage.

Has the 500th anniversary of the first voyage of Christopher Columbus added to the primary evidence about him— what he did, how he thought, what kind of man he was? Not by much.

But to expect dramatic discoveries to appear on cue for 1992 is unrealistic. In part, the anniversary celebration will have done its job if it erases a number of the apocrypha patched onto the figure of the Discoverer, as the 19th century called him. Some are obviously false, such as the tenacious story that Queen Isabella sold her jewels to pay for his first voyage, or that the *Santa María* was crewed by convicts, or that Columbus was trying to prove the world was round. (No educated person in the late 15th century, and no mariner either, believed otherwise.)

Columbus himself has been presented as Castilian, Catalan, Corsican, Majorcan, Portuguese, French, English, Greek and even Armenian. He was, in fact, Italian: born in Genoa in 1451, the son of a weaver.

Columbus' sense of his humble origins was crucial. He was determined to transcend them; his means would be navigation. Sometime between 1478 and 1484, the full plan of self-aggrandizement and discovery took shape in his mind. He would win glory, riches and a title of nobility by opening a trade route to the untapped wealth of the Orient.

This drive is one of the few attributes of Columbus that all the surviving sources agree on. It was clear to the crew of the *Santa María* as the little fleet was pitching and rolling west in 1492, with no land yet in sight and mutiny brewing. According to Bartolomé de las Casas' account, some of the men argued that "it was great madness and self-inflicted manslaughter to risk their lives to further the mad schemes of a foreigner who was ready to die in the hope of making a great lord of himself." They planned to pitch him overboard at night as he fiddled with his quadrant, trying to take a reading of the polestar.

Columbus was in fact a very rigid man, and his inflexibility combined with piety and opportunism to produce behavior not far from paranoid. His growing ambition encouraged the belief, typical of obsessed loners, that everyone except God was against him. He was so certain that his enterprise of the Indies was fulfillment of God's designs that he even greeted the wreck of the *Santa María* as a sign of divine approbation. He had an apocalyptic turn of mind.

Columbus could be extremely petty, as when he claimed for himself the prize money he had promised to the first crewman to sight westward land. His reports to the crown were absurdly self-serving, especially those composed after the first voyage, which are a tissue of hustling lies about "incredible amounts" of gold and spices— which, however, got him 17 ships for the second voyage. His fixations often skewed his charting, so that Columbus mistook islands for continental coasts and thus claimed to have found what he had not.

But lies and self-delusion, inflated claims, greed and chart errors were the common currency of exploration. Unlike others, Columbus got across the Atlantic and found something—not Asia, but something —in the West. The current prejudice against the word discovery, in the context of Columbus' efforts, is interesting. There has never been a shortage of claims and hypotheses about alternative "discoveries" of America. It seems quite certain that the first Europeans to reach the mainland of North America (which Columbus never did; the closest he got to it was Venezuela) were the Vikings, who created a short-lived settlement in Newfoundland around the year 1000.

One need not pay too much attention to other candidates: Ireland's St. Brendan, Jewish refugees fleeing Roman persecution, Japanese fishermen and, most recently, an unknown Spanish mariner who supposedly reached the Bahamas in the 15th century, struggled back across the Atlantic and entrusted his map and logs to Columbus, who concealed his knowledge of them to reap the glory of discovery for himself.

The point about discovery is not that someone floats ashore somewhere, by accident, leaving no traces. The essence of discovery is that the voyage is repeatable. It entails documentation—logs and records. The discoverer is the person who gets from known A to unknown B, returns to A, and can then get back to B again. Columbus' claim to be a discoverer is, admittedly, a function of European consciousness. It exists only in a European cultural frame—the native cultures and civilizations of America knew very well where they were. But this does not make it unreal. The achievement of Columbus' first voyage in 1492 was to open a route to the New World that could be sailed again, by himself and others, over and over—and was.

In this sense, he united the Western and Eastern hemispheres of the world across the Atlantic. No man had done so before. We should not allow our reaction against the myth of Columbus as Renaissance Ulysses, Romantic hero and near saint to obscure his actual achievement.

Exploring Columbus
The dispute over the legacy of Columbus should not obscure his real achievements

Bush's Choice for Schools

The Education Secretary is putting his political skills—and his ambitions—on the line to sell Choice to Capitol Hill

Author Alex Haley and his friend Lamar Alexander booked passage together in 1988 on a cargo ship from California to Australia, aiming to write books away from the distractions of their Tennessee home base. Every evening the pair would emerge from a day of writing in their cabins to watch the "green flash," which can sometimes be seen just before the sun disappears below the horizon. "He'd talk, and I'd listen," Haley recalls. "Lamar talked night after night about the desperate need to improve American education. It was in his marrow. He felt impotent to do the things that needed to be done."

Alexander is frustrated no longer. He is now the point man for George Bush's educational goals, including the idea of school Choice, and he is using his soft-spoken salesmanship to market them to Congress and the American public. The role is the most challenging yet for the man named by Bush as Secretary of Education in December 1990, whose mild and courteous demeanor masks a high-octane ambition. His goal is to transform the Department of Education, which Ronald Reagan once pledged to abolish, from a backwater operation into one of Washington's leading domestic agencies. Alexander, 51, brings political acumen to his job that was never seen under predecessors Lauro Cavazos and William Bennett. He learned from masters, serving first as an aide to Tennessee Senator Howard Baker and then in the Nixon White House before becoming a two-term Republican Governor. This background gives him a big advantage when he travels to Capitol Hill, as he often does, to lobby for his program: he understands compromise.

But behind the agreeable exterior is a flinty vision of American public education and its various ills that is sweeping in its condemnation. "The problem is the system," Alexander says flatly. He refers to the Supreme Court as "an obstacle" blocking the use of tax dollars for religious schools. He is wound tighter than he looks. His celebrated affability sometimes cracks when challenged—when he is asked, for example, why his younger son William attends a private rather than public school. "I chose it because I like it," he snaps.

The boyish-looking, sandy-haired native of the small Tennessee town of Maryville forgets nothing. "If he ever met you, he'll remember you," says Haley. Alexander is an inveterate notetaker, scribbling ideas and activities on handy scraps of paper.

The sense of discipline comes from his mother Florence, a no-nonsense woman who ran a nursery school in her backyard, and his late father Andrew, who served briefly as an elementary school principal. Lamar began piano lessons at four and studied diligently through his freshman year at Vanderbilt. Today he can deftly play Chopin or pound out rocket-top country piano, as he did in Bourbon Street watering holes while clerking for federal Judge John Minor Wisdom after his 1965 graduation from New York University law school.

As Governor, Alexander pushed through a 10-point program to improve public education in Tennessee (including classroom computers and merit pay for teachers) and a penny-on-the-dollar sales tax to pay for it. Bush liked what he saw and sought Alexander's counsel periodically on education matters. The two get along well, and Alexander's wife Honey is a friend of Barbara Bush's from Texas.

But not everyone is enamored of Alexander's record as an education Governor. "He brought education to the forefront as a topic at everyone's kitchen table," concedes Relzie Payton, president of the Tennessee Education Association, the state teachers' union. But Alexander was also a tireless self-promoter, she argues, whose follow-through was less impressive than his goals. Alexander's educational efforts in Tennessee have met with mixed success, and Payton adds, "Choice was mentioned, if at all, in passing while he was Governor."

So far, the new Education Secretary has received high marks for his energy and the caliber of his appointments. Directly under him as Deputy Secretary is David Kearns, 61, former chairman of Xerox Corp. Kearns will be, in Alexander's words, "my chief operating officer" and will spearhead a drive to raise $150 million from business for innovative schooling ideas.

Another interesting selection is Diane Ravitch, the incisive conservative thinker who has defended pluralism on college campuses against the assault of censorious "political correctness." Ravitch is in charge of the Office of Educational Research and Improvement and also serves as counselor to Alexander.

No one has ever accused Lamar Alexander of lacking confidence. "Five years from now, Choice will not be an issue," he serenely predicts. Instead, he insists, it will be the foundation for a transformed system of education that has long been his dream. Whether that is confidence or evidence of a quietly unbending temperament is something only he can prove.

157

Scandal at Stanford

The earthquake that rocked San Francisco in 1989 did $160 million worth of damage to nearby Stanford University. In 1991 tremors of a different sort rattled the élite Palo Alto–based institution—and may dent its coffers by as much as $200 million. A congressional investigation found that throughout the 1980s, Stanford routinely overcharged taxpayers for millions of dollars in research-related expenses. Among the charges: the university billed Uncle Sam for depreciation on a 72-ft. yacht; faculty discounts on tickets to athletic events; and a percentage of the cost of flowers, bedsheets, tablecloths and antiques for the president's house.

In January, Stanford agreed to refund $500,000 in government money used to maintain three university-owned houses and to pay back more than $180,000 on the yacht, a charge that the school said was an accounting error. By the fall, however, Stanford President

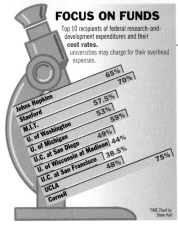

FOCUS ON FUNDS
Top 10 recipients of federal research-and-development expenditures and their **cost rates.** universities may charge for their overhead expenses.

Johns Hopkins	65% / 70%
Stanford	57.5%
M.I.T.	53% / 59%
U. of Washington	49%
U. of Michigan	44%
U.C. at San Diego	
U. of Wisconsin at Madison	38.5%
U.C. at San Francisco	48% / 75%
UCLA	
Cornell	

TIME Chart by Steve Hart

Donald Kennedy resigned as a result of the charges. Stanford's predicament raises troubling questions about how the government and universities spend taxpayer dollars intended for scientific research. At the center of the maelstrom is a set of arcane rules under which the government foots the bill for research and many of the overhead costs of doing research. These indirect costs include such university-wide expenses as administration, libraries, roads, utilities and building maintenance.

In order to recoup some of the skyrocketing costs of erecting new labs and technical libraries, schools have become increasingly aggressive about billing Washington for overhead. The government, meanwhile, faces a budget crunch that makes it less willing than ever to help universities expand or update their scientific infrastructure.

Universities had better be prepared for closer scrutiny. In 1992 Congress plans similar probes at five major universities. The aftershocks of the Stanford tremors will be felt for some time.

Promises: A. Delivery: D.

George Bush promised to be "the education President," but his marks for that endeavor have been decidedly mixed. In the spring of 1991, though, he apparently did some homework. Striving to fulfill his promise to launch a major domestic initiative, he presented an ambitious national plan called "America 2000: An Education Strategy" to improve troubled U.S. elementary and secondary schools.

Bush's goal of bringing about "a revolution in American education" was lofty enough, but the President hoped to perform a miracle: he offered relatively little federal money to back up his plan, which would be funded by $690 million shifted from existing programs. Among the more controversial proposals: nationwide standards for what youngsters need to know, monitored by uniform tests; report cards on each school's results; and the creation of 535 brand-new experimental schools, with businesses contributing $150 million or more to a research-and-development fund. Bush also favored replacing public school monopolies with parental choice among competing public and private schools, and recommended pay based on merit.

Food Fight

Throughout the '80s, federal food watchdogs napped to the sounds of a cacophony of false claims on food labels. The Food and Drug Administration virtually invited abuse by lifting its own longstanding ban against health promotions on food labels. But in 1991 the deregulatory winds shifted, and the sleeping sentry awakened. In a blaze of whistle blowing, the FDA, headed by tough new commissioner David Kessler (see *Society People*), cracked down. The agency began seizing products with misleading labels, developing new guidelines for nutritional information, and exposing hollow health claims.

The utterly novel vision: consumers should easily be able to tell what they are ingesting by reading what is written on food labels. Congress supplied the ammunition for the new crusade in 1990,

when it passed the Nutritional Labeling and Education Act, which requires new, straightforward labels for all foods, including fresh fruits and vegetables, beginning in 1993. Some restaurants have jumped on the bandwagon with knife and fork in hand; 80% of fastfood franchises have begun to provide nutrition information.

Regulators have targeted three major areas of label abuse: deceptive definitions, hazy health claims and slippery serving sizes. New labels will include standard definitions for such descriptive terms as high fiber, low fat and light; health claims will be certified on product packages. Although business executives grumble about the costs of relabeling, many manufacturers are philosophical about the reform movement. "This is not a fad," says Bob Pusey, a spokesman for Calistoga Mineral Water. "The thing we're all going to have to get used to is that the consumer has a right to know what's in food."

Cult of Greed

The Church of Scientology, started by science-fiction writer L. Ron Hubbard to "clear" people of unhappiness, portrays itself as a religion. But in reality the church is a highly profitable global racket that survives by intimidating members and critics in a Mafia-like manner. At times during the past decade, prosecutions against Scientology seemed to be curbing its menace. Eleven top Scientologists, including Hubbard's wife, were sent to prison in the early 1980s for infiltrating, burglarizing and wiretapping more than 100 private and government agencies in an attempt to block their investigations. In recent years hundreds of longtime Scientology adherents have quit the church and criticized it at their own risk. In various cases judges have labeled the church "schizophrenic and paranoid" and "corrupt, sinister and dangerous."

Yet the outrage and litigation have failed to squelch Scientology. The group, which boasts 700 centers in 65 countries, threatens to become more insidious and pervasive than ever. Scientology is trying to go mainstream, a strategy that has sparked a renewed law-enforcement campaign against the church. Many of the group's followers have been accused of committing financial scams, while the church is busy attracting the unwary through a wide array of front groups in such businesses as publishing, consulting, health care and even remedial education.

Most cults fail to outlast their founder, but Scientology has thrived since Hubbard's death in 1986. Scientology probably has about 50,000 active members, far fewer than the 8 million the group claims. But in one sense that inflated figure rings true: millions of people have been affected by Hubbard's creation. It is now run by David Miscavige, 31, a high school dropout and second-generation church member. Defectors describe him as cunning, ruthless and paranoid. His obsession is to gain respectability for Scientology in the 1990s. Among his tactics: hiring well-regarded public relations firms, sponsoring Ted Turner's Goodwill Games and buying huge quantities of Scientology books to propel titles onto the best-seller lists. As long as the organization's opponents and victims are successfully squelched, Scientology will continue to raise millions of dollars to achieve its ends.

Dr. Death Strikes Again

If you are dying, you may view Dr. Jack Kevorkian as a courageous crusader for your rights. If you are a doctor, he may seem more like a cheap purveyor of easy death. Either way, he has become the lightning rod of the right-to-die movement and a gifted promoter of a cause he desperately believes in—and shockingly abets. In October the doctor helped two more women kill themselves in Michigan. Lawmakers and doctors may debate the ethics of euthanasia endlessly; but while that argument unfolds, the activists have again decided to take life-and-death matters into their own hands.

In the vanguard is Kevorkian, a retired Michigan pathologist who appeared on every television talk show and news program in the country in 1990 in the 24 hours after he helped Alzheimer's patient Janet Adkins commit suicide. He hooked her up to a homemade contraption that allowed her to push a button and send lethal potassium chloride into her veins. A Michigan judge chose not to prosecute

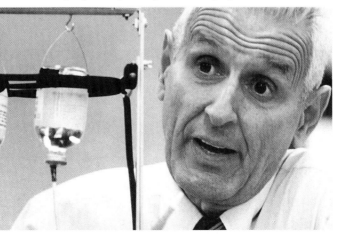

Kevorkian for murder, since the state has no laws against assisted suicide, but forbade him to use the machine again. Nonetheless, Dr. Death found a way around that injunction.

The two most recent recipients of his care were likewise from Michigan: Sherry Miller, 43, had multiple sclerosis, and Marjorie Wantz, 58, suffered from a painful pelvic disease. The two women were found dead in a cabin in the Bald Mountain recreation area, about 40 miles north of Detroit.

Since Kevorkian first detonated the euthanasia debate, the public's craving for information has grown. The strangest best seller in memory hovered for months at the top of the charts: *Final Exit,* by Derek Humphry, founder of the Hemlock Society, instructs people on how to die, or to kill. Humphry has urged physicians to assist in patient suicides. But much of the medical community remains deeply divided on this matter. Until the medical profession and state legislatures address the issue, a retired doctor with a bagful of poisons will be viewed as a savior by frightened people in search of final peace.

Day of Infamy

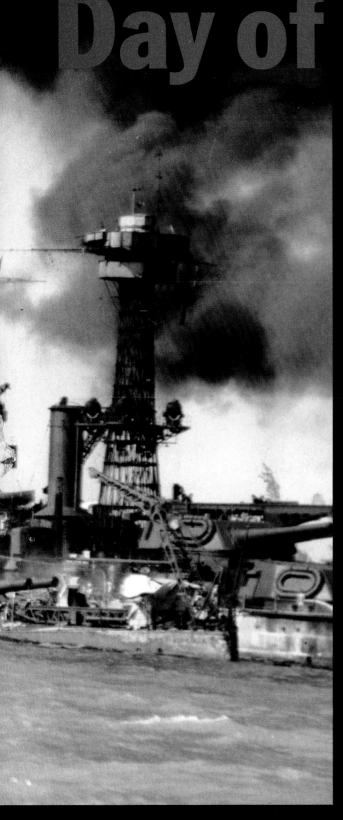

A half-century ago, Japan launched its surprise attack, and the world has never been the same since

The brass band on the stern of the U.S.S. *Nevada* kept on playing *The Star-Spangled Banner* for the 8 a.m. flag raising even after a Japanese bomber roared overhead and fired a torpedo at the nearby *Arizona*. The torpedo missed, but the bomber sprayed machine-gun fire at the *Nevada's* band and tore up its ensign. "This is the best goddam drill the Army Air Force has ever put on," remarked an *Arizona* sailor standing idly at the battleship's rail.

"Air raid, Pearl Harbor, this is no drill," said the radio message that went out at 7:58 a.m. from the U.S. Navy's Ford Island command center, relayed throughout Hawaii, to Manila, to Washington. But there was an even sharper sense of imminent disaster in the words someone shouted over the public address system on another docked battleship, the *Oklahoma:* "Man your battle stations! This is no shit!" Across the lapping waters of the harbor, church bells tolled, summoning the faithful to worship.

Almost alongside the *Oklahoma,* another torpedo hurtled through the air. After releasing it, recalled Lieut. Jinichi Goto, commander of the Japanese torpedo bombers, "I saw that I was even lower than the crow's nest of the great battleship. My observer reported a huge waterspout springing up . . . *'Atarimashita! [*It hit!*]'* he cried."

"I felt a very heavy shock and heard a loud explosion," said the *Oklahoma's* executive officer, Commander Jesse Kenworthy Jr., "and the ship immediately began to list to port. As I attempted to get to the conning tower over decks slippery with oil and water, I felt the shock of another very heavy explosion." Kenworthy gave the order to abandon ship. He barely made it over the rising starboard side as the giant battleship began to keel over, trapping more than 400 crewmen belowdecks.

Just as the *Oklahoma* capsized, a tremendous explosion tore open the *Arizona*. "A spurt of flame came out of the guns in No. 2 turret, followed by an explosion of the forward magazine," said a mechanic on the nearby tanker *Ramapo*. "The foremast leaned forward, and the whole forward part of the ship was enveloped in flame and smoke and continued to burn fiercely."

In Commander Mitsuo Fuchida's bomber circling overhead, antiaircraft fire knocked a hole in the fuselage and dam-

Smoke blankets bomb-ravaged *West Virginia* and *Tennessee* in the ruins of Battleship Row

aged the steering gear, but Fuchida couldn't take his eyes off the fiery death throes of the *Arizona*. "A huge column of dark red smoke rose to 1,000 ft., and a stiff shock wave rocked the plane," he recalled years later, when he had become a Presbyterian missionary. "It was a hateful, mean-looking red flame, the kind that powder produces, and I knew at once that a big magazine had exploded. Terrible indeed."

As operational commander of the Japanese attackers, Fuchida watched and controlled everything. It was Fuchida who had given, exactly at 7:49 a.m. on Dec. 7, 1941, the order to attack the strongest naval base in the world: *"To!* [the first syllable of *totsugekiseyo,* meaning: Charge!] *To! To! To!"* It was Fuchida who sent back to Tokyo the triumphant signal that the attack had caught the Americans by surprise: *"Tora!* [Tiger!] *Tora! Tora!"*

Now Fuchida led the attack on the *Maryland,* another of the eight battleships berthed at the U.S. Navy's Pacific Fleet headquarters. He saw four bombs hurtling toward their target. "In perfect pattern [they] plummeted like devils of doom. They became small as poppy seeds and finally disappeared just as tiny white flashes of smoke appeared on or near the ship."

Pearl Harbor is peaceful now, blue waves in the winter sunshine, an occasional toot of harbor traffic. A concrete canopy shrouds the rusted wreckage of the *Arizona,* the remains of more than 1,000 American servicemen entombed inside. Her flag is still raised and lowered every day on the mast emerging out of the quiet water.

In American mythology, Pearl Harbor still represents, even after a half-century, a classic moment of treachery and betrayal. Certainly it was a moment of historic surprise, a moment when the impossible happened, when warfare suddenly spread, for the first and only time in history, to virtually the whole world. This was the moment that changed Americans from a nation of provincial innocents, not only ignorant of the great world but proud of their ignorance, into a nation that would often have to bear the burdens of rescuing that world. The same cataclysm also changed the Japanese from a people trying to find their place on the rim of the great world into a nation that would eventually redefine that world and place itself at the very center.

Impersonally though the tides of history may seem to flow, in the case of Pearl Harbor, they were swayed by the force of a single

individual, a remarkably squat and broad-shouldered man, no more than 5 ft. 3 in. tall: Admiral Isoroku Yamamoto.

Admiral Yamamoto commanded Japan's combined fleet, but he disliked the imperial navy's cautious strategy. In case of war, its plan was to fall back and try to lure the U.S. Pacific Fleet into the Inland Sea between the Japanese home islands of Honshu and Kyushu. But as early as the spring of 1940, Yamamoto remarked to one of his officers: "I wonder if an aerial attack can't be made on Pearl Harbor."

Though Japan's military leaders had decided on war, they did not immediately agree to a surprise attack on Pearl Harbor. Yamamoto was adamant: "Japan must deal the U.S. Navy a fatal blow at the outset of the war. It is the only way she can fight with any reasonable prospect of success." But war games suggested that an attacking fleet would be spotted and badly mauled. As late as October, Yamamoto learned that the staff admirals, determined to concentrate on the drive into Southeast Asia, wanted to take away two or three of his six carriers. Yamamoto sent an aide to inform the navy's high command that if his Pearl Harbor plan was rejected, "he will have no alternative but to resign, and with him his entire staff." Yamamoto got his way.

The military set a new target date of Dec. 8 (Dec. 7 in Hawaii), and the Emperor and his military chiefs formally approved Yamamoto's attack plan on Nov. 3.

On Nov. 17, Yamamoto visited his training base in Saeki Bay to bid his men farewell. "Japan has faced many worthy opponents in her glorious history—Mongols, Chinese, Russians," Yamamoto said, "but in this operation we will meet the strongest opponent of all. I expect this operation to be a success." Fuchida, Commander Minoru Genda, who contributed several key ideas, and other officers joined him in eating *surume* (dried cuttlefish) for happiness and *kachiguri* (walnuts) for victory. Near portable Shinto shrines, they toasted the Emperor with sake and shouted, "Banzai!"

It took Vice Admiral Chuichi Nagumo's fleet five days to reach the rendezvous point at Hitokappu Bay in the Kuriles just north of

Japan's main islands. Fog swirled over the desolate outpost, and snow fell intermittently as the fleet steamed eastward at dawn on Nov. 26.

The armada boasted six carriers, led by Nagumo's flagship, the *Akagi,* 400 warplanes, two battleships, two cruisers, nine destroyers and a dozen other surface ships. At an average 13 knots, refueling daily, the attack fleet pursued a course 3,500 miles through the empty expanse of the North Pacific. Its orders provided that "in the event an agreement is reached in the negotiations with the United States, the task force will immediately return to Japan," but nobody expected that to happen.

Fuchida woke at 5 a.m. As he told American military historian Gordon Prange, he put on red underwear and a red shirt so that if he was wounded, his men would not be distracted by the sight of his blood. At breakfast one of his lieutenants said, "Honolulu sleeps."

"How do you know?" asked Fuchida.

"The Honolulu radio plays soft music. Everything is fine."

At 5:50 a.m. Nagumo's fleet reached the takeoff point, about 220 miles north of Pearl Harbor. The six carriers turned east into a brisk wind and increased speed to 24 knots. Nagumo's flagship was flying the celebrated Z pennant that Admiral Togo had flown at Tsushima in 1905. The flight decks tilted more than 10°, and the wind whipped spray over them.

"We could hear the waves splashing against the ship with a thunderous noise," Fuchida recalled later. "Under normal circumstances, no plane would be permitted to take off in such weather . . . There were loud cheers as each plane rose into the air." Once up, the pilots circled overhead until all 183 planes assigned to the first wave were airborne. At 6:15 Fuchida gave a signal, then led the way south.

Fuchida's bombers had to fly blind over dense banks of clouds, so they homed on the Honolulu commercial radio station KGMB. Over his receiver, Fuchida heard soothing music, then a weather report: "Partly cloudy . . . over the mountains. Cloud base at 3,500 ft. Visibility good." Fuchida flew on.

Two trainees operating a mobile radar unit at Opana, on Oahu's northern coast, were about to shut down when their watch ended at 7 a.m. Suddenly, Private Joseph Lockard noticed a large blip—"probably more than 50" planes—approaching southward from about 130 miles away. On the phone to Fort Shafter, Lockard reported to Lieut. Kermit Tyler "the largest [flight] I have ever seen on the equipment." The inexperienced Tyler figured that the planes must be a flight of the new B-17s expected from California. He told Lockard, "Don't worry about it."

As Fuchida's bombers neared Oahu, the U.S. destroyer *Ward* spotted an intruding submarine at 6:30 a.m. and opened fire from 50 yds. away. As the sub began diving, the *Ward* finished it off with depth charges. Lieut. William Outerbridge's report of his action was still ricocheting around headquarters when Fuchida arrived overhead.

"What a majestic sight," he said to himself as he counted the vessels lined up in Battleship Row in the dawn's early light. He pulled the trigger on his flare gun. That action was supposed to signal the

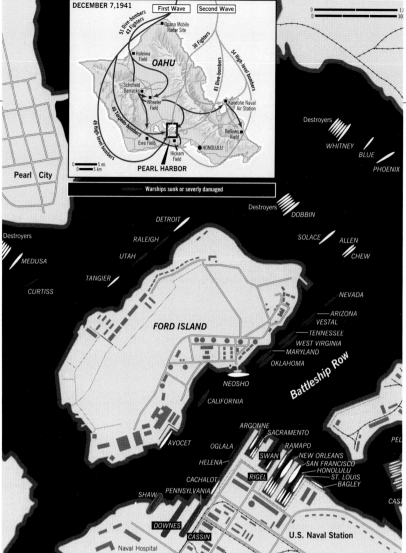

slow-moving torpedo bombers to take advantage of the surprise and strike first. But Fuchida's fighter pilots missed his signal to provide cover, so he fired again for the dive bombers to begin, and then the Japanese all attacked at once. Even when they made mistakes, it seemed that nothing could go wrong.

Within minutes, Pearl Harbor was pandemonium: explosions, screams, tearing steel, the rattle of machine guns, smoke, fire, bugles sounding, the whine of diving airplanes, more explosions, more screams. With Battleship Row afire, Fuchida's bombers circled over the maze of Pearl Harbor's docks and piers, striking again and again at the cruisers and destroyers and supply ships harbored there.

Other Japanese bombers swarmed over Hawaii's military airfields, Hickam and Wheeler, Kaneohe and Ewa. Dive-bombing and strafing the American planes neatly parked on the runways, they quickly won control of the sky. They wrecked hangars, warehouses, barracks—as well as the Hickam Field chapel and the enlisted men's new beer hall, the Snake Ranch. And in the midst of all this, a rainbow appeared over Ford Island.

To many of the Americans, the whole morning had a dreamlike unreality. Disbelief had been the overwhelming first reaction—this couldn't be happening, it was a trick, a drill, a silly rumor, a prank—disbelief and then pain and then anger, and still disbelief.

Admiral Husband Kimmel, the U.S. Pacific Fleet chief in Pearl Harbor, was preparing for his golf game with Lieut. General Walter Short, Hawaii's commander, when an officer phoned him with the news that Japanese planes were attacking his fleet. The admiral was still buttoning his white uniform as he ran out of his house and onto the neighboring lawn of Captain John Earle, which had a fine view of Battleship Row. Mrs. Earle said later that the admiral's face was "as white as the uniform he wore."

"The sky was full of the enemy," Kimmel recalled. He saw the *Arizona* "lift out of the water, then sink back down— way down." Mrs. Earle saw a battleship capsize. "Looks like they've got the *Oklahoma*," she said. "Yes, I can see they have," the admiral numbly responded.

General Short, who couldn't see the explosions, bumped into an intelligence officer and asked, "What's going on out there?"

"I'm not sure, general," Lieut. Colonel George Bicknell replied, "but I just saw two battleships sunk."

"That's ridiculous!" said Short.

Down on Battleship Row, Fuchida's bombers kept pounding the helpless battlewagons. The *West Virginia* took six torpedoes, then two bombs. One large piece of shrapnel smashed into the starboard side of the bridge and tore open the stomach of the skipper, Captain Mervyn Bennion. A medic patched up the dying man's wound, and a husky black mess steward, Doris Miller, who had once boxed as the ship's heavyweight champion, helped move the stricken captain to a sheltered spot.

Fire and smoke swirled around the bridge. Bennion told his men to leave him; they ignored him. He asked them how the battle was going; they told him all was well. After Bennion died, an officer told Miller to feed ammunition into a nearby machine gun. Like other blacks in the Navy of 1941, Miller had not been trained for anything but domestic chores, but he soon took charge of the machine gun and started firing away. A young ensign recalled later that it was the first time he had seen Miller smile since he last fought in the ring.

As Admiral Kimmel stood near a window, a spent machine-gun bullet smashed the glass and hit him lightly in the chest. Kimmel— who would soon, like General Short, be dismissed from his command—picked up the bullet. To an aide, he observed, "It would have been merciful had it killed me."

Fuchida's surprise attack lasted only about half an hour. Then, after a short lull, a second wave of 171 more planes roared in. By now the Americans were on the alert and firing at anything in sight. Twenty planes flying in from maneuvers with the *Enterprise* came under heavy American fire; two were shot down.

The battered *Nevada* (its band having finished *The Star-Spangled Banner*) managed to get up enough steam to proceed majestically out into the channel to the sea. Despite a gaping hole in its bow, its guns were firing, and its torn flag flew high. As it edged past the burning *Arizona,* three of that doomed ship's crewmen swam over, clambered aboard and manned a starboard gun.

"Ah, good!" the watching Fuchida said to himself as he saw the slow-moving *Nevada.* At his signal, all available bombers attacked in an effort to sink it and block the channel to the sea. Bombs ignited huge fires in the ship's bow. It escaped total destruction only by deliberately running aground.

The great attack was really fairly short. The first bombers returned to their carriers just after 10 a.m., scarcely two hours after they had descended on Battleship Row. Fuchida lingered to observe and photograph the damage and was the last to return to Nagumo's fleet. It was still only noon.

Stirred by their success, Fuchida and Genda argued fiercely for renewing the attack. The oil-storage tanks had not been hit, and the raiders had not found any of Kimmel's three carriers (the *Lexington* and *Enterprise* were at sea, the *Saratoga* undergoing repairs). But Admiral Nagumo, who had mistrusted the plan from the start, felt he had accomplished his mission and saw no reason to risk his fleet any further. Back in Japan, Yamamoto strongly disapproved of Nagu-

mo's decision to withdraw but accepted the tradition that such decisions are left to the combat commander on the scene.

On the capsized hull of the *Oklahoma,* Commander Kenworthy strode up and down for hours listening for raps and banging from the men trapped inside. Some survivors were finally pulled to safety through holes cut in the hull, but others drowned in the water rushing through the openings. Kenworthy wouldn't leave until the last of 32 survivors had been saved. By then it was Monday afternoon. Six sailors caught inside the *West Virginia* died just before Christmas—after two weeks of incarceration.

In terms of casualties and destruction, this was one of the most one-sided battles in history. The U.S. lost 2,433 killed (about half of them on the *Arizona*) and 1,178 wounded. The Japanese, who had expected to sacrifice as much as one-third of their force, lost 55 airmen, nine crewmen aboard five minisubs and approximately 65 on one sunken submarine. The U.S. lost 18 surface warships, sunk or seriously damaged; the Japanese none. The U.S. lost 188 planes destroyed and 159 damaged; the Japanese lost 29. Yet three of the five wrecked U.S. battleships (the *California, Nevada* and *West Virginia*) were eventually restored to service, and all the lost warplanes were eventually replaced—more than replaced—by the bombers that struck Tokyo and Hiroshima.

If Pearl Harbor seemed an American disaster, it proved a Japanese disaster as well. Winston Churchill knew that when he gloated at the news: "So we had won after all!" So did U.S. War Secretary Henry Stimson, who felt "relief. . . that a crisis had come in a way which would unite all our people." So did Admiral Yamamoto, who predicted that he would run wild for only a year. Pearl Harbor united Americans in rage and hatred, and thus united, powerful and determined, they would prove invincible.

The sinking of the U.S.S. *Arizona*, the final resting place of 1,102 American sailors

Science Under a Shadow of Doubt

By MICHAEL D. LEMONICK

It was a good year for technology—military technology at least. The allies who defeated Saddam Hussein's army in the Persian Gulf did it with a remarkable array of high-tech weaponry. The war was won in part thanks to such advanced weapons as the Stealth fighter, whose radar-absorbing shape and skin shrank it to the apparent size of a bird on enemy screens; smart bombs, guided by lasers and computerized maps not just to specific buildings in Baghdad, but to the air shafts where detonation insured maximum damage; and hand-held navigation receivers tied into overhead satellites that let soldiers on the ground pinpoint their locations to within a few feet, even at night.

But for the rest of science, things did not look so bright. A series of scandals and fiascoes seriously undermined America's faith in its scientists. David Baltimore, the president of Rockefeller University, resigned in the aftermath of an investigation of his role in supervising a fraudulent laboratory paper. Donald Kennedy, president of Stanford, resigned over charges his university had fleeced the government out of research funds. Robert Gallo, of the National Cancer Institute, acknowledged that his "discovery" of the HIV virus that causes AIDS was really a re-discovery of something uncovered by French scientists. In space, the Hubble telescope's gyroscopes began to fail, compounding the mess caused by its improperly ground mirror, while the Galileo spacecraft sped on its way to Jupiter, working perfectly—except for a stuck antenna that could keep the probe from sending information back to Earth.

Things were not so rosy for the environment, either. As the clearing of once-remote jungles and rain forests continued virtually unchecked around the world, researchers began to realize that the destruction was not limited to plant and animal species, soils and the general health of the earth's atmosphere. Entire peoples are being wrenched from their traditional lives, and a vast storehouse of invaluable knowledge about the natural world is disappearing wholesale. The ozone crisis also worsened, even though the world's industrial nations have agreed to phase out by the year 2000 the chemicals that destroy this vital component of the stratosphere. The Antarctic ozone hole, it turns out, is no longer confined to Antarctica. Ozone has started to disappear in temperate zones as well, including the continental U.S. The result: an extra dose of solar ultraviolet light, threatening an increase in already elevated levels of skin cancer. In the U.S., the Bush Administration declared that it would abide by a campaign pledge of "no net loss of wetlands," but that it would do so by changing the official definition of what a wetland is—thus opening up vast areas for development that have hitherto been protected.

In medicine too there were plenty of rough spots. An epidemic of cholera raged through South America. A new, deadly and drug-resistant strain of tuberculosis emerged in the U.S. Breast cancer, the leading cause of death in women between 35 and 50, is a growing risk. The AIDS epidemic entered a new phase, with public health officials tracking the disease's emergence among people who thought themselves risk free. In Africa the infection is passed more often by heterosexual than homosexual acts, and in the U.S., two victims—Kimberly Bergalis and Magic Johnson—brought home the fact that no one is immune. Bergalis is thought to have been infected by her HIV-positive dentist, while Johnson claims to have been exclusively heterosexual. The facts are less important than the public's new awareness that even when the odds are low, medical professionals must take hygienic precautions and everyone must practice safe sex.

That is not to say, however, that there was no good news at all. NASA, for example, did a few things right. It launched the first satellite in the Mission to Planet Earth program, which will study the earth from space to get a better understanding of environmental problems and how to solve them. And the Magellan spacecraft, working almost flawlessly, sent back the most detailed images ever taken of Venus—including evidence of volcanoes that are erupting. In medicine, the growing problem of infertility in the U.S. is yielding to a growing arsenal of therapies. Thanks to in-vitro fertilization, surgery and sophisticated drugs, couples who once would have given up on biological children can now have them. Even women past menopause can now bear children, and in one case a woman was able to act as a surrogate mother for her own daughter. In October, Arlette Schweitzer gave birth to her granddaughter.

It also turned out that several of the chemicals scientists have been warning us about are not quite as dangerous as advertised. The radon gas that seeps into basements, the Alar pesticide that clings to the surfaces of apples, the asbestos wrapped around pipes and pressed into ceiling tiles and even the dioxin that forced the evacuation of the entire town of Times Beach, Missouri, all had their toxicity revised downward. None of them promotes good health, but none appears to be an inevitable cause of environmental disease, either.

Finally, there were events that were neither good nor bad news; they were just plain fascinating. A Princeton astrophysicist presented calculations showing that time travel could, under certain extremely improbable circumstances, be possible. A pair of British jokers revealed that the "crop circles" appearing in farm fields over the past several years, which had spawned an entirely new branch of paranormal investigation, were the result of a stunt they had dreamed up after a few pints of beer. And thousands of people snatched up virtually every hotel room in Hawaii and Baja California to gawk as the moon slowly swallowed, then disgorged, the sun, in the last total eclipse over any part of the U.S. in the 20th century.

Science Under Siege

Beset by a budget squeeze, cases of fraud, relentless activists and a skeptical public, American scientists are under the microscope

Without scientific progress the national health would deteriorate; without scientific progress we could not hope for improvement in our standard of living or for an increased number of jobs for our citizens; and without scientific progress we could not have maintained our liberties against tyranny.

—Vannevar Bush, presidential science adviser, in *Science: The Endless Frontier*, 1945

It was the glory of America. In the decades following World War II, U.S. science reigned supreme, earning the envy of the world with one stunning triumph after another. Fostered by the largesse of a government swayed by Vannevar Bush's paean to science, it harnessed the power of the atom, conquered polio and discovered the earth's radiation belt. It created the laser, the transistor, the microchip and the electronic computer, broke the genetic code and conjured up the miracle of recombinant DNA technology. It described the fundamental nature of matter, solved the mystery of the quasars and designed the robot craft that explored distant planets with spectacular success. And, as promised, it landed a man on the moon.

Now a sea change is occurring, and it does not bode well for researchers—or for the U.S. While American science remains productive and still excels in many areas, its exalted and almost pristine image is beginning to tarnish.

European and, to a lesser extent, Japanese scientists have begun to surpass their American counterparts. In the U.S. the scientific community is beset by a budget squeeze and bureaucratic demands, internal squabbling, harassment by activists, embarrassing cases of fraud and failure, and the growing alienation of Congress and the public. In the last decade of the 20th century, U.S. science, once unassailable, finds itself in a virtual state of siege.

"The science community is demoralized, and its moans are frightening off the young," says Dr. Bernadine Healy, director of the National Institutes of Health. "You have never seen such a depressed collection of people," says Stephen Berry, a University of Chicago chemist. "It's the worst atmosphere in the scientific community since I began my career more than 30 years ago."

In public perception, at least, that atmosphere has been fouled by a multitude of headline-grabbing incidents:

▶ In space, the inexcusable myopia of the $1.5 billion Hubble telescope, the balky antenna that endangers the $1.3 billion Galileo mission to Jupiter, and even the *Challenger* disaster and the shuttle's subsequent troubles gave space science a bad name.

▶ The circus atmosphere that accompanied the 1989 announcement that cold fusion had been achieved, the subsequent debate among scientists and the eventual widespread rejection of the claim evoked public exasperation and ridicule in the press.

FRAUDS AND EMBARRASSMENTS

PONS AND FLEISCHMANN The "discovery" of cold fusion grabbed headlines, but chemists Stanley Pons and Martin Fleischmann found something that probably does not exist. After the initial excitement, they won more scorn than research grants.

DAVID BALTIMORE When someone claimed results were falsified in an immunology paper he had supervised, Baltimore blamed the whistle blower rather than his colleague. But an inquiry found the study was indeed faked.

A STRING OF BLUNDERS, FIASCOES AND TRAGEDIES IN SPACE

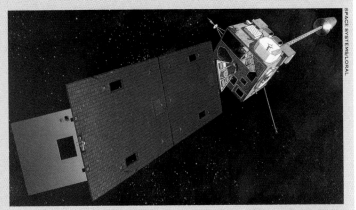

GOES NEXT: WEATHER SATELLITES The only weather satellite currently photographing the U.S. is the GOES 7, which was originally expected to be functional only through early 1992. Careful use of fuel may add another year. But the next generation of satellites, ordered from NASA by the Weather Service back in 1986, is three years behind schedule, $500 million over budget and plagued with problems. One glitch is in the sensors that monitor air temperature and humidity. Another is in the instrument that photographs cloud systems. The images are distorted in part because of cheap wiring in the electronics. If GOES 7 dies early, the U.S. may have to borrow satellites from the Japanese or the Europeans.

CHALLENGER The moon landings and planetary probes of the late 1960s and '70s gave NASA a reputation for near infallibility. Then came the 1986 *Challenger* explosion. The primary cause was a low-tech O-ring, meant to keep hot gas from escaping from the spacecraft's booster engines. Engineers had warned NASA launch officials that the rings could crack in cold weather, but the danger was ignored on that cool, tragic January morning.

HUBBLE SPACE TELESCOPE A $1.5 billion instrument designed to take the sharpest pictures of the heavens in history is half blind, thanks to an egregious goof. The Perkin-Elmer Corp. ground the Hubble's main mirror to the wrong curvature, which means it cannot focus light properly. A test on the ground could have confirmed the error before the launch, but nobody insisted strongly enough that hints of a problem be followed up.

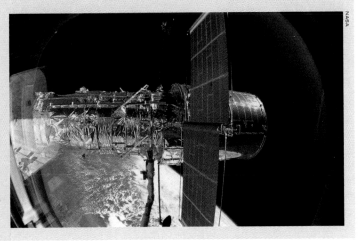

▶Nobel laureate David Baltimore's long-standing refusal to concede that data reported by a former M.I.T. colleague in an immunology paper Baltimore had co-signed was fraudulent, and the shoddy treatment of the whistle blower who spotted the fraud, aroused public suspicion about scientific integrity. The controversy led to Baltimore's resignation as president of Rockefeller University, one of the U.S.'s most prestigious research universities.

▶A congressional probe, which revealed that Stanford University had charged some strange items to overhead expenses for projects funded by federal science grants, mortified university president Donald Kennedy, led to his resignation and raised questions about misuse of funds at other universities.

▶Bowing to the demands of pro-lifers, the Bush Administration continued a ban on federal funding for fetal-cell transplants, despite the fact that the use of such tissue has shown promising results in treating Parkinson's disease and other disorders. Frustrated U.S. re-

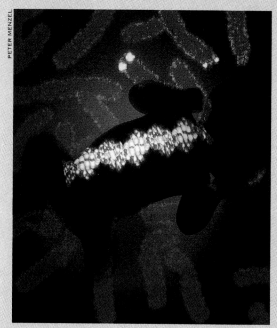

SPACE STATION FREEDOM

The station was going to be a combination space factory, biological lab and construction platform for interplanetary forays. It was also going to cost $8 billion. Now, having survived a death threat from Congress, the official cost is up to $30 billion (independent estimates run as much as $40 billion). And its missions are down to just two: studying the health effects of space travel and fashioning new materials in low gravity. Most space scientists think Freedom is a farce. Aerospace companies love it.

HUMAN GENOME PROJECT

The pride of biologists is a $3 billion attempt to identify each of the 50,000 to 100,000 genes carrying human-hereditary information. This will make it easier to understand—and perhaps cure—genetic diseases. Few people doubt the value of studying important genes, but critics wonder why it is necessary to have a map of every bit of genetic material.

SUPERCONDUCTING SUPERCOLLIDER

The elementary-particle accelerator under construction in northern Texas literally surrounds its hometown of Waxahachie. The SSC's oval tunnel, through which particles will hurtle at nearly the speed of light, will be 85 km (53 miles) around. Physicists need a device this size to solve fundamental mysteries about matter. But the price, originally $4.4 billion, has almost doubled. Even some physicists wonder whether the knowledge will be worth the money.

searchers watched helplessly as their European counterparts moved ahead on medical applications for fetal tissue.

▶ In several raids on research laboratories, animal-rights activists destroyed equipment and "liberated" test animals, setting back experiments designed to improve medical treatment for humans.

▶ Although gadfly activist Jeremy Rifkin failed in a legal attempt to delay the first human-gene-therapy experiment in 1990, he skillfully used the courts to set back by months, and even years, other scientific trials involving genetically engineered organisms or substances.

To many researchers, however, the single greatest threat to U.S. science, and a source of many of its troubles, is money—or a lack of it.

In June the House of Representatives made a choice, and it did not sit well with scientists. The House voted to designate $1.9 billion of NASA's fiscal 1992 budget to continued work on the proposed space station, which could eventually cost as much as $40 billion. Because of the budgetary restraints, that money may be cut from other projects supported by NASA and the National Science Foundation (NSF). And two huge science ventures are already siphoning off significant chunks of the federal budget: the Human Genome Project, a 15-year, $3 billion program to identify and map all 50,000 to 100,000 genes and determine the sequence of the 3 billion code letters in human DNA; and the superconducting supercollider, a high-energy particle accelerator to be built in Texas at an estimated cost of $8.2 billion.

Several planned NASA science projects could immediately suffer or even be eliminated because of the space-station vote. They include the Comet Rendezvous Asteroid Flyby mission, in which an unmanned spacecraft would make close approaches to Comet Kopff and an unnamed asteroid; the Advanced X-Ray Astrophysics Facility, which will investigate X-ray sources in space; and the Earth Observing System for weather and pollution studies.

Scientists were dismayed. Daniel Kleppner, an M.I.T. physicist, pointed out that the money spent on the space station this year will be almost as much as the total fiscal 1990 NSF budget, a major source of federal funding for all the sciences except biomedicine.

These days scientists often pick their fields of research with an eye to the whims of funding agencies. University jobs are hard to find, and because of tight budgets, positions will not become more plentiful until the older professors, the majority of them hired in the bountiful, go-go 1960s, retire. When a university slot does open, hundreds of graduate students may apply for it. Industry too has little to offer newly graduated scientists. Saddled with debt and under pressure to turn out favorable quarterly reports, companies have cut back on money spent for research and development.

Money is so tight that many scientific institutions are finding it difficult to maintain the equipment they have, much less buy new instruments. At Kitt Peak in Arizona, the structure of the solar telescope was beginning to corrode because astronomers, strapped for funds, had put off painting it. This year they could wait no longer, and instead of buying a new, badly needed $100,000 infrared detector, they put the available money into a paint job.

The budget constraints are part of an even deeper problem—Congress is reflecting an erosion of public confidence in the scientific establishment. The message from Washington is clear: science will receive no more blank checks and will be held increasingly accountable for both its performance and its behavior.

Some of this burgeoning antiscience sentiment springs from the well-meaning but naive "back to nature" wing of the environmental movement, some from skillful manipulation by demagogues and modern-day Luddites. And some is misdirected; science is often blamed for the misdeeds of industry and government.

But scientists too must shoulder their share of the blame. Cases of outright fraud and waste, sloppy research, dubious claims and public bickering have made science an easy target for its critics.

In Washington the new sock-it-to-science stance is personified by Michigan Democrat John Dingell, who has taken the lead in investigating the wrongdoings of researchers. Many scientists consider his intrusion into their domain dangerous because it threatens their long-held notion that science should be self-governed, self-regulated and self-policed. Because of his badgering of scientists at congressional hearings, Dingell has been charged with practicing McCarthyism.

Despite his abrasive manner, however, he has rooted out some serious abuses in science. The Congressman makes a legitimate argument that science is a social tool and should be directed and regulated in the same manner as other social tools, such as defense and education.

Congressional pressure on science has been countered by a growing pressure on Congress—by institutions and researchers lobbying for science funds. Influencing the lawmakers has become so critical that science is recruiting the professionals of persuasion. Many universities pay $20,000 a month each for the services of Cassidy & Associates, a science-lobbying firm that has been successful in getting federal money earmarked for its clients.

Too often, science lobbyists find easy pickings on Capitol Hill, where Congressmen, courting votes, can win generous sums for research projects in their home districts by simply slipping riders onto appropriation bills. Federal legislators in fiscal 1991 approved at least $270 million for pork-barrel science projects. In many cases, this kind of financing supports projects of dubious value while more worthy endeavors go begging.

For all the lobbying, the scientific community has reached no consensus about the worthiness of various projects. Molecular biologists and particle physicists find it impossible to agree on the relative merits of the Human Genome Project and the superconducting supercollider.

What is the alternative? Researchers blanch at the thought of a scientifically illiterate public allotting the available funds through the political process. Yet if the science community cannot establish its own priorities, it is inviting Congress and the White House to make all the choices, for better or worse.

While striving for harmony, scientists would do well to put their house back in order. They should avoid cutting corners or misusing funds to make financial ends meet. They must come down hard on transgressors, give whistle blowers a fair hearing and not stonewall in defense of erring colleagues. And they should discourage the ill-conceived practice of hastily calling press conferences to announce dubious results that have not been verified by peer review.

Equally important, scientists should redouble efforts to help educate Congress, the press and the public about the importance and benefits of some of their more esoteric work. More aggressive promotion of science's success stories would certainly enhance the image of researchers, help restore waning public trust in science and lessen the clout of antiscience activists.

Nearly a half-century ago, Vannevar Bush's clarion call launched America into its golden age of science. His words still ring true today, despite the social and economic woes besetting the U.S. In fact, a vigorous science program might generate the wealth needed to solve these problems. To create that wealth, the U.S. must increase its investment in science, both by allocating more dollars and by making certain that the dollars already appropriated are spent more wisely.

Native Wisdom

Lost tribes, lost knowledge: when native cultures and traditions disappear, so does a trove of scientific and medical wisdom

One horrible day 1,600 years ago, the wisdom of many centuries went up in flames. The great library in Alexandria burned down, a symbol for all ages of the vulnerability of human knowledge. The tragedy forced scholars to grope to reconstruct a grand literature and science that once lay neatly cataloged in scrolls.

Today, with little notice, more vast archives of knowledge and expertise are spilling into oblivion, leaving humanity in danger of losing its past and perhaps jeopardizing its future as well. Stored in the memories of elders, healers, midwives, farmers, fishermen and hunters of the estimated 15,000 cultures remaining on earth is an enormous trove of wisdom.

This largely undocumented knowledge base is humanity's lifeline to a time when people accepted nature's authority and learned through trial, error and observation. But the world's tribes are dying out or being absorbed into modern civilization. As they vanish, so does their irreplaceable knowledge.

Over the ages, indigenous peoples have developed innumerable technologies and arts. They have devised ways to farm deserts without irrigation and produce abundance from the rain forest without destroying the delicate balance that maintains the ecosystem; they have explored the medicinal properties of plants; and they have acquired an understanding of the basic ecology of flora and fauna. If this knowledge had to be duplicated from scratch, it would beggar the scientific resources of the West. Much of this expertise and wisdom has already disappeared, and if neglected, most of the remainder could be gone within the next generation.

Until quite recently, few in the developed world cared much about this cultural holocaust. The prevailing attitude has been that Western science, with its powerful analytical tools, has little to learn from tribal knowledge. The developed world's disastrous mismanagement of the environment has somewhat humbled this arrogance, however, and some scientists are beginning to recognize that the

world is losing an enormous amount of basic research as indigenous peoples lose their culture and traditions.

The most intractable aspect of the crisis is that it is largely voluntary. Entranced by images of the wealth and power of the First World, the young turn away from their elders, breaking an ancient but fragile chain of oral traditions. For an elder, it is difficult to persuade an ambitious young native that he is better off hunting boar with blowpipes than reaching for the fruits of "civilization," even if those fruits might translate into a menial job in a teeming city. For the well-fed, well-educated visiting scientist to make that argument can seem both hypocritical and condescending.

The pace of change is startling. As many as 10,000 members of Borneo's Penan tribe still led a seminomadic life of hunting and gathering at the beginning of the 1980s. But the logging industry has been destroying their woodlands, and the Malaysian government has encouraged them to move to villages. Now fewer than 500 Penans live in the forest. When they settle into towns, their expertise in the ways of the forest slips away. Villagers know that their elders used to watch for the appearance of a certain butterfly, which always seemed to herald the arrival of a herd of boar and the promise of good hunting. These days most Penans cannot remember which butterfly to look for.

The number of different tribes around the world makes it impossible to record or otherwise preserve more than a tiny percentage of the knowledge being lost. Since 1900, 90 of Brazil's 270 Indian tribes have completely disappeared, while scores more have lost their lands or abandoned their ways. More than two-thirds of the remaining tribes have a population of fewer than 1,000. Some might disappear before anyone notices.

A recent study by M.I.T. linguist Ken Hale estimates that 3,000 of the world's 6,000 languages are doomed because no children speak them. Researchers estimate that Africa alone has 1,800 languages, Indonesia 672 and New Guinea 800. If a language disappears, traditional knowledge tends to vanish with it, since individual language groups have specialized vocabularies reflecting native people's unique solutions to the challenges of food gathering, healing and dealing with the elements.

The most immediate tragedy in the loss of knowledge and traditions is for the tribes themselves. They do not always die out, but the soul of their culture withers away. The price is real as well as psychological when native peoples lose their grip on traditional knowledge.

In the island nation of Papua New Guinea, in the Coral Sea, jobless people returning to highland villages from the cities often lack the most rudimentary knowledge necessary to survive, such as which rot-resistant trees to use to build huts or which poisonous woods to avoid when making fires for cooking. Many of the youths, alienated from their villages by schooling and exposure to the West, become marauding "rascals," who have made Papua New Guinea's cities among the most dangerous in the world.

It is difficult for an outsider to imagine the degree to which novel ideas and images assault the minds of tribal adolescents moving into the outside world. They get glimpses of a society their parents never

173

Top row: Highland tribespeople, Papua New Guinea
Middle row: Pygmies, Bayanga, Central African Republic
Bottom row: Nomadic Penans, Sarawak, Malaysian Borneo

encountered and cannot explain. Students who leave villages for schooling in the cities of Papua New Guinea learn that people, not the spirits of their ancestors, created the machines, dams and other so-called cargo of the modern world. Once absorbed, this realization undermines the credibility and authority of elders.

If the developed world is to help indigenous peoples preserve their heritage, it must first recognize that this wisdom has value. Western science is founded on the belief that knowledge inexorably progresses: the new and improved inevitably drive out the old and fallible. Western science also presumes to be objective and thus more rigorous than other systems of thought. Guided by these conceits, scientists have often failed to appreciate tribal knowledge.

Attitudes are beginning to change, however. Scientists are learning to look past the myth, superstition and ritual that often conceal the hard-won insights of indigenous peoples. Sometimes the lessons have come in handy: during the gulf war, European doctors treated some wounds with a sugar paste that traces back to Egyptian battlefield medicine of 4,000 years ago.

Michael Balick, director of the New York Botanical Garden's Institute of Economic Botany, notes that only 1,100 of the earth's 265,000 species of plants have been thoroughly studied by Western scientists, but as many as 40,000 may have medicinal or undiscovered nutritional value for humans. Many are already used by tribal healers, who can greatly help scientists focus their search for plants with useful properties.

Balick walks tropical forests with shamans in Latin America as part of a study, sponsored by the National Cancer Institute, designed to uncover plants useful in the treatment of AIDS and cancer. The 5,000 plants collected so far, says the NCI's Gordon Cragg, have yielded some promising chemicals. If any of them turn out to be useful as medicines, the country from which the plant came would get a cut of the profits.

Preserving tribal wisdom is as much an issue of restoring respect for traditional ways as it is of creating financial incentives. Balick has made it part of his mission to enhance the status of traditional healers within their own communities. He and his colleagues hold ceremonies to honor shamans, most of whom are religious men who value respect over material reward. In one community in Belize, the local mayor was so impressed that American scientists had come to learn at the feet of an elderly healer that he asked them to give a lecture so that townspeople could learn about their own medical tradition. Balick recalls that this healer had more than 200 living descendants, but that none as yet had shown an interest in becoming an apprentice. The lecture, though, was packed.

Such deference represents a dramatic change from past scientific expeditions, which tended to treat village elders as living museum specimens. Balick and others like him recognize that communities must decide for themselves what to do with their traditions. Showing respect for the wisdom keepers can help the young of various tribes better weigh the value of their culture against blandishments of modernity. If young apprentices begin to step forward, the world might see a slowing of the slide toward oblivion.

A Chronicler of Elders' Wisdom

Papua New Guinea is a raucous teenager of a country, boiling with the vitality and conflict that come with its kaleidoscope of cultures. The stresses between traditional ways and the demands of modern commerce bedevil the island north of Australia with near anarchy in the cities, persistent tribal wars in the highlands and intermittent insurrection in the province of Bougainville. While many of New Guinea's people have become alienated from traditional ways during these growing pains, Saem Majnep, a simple man from the highlands, has responded by making it his cause to preserve tribal learning and restore respect for the accumulated wisdom of 800 peoples.

A diminutive man from the Kalam people of the Kaironk valley, Majnep is a living bridge between the subsistence life of a remote part of New Guinea's highlands and the world of science. In recent years, he has served as a collaborator on several scientific monographs published by Oxford University Press. Hired as an adolescent in 1959 to translate for New Zealand ornithologist Ralph Bulmer, Majnep soon found

Saem Majnep teaches his compatriots that their knowledge of plants and animals is of lasting value

himself being interviewed for his familiarity with the feeding and breeding habits of birds that Bulmer was studying in the region.

Bulmer's respect for the knowledge of the Kalam people had a profound effect on Majnep. After assisting Bulmer, Majnep went on to work as a technician at the University of Papua New Guinea. Bulmer is now dead, and Majnep has returned to his village, where he continues to record his people's observations of animals and plants. "If you stay in your village, it is easy to pick up this learning because it is still all around you," he says. "But when people go to Madang [the nearest city], they lose it very quickly." Throughout the country, though, Majnep notes that the younger generation feels shame rather than pride in what their ancestors knew.

Alarmed at how easily this wisdom slips from its fragile perch in oral traditions, he also spends a good deal of time speaking to other tribes in New Guinea, either in person or on the radio, exhorting them to take pride in their culture. "I am an uneducated man," he tells them, "but white people value what I know."

With bountiful soils that make subsistence living an attractive alternative to workaday jobs, New Guinea's tribal life is still vibrant. Majnep says his biggest concern is the misuse of the land, as people abandon traditional crop rotation and forget about taboos that used to protect the forest. Still, people like Majnep raise hopes that the island nation may find an accord between tradition and modernity. ∎

Resurrecting a Wondrous Craft

George Dyson has set himself a task even more difficult than preserving the wisdom of a vanishing culture: reviving an art that is already lost. The son of a Princeton physicist, Dyson, 38, was fascinated by 18th century accounts of Aleutian kayakers, who were said to have sustained speeds of 10 knots on the open ocean in their 15-ft. to 30-ft. craft, defying the apparent limits imposed by the length of the boat and human endurance. For two decades, Dyson, a self-taught boatbuilder, has worked to rediscover the technological secrets of these fabled vessels, or baidarkas, as Russian colonists called them.

For more than 5,000 years, Aleut Indians plied the islands off Alaska in craft made of animal skins and bone. Over time these craft diverged in design from other kayaks. They evolved curiously split bows, sterns that were wide at the top but V-shaped at the bottom, and bone joints that made the vessels 100 times as flexible as modern boats. The Aleuts became shaped to the demands of kayaking vast distances, developing huge upper bodies from relentless paddling and bowed legs that allowed them to sit confined for hours. By the time the

George Dyson plumbs the secrets of baidarka design in his Bellingham, Wash., workshop

Russians arrived in pursuit of sea-otter pelts in 1741, the Aleuts had established a marriage of man and technology near perfect for hunting sea mammals.

The baidarka changed markedly under the influence of the Russians and then began to disappear with the end of the sea-otter hunts in the last century. After World War II, the Aleuts switched to motor-powered craft. In his efforts to reconstruct the original kayaks, Dyson, based in Bellingham, Wash., relies on early accounts of explorers and sea captains.

The most intriguing elements of baidarka design are those that show the Aleuts' rejection of typical kayak forms in favor of a distinctive approach. Dyson speculates that the forked bow prevents the boat from submarining in waves. It also gives the kayak the speed advantage of a longer, slenderer craft, and may set up a wave that counteracts the drag-inducing bow wave of ordinary designs. The oddly configured stern may help the kayak make the transition from a vessel that pushes through the water to one that planes on top of the water.

Dyson believes that the baidarka will have a robust future, influencing the shape of modern sport kayaks. Physicist Francis Clauser designed a forked-bow craft for a syndicate in the 1986-87 America's Cup race. Dyson still speaks of the genius of the Aleut kayak builders with reverence: "Modern science has recognized all the elements that went into the baidarka, but nobody put them together to achieve a synthesis the way the Aleuts did." ∎

Proving the Worth of A Healing Art

Bernard N'donazi has the gentle manner of a country doctor, but his mildness conceals fierce commitment to a mission that began to take shape 28 years ago, following the destruction of one of his tribe's central institutions. As a boy, N'donazi endured an initiation rite of the Souma tribe in the Central African Republic, during which an incision was made in his side and his intestine was briefly exposed. This ceremony marked the transition to adulthood and followed months of instruction in the use of plants and herbs in healing. Bernard, now in his late 30s, was among the last of his cult to be initiated. Acting in deference to a Catholic abbot who regarded the traditions as pagan, N'donazi's father, a convert, ordered the destruction of the male house, where boys acquired the learning of their elders. With that, a cultural and medical tradition that extended back to antiquity went up in flames.

This might have been the end of the line had not the younger N'donazi gone on to pursue a career in Western medicine. During his training in Africa, Europe and the U.S. as a health technician, he discovered that many Western medicines are derived from plants. Angered that a European

Bernard N'donazi studies the medicinal properties of plants in his lab in the remote town of Bouar

missionary might dismiss traditions that he had never witnessed, N'donazi began to direct his energies toward revalidating the healing wisdom of Central African tribes.

N'donazi's base is a clinic and research facility he founded in the remote town of Bouar. There he collects plants used by healers for laboratory analysis in order to distinguish those with biomedical value from those that have only a placebo effect. His staff dispenses both Western drugs and low-cost and proven traditional preparations.

Though modest about his work, the healer takes pleasure in recounting one triumphant moment of vindication. Last year he was approached by nuns from a Catholic mission hospital who asked him to help an extremely sick man whose chest was being eaten away by a subcutaneous amoebic infection that had not responded to drugs. Using a method learned from his father, N'donazi applied washed and crushed soldier termites to the open wounds. The patient, Thomas Service, made a remarkable recovery. In gratitude, he now appears at the clinic every Sunday bearing a gift for N'donazi. When a visitor asks how Service feels, the diminutive man shyly shows his healed chest and says the fact that he has walked 11 miles from his village speaks for itself.

Alas, some of the secrets of the male house remain lost. During his initiation, N'donazi recalls, he was given a plant to chew that numbed the pain of the incision. He wistfully notes that he has not since been able to find that natural anesthetic. ∎

A Puzzling Plague

What is it about the American way of life that makes more and more women contract breast cancer?

In the bad old days, some 20 years ago, no one had the heart even to talk about it. Breast cancer struck the most evident of a woman's assets, where the motherly and the erotic are joined. And treatment of the disease was a nightmare of pain, disfigurement and uncertainty. A seemingly healthy woman with nothing more than a tiny lump in her breast could agree to have a biopsy performed and not know whether she would awake from surgery with a small bandage on her breast—or no breast at all.

Much has changed since then. For one thing, breast cancer is widely discussed. Celebrity after celebrity—a veritable Breast Cancer Hall of Fame—has stepped forward to demystify the disease and soften its stigmas, beginning with Shirley Temple Black, Ingrid Bergman and Betty Ford, and more recently including Nancy Reagan and Gloria Steinem. Lessons on cancer detection and the importance of mammograms are the subject of elaborate public information campaigns.

More important, the surgical and post-surgical options have multiplied, and doctors now wait after a positive biopsy to discuss these options before moving in to amputate. In 1990 a consensus meeting convened by the National Institutes of Health formally rec-ommended lumpectomy, the removal of a cancerous lump plus a small amount of surrounding tissue, followed by radiation therapy, as an equally effective alternative to breast removal in many cases. And the success rate for treatment is up—not dramatically, but up.

But there is also bad news about breast cancer. The number of cases continues to soar. According to the National Cancer Institute, the U.S. incidence increased 32% between 1982 and 1987. Only lung cancer is rising faster. Cancer is the leading cause of death for women 35 to 50, and breast cancer is the most common malignancy in this age group. All in all, an American woman has a 1-in-10 chance of developing breast cancer over the course of her lifetime, and that risk keeps on rising.

The big question is why. Most experts on the disease agreee that part of the increase can be attributed to earlier detection of tumors. The widespread use of mammograms, a low-dose X ray of the breasts, has meant that more women are discovering their tumors in the early stages, before a lump can be felt. Nonetheless, most investigators of the epidemic believe early detection is only part of the story. They look at the fact that breast cancer is far less common in other parts of the world and conclude, ominously, that the answer lies in some facet of the American life-style. Many researchers around the world are pointing to a component of the Western way of life: a diet rich in fat. Researchers have known for more than 40 years that high-fat diets promote the growth of mammary tumors in laboratory animals. They have also observed that the varying rates of breast cancer in various countries correlate neatly with the amount of fat in a nation's diet. The U.S., Britain, and the Netherlands, which have some of the world's richest diets, also have among the highest breast-cancer rates. Meanwhile, in

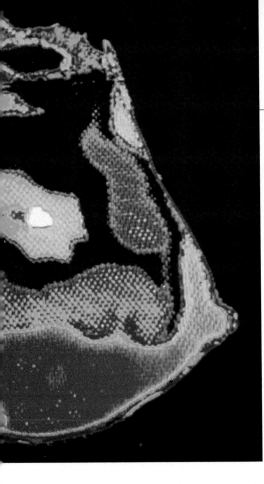

countries such as Japan, Singapore and Romania, where the diet is very lean, the incidence of breast cancer is one-sixth to one-half the U.S. rate.

Researchers have found that when Japanese move to the U.S., their previously low breast-cancer mortality rate rises to match the higher rate of their adopted country within a generation or two, as diet and life-style change. Japanese researchers are also convinced. Breast cancer is one of the fastest-growing diseases among Japanese women, with the incidence up 58% between 1975 and 1985. "The largest factor behind the sharp rise is the Westernization of eating habits," says Dr. Akira Eboshida, of the Health and Welfare Ministry's Disease Control Division. "We are eating more animal fat and less fiber."

Despite such evidence, not everyone shares the conviction that fat is the villain. Critics point out that statistical correlations are not the same as proving cause and effect. According to Dr. Walter Willett at the Harvard School of Public Health, overall calories may play a larger role than fat: Americans may simply be eating too well. Willett points out that breast-cancer rates tend to be highest in prosperous countries where people are well nourished. In such lands of plenty, girls begin to menstruate at an earlier age, women tend to have their children later in life and menopause also comes later. Late menopause (after 50), delayed childbearing (after 30) and early onset of menstruation (before 12) are all acknowledged "risk factors" for breast cancer. Ironically, better education and job opportunites for women have furthered the trend toward postponed motherhood and childlessness (also a risk factor).

Doctors have long been convinced that some people are genetically predisposed to develop breast cancer. A woman whose mother or sister had the disease before menopause has five to six times the usual risk of developing it. If either one had the disease in both breasts, then the woman's risk is five to 10 times the norm.

Though scientists do not know how breast cancer begins, they do have some ideas about how it progresses. The female hormone estrogen, which is produced in the ovaries and causes a young girl's breasts to develop, also plays an unmistakable role in promoting the growth of tumor cells. Why do childlessness, late menopause, early onset of menstruation and delayed childbearing all increase the risk of breast cancer? One likely explanation is that all involve a prolonged uninterrupted presence of high levels of estrogen in the bloodstream.

Researchers focusing on the role of fat in the development of cancer have been particularly intrigued by the estrogen connection. Biologists have long known that estrogen is produced not only in the ovaries but also in fat cells. Obese women have higher levels of estrogen than thin ones—a probable factor in their greater risk of breast cancer after menopause.

But it has been only in the past five years that researchers have found a link between estrogen levels and fat in the diet. Women who eat lots of hamburgers, thick shakes and other fatty foods have higher levels of estrogen and especially large amounts of the "biologically active" form; when women switch to a very low-fat diet (20% of total calories), their estrogen levels quickly drop 20%. Advocates of the dietary-fat theory regard this observation as a crucial bit of supporting evidence.

Until the government funds a long-term dietary study and until the work is completed, the value of an ultralow-fat diet in preventing breast cancer will remain open to question. For women 40 or over, however, there is one bit of medical counsel that has almost unanimous approval: Get a mammogram. Now. And do it regularly. A 1987 study found that for women whose tumors were discovered early by mammograms, the five-year survival rate was about 82%, as opposed to 60% for a control group. And if that is not incentive enough, early detection through mammography can sometimes bring another bonus: removing the tumor with a lumpectomy procedure rather than a mastectomy. The American College of Radiology advises patients to choose a high-volume accredited facility. One sign that a mammogram is up to snuff: the ouch factor. To get a good picture, the mammography machine must compress the breast. "If you're not uncomfortable," says Dr. Sarah Fox, a UCLA professor of family medicine, "you're probably getting a bad mammogram."

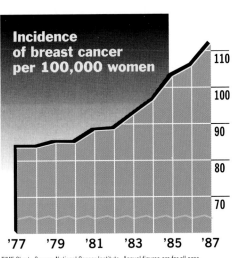

Incidence of breast cancer per 100,000 women

110
100
90
80
70

'77 '79 '81 '83 '85 '87

TIME Chart Source: National Cancer Institute Annual figures are for all ages

The Double Dawn

An eclipse reveals that the sun is bigger, hotter and denser than we thought

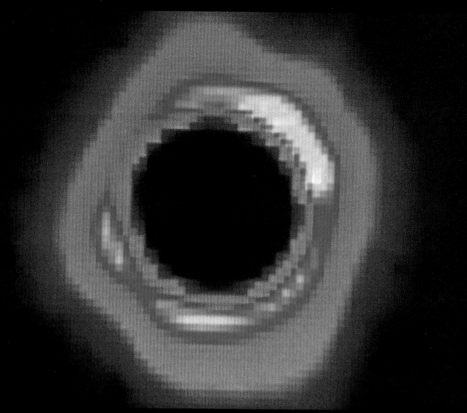

Infrared image of the solar eclipse recorded from observatory on Mauna Kea, Hawaii

High on the mountaintop, where the life-giving star is worshiped, no one slept a wink. On Hawaii's Mauna Kea, home to the world's greatest concentration of high-powered telescopes, a total of 250 scientists, journalists and guests had gathered on July 11, waiting for the last eclipse visible from the U.S. in the 20th century.

At 6:30 a.m. the celestial show began. Like a devouring sky god, the moon's shadow appeared. Soon it obscured all but a thin lower crescent that gleamed against the darkening sky like the Cheshire Cat's smile. Next the corners of the smile vanished, leaving a single dazzling gem of brilliance at the bottom of a circle of light—the so-called diamond-ring effect. At 7:28 the solitaire blinked out. And, as if the hand of God had thrown a switch, day turned to night.

Left in the sun's place was a black orb surrounded by a wide, shimmering halo—the solar corona, visible only during an eclipse. From the 12 o'clock position, an enormous red-orange flame flared beyond the halo; smaller "prominences" appeared at the 3 and 6 o'clock positions. Then, with stunning suddenness, the four minutes of totality ended, another diamond ring appeared, and the

shadow of the moon could be seen fleeing across the Pacific.

From the standpoint of science, the eclipse was something of a letdown. Thin clouds above Mauna Kea interfered with the quality of data gathered through telescopes. Even more damaging to the infrared readings was the fine dust accumulating in the atmosphere since the June explosion of Mount Pinatubo in the Philippines.

Still, most of the Mauna Kea scientists were elated. One discovery: the sun is bigger, hotter and denser than previously thought. Observations of invisible wavelengths that represent hydrogen emissions found that the sun's chromosphere, or lower atmosphere, extends 6,000 km (3,700 miles) beyond what is normally visible, considerably farther out than previously believed.

For the ultimate spiritual experience, no eclipse site could surpass the ancient Olmec pyramids at Cacaxtla, Mexico. There the sun's pas de deux with the moon, lasting nearly six minutes, led many to fall to their knees. With Mars, Mercury, Venus and Jupiter suddenly bursting into view, what else could those watching do but give thanks to the gods and pray for the opportunity to view the double dawn again in their lifetime?

Thin Skins and Fraud at M.I.T.

The case should have been settled nearly five years ago. That is when an obscure postdoctoral fellow at M.I.T. first charged that a celebrated scientific article signed by some of the university's leading biologists—including Nobel laureate David Baltimore—was based on data that had been fudged. But rather than reopen the experiment (which involved introducing foreign genes into a mouse and observing the effect on the animal's own genes), the scientists, led by Baltimore, closed ranks. The junior researcher, Irish-born Margot O'Toole, was asked to give up her place in the lab. The senior scientist accused of misconduct, a gifted Brazilian immunologist named Thereza Imanishi-Kari, went on to win a prestigious appointment at nearby Tufts University.

But the story did not end there. Some tenacious watchdogs at the National Institutes of Health found that Imanishi-Kari faked her results and that Baltimore failed to take the allegation seriously enough.

Those conclusions came only after probes by two different NIH committees and three separate congressional hearings over the past three years. The highlight

was an icy confrontation in May 1989 between Baltimore and John Dingell, the powerful chairman of the House Subcommittee on Oversight and Investigations. Dingell called in the Secret Service, which found a pattern of data falsification that began before the 1986 paper was published and continued, in a clumsy effort to cover up earlier misdeeds, into the late 1980s. The report raised questions about whether some crucial experiments were ever performed at all. Faced with the evidence, in late March Baltimore finally moved to distance himself from the work done by Imanishi-Kari. In a statement, he acknowledged that "very serious questions" had been raised, and for the first time asked that the original paper be retracted. He left it to Imanishi-Kari—who faces a possible cutoff of federal research funding—to explain what went wrong.

But the apology proved to be too little, too late. Irrevocably tarnished by the affair, Baltimore resigned from his prestigious position as president of Rockefeller University in December. He seems to have worried more about a colleague's reputation than about the truth of a junior researcher's complaint. In the end, he damaged not just his own reputation but science's as well.

The 4,000-Year-Old Man

One day a long time ago, a young man bundled himself up in a weatherproof leather coat, shouldered a crude wooden backpack, grabbed a knife, a bow and an ax, and headed into the Tyrolean Alps, which run between today's Austria and Italy. High up in the mountains, at about 3,200 m (10,500 ft.), something happened—an accident, a violent blow—that took his life and left him to be swallowed by the Similaun Glacier. There he lay, locked in a crevasse, buried, frozen, forgotten.

Now, 4,000 years later, he has turned up—remarkably well preserved—a messenger from the ancient past. Stumbled upon at the glacier's edge by a pair of German climbers, the mummified corpse was identified as a rare human specimen from the early Bronze Age, possibly the oldest ever found in Europe. Although hundreds of Bronze and Iron Age bodies have been found in the bogs of northwest Europe, the "Iceman from the Similaun," is much better preserved.

The Iceman has already yielded a trove of detail, providing a glimpse into a murky period of European history, when Central Europe was populated largely by preliterate farmers who supported themselves with mixed agriculture and hunting. He was a 20- to 40-year-old man, about 1.6 m (5 ft. 3 in.) tall, with tattoos in the shape of crosses and lines. The wear on his teeth suggests a diet of meat and stone-ground meal. Well equipped for an Alpine trip, he wore a jacket of tanned leather stitched together with fine thongs. His leather boots were lined with hay to keep out the winter chill.

What was he doing in the mountains? He was probably not a hunter, since most of the deer, badgers and wild pigs would have been found in forests at lower altitudes. He may have been searching for precious metals. He could have been on the run, hiding from enemies in the mountain passes. Or, says Professor Konrad Spindler at the University of Innsbruck, where the Iceman was flown for detailed study, he may simply have been on his way to visit the next valley—a trip disastrous for him but lucky for scientists 40 centuries in the future.

A Mission Close to Home

America's space program has spent billions of dollars to explore the clouds of Venus and the craters of Mars. But in the future, NASA's researchers will need to pay closer attention to their home planet. As the earth's air, land and seas become ever more threatened by human overpopulation and industrial pollution, measuring the extent of the damage has become one of the most urgent missions of science.

In early September the space shuttle *Discovery* deployed the first satellite in the Mission to Planet Earth, an ambitious, long-range program to monitor the planet's pulse. This particular satel-

lite carries four instruments to measure how badly the fragile ozone layer, which protects the earth from the harmful ultraviolet rays in sunlight, is being depleted. Much more is on the drawing boards. During the next 15 years, NASA hopes to spend $30 billion to $40 billion to launch satellites that will study the impact of such forces as global warming, deforestation and desertification. Despite its importance, the mission has not escaped criticism: the mammoth price tag is a concern. Budget Director Richard Darman reportedly quipped, "I didn't know we needed a $30 billion thermometer."

NASA's plan also calls for two large space platforms that would wind up holding the majority of the earth-sensing equipment.

In response to the criticisms, Congress and the White House have put pressure on NASA to improve its proposal, perhaps by launching six smaller space platforms instead of two large ones. Says Edward Frieman, chairman of an "engineering review panel" set up by NASA to study suggestions for the mission: "We found ways to do it faster and make it more flexible, but not cheaper."

Cheaper ways might be found if the project's budget were not partly the product of pork-barrel politics. NASA has learned a lesson from the Pentagon: a program will fly politically if it involves a popular cause, promises to spread lots of money through key congressional districts and also guarantees contracts to companies with strong lobbying clout in Washington.

In this case, NASA appears to have picked a winner. The agency needs to refine its plans, but Congress will eventually come up with $30 billion or more, if that's what it takes. After the disasters with the shuttle program, the Hubble telescope and the Galileo probe to Jupiter, the Mission to Planet Earth gives NASA a chance to take a flight back to respectability.

Death in the Time of Cholera

Many doctors think of cholera, a disease that robs the body of fluids, as a kind of Lazarus syndrome. Victims are brought to a clinic or hospital with no apparent blood pressure or pulse, taking only shallow breaths. But if there is any life in them at all, doctors report, they can be brought back. This year the first epidemic of cholera on the South American continent in this century was raging. The epidemic, which is spread through contaminated food and water, started in Peru and surged into neighboring countries, overwhelming medical resources in many areas and striking mostly the very poor in shantytowns, mountain villages and remote jungle settlements.

By one estimate, as many as 6 million people may fall ill over the next three years, with the death toll reaching 40,000. Brazil reported its first cases in April, in the Amazonian jungle on the border with Peru.

Scientists do not know exactly why cholera periodically explodes into epidemics. The bacteria that cause it are part of the aquatic ecosystem, helping to break down dead shellfish. Cholera germs travel up the food chain by attaching themselves to plankton, which are eaten by fish and then by people. Studies by Rita Colwell, professor of microbiology at the University of Maryland, suggest that a plankton bloom, a rapid growth like the one reported off the coast of Peru earlier this year, may help trigger epidemics.

Quick treatment can easily save lives. Large amounts of a simple solution of sodium and potassium salts and sugar can rapidly replace the body's fluids. Antibiotics speed up the recovery time. Unfortunately, in Latin America, distributing medicines can be difficult,

especially in remote areas.

Even so, the epidemic may not be as devastating in other countries as it has been in Peru, where relief efforts have been hampered by a strike among health-care workers. When Bolivia tried to send doctors to the Andean village of Puno, where an outbreak was beginning, the medical team was asked to stay home. Finally the strikers allowed a limited number of Bolivian technicians to disinfect Puno's sewage pipes with chlorine.

Even with the staunchest efforts, cholera's march through Latin America could mean trouble for years to come. The only effective solution is good public sanitation. But according to the World Health Organization, providing safe water and sewage treatment in Latin America could cost $50 billion over the next decade—a staggering sum for countries that are already deeply in debt and struggling with the problems of crushing poverty.

Erupting on Schedule

When 15,000 anxious Americans were evacuated from Clark Air Base in the Philippines in June, they didn't know what to think. Were they in real danger or the victims of a false alarm? Within 48 hours, they got their answer. Nearby Mount Pinatubo, after sleeping quietly for more than 600 years, suddenly erupted in a series of explosions that shot plumes of steam and ash as far as 30 km (20 miles) into the sky. Debris rained down on surrounding villages, and a giant mushroom cloud was visible 100 km (62 miles) away in Manila.

Thanks to advance warnings and speedy evacuations, tens of thousands moved to safety; but the continuing mud slides have killed more than 700. The swift action by the government reflected the improving ability of scientists to monitor volcanic activity and identify the telltale events that presage eruptions.

Mount Pinatubo's blasts came just one week after Japan's Mount Unzen blew its top, killing at least 38 people. But the toll could have been much higher if scientists had not sounded the alarm that an eruption was imminent. In fact, many of those killed were journalists and volcanologists drawn to the mountain by the warnings, whereas most residents of the area fled to safety.

The number of eruptions these days is not abnormal, but human populations near the fiery mountains have been growing rapidly. Never before have the volcanoes posed such a serious threat. Some volcanologists believe, for example, that Mount Fuji has entered an active phase, raising the specter of a giant eruption only 100 km (62 miles) from Tokyo. But scientists hope to foretell most major eruptions, employing a combination of seismometers, chemical sensors mounted on airplanes and laser-based devices to measure the physical swelling of mountain slopes—and their record is increasingly impressive. Since 1980 Mount St. Helens has erupted 22 times, and 19 of those episodes were predicted by U.S. volcanologists.

"When a nice little hill covered with lush vegetation finally wakes up," observes Smithsonian Institution volcanologist Tom Simkin, "it's going to cause a lot of damage." Fortunately, scientists were able to see that some nice little hills in the Philippines and Japan were turning nasty while people had time to get away.

Born Gay?

Gay men often claim that even as children they knew they were somehow "different" from other boys. Many say that sense even preceded puberty. And yet, though researchers have tried for decades to identify a biological basis for homosexuality—which seems to be present in all human societies—they have mostly come up dry.

Now new research offers evidence that there may indeed be a physiological basis for sexual orientation. In a study of 41 brains taken from people who died before age 60, Simon LeVay, a biologist at San Diego's Salk Institute for Biological Studies, found that one tiny region in the brain of homosexual men was more like that in women than that in heterosexual men.

That specific part is found at the front of the hypothalamus in an area of the brain that is known to help regulate male sexual behavior. Within this site, LeVay looked at four different groupings of cells, technically referred to as the interstitial nuclei of the anterior hypothalamus (INAH), and found that the areas of most of the women and homosexual men were about the same size. In straight men this region was on average twice as large—or about the size of a grain of sand.

LeVay's findings are certain to trigger a good deal of controversy. Many technical aspects of the study are subject to question, as the author concedes. He cannot be certain, for instance, that all the heterosexual men in the control group were heterosexual. And since the AIDS virus attacks the brain (26 of the 41 people died of AIDS), the size difference could be an artifact of the disease. It is also possible that the difference actually has nothing to do with sexual orientation or that it is the result rather than the cause of homosexuality.

"My freshman biology students know enough to sink this study," declares Anne Fausto-Sterling, professor of medical science at Brown University. Others are more receptive to LeVay's work. "It makes sense," says Laura Allen, a neuroanatomist at the University of California, Los Angeles. Finding a difference in the INAH, which influences male sexual behavior, she says, "is what one would expect."

LeVay and others hope their work will enable humans to view homosexuality as a normal variation of sexual behavior.

The Arts: News of Another Kind

By CHRISTOPHER PORTERFIELD

In February 1991, tensions at the Théâtre Royal de la Monnaie in Brussels were running high, even by the standards of an opera house. Outside, the world was gripped by anxiety over the gulf war. Onstage, rehearsals were in progress for a new opera on a politically explosive subject: *The Death of Klinghoffer,* by American composer John Adams, about the brutal murder of a wheelchair-bound American Jew by Palestinian terrorists aboard the Italian cruise ship *Achille Lauro* in 1985. Some Belgians urged a postponement of the premiere, fearing that it might incite further terrorism. As it turned out, their fears proved groundless, but their respect for the work's potency was impressive. How long has it been, one wonders, since anybody felt that way about an opera?

The arts, often regarded as an adjunct to, or a relief from, the news, are actually news of another kind. Sometimes, as in the case of *Klinghoffer,* they cut close to the headlines, and 1991 was a year bristling with examples of such immediacy. Innumerable books, plays, paintings and pieces of music took account, explicitly or implicitly, of the ravages of AIDS, just as many performances or exhibitions were mounted as memorials or as rallies for AIDS research. On another front, rap music produced blistering bulletins from the streets of America's ghettos. Albums by black groups like N.W.A. (Niggas With Attitude) and Public Enemy took the poverty, frustration— and, alas, the hostility and bigotry—of contemporary inner-city life and put it, as a rap lyric might say, in your face.

Even the usually sedate realm of art museums resounded with the sociopolitical controversies of the day. Washington's National Museum of American Art ventured into the cross-fire of revisionist American history and politically correct attitudes toward Native Americans with an exhibition showing how George Catlin, Albert Bierstadt and other artists recast the harsh conquest of the West as a heroic and exculpatory myth of Manifest Destiny.

Another pattern of 1991 was the emergence, on the inside, of many erstwhile outsiders; voices previously stifled or muted began to be heard more clearly. In Hollywood it was a good year for women on both sides of the camera. They were frequently portrayed, for a change, in strong, independent, assertive roles, nowhere more so than in the breakthrough gender-bender *Thelma & Louise.* That film fused the (male) conventions of the buddy movie and the road movie in a feminist picaresque that turned a crime spree into a voyage of self-discovery and self-affirmation. Women also came into their own as directors of several movies. The most auspicious arrival: Jodie Foster's. A child star at 10 and an Oscar-winning actress at 25, Foster proved herself equally precocious at 28 in the skill and shrewdness with which she directed her first film, *Little Man Tate.*

Part of the women directors' triumph was that they took on the same genres as male directors—not just delicate "women's movies."

But Hollywood's other new wave, black directors, were prized precisely because they could turn out authentic, gritty portrayals of black life. The *eminence noire* of this group was unquestionably Spike Lee, whose fifth film, *Jungle Fever,* delved forcefully if not always coherently into interracial sex, black vs. black bias and the scourge of drugs. Among the younger black directors whose way Lee had helped to clear, two were making stunning debuts: Matty Rich, 19, with *Straight Out of Brooklyn,* and John Singleton, 23, with *Boyz N the Hood*—both harrowing autobiographical accounts of the odds against moral or even physical survival in the ghetto.

Ethnic authenticity was central too to issues that tapped into Asian roots. Amy Tan and a constellation of Chinese-American writers produced books celebrating the pain and humor of the immigrant experience. On the other hand, Asian Americans lost a highly publicized battle when they failed to secure the casting of one of their own in the role of the Eurasian pimp in the splashiest Broadway musical of the year, *Miss Saigon.* Producer Cameron Macintosh threatened to cancel the production if English actor Jonathan Pryce was not allowed to repeat his London performance.

As America's baby boomers slid a little deeper into middle age (and the century rolled closer to its end), it seemed fitting that some of the year's most stirring feats were achieved by figures on the downhill side of 40. That old master of the art of baseball, Nolan Ryan, pitched his record seventh no-hitter at 44, striking out batters who hadn't been born when he began his major-league career. Onetime Beatle Paul McCartney, 49, conquered new musical worlds with his *Liverpool Oratorio,* though if anything he put rock 'n' roll too far behind him in the process. Some daring leaps taken by older artists, however, ended in flops. Norman Mailer, 63, published his monumentally ambitious *Harlot's Ghost* (ten years in the making, 1,310 pages in length), and while some of it hummed with Mailerian electricity, too much made the reader feel as if he were locked up in a document room in the basement of CIA headquarters.

But works of art can be fitted into only so many categories. For every one in 1991 that reflected a social concern or illustrated a trend, there was another that floated blithely free of issues, that went its own inspired way. Anne Tyler's luminous novel *Saint Maybe* was such a work, as were the mystically calligraphic paintings of Brice Marden and the heartbreakingly comic *Dancing at Lughnasa,* by playwright Brian Friel. And in the end these creations were no less immediate or relevant than the most politically aware works of the year. At their best, all of them, the zealously significant as well as the unabashedly quotidian, dispatched reports from the same place: the frontiers of the human soul. This is the essence of art and the quality that gives it a claim to permanence. It is what makes art, as Ezra Pound said, news that *stays* news.

Thelma & Louise

Thelma & Louise is in the honorable line of movies whose makers, without quite knowing what they were doing, sank a drill into what appeared to be familiar American soil and found that they had somehow tapped into a wild-rushing subterranean stream of inchoate outrage and deranged violence. Like *Bonnie and Clyde*, *Easy Rider* and *Dirty Harry*, it began as an attempt to vary and freshen traditional generic themes but ended up taking its audience on a trip much deeper, darker, more disturbing than anyone dreamed they were going to make. Screenwriter Callie Khouri's tale tells of two women—Susan Sarandon's Louise and Geena Davis' Thelma—who shed their men and end up on a liberating but self-destructive crime spree. The film cheers one's argumentative spirit, stirs one's critical imagination and awakens one's protective affection.

Terminator 2

Terminator 2, James Cameron's sequel to his wonderfully reverberant 1984 thriller, is a humongous, visionary parable that intermittently enthralls and ultimately disappoints. *T2* is half of a terrific movie—the wrong half. For a breathless first hour, the film zips along in a textbook display of showmanship. But then it stumbles over its own ambitions before settling for a conventional climax with a long fuse. This time around, Arnold Schwarzenegger is back as a kinder, gentler T-man, now on the side of the angels. His mission is to protect Sarah (Linda Hamilton) and her young son (Edward Furlong) from an even more efficiently psychopathic cyborg (Robert Patrick). *T2* is a macho movie that scorns the male-stud ego: the picture believes the only good man is a mechanical man. And it parades its fabulous film technology while predicting that the world could end when military technology runs amuck.

Little Man Tate

For 25 of her 28 years Jodie Foster has been an actress, and her film, *Little Man Tate,* stands as both an artful commentary on growing up onstage and a calling-card film for a director who promises much and delivers most of it. Reverberations from Foster's extraordinary youth pulse through Scott Frank's script and inform the fierce care the director took in realizing it. The story involves a gifted child (Adam Hann-Byrd), his sympathetic teacher (Dianne Wiest) and his mother (Foster), a defiant single parent, torn between love and loss. The women enact a kind of custody battle, each offering part of what the child needs, as the film asks: How many mothers can divide a boy's loyalty? And the answer is: Both of them. In the wrong hands, this material could get twee and reductive, but the comforting dream of communion at the picture's end can't erase its careful wit about good people in desperate situations.

Cape Fear

Martin Scorsese's style reconciles art-house finesse with B-movie excess; *Cape Fear* carries his familiar themes of guilt and obsession. The film is violent, excessive and, above all, entertaining: it anticipates, satisfies and then trumps the moviegoer's expectations. It plunders film history and creates, in Robert DeNiro's character, a loner driven to impossible extremes by the voices inside him, a brother to *Taxi Driver's* Travis Bickle and *Raging Bull's* Jake LaMotta. From the first images of this remake of the 1962 sicko classic—weird creatures shimmering just below sea level like monsters of the id, DeNiro's eyes burning through the screen—*Cape Fear* has been Bobbyized and Martyized. A worthy addition to the Scorsese canon, the film meets the challenge of starting at fever pitch and then ascending to a climax that plays like a hurricane of hysteria.

JFK

Oliver Stone screams bloody murder for a living. Oddly enough, Stone's tortured artistic mission—dispensing downers to a movie public famously addicted to escapism—has its upside. He pours so much dramatic juice into the hemlock blender that folks go to his films, and official Hollyood has rewarded him with three Oscars.

JFK, his attempt to explain the Kennedy assassination, is an electrifying melodrama. Whatever one's suspicions about its use or abuse of the evidence, *JFK* is a knockout. Part history book, part comic book, the movie rushes toward judgment for three breathless hours, lassoing facts and factoids by the thousands, then bundling them together with an incendiary device that would frag any viewer's complacency. Tip-top tabloid journalism, *JFK* is seditiously enthralling; in its craft, wondrously complex.

Boyz N the Hood

One man created the market for black-movie rage: Spike Lee. This acerbic auteur has carved a niche for fierce minority movies—a niche that can be enlarged by other directors who are even younger, more choleric, closer to the action if not to the edge. Call them the Spikettes. Leading their summer charge on the box office was John Singleton, whose *Boyz N the Hood* was a slice of fictionalized autobiography: a life story that could have been a death warrant. Lame as moviemaking craft, the picture is nonetheless a harrowing document true to the director's South Central Los Angeles milieu; he paints it black. The boys in the neighborhood have a choice: dying poor from drugs or dying rich selling them. *Boyz N the Hood* functions both as a condemnation of the world outside any big-city movie house and an inspiration to those aspiring outsiders who would change history by filming it.

Beauty and the Beast

Disney's 30th animated feature, *Beauty and the Beast,* is close to seamless. Its animators' pens are wands; their movement enchants. Enchantment is at the heart of the story too. A selfish prince lives under the curse of a righteous witch: that he be a beast, confined to his castle, until he can love and be loved. Pretty Belle will be his cure—if she can shake off her revulsion at being his prisoner and shiver out of the clutches of Gaston, a way-too-handsome galoot. With an emotional resonance rare in movies and a pleasing score by Howard Ashman and Alan Menken, *Beauty and the Beast* gets all the comic leavening it needs from a nice modification of the Seven Dwarfs: the prince's household staff have been changed into candlesticks, teapots, clocks and armoires. The voluptuousness of visual detail offers proof that the Disney studio has relocated the pure magic of the *Pinocchio-Dumbo* years.

Hook

Welcome to '90s revisionism run riot. In Steven Spielberg's overblown *Hook,* Robin Williams is a Peter Unprincipled, grounded in all the latest guilts and anxieties, including a wife and two kids whom he neglects, owing to the press of the greed business. It requires a great deal of whirring and clanking of plot machinery to make us believe this is the One True Peter. He's carrying too much baggage, and so is the movie. The sets are spectacular, but their scale and luxe become oppressive. John Williams' score, all thunder, lightning and self-importance, reinforces the film's charmlessness, and Dustin Hoffman's Hook emblematizes it. He's broody and self absorbed, utterly gleeless in his villainy. But then even Robin Williams, that freest of comic spirits, never has a truly antic moment. As Tinkerbell, though, Julia Roberts is ingenuous, unaffected and what *Hook* is only some of the time—light on her wings.

Bugsy

Bugsy is elegantly made, wickedly perverse and very smart. Screenwriter James Toback writes dialogue as if it had not gone out of style; director Barry Levinson envisions old-time Hollywood as sleek, hard and distracted by its own overnight success. Annette Bening gives a remarkable performance, proposing the intriguing possiblity that a kept woman can also be a liberated woman, sharing her character's fears and vulnerabilities only in a few private moments with the camera. But the picture belongs to producer/star Warren Beatty. He is not a star appearing, but an actor acting—mercurially, hypnotically. Like the film, he is metaphorically but ferociously at grips with American ambiguities: infamy as a form of fame, violence as an aspect of the visionary, bold greed as relief and corrective for our pious official hypocrisies.

The Silence of the Lambs

The lacerating suspense of Thomas Harris' novel is missing from this earnest adaptation of *The Silence of the Lambs*, but if you haven't read the book about an FBI trainee tracking one serial killer with the help of another, you ought to see the movie. As Clarice Starling, Jodie Foster is the young agent whose nerve and empathy battle an army of dysfunctional men, from serial killers to asylum wardens, and save a woman trapped in a hole of sexual depravity. Anthony Hopkins' portrayal of serial killer Hannibal ("the Cannibal") Lecter is brilliantly chilling. The movie's main attraction isn't the thriller elements: it's the intellectual tug-of-war between Foster and Hopkins. Sweeping the early awards voting, the movie was voted best film of 1991 by the New York Film Critic's Circle and also won awards for stars Foster and Hopkins and director Jonathan Demme.

Miss Saigon

Miss Saigon is a cracking good show. It blends a love story and a spectacle with tragic social commentary about what the West symbolizes to the Third World, which is not peace and freedom so much as money and security. The plot is the sad, simple story of a soldier and a peasant woman. The stage mechanics feature that famous (or infamous) last helicopter taking off from the U.S. embassy in 1975. But the themes could not be bigger: geopolitical rescue missions that turn into fiascoes, the sheer randomness of how riches are distributed on this planet.

The blasted hopes of Kim, a country maiden turned bar girl turned bride-to-be turned stateless refugee, are a paradigm for all the promises that Western powers made but failed to keep in Vietnam and other colonies. Her yearning is echoed comically and tragically in her sometime pimp, a Eurasian hustler called the Engineer, whose vision of the U.S. is a pathetic pop mishmash of the Statue of Liberty, big white Cadillacs and Fred Astaire.

As Kim, Lea Salonga is incandescently in command of the stage; Jonathan Pryce as the Engineer gets the sardonic laughs owed to his Dickensian lampoon of a conniver, yet Pryce has transmuted him into a full-blown tragic figure, a victim of global politics all the sadder for being so streetwise.

The Ride Down Mt. Morgan

Any new play by Arthur Miller is an important event in American culture. One as theatrically bold and intellectually subtle as *The Ride Down Mt. Morgan* is reason to shout for joy: robustly funny, full of fantasy and hallucination yet easy to follow, it is free of the world-weary, elegiac tone of the four slight one-acts that had been Miller's sole stage output in the previous decade. At 76, the playwright has recaptured the vigorous voice and zest of middle age and has found a fresh, indeed engagingly oddball, way to revisit his accustomed theme of how to assess rugged individualism—as personal integrity or social irresponsibility. The text abounds in unusually shapely language for Miller, and in jokes. The production is not, alas, quite as polished. Tom Conti looks too young to play Miller's antihero, who rises from his hospital bed to engage the play's moral dilemma: whether to mire oneself in decency or succumb to seductive selfishness. Only one fact jars: this world premiere is delighting audiences not on Broadway but in London's West End.

The Secret Garden

Vibrant and thought provoking to look at, melodic and poignant to hear, movingly acted and blessed with the dazzling 11-year-old star Daisy Eagan, *The Secret Garden* is the best American musical of the spring Broadway season. It is that rarest of entertainments, a story fascinating to children that unfolds in a manner both sophisticated and stimulating for adults.

Fittingly, Frances Hodgson Burnett's novel has been translated by what is believed to be a Broadway first, an all-female creative team. Producer Heidi Landesman also designed the allegorical, imagistic set; director Susan Schulman has laced the narrative with ghosts and wraiths of memory. Composer Lucy Simon blended folk music with art songs fitting the moneyed manor-house setting. Librettist-lyricist Marsha Norman made songs vehicles for thoughts characters would never merely speak.

The first act takes a long, slow time setting things up. The second act thrillingly resolves them. Like the novel, this adaptation rewards patience with a satisfying surge of emotion, a sense that God's in his heaven and all's right with the world.

Lost in Yonkers

In the pivotal scene of Neil Simon's wonderful *Lost in Yonkers,* the mildly retarded 35-year-old Bella sits her family down to tell them her plan to marry a similarly handicapped usher whom she has met at a local movie theater. The scene ought to be agony. Yet as it plays out, spectators who were crying with laughter one moment are left simply crying, without any sense of having been manipulated. The ability to find humor in unlikely places, then shift emotional gears with no machinery showing, makes Simon a great comedist.

Simon is commercially the most successful playwright in history. Yet rather than rely on formulas, Simon uses success to keep testing audiences and himself. At the heart of this new play is a dysfunctional family: a mother who was abusive and four middle-aged children who still suffer the weaknesses she inflicted in teaching them to be strong. As the matriarch, Irene Worth, 75, lives up to her legendary reputation. But the play belongs to Mercedes Ruehl, as Bella, who veers from Gracie Allenesque comic illogic to mistrustful tantrums and wistful dreams. If Simon's terrain is the border country between laughter and tears, Bella's is the no-man's-land between hope and despair. It is a terrible place to live, and an unforgettable one to visit.

Dancing at Lughnasa

A good dramatist defines a theme, shapes a story to illumine it and moves clearly and logically toward an emotionally satisfying conclusion. A great dramatist can make quicksilver leaps from theme to theme, fragment a story into seemingly disparate shards and play games with character and chronology, yet achieve a conclusion that is even more emotionally satisfying because of the sense of surprise and revelation in how it all comes together. For more than three decades, Ireland's Brian Friel has been a good dramatist. In *Dancing at Lughnasa* he has become a great one.

The title refers to a merry harvest festival in County Donegal. But the action never leaves the cottage of the five Mundy sisters, living poor and unmarried in the hard year of 1936, with no entertainment but a balky old radio and their Celtic gift for chat.

From this simple setting, Friel evokes great sadness, but also great joy, in vivid exchanges of everyday talk and, most boldly, when the sisters erupt, at home and alone, in life-embracing energy. The cast members, from Dublin's Abbey Theater, are amazingly fresh and spontaneous, yet the performances also have the delicacy and nuance that come from long consideration. In a lifetime of theatergoing one would be lucky to see a dozen ensembles this good or any that are better.

Nick & Nora

When the curtain rises on the only new American musical of Broadway's 1991-92 season, derived from the beloved *Thin Man* movies, the only character onstage is a dog. That turns out to be depressingly symbolic. The show is a crashing bore—cranky and arbitrary as a love story, tedious and pointless as a murder mystery, hamhanded as comedy, clubfooted as dance, at best wanly pleasant as music. After three months of "previews," it closed in a week.

A few scenes work, some quite well. The final 10 minutes achieve a truth and simplicity underscoring the barren brittleness of what has gone before. But ultimately the show fails at its most basic task: making audiences care about, or for that matter simply believe in, its characters. This failure is a pity for everyone involved, and for the American theater. As the cost of Broadway production soars and the number of new shows per season plummets, each arrival becomes precious—especially the handful of big musicals, the Great White Way's economic mainstay and artistic signature.

Mao II

What do authors and terrorists have in common? That is one of the many questions raised in this novel, Don DeLillo's 10th, which bristles with unsettled and unsettling impressions: "Years ago I used to think it was possible for a novelist to alter the inner life of a culture. Now bomb-makers and gunmen have taken that territory. They make raids on human consciousness."

The speaker is not DeLillo, but his main character, Bill Gray, 63, a famously reclusive writer à la Salinger or Pynchon. But *Mao II* is not really about the paranoia of a writer; Gray is one extreme in a taut, fully dramatized dialectic about the future. Opposed to him are the forces epitomized in this novel by the image of Mao Zedong, all those who argue that the world has grown too crowded for the individual and that the only salvation lies in the dissolution of personalities into the single-headed throng. DeLillo's gifts—terse, electric dialogue, descriptive passages of insidious beauty—have never been more apparent or put to better use. As it races toward several shattering conclusions, *Mao II* triumphs as a thriller of ideas.

Saint Maybe

Saint Maybe, Anne Tyler's 12th novel, draws on the strengths of its predecessors while investigating more thoroughly than Tyler has ever attempted before the sources and aftereffects of religious faith. The burden of the novel records young Ian Bedloe's attempts to atone for a guilt that is beyond the power of reason or common sense to assuage; a moral blunder has become a millstone on his young life. Since crime is ordinarily more interesting than punishment, Tyler's emphasis on his long reparation is both risky and audacious. The more her hero becomes dedicated to religion and self-sacrifice, the further he diverges from the alert, sexually aware, engrossing young man he seems to be in the opening pages. Ian, in short, becomes a stick-in-the-mud. Tyler largely salvages this problem by focusing on the mud—the rich, roiling life that surrounds her ascetic main character. Seen this way, the moral message of *Saint Maybe* oddly resembles a medieval tapestry: at the center is an event of allegorical significance, but off to one corner is a cat, stealing — and then regurgitating — an oyster at a Christmas dinner.

Illiberal Education

In the spring of 1991 Conservative polemicist Dinesh D'Souza lived every nonfiction author's fantasy: to publish at precisely the correct moment. Like the cavalry in an old-time western racing over the hill to save the wagon train from the thunderous Indians—oops, misunderstood Native Americans—*Illiberal Education: The Politics of Race and Sex on Campus* arrived just as public outrage was building to a peak. Liberals and conservatives alike had suddenly joined forces to ridicule the excesses of left-wing policies and posturing in academia.

The rewards of being topical carry with them the risks of over-familiarity. That is the problem with the six case studies that make up the heart of *Illiberal Education*. D'Souza amply documents the prejudice against Asian Americans in the admission policies of Berkeley, the absurdities of recasting the introductory civilization course at Stanford to purge many Western white male thinkers, the affront to civil liberties in the racial-speech code at the University of Michigan, along with analogous flaps at Howard, Duke and Harvard. But he rarely transcends his material; the writing is earnest, the details repetitive and the analysis predictable. Many of the best quotes and anecdotes in the book turn out to be secondhand prose, and D'Souza's interview style is that of a patronizing pedant. *Illiberal Education* disappoints because it never delves beneath the surface of its all-too-easy targets. Like the Broadway theater, liberal education always seems in peril. Luckily for D'Souza, equally constant is the off-campus demand for books direly proclaiming the end of Western Civilization courses as we knew them. Not to worry; Shakespeare will survive.

Harlot's Ghost

At first glance Norman Mailer's much anticipated and superhyped new novel beggars description. Saying, for openers, that it is very, very long is like observing that the Grand Canyon is quite roomy. The next step is to point out that mind-boggling immensity seems to be one of the points of the exercise. Mailer's narrator, an aging CIA hand named Herrick ("Harry") Hubbard, who has written the two manuscripts that make up the bulk of the book—1,310 pages—notes that he has been guided by Thomas Mann's assertion that "only the exhaustive is truly interesting." By that standard alone, Harry and Mailer have produced the most interesting book in recent memory.

Unfortunately, other criteria for engaging a reader's attention also exist: plot, suspense, characterization, dialogue, effective prose. In all these areas, *Harlot's Ghost* runs into serious difficulties. The first 100 pages or so are a burst of bravura storytelling, fine and engaging, comparable to the best passages that Mailer has ever written. Then the joyride turns into a forced march, as Harry shackles himself to chronology and tells the story of his life in the CIA. Mailer finally does not use history, but succumbs to it.

Immortality

Not everyone will be pleased to hear that a character named Mr. Kundera moves through the pages of this novel. Even more dispiriting, this Mr. Kundera is an author, and the book he is writing turns out to be the very one that readers of *Immortality* will hold in their hands. What the world scarcely needs at this moment is more self-referential fiction.

Happily, *Immortality* is gripping and exhilarating, swinging easily, almost imperceptibly, from narrative to rumination and back again, collapsing the distinction between action and concepts. Milan Kundera's characters must cope with their emotions and with the stresses of daily life in contemporary Paris; but they also embody a number of nagging problems of existence. What does it mean to be a person in the waning years of the 20th century? If images have become reality and if people lack the power to control how they are perceived by others, what happens to the notion of the unique, inviolable self?

In its inventiveness and its dazzling display of what written words can convey, *Immortality* gives fiction back its good name.

The Journals of John Cheever

When John Cheever died in 1982, he left a legacy of 12 books. Eleven cannot fail to enhance his reputation; one is likely to erode it. *The Journals of John Cheever* occasioned more chatter than anything the author published in his lifetime, because they reveal a private face unlike the mask that Cheever contrived for public view.

In 1961 Cheever published a list of subjects he considered off limits: it included explicit scenes of sexual commerce, alcoholism and homosexuality. Later he dealt with some of these proscribed items, but never in the tone of the journals. Here they appear in a harsh floodlight, personified by Cheever himself. The author's idiosyncrasies are no longer secret: his daughter Susan described him as "the worst kind of alcoholic;" her brother Ben recalled that Cheever was "bisexual all his life . . . He liked good-looking younger men." Still, these were posthumous comments, made by members of the family that Cheever alternately cherished and regarded as a self-inflicted wound. In his notebooks, the author discloses himself in passages that seem to have been meant for an audience of one.

With a comparatively small body of work, Cheever established himself as the Chekhov of the American suburb, investing railroad stations, tract houses and their owners with an amalgam of poetry, comedy and pathos. But that was in his fiction. The journals written before his renunciation of liquor, if not infidelity, reveal a blundering father, a conniving lover and a narcissistic mind. According to *New Yorker* editor Robert Gottlieb, Cheever wanted his notebooks to be published; the family is simply honoring his wishes. How much honor accrues to the request will be debated for years to come.

Bland on the Run

Since the death of Irving Berlin, Paul McCartney is probably the world's most famous musical illiterate. He freely admits that his repeated attempts to learn to read music have failed. But that hasn't kept the erstwhile "cute" Beatle and Wings captain from having a go at an oratorio, written in the High Church/High Seriousness manner that has attracted English composers as disparate as Handel, Elgar and Andrew Lloyd Webber.

McCartney's quasi-autobiographical *Liverpool Oratorio*, commissioned for the 150th anniversary of the Royal Liverpool Philharmonic Orchestra and Choir, was first performed in McCartney's native city last July and received its U.S. premiere in November at New York City's Carnegie Hall.

McCartney enlisted a little help from a friend for the composing chores: Carl Davis, an American-born film composer and accomplished pastiche artist. After McCartney wrote the text and invented

the tunes, Davis arranged them slickly for soprano, boy soprano, chorus, cathedral choir and full orchestra.

The result is a big, sprawling, high-minded and honorably intended work that never quite comes into focus. The story concerns a Liverpool boy named Shanty, born during the air raids of 1942. The second, third and fourth sections detail typical adolescent angst. In the oratorio's second half, the hero meets Mary Dee, marries her, impregnates her, fights with her and finally, after a traffic accident that almost claims her life and that of their unborn child, reconciles with her.

Shanty's wedding music stands out as a luminous love song, but overall the oratorio is rambling and generic; there is nothing to match the economy and effect of such "classical" McCartney tunes as *Eleanor Rigby* and *Yesterday,* and you certainly can't dance to it. One waits in vain for the real McCartney to loosen his tie and do something a little rude. His vital rock roots remain a band on the run.

Hats Off to a Genius!

Though very much a child of the 18th century Enlightenment in Austria, Wolfgang Amadeus Mozart is probably the most universally beloved of classical composers. So while the 200th anniversary of his death was celebrated in 1991 with concerts and exhibits in London and Paris, there also were Mozart festivals in more unexpected places, ranging from Bartlesville, Okla., to Dunedin, New Zealand. When all the cheering finally died, it was probably the largest and

loudest celebration of any artist in human history. Said one New Yorker who prefers Puccini: "Where can I hide?"

The bicentennial celebrations were not all musical. The British, for example, staged a weekend of billiards tournaments to commemorate Mozart's fondness for planning carom shots while he composed music, and vice versa. Japanese entrepreneurs sold Mozart dolls, Mozart watches, even Mozart sake manufactured to the strains of Mozart's music.

In the composer's native Salzburg, the high shrine of Mozartism, the festivities started Jan. 2, when the celebrated Salzburg Marionettes presented the first of the seven Mozart operas the troupe has in its repertoire. In Vienna, where the composer spent his last 10 years, the Staatsoper and the Volksoper played Mozart operas all season.

New York City's Lincoln Center wins the prize for endurance: during a 19-month period beginning January 1991, every note the composer ever wrote will be played. While Mozart was not the twit popularized in the play and movie *Amadeus,* he did like jokes and games, and he had a rich sense of his own gifts. It is easy to guess that he would have enjoyed his bicentennial enormously.

The Success of Klinghoffer

Few operas in history have been as instantly controversial as *The Death of Klinghoffer.* To begin with, the subject matter is politically incendiary: the brutal 1985 murder of a wheelchair-using American Jew by Palestinian terrorists aboard the cruise ship *Achille Lauro.* Further, the opera is the second collaboration by composer John Adams, librettist Alice Goodman, choreographer Mark Morris and director Peter Sellars, the people behind *Nixon in China.* That dazzling 1987 opera left a trail of argument in its wake as it made its way across America and Europe. Surely, *Klinghoffer* would be even more provocative than its predecessor. Wouldn't it?

The Belgians thought so. When the opera had its world premiere in Brussels in late March, security was tight. But surprise: *Klinghoffer* is not that kind of provocateur. This sweet, sorrowful work upended everyone's expectations. It is not a docudrama but rather a stylized, subtle *Rashomon*-like retelling of the tragedy. It takes no prisoners, and takes no sides either. Confusion is captain, and perspectives shift like ocean waves. Along with Leon Klinghoffer, truth becomes a casualty.

In his most flexible score to date, Adams has erected huge choral pillars to frame the action and provide context. In between, he spins out long, shimmering arias whose sinuous lines deny the listener the security of a conventional verse-chorus-verse structure. Once a card-carrying minimalist, the composer now weds a sturdy rhythmic pulse with a freer melodic and harmonic idiom that can evoke with equal aplomb a Monteverdi arioso, a Mendelssohn scherzo or *Duke of Earl.*

Goodman writes vigorous, stark verse whose impact is almost physical, combining flights of fancy with earthy images and expressions. The work has some flaws: the comic prologue seems superfluous, and the dense text demands supertitles. But none of this should impede its success. Adams, Goodman, Morris and Sellars are the foremost creative team working today on the operatic stage—and perhaps on any stage.

With Attitude

Here's a representative lyric from *Efil4zaggin,* the latest album by the rap group N.W.A. (Niggas with Attitude): "This is the bitch that did the whole crew/ She did it so much we made bets on who the ho would love to go through . . . / And she lets you videotape her/ And if you got a gang of niggers the bitch'll let you rape her."

In early summer *Efil4zaggin*—"niggaz4life" backward—was one of the best-selling pop albums in America. It was at the very top of *Billboard's* main chart—without benefit from a video on MTV, without the help of a hit single and, most amazingly, without getting much play on radio stations. N.W.A. raps nasty and righteous, with real ghetto heat, and doesn't give an inch: their fury is incendiary. Everything good about N.W.A.—and a lot that isn't—is straight street: smarts, attitude, language, beat. The album is a rap mural of ghetto life, spray-painted with blood. It is for hard-case rappers, and it is no sellout.

But if street-seasoned blacks won't be surprised by *Efil4zaggin,* they may be surprised by the company they're keeping. A major factor in the album's startling success was the appeal it had for another crucial segment of the record-buying public: white middle-class teenage males. Timothy White, editor of *Billboard,* thinks N.W.A.'s attraction for white male teens is "danger at a safe distance."

The fact is, *Efil4zaggin* is an entire open season for negative stereotyping. That's the classic rap posture, black male division, of course: turning the comic-book white fantasy of the black male as a murderous sexual stud into a hyperbolic reality.

Women, even more than cops, take the brunt of the abuse on the album. Listening to a continual obscene litany about bitches and hos is an exercise in brutalization. In Britain, Sinéad O'Connor has backed off her support of the group, saying their "attitudes have become increasingly dangerous. The way they deal with women in their songs is pathetic." N.W.A has serious stuff to say, but they are stifled by their ravening sexism. No excuse cuts it. Until that attitude changes, "the world's most dangerous group," as it bills itself, will be a threat above all to itself.

Misfit Metalheads

For the original cover of their monstrously successful 1987 debut album, *Appetite for Destruction,* Guns N' Roses selected a painting of a sinister robotic figure towering over a ravished female with her undergarments around her knees. The album, whose leitmotivs were violent sex, drug abuse, alcoholism and insanity, sold 14 million copies. Buoyed by this success, the Gunners in 1988 exhumed some archival material and released a stopgap, extended-play album that bashed police, "niggers," immigrants and "faggots." The record sold 6 million copies.

Buoyed by *this* success, the Gunners then made rock-'n'-roll history by simultaneously releasing two completely different albums with virtually identical covers: *Use Your Illusion I* and *Use Your Illusion II.* This time out, the Gunners, while clinging to their trademark bitch-slapping posture, have also introduced such engaging new subjects as bondage, the lure of homicide and the pleasures of drug-induced comas. They offer a song called *Pretty Tied Up,* accompanied by a drawing in the lyric sheet of a naked, bound and blindfolded woman. They also graphically invite the editor and publisher of *Spin* magazine, Bob Guccione Jr., to perform oral sex on the Guns N' Roses' irrepressible lead singer, W. Axl Rose.

When the two albums went on sale at midnight in late September, many large stores stayed open to accommodate sometimes raucous crowds of buyers who had milled about for hours. Nationwide, the albums sold an estimated 500,000 copies within two hours of going on sale, and 1.5 million copies within three days.

It would be unfair to attribute all, or even most, of Guns N' Roses' success to their unrelentingly sexist and uncompromisingly violent lyrics or their forays into xenophobia, racism and sadomasochism. Rock 'n' roll has always been filled with sexist, violent bands, but very few of them sell 14 million copies the first time out of the chute. What sets the Gunners apart is that they are a genuinely electrifying band that neither looks nor sounds like the interchangeable Whitesnakes, Poisons and Bon Jovis that make up the drab MTV universe. The new albums are exciting, well-produced records, with plenty of catchy rockers and only a handful of duds. The guitars are hot, the drumming is hot, the vocals are red-hot. What the Gunners *play* is very, very good. What the Gunners *say* is very, very bad. Of 30 songs on the new albums, 10 contain the *F* word. Anyone who can get past the offensive lyrics will be buying one of the best rock albums of the year. Or two of them.

From the Dud Museum

The exhibit of new paintings by David Salle at New York's Gagosian Gallery in the spring had one tiny merit. It reminded you how lousy and overpromoted so much "hot," "innovative" American art in the 1980s was. If Julian Schnabel is Exhibit A in our national wax museum of recent duds, David Salle is certainly Exhibit B.

In the '80s, Salle became about as successful as a young artist could get, analyzed at length in the art magazines, pursued by bleating flocks of new collectors. In 1987, when he was only 34, the Whitney Museum gave him a full-dress retrospective, a striking example of that institution's passive-masochistic relation to the art market.

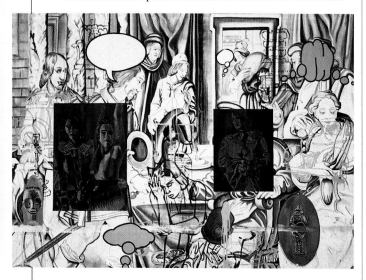

Yet is there a duller and more formula-ridden artist in America than Salle in 1991, as he approaches the big Four-Oh? His work, essentially, is a decoction from three other artists. From Robert Rauschenberg, Salle learned about piling unrelated images onto a canvas, the difference being that Salle hasn't a trace of the lyrical sharpness and poetic force of vintage Rauschenberg. From his German contemporary Sigmar Polke, Salle learned about hand painting his mass-media images. And from the late paintings of Francis Picabia, he extracted the banal mannerism of painting figures and things as though they were transparent, drawing them over the top of other things and figures.

One says "drawing" out of force of habit. At any rate, it is done with line. (It has to be, since Salle has no discernible sense of color: his range goes from putty to nasty anilines, but in this show a washed-out gray was the key.) Drawing is not what the artist does. He never learned to do it, and probably never will. He is incapable of making an interesting mark. The line has all the verve of chewed string. Mostly he traces, from slides projected on the canvas, often appropriating images from the Old Masters. And he traces very badly.

The next step is to patch in some disconnected quotes from modern life, like a comic-strip balloon or a nude, repeating them from picture to picture to lend an air of profundity to the series. Why? Because Salle, as everyone now knows, has discovered important metaphors of the meaningless overload of images in contemporary life. Thus his pictures enable critics to kvetch soulfully about the disassociation of signs and meanings and praise what all good little deconstructors would call their "refusal of authoritarian closure," meaning, roughly, that they don't mean anything in particular.

Lines That Go for a Walk

Brice Marden's "Cold Mountain" paintings of 1988-91—six of them, big ones, 9 ft. by 12 ft.—are a show and a half. How fast, how silently, the sight of a real sensibility at full stretch can cut through the visual jabber and white noise of so much of the gallery scene! On the evidence of these new works, Marden, 53, is now the finest American abstract painter of his generation.

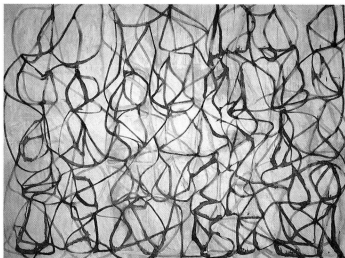

Every artist has prototypes, artists he or she admires and learns from—an internal homage that never ends. The problem is to subdue their authority, to bring their lessons into line with one's instincts. The artist who does this may be called mature. So with Marden, who with this show of huge, pale canvases covered with a loose tracery of inky line has reconciled his inheritance as a late modern American painter—chiefly, the work of Jackson Pollock—with his interests in Oriental art. Marden has made intense and complicated images out of this dialogue. His internal argument about his sources is settled, and the show is an exhilarating vindication of the expressive reach of abstract art: an argument for beauty.

"The line," wrote Paul Klee back in the days of the Bauhaus, "likes to go out for a walk." This is true of Marden's paintings, which at first sight seem to consist of nothing but line, moving across the surface in an improvised way—a maze making itself. There is a small amount of color in the paintings, but the prevalent hue of the gray-to-silver monochrome seems to change from canvas to canvas, emitting different tints of light. Marden scrapes back and sandpapers the canvas, leaving the ghosts of one layer of paint behind the other; this subtlety plays off against the roughness of the lines.

There is also a lot of blurring of the line itself; it is blotted when too dark or scrubbed so that smears are left; drips run down and impede its forward movement. The effect is to slow up the progress of the line enough to keep it from looking glib.

These are bold paintings, but not in a macho way. You don't get the image all at once, and the size of the canvases is meant not so much to impress you in the familiar, take-it-or-leave-it American fashion as to draw you slowly into the web. This, too, is part of Pollock's often misunderstood legacy. Looking at the "Cold Mountain" paintings one inevitably thinks of nature: thin they are, and austere, but also full of light and space. They suggest mountain landscapes, rocks half-effaced by blowing mist, sharp things incompletely seen.

How the West Was Spun

The first photograph in the catalog of "The West as America: Reinterpreting Images of the Frontier, 1820-1920," the large and deeply interesting show at Washington's National Museum of American Art, has to be one of the funniest ever seen in a museum. It is of Charles Schreyvogel, a turn-of-the-century Wild-West illustrator, painting in the open air. His subject crouches alertly before him: a cowboy pointing a six-gun. They are on the flat roof of an apartment building in Hoboken, N.J. Such was the "authentic West" of Schreyvogel and other painters like Frederic Remington and Charles Russell, circa 1903.

It is the right emblem for this show. Religious and national myths are made, not born; their depiction in art involves much staging, construction and editing, under the eye of cultural agreement. Whatever the crucifixion of a Jew on a knoll 2,000 years ago looked like, it wasn't Tintoretto. And the American West of the 19th century was rarely what American artists set out to make it seem.

What they left, instead, is a foundation myth in paint and stone. Its main character is God, the approving father, as manifested in the landscape. Its human actors are frontier scouts and settlers, cavalrymen and trappers and the American Indians—noble at first, then seen as degenerate enemies of progress as their resistance grew and finally as doomed phantoms. Its stage material includes the Conestoga wagon, the simple cabin, the teepee, the isolated fort and, at the end, symbol of absolute victory over nature, the California sequoia with a road cut through its trunk.

Among the painters of this myth were George Catlin, friend of the explorer William Clark and indefatigable painter of native tribes; George Caleb Bingham, that vigorous orderer of American genre scenes; the landscapists Albert Bierstadt and Thomas Moran; and a host of lesser figures, who also played their part in the creation of a heroic imagery of national conquest.

The exhibition shows how the vast exculpatory fiction of Manifest Destiny wound its way round the facts of conquest and turned them into art. It therefore does a valuable service, even in the banal aesthetic quality of much of the work in it—those earnest efforts of small talents whose work would not be worth studying except for the clarity with which it enshrines the obsessive themes of an expansionist America.

Zeitgeist in a Box

Big, narrative, tie-it-all-together museum exhibitions remain irresistible, but they are rarely as well done as "The 1920s: Age of the Metropolis." How do you put a zeitgeist in a box, albeit a box the size of a museum? Led by Jean Clair, the director of the Musée Picasso in Paris, six curators have set out to raise and question the

ghosts of the queen cities of Modernism: Paris, Berlin and New York—with detours to London, Weimar (for the Bauhaus), Cologne (for Dada) and Moscow (for Constructivism)—in the decade between the end of World War I and the 1929 Depression.

There are 688 works, ranging from Deco vases to documentary photos, from tiny collages to a De Havilland biplane and a huge, sleek Type 41 Bugatti Royale, the ultimate dream machine of the 1920s, with sharkskin-inlaid running boards. Even the school kids, who race through the rooms of painting and sculpture, fall into an awed hush in front of this one, as their ancestors were once supposed to shut up before a Rembrandt.

The show steers a didactic course through the recurrent images of jazz-age dreaming. No phase of modern art showed such profound doubts about the present, such anguish in the face of inhuman technology, or threw off such febrile dreams about new social orders. The city was seen as the mill of oppression, grinding women down into whoredom and men into anonymity. German artists like George Grosz and Karl Hubbuch imagined it as a grotesque theater, full of libido and irony.

Allied to this was the city as tomb, both futuristic and archaic, a kind of Mayan ruin referring only to itself, incomprehensible to its antlike inhabitants. This vision left its most startling images in the expressionist cinema. Then there is the international preoccupation with a benign Utopia—Europe's reaction against the horror of war —whose "spiritual" symbol was glass architecture.

In the 1920s Modernism was not only a vehicle for political protest or idealist reverie. It also became, for the first time, chic: it entered the salons and diffused through the decorative arts, especially in France. The birth of Art Deco is one of the themes of this show— designers' homages to larger avant-garde ideas: a Cubist table lamp, for instance, or "skyscraper" furniture. "Age of the Metropolis" is an intelligent wide-screen movie, generous in spirit, provocative and full of good things.

Wizard of Whiff

Many men in their middle years could identify with how this 44-year-old felt before dragging himself off to work. A pounding headache, an aching back, sharp pains in his heel, all added up to the poignant self-diagnosis: "I feel old today."

Who could blame Nolan Ryan for feeling the cold chill of his own mortality as he braced himself to start his 711th game in the majors? Sure, Ryan bestrode the baseball record book like a colossus, with more strikeouts and more no-hitters than any pitcher in history. But decay is an inevitable stage in the human condition. And Ryan was facing the powerful Toronto Blue Jays, whose youthful lineup included three players who had not even been born when the Texas Rangers' star broke into the big leagues back in 1966.

With all these aches and pains, Ryan's fate was predictable; he was carried from the field. But the only injury was to the Blue Jays; Ryan's joyous teammates hoisted him to their shoulders after he pitched his seventh no-hitter, a time-warp classic that even the self-effacing Texan described as "my most overpowering night." Only

two Blue Jays reached first base on walks; only four hitters managed to loft fly balls to the outfield. The scorecard for the game looked like a bowl of Special K, the letter baseball uses to symbolize each of Ryan's 16 strikeouts.

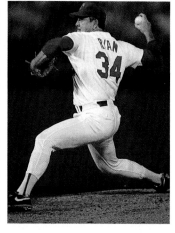

Earlier on the same magical day, the Oakland A's left fielder Rickey Henderson purloined third base against the New York Yankees to eclipse Lou Brock's career record of 938 stolen bases. Afterward, Henderson crowed, "Today I'm the greatest of all time."

Still in his prime at 32, Henderson predicts that his theft total could reach 1,600 by the time he retires. Of course, ageless Nolan Ryan may yet be out on the mound even then, throwing heat, defying defeat and blazing new standards for the game's élite.

Yo, Michael! You're the Best!

Michael Jordan is an icon who grows more revered by the day. When Jordan led the Chicago Bulls to their first N.B.A. championship in June against the Los Angeles Lakers, he removed the last shadow on a peerless career: the notion that great players who never win a title are somehow less great than those who do. In conquering the Lakers, Jordan did the very thing that is hardest for a virtuoso talent: he used his genius to raise the talents of those around him.

Countless odes have been sung to Jordan's uncanny, unearthly, preternatural ability to defy gravity. But amid the oohing and aahing over his impossible dunks, something important is usually overlooked: Jordan's passing. It was Michael's sharp assists to guard John Paxson, not his 30 spectacular points, that won the day and the series. Jordan's passing violates two sacrosanct rules: don't go up in the air unless you know what you're going to do there, and don't throw the ball crosscourt. Jordan found the open man because he has a map of the court and all its players inside his head. Now that he has won an N.B.A. championship, he doesn't really have anything left to prove—except, of course, that he can do it again.

The Last Shall Be First

They picked Cinderella for last place too, and she did all right. But even in a fairy tale, no one expects Prince Charming to be that ungainly lad who had been kept in the cellar for the past three years.

The improbable is for fables: baseball, right now at least, is the art of the impossible. In a century of the sport, no team had vaulted in a single year from worst in its league to best. This year two teams did. After a decade or so of balky, highly paid superstars, the Minnesota Twins and Atlanta Braves built their franchises on gonna-bes and has-beens. The Braves sported new good young talent: Steve Avery, David Justice and John Smoltz. The Twins featured older stars—Kirby Puckett, Jack Morris and Chili Davis—who brought gravity and intensity to the contests. Call it postmodern baseball.

And when the World Series was over—when the last hanky had been waved and the last tomahawk chopped—many Americans described the 7-game matchup as the greatest of all time. With extra innings, home-run heroics, plays at the plate, and glowering pitchers dueling past prime time, the games were a celebration of the sport. Oh, yes: the Twins won.

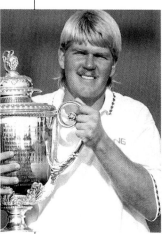

Daly Double

The week after his awesome display of power won him the 1991 P.G.A. Championship, John Daly got ready to hit a few practice balls in preparation for the International tourney at Colorado's Castle Pines Golf Club. As word spread that he was on the practice tee, a crowd gathered, whistling appreciatively as he casually knocked iron shots into the far reaches of the range.

Then he took out his titanium-shafted Cobra driver, and the whistles turned to disbelieving laughter as he started launching balls over the road beyond the driving

range. Nearby pros broke off their own practice regimens to watch the ballistic display. A few minutes later Daly headed for the course. His first drive was a monster 364-yd. shot, followed by a 280-yd. 3-iron blast. In short order, Daly turned the 644-yd., par-5 first hole, the longest on the P.G.A. tour, into an ordinary par 4.

Daly makes fans remember that golf is a thrilling sport. Rarely pausing for more than a quick glance, Daly plays as though he were being pursued by revenuers. His simple philosophy—"I just hit it as hard as I can, and if I find the ball I hit it again"—strikes a responsive chord in galleries. Moreover, Daly is a self-made player. He says he learned to hit the ball by watching Jack Nicklaus on TV, and by experimenting with what felt natural on a rural nine-hole course in Dardanelle, Ark. Having triumphed in the P.G.A., he improved on his victory by promising $30,000 of the $230,000 prize to the children of a spectator killed by lightning at the tournament.

Get Mad, Jimbo!

Over the years, Jimmy Connors has treated spectators to phenomenal displays of tennis and temper—and at the 1991 U.S. Open, he exhibited both again. In the second set of a match against Aaron Krickstein, Connors flared up when the umpire overruled a linesman and called one of his passing shots wide. In a one-minute tantrum, the 39-year-old, five-time Open winner called the offending official "a bum," "a son of a bitch" and "an abortion." From then on, Connors played brilliantly, and he took the 4-hr. 41-min. match in a tempestuous tie-breaker, before advancing again three days later.

The abuse, though it drew no penalty from Open officials, appalled onlookers. Some Connors watchers, however, recognized that such displays may be an integral, even calculated, part of Connors' game. "The world may see a spoiled brat," observes David Pargman, a sports psychologist at Florida State University, "but some élite athletes turn on the anger strategically." Anger steps up the body's pitch: blood pressure rises, heart and respiration rates quicken, and adrenaline surges.

Connors' performance was the adrenaline in this Open. He thrilled crowds—and inspired the middle-aged everywhere—before bowing out in the semifinal round. The consensus verdict: Connors may not have lasted until the final match—but the 1991 Open belonged to him.

Tragedy of an Ex-Champ

Mike Tyson has inspired many epithets: the Mighty Joe Young of boxing, Don King's twisted Trilby, America's most volcanic son-in-law. For three years he was also known as the heavyweight champion of the world. But the organizer of the Miss Black America Pageant topped all name callers. In a $21 million lawsuit alleging sexual assault of 11 of the 23 contestants at July's competition, J. Morris Anderson charged the ex-champ with being "a serial buttocks fondler."

Tyson was staggered by the body punches of accusations stemming from his appearance at the Indianapolis pageant. An 18-year-old contestant says the fighter raped her in a hotel room. Miss Black America of 1990, the first to make the buttock-fondling charge, sued Tyson for $100 million. The allegations—and a later injury—aborted Tyson's November fight with current title holder Evander Holyfield—the ex-champ's chance to recapture his old glory and the awe he once commanded in and outside the ring.

A champ is expected to be a role model: a monster at work, a gentleman at play. But Tyson also needed to live out the fight-fan's fantasy—and maybe his own—that he is the world's baddest stud. His worst offense may be in believing that he is what he does.

Lo-o-ong Jump

The record had stood unapproachably majestic for 23 years, a distance of 29 ft. 2½ in., about the length of a medium-size truck, easily traversed by a motorcycle daredevil propelled off a ramp—but not by unaided tendon, sinew, flesh and blood. Only a few dared challenge the long-jump record—the oldest and most awesome in track and field—set in 1968 when the American Bob Beamon flung himself through the thin Olympic air of high-altitude Mexico City. Beamon never got close to his record again.

If anyone might have been expected to break Beamon's record, Carl Lewis was it. He is the king of track and field. In late August, Lewis proved he could still be the fastest human alive, when he set a new world record of 9.86 sec. to take the 100-m gold medal at the World Track and Field Championships in Tokyo. He turned in the greatest sequence of long jumps ever recorded. No one had ever soared so far and so consistently over six tries, all well past 28 ft., brushing against the record.

Limbering up in Lewis' shadow was Mike Powell, 27, an American who had chafed under the superstar's decade-long domination of track and field. Powell's first four tries were unimpressive. But the fifth came with a veritable thunderclap. He had broken Beamon's mark by a full 2 in. From the sidelines the eclipsed Lewis watched Powell claim victory, brushed off tears and walked away.

It's Coming Back to Me Now

A reasonable citizen may wonder what George Foreman, Bjorn Borg, Larry Holmes, Sugar Ray Leonard, Nancy Lieberman Cline, John McEnroe, Jim Palmer, Mark Spitz and Jill Sterkel have in common. A reasonable answer might be they're nuts. They all tried comebacks in 1991, holding high the torch for middle-aged wheezers everywhere.

It could be that these veteran athletes aren't being unrealistic. "We've always had this dogma that the human body peaks at age 26 to 28 and then goes into a slow decline," says Rick Sharp, a professor of exercise physiology at Iowa State University. "But in fact, what we were seeing was not the effects of aging per se, but of increasingly sedentary lifestyles."

Athletic ability consists of three elements. Endurance generally peaks in the late 20s and is sustainable into the mid-30s, then deteriorates slowly. Strength peaks later, perhaps not until the 40s, then deteriorates even more slowly. Coordination, including reflexes, can be maintained at nearly 100% capability until 50.

Consider George Foreman, 42. He isn't spoiled, folks, just nicely ripened. He trains hard, sparring with four partners in succession for 21 consecutive minutes, pushing, slogging that thunderous right hand, crowding. In his April fight against Evander Holyfield, he fought with honor to the final bell. Holyfield retained the crown; Foreman's was a different sort of laurel.

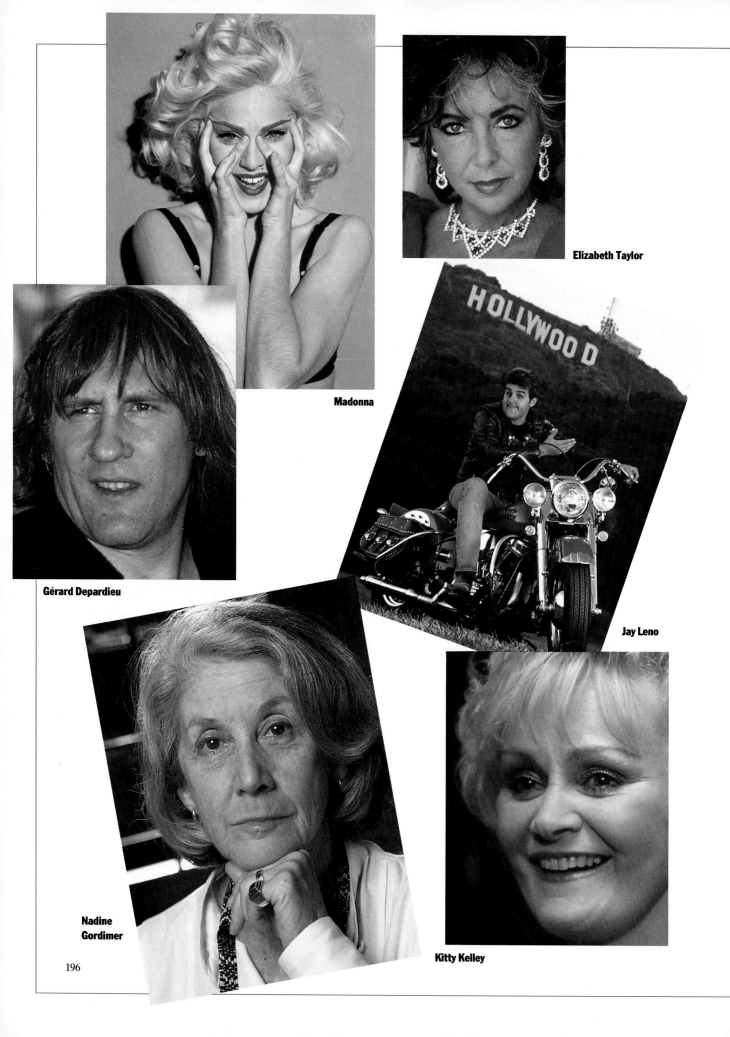

Elizabeth Taylor

Madonna

Gérard Depardieu

Jay Leno

Nadine Gordimer

Kitty Kelley

John Singleton

He is only 23 years old, but movie director John Singleton's first film, *Boyz N the Hood*, about young black males coming of age in the gang-ridden inner-city war zone known as South Central Los Angeles, grossed $56 million in four months. Singleton grew up in South Central, where "from the time I was born, I looked out the window and there was this 70-ft. screen (a drive-in theater) with movies on it." He read widely and enrolled at the University of Southern California film school, where he won three prizes for as many screenplays. "I bring a street sensibility to the business of Hollywood," he says. "It helps me survive. Here, instead of a trusty gun, you need a good lawyer and an agent."

Madonna

For a long time, Madonna seemed like a rebelette without a cause vamping for the world's attention. Now she has it. Not content to continue spinning out mere dance-floor fodder, she has used her bully pulpit to preach scantily clad homilies on bigotry, abortion, civic duty, power, love, death, safe sex, grief and the importance of families. At 33, she has three world tours, 20-plus music videos, seven feature films and eight albums under her Boy Toy belt. Her 1991 catharsis was *Truth or Dare*, a panoramic, emetic, beauty-marks-and-all feature-length autobiographical documentary shot during her Blond Ambition tour. "I am not going to be anybody's patsy," she declared. "I am not going to be anybody's good girl."

Nadine Gordimer

In 1991 Nadine Gordimer, 68, became the first woman in 25 years to win the Nobel Prize for Literature. The news pleased readers and critics of her 20 works of fiction and prompted an interesting response in South Africa, where she has lived all her life, and where three of her books were once officially banned. President F.W. de Klerk congratulated her for "this exceptional achievement, which is also an honor to South Africa." Such praise from a South African head of state would not so long ago have been unthinkable. For nearly 40 years Gordimer has spoken out against apartheid; yet she told TIME, "That's not my subject. My subject has been living in that country and the people who live there."

Pee-wee Herman

Alas, poor Pee-wee. His hyperkinetic nerdiness was irresistible to millions of children—and others. But in mid-summer, Pee-wee was slaughtered by bad publicity. Paul Reubens, 39, the actor who played the Pee-wee character, was arrested in a Sarasota, Fla., porn-movie theater and charged with "exposure of sexual organs," which means masturbation. Result: a kangaroo court, endless jokes, public hanging and quick burial on TV boot hill. CBS yanked the remaining repeat episodes of *Pee-wee's Playhouse;* Disney-MGM Studios pulled a two-minute clip featuring Pee-wee at its Orlando theme park.

Alexandra Ripley

"Margaret Mitchell is a better writer," said Alexandra Ripley, "but she's dead." Ripley, 57, had tangled with the ghost of Mitchell in writing *Scarlett,* the carefully prepared, shrewdly promoted, authorized sequel to *Gone With the Wind*. The "publicity foreplay is more exciting than what goes on between the covers," pronounced TIME's R.Z. Sheppard, speaking for most critics. But Ripley had the last laugh: *Scarlett* became the biggest best-seller in many years. Although her contract with Mitchell's estate provided for a sequel to the sequel, Ripley claimed she would not write it. But tomorrow is another day.

Kitty Kelley

When America's slash biographer, Kitty Kelley, 49, published *Nancy Reagan: The Unauthorized Biography,* many bookstores sold out their copies. The book dug up every catty comment uttered about Nancy. Turning the tables, TIME interviewed journalists who had investigated Kelley. Their conclusion: she practices the same kind of petty reprisals she has confronted in her Hoovering of public figures. When Washington *Post* critic Jonathan Yardley panned an earlier book, he received a gilded box containing fish heads, and a card signed "From the friends of Kitty Kelley."

Elizabeth Taylor

The couple had eleven marriages between them. But this ceremony stood out. Elizabeth Taylor, 59, wed blue-collar hero Larry Fortensky in Michael Jackson's backyard, to the tune of roaring press helicopters overhead. The service was performed by a spiritual psychotherapist (anybody can get a priest) in a gazebo. All in all, it was the craziest media event since Sean married Madonna. In a '90s update on "meeting cute," Liz found her construction-worker husband when both were enrolled in rehabilitation programs at the Betty Ford Center.

Jay Leno

The world had long known that anvil-jawed Jay Leno, *The Tonight Show's* exclusive guest host since 1987, was bound to succeed Johnny Carson. But when NBC made it official in June, press tattle hinted that David Letterman, who gave Leno his first sustained TV exposure, was furious and planned to sue NBC to break his contract. He didn't. Once upon a time, the ringmaster of Stupid Pet Tricks was indeed Carson's heir apparent, Bonnie Prince Dave. But now Leno will assume command over the United Kingdom of Late Night. Letterman gets to keep Wales.

Gerard Depardieu

Kevin Costner's *Dances with Wolves* won seven statuettes at the 1991 Oscar awards, but it was one of the evening's losers who provided the biggest flap. Gérard Depardieu, who was nominated for Best Actor for *Cyrano de Bergerac,* was a no-show at the ceremony. Even so, he was at the center of a fire storm over comments about his wild days as a youth. The ruckus stemmed from a TIME story about the French film star published in late January. Depardieu, 42, was asked about his 1978 remark to a film magazine: "I had plenty of rapes, too many to count." Asked by TIME if he had participated in rapes, Depardieu said yes. "But it was absolutely normal in those circumstances," he added. The admission drew an outcry, and the star later denied making the statements and threatened TIME with libel. Interestingly, while Americans were shocked by the star's blasé attitude, the French came to Depardieu's defense, seeing the brouhaha as an example of American prudishness.

TIME
The Weekly Newsmagazine

■ Frank Capra

Their basic business being the creation of images, not many movie directors contribute a word to the language. But Frank Capra did. The word, of course, is Capraesque. To most people the term signifies almost any improbable but inspirational story in which an idealistic little guy, though his principles may waver, ultimately triumphs first over self-doubt, then over the big guys determined to exploit him and his class. The movie that epitomizes all this is *It's a Wonderful Life*. Which is too bad. For Capra was a moviemaker whose range and gifts far exceeded any one-picture definition. The emphasis on the heartwarming content of his films has obscured the sometimes heartstopping skill with which he orchestrated his themes. It is because his technique was so sophisticated that he achieved the whopping suspensions of disbelief his stories required.

A Sicilian immigrant who revered America for the opportunities it offered him, Capra knew in his bones the kind of life he would later celebrate; he crammed his frame with people who talked and moved just a little faster, a little more eccentrically than they did in real life. He achieved his breakthrough with his 24th film, *It Happened One Night*; its success gave him the budget clout to make his great trilogy of *Mr. Deeds Goes to Town* (1936), *Mr. Smith Goes to Washington* (1939) and *Meet John Doe* (1941).

In Capra's last years, official, award-giving America insisted on honoring him as a man of simple sentiment. His nature and achievements were much richer and more complex than that, and they cry out for history's healing revisionism.

■ Graham Greene

No serious writer of this century more thoroughly invaded and shaped the public imagination than did Graham Greene, who died in April at 86. Millions who have never read him are nonetheless familiar with his vision. Versions of Greene scenes can be found in daily headlines or wherever entertainment flickers: the dubious quest, undertaken by a flawed agent with divided loyalties against an uncertain enemy; the wrench of fear or of violence that confronts an otherwise ordinary person with a vision of eternal damnation or inexplicable grace.

Birth and circumstances drove Greene to a life on the edge. He found himself a double agent at a tender age, a student at the Berkhamsted School, where his father reigned as headmaster. Naturally, his classmates made his life miserable, and Greene sought retreat in voracious reading. At Oxford he dabbled in writing and later drifted into newspaper work. He converted to Roman Catholicism, and his beliefs served in his fiction both as a stern gauge by which to measure the behavior of fallen mortals and as a powerful source of divine mercy.

His first published novel, *The Man Within* (1929), enjoyed a modest success and was made into a film. Greene learned and used the economies of filmed narration—the quick cuts, the disembodied perspective, the interpolated conversations. His greatest fiction spanned the years 1938 to '51: *Brighton Rock* (1938), *The Heart of the Matter* (1948), *The End of the Affair* (1951) and, most hauntingly, *The Power and the Glory* (1940). The pilgrimage of the nameless "whiskey priest," on the run in a Mexican state from a sectarian tyranny, remains a thrilling adventure of despair and irrational redemption.

■ Joseph Papp

He was born into an America that still believed in the limitless potential of self-education and upward mobility, that considered high art and great ideas accessible to ordinary working people. He grew up in a Brooklyn household where Yiddish was the mother tongue; his father made trunks by hand and peddled peanuts from a pushcart. Young Yosl Papirofsky awakened to the arts in public schools. In junior high school he discovered Shakespeare, memorizing a speech from *Julius Caesar* as a class assignment and liking it so much he mastered another for fun. He didn't go to college: his family had no money, and his country went to war.

When he died in October at 70, having been the most influential figure in the American theater over the past quarter-century, Joseph Papp was recalled as an impresario, nonprofit-institution builder, star-maker and celebrity. In early years, when his theater was a flatbed truck and a stretch of grass in a park, he nurtured Colleen Dewhurst and James Earl Jones. Later Robert De Niro, Al Pacino and Michelle Pfeiffer would turn to him for a chance at something serious. Playwrights David Rabe and David Henry Hwang ripened with Papp; so did Vaclav Havel. His productions won three Pulitzer Prizes and 28 Tony Awards—nine for *A Chorus Line,* which had a record run on Broadway from 1975 to 1990.

Papp's vital legacy was neither his shows nor his institution but his audiences. He always saw himself as a belligerent radical. Yet his passion was a deeply conservative idea: that art, culture and tradition should form a central force in the life of every human being.

■ Theodor Seuss Geisel

He was one of the last doctors to make house calls—some 200 million of them in 20 languages. By the time of his death at 87, Dr. Seuss occupied a unique and hallowed place in the nurseries of the world. Actually, the title was as imaginary as the name: the first doctorate Theodor Seuss Geisel ever earned was an honorary one, given by his alma mater, Dartmouth. Following college and Oxford, he and his wife returned to the states in time for the Depression, and Theodor fed his soul by trying to write serious novels and filled the refrigerator by concocting an ad campaign for a spray insecticide: "Quick, Henry, the Flit."

Successful but frustrated, he amused himself by writing a volume for the very young: *And to Think That I Saw It on Mulberry Street*, which became an instant hit. The Seuss style was born fully developed: looping, free-style drawings; clanging, infectious rhymes; and a relentless logic.

In the 1950s Seuss began a one-Dr. battle against illiteracy. For beginning readers he created an overnight success, *The Cat in the Hat*, with a vocabulary of 220 words. Best seller followed best seller; prize followed award. Generations devoured *Green Eggs and Ham* and *Yertle the Turtle*. He was given an Oscar for the animated cartoon *Gerald McBoing-Boing*, Emmys for Grinch TV specials, a Pulitzer citation. The childless author eventually lost interest in writing for grown-ups. He proclaimed that "adults are obsolete children, and the hell with them." Reason enough to believe:

> It was T.S. Geisel who provoked all the chortles,
>
> But it's old Dr. Seuss who has joined the immortals.

■ I.B. Singer

It was easy for Isaac Bashevis Singer to believe in miracles. He was proof that they existed. In 1935 the rabbi's son journeyed from Warsaw to New York City to visit his brother, novelist Israel Joshua Singer, and thereby escaped the Holocaust. He described vanished worlds in a dying language to a dwindling audience and was awarded the 1978 Nobel Prize for Literature. He was unknown at 40, but in July, when I.B. Singer died of a stroke at the age of 87, he was the most applauded Polish-born writer since Joseph Conrad.

Singer had every right to act the celebrity, yet he was never at home in the modern style. His works were often published first in Yiddish and later in translation. Saul Bellow brought him wide recognition by rendering the poignant anecdote *Gimpel the Fool* in English. But royalties were slow to arrive, and for many years Singer lived modestly on the earnings of his second wife Alma, a buyer at Saks Fifth Avenue.

When I.J. Singer died in 1944, I.B. assumed the literary role. But the elder brother had been a rationalist and a radical. The younger one was apolitical and haunted by "a God who speaks in deeds, not in words, and whose vocabulary is the universe." The biblical and supernatural tales of youth provided the underpinnings of his work. As his rickety Yiddish typewriter chattered away, the ghettos of the Middle Ages rose up again, with a cast of erotic shtetl dwellers and phosphorescent imps. The Jews of 20th century Europe, consumed by the Nazi death camps, were granted the powers of speech and lust. None of his novels, plays, autobiographies or children's books could be categorized—except as productions of the last authentic teller of folktales.

■ Martha Graham

Martha Graham finally retired from the stage at 75, but the decision came hard. A friend suggested she must remember that she was not a goddess but a mortal. "That's difficult," Graham replied, "when you see yourself as a goddess and behave like one."

When she died in April, at 96, dance lovers could hardly believe she had succumbed to any physical weakness. She was the reigning deity of modern dance. If she did not invent it—there are always forerunners in any movement—she embodied it, propagated it, imposed a clear discipline and aesthetic on a new, inchoate art. Her personal flair—her Easter Island mask of a face, her extravagantly theatrical wardrobe—made her slightest gestures, onstage or off, indelible.

The hallmark of her choreography, as well as her performances, was fierce concentration and intensity. She went for the biggest, broadest gesture, the most vivid rage, the most startling image of love. What interested her was not the airiness and elevation of ballet. She made the earth her touchstone and reveled in the downward pull of gravity.

Her early dance inspiration was surprising: Ruth St. Denis, who charmed audiences with free-form creations perfumed with the exoticism of the Orient. Entranced, Graham joined the Denishawn company, but left in 1923 to try Broadway dancing. By 1926 she had formed a group and the masterpieces began to flow, as they would over several decades. There was a cluster of distinctively American works, such as *Letter to the World*, about Emily Dickinson, and the ever vernal *Appalachian Spring*. Though a quintessential modernist, she was attracted to doomed classical heroines: Clytemnestra, Medea, Alcestis, Phaedra. At the heart of her artistic revolution lay an indomitable commitment to honesty in motion.

■ **Claudio Arrau,** 88, one of the premier piano virtuosos of the 20th century. Born in Chile in 1903, for the next eight decades Arrau would dazzle audiences worldwide with a unique blend of brute strength and introspective clarity. Critics hailed his performances of Liszt, Chopin, Brahms and Debussy.

■ **Lee Atwater,** 40, former chairman of the Republican National Committee. A savvy political strategist who managed George Bush's 1988 presidential campaign, Atwater was often criticized for his "pit bull" style, as in his use of the Willie Horton commercial during the 1988 campaign.

■ **Klaus Barbie,** 77, "the Butcher of Lyons," the Gestapo commander who ordered the execution and deportation of thousands of French citizens, mostly Jews and Resistance members. In 1983 the Bolivian government expelled Barbie, and he was returned to France, where he was convicted in 1987 of crimes against humanity and sentenced to life in prison.

■ **John Bardeen,** 82, a co-inventor of the transistor, the tiny device that heralded the revolution in modern, miniaturized electronics and earned him a Nobel Prize in 1956. Later he won a second Nobel (with two others) for their theory of low-temperature superconductivity.

■ **James ("Cool Papa") Bell,** 87, fleet-footed Baseball Hall of Famer. From 1922 to 1936 and from 1942 to 1950, Bell compiled an estimated .340 average in the Negro leagues as a pitcher and outfielder for nine different teams.

■ **Paul Brown,** 82, football innovator who founded and coached the Cleveland Browns and the Cincinnati Bengals. He started the Browns in 1946, and by the time he was fired as the coach 13 years later, the team had won three N.F.L. championships.

■ **Miles Davis,** 65, jazz trumpeter whose restless ear compelled him to invent new sounds. "Don't play what you know," Davis said. "Play what you hear." His music was about taking risks, and it went through enormous changes as Davis reworked bop, cool jazz or fusion. His single rule—never go back—sent him in recent years into unexplored regions of electrified jazz and funk that disappointed some loyalists.

■ **Christian de la Croix de Castries,** 88, aristocratic French cavalry officer and brigadier general who doggedly defended but finally lost the Vietnam fortress of Dien Bien Phu in a grueling 57-day siege. The 1954 defeat led directly to the signing of a truce agreement in Geneva that divided Vietnam into a communist north and pro-Western south.

■ **Colleen Dewhurst,** 67, raspy-voiced Tony Award–winning actress. Although she appeared in a number of television and feature films, Dewhurst was most identified with the dramas of Eugene O'Neill on Broadway. She played the forlorn, drug-plagued Mary Tyrone in *Long Day's Journey into Night* and the murderous Christine Mannon in *Mourning Becomes Electra.* Dewhurst won a 1974 Tony as best dramatic actress for her portrayal of Josie Hogan in *A Moon for the Misbegotten.*

■ **Leo Durocher,** 86, combative baseball manager who piloted the Brooklyn Dodgers and the New York Giants into three World Series and whose hard-boiled comment about a rival team ("Nice guys finish last") captured the unforgiving side of American sports.

■ **Clarence Leo Fender,** 81, inventor of the 1954 Stratocaster, the electric guitar whose design has become an industry standard. Favored by rock legends such as Buddy Holly and Jimi Hendrix, the Strat has been used to play everything from country to blues to heavy metal.

■ **Eugene Fodor,** 85, peripatetic creator of travel guides. Fodor invited readers not only to see the sights but also to immerse themselves in foreign cultures' different mores. More than 3 million guides, covering 93 countries, encompassing 128 titles and several languages, are sold worldwide each year.

■ **Margot Fonteyn,** 71, legendary prima ballerina. She distinguished herself in a 50-year career with a classical, graceful but passionate style. Memorable performances in *The Sleeping Beauty, Swan Lake, Giselle* and *Romeo and Juliet* thrilled audiences worldwide. In 1962, at 42, Dame Margot started a dynamic partnership with Rudolf Nureyev, who was 19 years younger. They danced together until the late 1970s. Said Nureyev: "For me she represents eternal youth."

■ **Ernest ("Tennessee Ernie") Ford,** 72, avuncular, pipe-puffing country singer whose recording of *Sixteen Tons,* Merle Travis' paean to the workingman, was one of the biggest-selling hits of the 1950s. Host of television variety shows in the 1950s and '60s, Ford especially loved singing hymns and spirituals and sold more than 24 million gospel-music albums.

■ **Charles Goren,** 90, contract-bridge champion whose syndicated newspaper column and how-to books became synonymous with the game. Goren, who became known as Mr. Bridge in the 1950s, introduced a point-counting system that is still used by most American bridge players.

■ **Bill Graham,** 60, rock-concert promoter who ushered the psychedelic era onstage. In the late 1960s, Graham's Fillmore West in San Francisco and Fillmore East in New York City were spawning grounds for the careers of the Grateful Dead, Jefferson Airplane, Janis Joplin, Santana and other counter-culture stars.

■ **Harold ("Red") Grange,** 87, artful, wing-footed running back (the "Galloping Ghost"), whose heroic exploits gave professional football its first and decisive respectability while he played with the Chicago Bears in the 1920s and 1930s.

■ **Howard Head,** 76, inventor of the Head metal ski and the Prince tennis racket. An aircraft engineer, he applied his expertise to replacing the bulky wooden ski with an aluminum model. The new product was as big a hit with weekend skiers as with Olympic medal winners. Later, Head joined the Prince Manufacturing Co. and revolutionized the tennis racquet. His design improved the game of countless players by almost quadrupling the sweet spot of the racquet.

■ **Soichiro Honda,** 84, pioneering Japanese manufacturer who built his motorcycle company into a global automotive giant. A hands-on mechanic as well as a visionary, Honda scored his first success in postwar Japan by selling bicycles powered by military-surplus engines. Defying government bureaucrats who tried to limit Japan's auto industry to a few dominant firms, Honda began making cars in 1963, and in 1982 became the first Japanese automaker to build cars in the U.S.

■ **Klaus Kinski,** 65, actor who created haunting portraits of tortured protagonists in Werner Herzog's films, most notably the power-mad conquistador in *Aguirre, the Wrath of God* and the possessed soldier in *Woyzeck*. He was the father of film actress Nastassia Kinski.

■ **Jerzy Kosinski,** 57, brooding Polish-born author of *The Painted Bird, Steps* and *Being There*. In his writings, Kosinski explored themes drawn from his hellish childhood as a Jew in Nazi-occupied Poland and its reverberations in his adult life.

■ **Edwin Land,** 81, an inventor of instant photography and founder of Polaroid Corp. Land patented more than 500 inventions, including instant X rays, polarized sunglasses and a 3-D movie projector.

■ **Michael Landon,** 54, boyishly handsome actor, best known for playing Little Joe Cartwright in *Bonanza,* and writer, director and producer of television hits. In 1957 Landon starred in the cult film favorite *I Was a Teenage Werewolf*. His part in *Bonanza,* which aired from 1959 to 1973, made him a household name. Landon subsequently starred in and wrote many of the episodes of *Little House on the Prairie,* solidifying a reputation for creating wholesome family entertainment.

■ **David Lean,** 83, the rajah of imperial cinema. An old-fashioned adventurer, Lean saw the whole world as a sumptuous back lot. He bivouacked in Sri Lanka for *The Bridge on the River Kwai,* on the Irish coast for *Ryan's Daughter,* and in Jordan, Morocco and Spain for his masterpiece, *Lawrence of Arabia*. The director's films, which won 28 Academy Awards, spread the most intimate emotions—a lover's restlessness in *Doctor Zhivago,* a child's rootlessness in *Oliver Twist*—on a huge, beautiful canvas.

■ **Fred MacMurray,** 83, television's quintessential father figure. Adept at comedy and drama, MacMurray's stage, film and TV career spanned five decades. Although he played the proverbial good guy in Disney movies and in TV's *My Three Sons,* MacMurray's most memorable roles went against type: a crooked insurance agent in *Double Indemnity* (1944), a cowardly, ambitious Navy lieutenant in *The Caine Mutiny* (1954) and a philandering husband in *The Apartment* (1960).

■ **Belinda Mason,** 33, AIDS activist and writer. Mason became infected with the HIV virus in 1987 while receiving a blood transfusion. She became an AIDS-rights advocate and was named by President Bush to the National Commission on AIDS. She was critical of the Administration, saying it treated the AIDS epidemic as a moral issue instead of as a public-health crisis.

■ **Floyd McKissick,** 69, maverick civil rights leader. In 1947 McKissick helped lead the first integrated bus ride through the South. Four years later, following a protracted legal battle, he won admission to the all-white University of North Carolina Law School. As director of the Congress of Racial Equality, McKissick stressed the need for blacks to seek economic as well as political power. In 1972 he surprised his supporters by switching from the Democratic to the Republican Party.

■ **Yves Montand,** 70, durable French entertainer who in later life achieved international film stardom. The Italian-born Montand gained fame as a singer and protégé of his lover Edith Piaf, with whom he appeared in his first film *(Star Without Light)*. He won highest acclaim for his role as a scheming peasant in Claude Berri's two-part film adaptation of Marcel Pagnol's *Jean de Florette* and *Manon of the Spring*.

■ **Robert Motherwell,** 76, founding member of the Abstract Expressionist school of American painting. He was especially renowned for the series he painted from 1949 to 1976 known as *Elegies to the Spanish Republic,* a sequence of funereal images that evoke prison bars and bullfighters' hats. Lauding Motherwell's collages, TIME art critic Robert Hughes said he was "the only artist since Matisse in the '50s to alter significantly the syntax of this quintessentially modernist medium."

■ **Arthur Murray,** 95, ballroom-dancing teacher. Murphy sought to overcome shyness and an ungainliness by learning dancing from a girlfriend. In the 1920s, through a thriving mail-order business and studios, he capitalized on the dance craze sweeping the country; among his students were Lowell Thomas and the Duke of Windsor. By his retirement in 1964, Murray had parlayed his nimble feet and business skills into an empire of 350 franchised studios that grossed $25 million a year.

■ **Harry Reasoner,** 68, avuncular television newsman who brought a droll flavor to his reporting for CBS News, especially on *60 Minutes,* which he helped launch in 1968.

■ **Lee Remick,** 55, graceful, versatile actress who won an Academy Award nomination for Best Actress for portraying a tormented alcoholic in 1962's *Days of Wine and Roses*. Her 1966 performance on Broadway in *Wait Until Dark,* as a blind woman terrorized by criminals, resulted in a Tony nomination.

■ **Tony Richardson,** 63, director who helped lead the "Angry Young Man" revolution in British drama in the 1950s and '60s. Richardson won acclaim for his staging of John Osborne's *Look Back in Anger* in 1956. He directed Laurence Olivier in the film *The Entertainer* (1960), and won a 1963 Academy Award for best director for his uproarious version of *Tom Jones*.

■ **Gene Roddenberry,** 70, visionary television producer and creator of *Star Trek*. His series (1966-69) imagined a future of intergalactic travel that spawned millions of passionately devoted fans—"Trekkies"—and six motion pictures.

■ **Florence Seibert,** 93, biochemist who developed a process that made intravenous transfusion safe and refined an accurate skin test for tuberculosis.

■ **Rudolf Serkin,** 88, one of the world's most brilliant concert pianists and teachers. A skilled technician, he hailed from the Viennese tradition that mingled the instrument's classical and romantic styles. In 1950 he helped found the Marlboro Music Festival in Vermont.

■ **Danny Thomas,** 79, comedian and philanthropist. In the 1950s and '60s he starred in the television series *Make Room for Daddy* and *The Danny Thomas Show* as the family's cranky but kind patriarch.

■ **Robert Wagner,** 80, influential mayor of New York City from 1954 to 1965. Widely regarded as one of the best mayor's in the city's history and admired for his integrity, Wagner managed to defeat Tammany Hall, the Democratic Party machine that influenced city and state politics for 150 years.

INDEX

Cover: (left to right) Thomas Hartwell; David Burnett/Contact; Dennis Brack/Black Star; Terry Ashe ● **Contents** 4 (top) Rick Maiman/Sygma; (bottom left) Joel Simon Images; (bottom right) Anthony Suau/Black Star ● 5 (top left) Ted Thai; (top right) Stephanie Compoint/Sygma; (middle) Steve Hart/TIME; (bottom left) Lawrence Burr/Gamma Liaison; (bottom right) Roland Neveu/MGM ● **Essay** 8 Najlah Feanny/SABA ● **Patterns** 12/13 Nigel Holmes/TIME ● 14/15 Holmes, Telak/TIME ● 16/17 Joe Lertola/TIME ● 18/19 Hart, Lertola/TIME

Gulf 20 Rick Maiman/Sygma ● 22/23 John McCutcheon/DOD Pool ● 24 G. Preston Saloom/SIPA ● 25 (top) Susan May Tell/SABA; (bottom) Apesteguy-Duclos-Morvan/Gamma Liaison ● 26/27 Nigel Holmes/TIME ● 28/29 Noel Quidu/Gamma Liaison ● 32 Michael Gangne/AFP ● 33 Lertola,Pugliese/TIME ● 34 (both) Iraqi TV/ABC News ● 35 Ali Yurtsever/Gamma Liaison ● 36 Charles Platiau/DOD Pool ● 38/39 Ken Jarecke/Contact ● 40 Wesley Boxce/SIPA ● 42 Pascal Guyot/AFP ● 43 Cynthia Johnson ● 44/45 Nigel Holmes/TIME ● 46/47 Coskin Aral/SIPA ● 47 Christopher Morris/Black Star ● 48 (left) Diana Walker; (right) Peter Kurz/Gamma Liaison ● 49 (top) Ken Jarecke/Contact; (middle) AP; (bottom) Brad Markel/Gamma Liaison

Nation ● 50 Joel Simon Images ● 52 David Burnett/Contact ● 53 David Burnett/Contact ● 54 (clockwise from top left) Dennis Brack/Black Star; Dennis Brack; Dennis Brack; David Burnett/Contact ● 56 Terry Ashe ● 57 David Burnett/Contact ● 58 Dennis Brack/Black Star ● 59 Michael Schumann/SABA ● 62 P.F. Bentley ● 63 (top) Douglas Burrows/Gamma Liaison; (bottom) Roger Sandler/Black Star ● 64 Charles Tasnadi/AP ● 65 (top) William Meyer-Milwaukee Sentinel/SABA; (bottom) Riverside Press Enterprise ● 66 (both) Ron Haviv/SABA ● 67 John W. McDonough/Sports Illustrated ● 68 (left) Brad Markel/Gamma Liaison; (right) Terry Ashe ● 69 (top left) John Duricka/AP; (top right) Terry Ashe; (bottom) Dirck Halstead ● 70 Jack Affleck-Vail ● 71 (top) Ken Heinen; (bottom) Shepard Sherbell/SABA

World 72 Anthony Suau/Black Star ● 74/75 Shepard Sherbell/SABA ● 76 Frederick Stevens/SIPA ● 77 Liu Heung Shing/AP ● 78/79 Nigel Holmes/TIME ● 80 Boris Yurchenko/AP ● Filip Horvat/SABA ● 82/83 Pugliese, Lertola/TIME ● 84 AFP ● 85 Paul Pugliese/TIME ● 86/87 (top) David Brauchli/Reuter-Bettman ● 87 Paul Pugliese/TIME ● 88 Paul Walters—SWNS/SIPA ● 89 Thomas Kienzle/AP ● 90 (left) Apesteguy-Merillon-Simon/Gamma Liaison ● 90/91 Apesteguy-Merillon/Gamma Liaison ● 92 (top) William Campbell ● 94 (top) Ron Haviv/SABA; (middle) Peter Magubane; (bottom) Contact ● 95 (top left) Brian F. Alpert/Keystone; (top right) Barry Iverson; (middle) Jeffery Aaronson; (bottom) Noburu Hashimoto/Sygma ● 96 (top) Marguerite Michaels; (middle) Alexander Joe/AFP; (bottom) Raul deMolina/Shooting Star ● 97 Rakesh Sahai/Black Star ● 98 Michel Setboun/JB Pictures ●

Man of the Year 100/101 Ted Thai ● 102 Ted Thai ● 103/104/105 Video Images Courtesy of CNN; copyrights 1990, 1989, 1988, 1986 ● 106/107 Ted Thai ● 108 (top left) Doug Bruce/Picture Group; (top right) Harrison McClary/SIPA; (bottom) Barbara Pyle ● 109 Ted Thai ● **Images** 110/111 David Turnley-Detroit Free Press/Black Star ● 112 (left) Ken Jarecke/Contact ● 113 Tony O'Brien/JB Pictures ● 114/115 Stephanie Compoint/Sygma ● 116/117 Anthony Suau/Black Star ● 118/119 Alberto Garcia/SABA ● 120 Pablo Bartholomew/Gamma Liaison ● 121 (top) SNS/SIPA; (bottom) NASA/JPL

Business 122 Steve Hart/TIME ● 124/125 Nigel Holmes/TIME ● 129 (top) Eli Reed/Magnum; (middle) Dilip Mehta/Contact; (bottom) Filip Horvat/SABA ● 130/131 Michael Witte/TIME ● 132 (left) Lawrence Barnes/Black Star; (right) Louis Psihoyos/Matrix ● 134 (top) Doug Menuez; (middle) Ed Kashi; (bottom) Andy Freeberg ● 136 Rick Maiman/Sygma ● 137 (bottom left) Philip Burke/TIME ● 138 (top left) Douglas Burrows/Gamma Liaison; (bottom right) Andrew Sacks ● 139 Lawrence Barns/Black Star

Society 140 Ken Robbins ● 142 The Granger Collection ● 143 (all) The Granger Collection ● 144 (left and middle) The Granger Collection; (right) Courtesy Colorado Historical Society ● 145 (left) Culver Pictures, Inc.; (middle) Eastman House Collection; (right) Culver Pictures Inc. ● 146/147 Mitch Kezar ● 148 Steve Liss ● (top) Richard Bowditch; (bottom) Susan Lapides ● 150/151 Arnold Roth/TIME ● 152 (top left) Photofest; (top right) Everett Collection; (bottom left) Everett Collection; (bottom right) Everett Collection ● 154 Katherine Lambert ● 155 Per Breiehagen ● 156 The Granger Collection ● 157 Dennis Brack/Black Star ● 158 Cynthia Johnson ● 159 (bottom) Gary Porter-Detroit News/Gamma Liaison ● 160/161 U.S. Navy ● 162/163 U.S. Navy ● 164 Paul Pugliese/TIME ● 165 Fox Movietone News

Science 166 Lawrence Burr/Gamma Liaison ● 172/173/174/175 William Coupon ● 176 Tom Raymond/Medichrome ● 177 Howard Sochurek/The Stock Market ● 178 Robin Shanabargar/Amber Engineering, Inc. ● 179 (top) Rockefeller University; (bottom) Hinterleither/Gamma Liaison ● 180 (top) NASA; (bottom) Alejandro Balaguer/Sygma ● 181 (left) Ivan Cappellen/REA/SABA; (right) Ron Haviv/SABA

Arts 182 Roland Neveu/MGM ● 184 (left) Roland Neveu; (middle) Zade Rosenthal; (right) Suzanne Hanover ● 185 (left) D. Stevens; (middle) Walt Disney; (right) Murray Close/Tri-Star ● 188 (left) Mario Ruiz; (right) Diana Walker ● 189 (left) Nancy Crampton; (right) Aaron Mannheimer ● 190 (top) David Modell/Katz; (bottom) Superstock ● 191 Peter Dokus/Ruthless/LGI; (bottom) Kevin Mazur ● 192 (left) Gragosian Gallery; (right) Plane Image, Inc. ● 193 (left) National Cowboy Hall of Fame & Western Heritage Center; (right) Institut Francais D/Architecture—Paris ● 194 (top) Phil Huber; (left) Duomo ● 195 (top) Allsport; (bottom) Manny Millan/Sports Illustrated ● 196 (clockwise from top left) Steven Meisel; Helmut Newton/Sygma; Wayne Williams/Outline; Cynthia Johnson; James Keyser; Alexis Duclos/Gamma Liaison

Milestones 198 (top left) TIME; (top right) Enrico Ferorelli; (bottom) Snowdon/Camera Press ● 199 (top) Abe Frajndlich/Sygma; (bottom left) Bob Sacha; (bottom right) Barbara Morgan/Morgan Press, Dobbs Ferry, NY